The New Geo-Governance

GOVERNANCE SERIES

Governance is the process of effective coordination whereby an organization or a system guides itself when resources, power and information are widely distributed. The study of governance entails probing the pattern of rights and obligations that underpins organizations and social systems; understanding how they coordinate their parallel activities and maintain their coherence; exploring the sources of dysfunction; and suggesting ways to redesign organizations whose governance is in need of repair.

The Series welcomes a range of contributions to the ongoing discourse on governance – from conceptual and theoretical reflections, ethnographic and case studies, and proceedings of conferences and symposia, to works of a very practical nature. The Series publishes works both in French and in English.

The Governance Series is part of the publications division of the Program on Governance and Public Management at the School of Political Studies. Eight volumes have previously been published within this Series. The Program on Governance and Public Management also publishes electronic journals: the quarterly www.optimumonline.ca and the biannual www.revuegouvernance.ca

The New Geo-Governance:
A Baroque Approach

Gilles Paquet

University of Ottawa Press

The University of Ottawa Press gratefully acknowledges the support extended to its publishing programme by the Canada Council for the Arts and the University of Ottawa.

We also acknowledge with gratitude the support of the Government of Canada through its Book Publishing Industry Development Program for our publishing activities.

National Library of Canada Cataloguing in Publication

Paquet, Gilles, 1936-
The new neo-governance : a baroque approach / Gilles Paquet.

Includes bibliographical references and index.
ISBN 0-7766-0594-1

1. Geopolitics. 2. Territory, National. 3. Natural resources. 4. Global commons. I. Title.

JC319.P26 2005   320.1'2   C2005-902565-4

Canada word mark

University of
Ottawa Press

Cover design: Laura Brady
Interior design and typesetting: Brad Horning

ISBN 0-7766-0594-1   ISSN 1487-3052

Published by the University of Ottawa Press, 2005
542 King Edward Avenue, Ottawa, Ontario K1N 6N5
press@uottawa.ca / www.uopress.uottawa.ca

Printed and bound in Canada

"To prescribe methods automatically blocks
the development of better methods"

Jane Jacobs

Table of Contents

PART 3: OCEAN GOVERNANCE

PART 4: THE NEW STEWARDSHIP

List of Figures and Graphs

Preface

"Things fall apart;
the center cannot hold.
Mere anarchy is loosed upon the world"
W. B. Yeats

The Forum for the Future of the OECD has produced a most interesting set of studies in the last few years focusing on the prospects for the long-term transformation of our "geo-socio-technical systems" over the next few decades. While the overall tone of the four reports (on technology, economic growth, diversity and creativity, and governance) has been positive, many perils likely to haunt the current transition period have also been underlined.

The major challenge, identified but addressed only obliquely by the four reports, had to do with geo-governance. It has become clear that the technological, economic, and social dynamisms require new ways to ensure effective coordination in a world where power, resources, and information are bound to be ever more widely and asymmetrically distributed, both organizationally and spatially.

Whether one scrutinizes the economy, the polity, the society, or the technological order, the centre cannot hold. There has been an implosion of all the traditional behemoths—and of the models used to map them—be they centrally planned economies, so-called totalitarian or mass society regimes, or centralized information or innovation systems. All modern effective systems have tended to become more decentralized and distributed, organizationally or spatially, or both.

Moreover, the multiplex relationships that used to hold these diverse systems together, and to help them re-enforce one another, have also fizzled out. The old linkage between state, nation, and territory, that provided much of the social glue, has been shaken loose: states and nations (and the related notions of citizenship, identity, etc.) had for us come to be associated with territory, only to now be developing in a more footloose and "de-territorialized" direction.

As a result, the hierarchical and authoritarian geo-governance nation-state structures that had been in good currency for the last century are proving to be rather ineffective in meeting the coordinating needs of socio-technical systems that are continually stirred by new technologies, globalization, greater social differentiation, and higher interdependency.

At the core of the new geo-governance challenge is the need to improve the basic capacities to integrate, mobilize, and transform our socio-technical systems in fundamental ways: first, by finding new ways to get increasingly heterogeneous and temporary groups to work together; second, by inventing new incentive reward systems, by designing new organizational forms, and by building the requisite degree of trust, integrity, and legitimacy in these structures to mobilize the minds, hearts, and souls of these diverse groups to some form of collaboration; three, by ensuring that the requisite learning loops and infrastructures are in place to catalyze collective intelligence and social learning, and, thereby, to effect the appropriate capacity to transform.

In a nutshell, what is needed is a new regime of geo-governance, capable of providing a "chaordic" form of integration—i.e., a form of organization capable of mixing chaos and order, of defining ensembles of norms, values, and rules likely to generate concurrently the requisite coherence and instability, for both are required to underpin the sort of social learning, creativity, and resilience that is needed.

Many have simply refused to acknowledge the centrality of this new geo-governance challenge, and/or have denounced the supposedly utopian nature of any new geo-governance regime capable of meeting this challenge. This is neither realistic nor practical. My sense is that we are facing a stark challenge and we have no choice but to search for workable practical responses even if we know that they will be neither simple nor perfect.

What is provided in this volume is an attempt at baroque thinking because it is the only strategy likely to work in the face of such a challenge. We will not search for ready-made solutions, but for ingenious responses. And if, despite the breadth of concepts and the rich harmonies and ornamentation, the responses are messy, and the rough pearls that we distill are not perfectly round—irregularly shaped pearl being the original meaning of the word "barroco" (Tapié 1961) —so be it! Important baroque principles are polyphony, counterpoint, contrast between large and small forces, a struggle between freedom and order: it is best illustrated by the music of Bach, which is marvellously complex, worked out in wonderful structures, and follows all sorts of rules, but in which there is also a lot of breaking of rules.

This book has been in the making for some seven years and many themes have been developed for the diversity of the readership mentioned in the acknowledgements. This has led to some leitmotifs being presented more than once. I have endeavored to eliminate tedious repetitions while preserving the reiteration of some useful leitmotifs.

I have a major debt of gratitude to colleagues who have commented on some of my work, not always favourably but always most helpfully, and to those who have brought to my attention much relevant material: John Curtis, George Emery, Monica Gattinger, Robin Higham, Luc Juillet, Dan Lane, Paul Laurent, John Meisel, Marie-France Paquet, Tim Ragan, Jeffrey Roy, and Chris Wilson. I must single out the help of Kevin Wilkins who has contributed substantially to the development of the section on ocean governance, and of Ruth Hubbard whose collaboration on chapter 4, and whose comments and suggestions on the whole project, were most helpful in the final stages of this work.

Preliminary versions of portions of this book have been published or presented in various places. I would like to thank the colleagues who have provided the invitations to these various forums: Pierre Boyer, Linda Cardinal, T. J. Courchene, Chad Gaffield, Fabien Gélinas, David Headon, Michael Howlett, Riel Miller, Sue Nichols, and Jean-Pierre Wallot.

The multifaceted help of Danna Campbell and Diane Fontaine is gratefully acknowledged.

Finally, I must acknowledge the editorial assistance of Anne Burgess and Marie Clausén, and the financial assistance of the SSHRC (410-97-0899; 410-2001-0367) and of the GEOIDE Network.

Introduction

Geo-governance: Some Scaffolding

"While the incalculable strings gather in
what's hers to gather in"
Two lines from George Johnston's poem
Elaine in a bikini

Many observers have announced the demise of the Westphalian nation state as the dominant system of geo-governance. Supposedly, the erosion of this dominant jurisdiction is ascribable to a nexus of forces: the pressure emanating from the ever expanding expectations of a more globally-focused citizenry, the expansion and greater complexity of the domains to be governed, nation states' weaker capacity to govern in the face of the greater mobility of labour, capital, etc. The territorial nation state has become, if one accepts this scenario, less congruent with contemporary realities, and less capable of providing an effective governance regime.

In the existing process of governance, much remains that is mediated by the national state context, and by nation-state regimes (McCallum 1995; Nitsch 2000), but there is no denying that the erosion of its dominion forges on.

While the governance capabilities are not necessarily as tightly packaged in national territorial niches as they were in earlier times, the territorial nation still plays the role of an echo box, through which much must be arbitrated (Paquet 2000b). However, in recent decades, both external forces and internal tensions have fundamentally transformed the innards of geo-governance systems. New forms of distributed governance arrangements have emerged, based on a more diffused pattern of power, and on a new valence for the various meso-systems (Storper 1996; Elkins 1995).

This new pattern of geo-governance is still without a formal name. Following Walter Truett Anderson, we have labelled it "ecologies of governance" (Anderson 2001).

Some still insist on "national packaging" as a matter of convenience. But the new realities bear little resemblance to the old Westphalian construct. This new pattern has vested infra-national communities with new powers, has built on new principles of cooperation/competition within and across national boundaries, and has been rooted in new capabilities that are much less state-centred (Paquet 1999b).

The new dynamic also involves more complex mixes of intertwined relations, networks, and regimes, and governance capabilities that are more diverse and seemingly more disconnected than was the case in the old nation-state-centred governance world. These new complexities do not change the fact that geographical space still remains a fundamental element of the present governance regime, but its relative importance has diminished.

In this introductory chapter, I sketch a very simple framework based on social learning as the most useful lens through which one can examine the current challenges.

Governance and the dispersive revolution

As technological change, economic growth, and socio-cultural effervescence increased, a dispersive revolution led organizations to adapt to the new circumstances by various processes of disintegration, and quasi-reintegration in more diffuse patterns.

The new circumstances created the need for a heightened capacity for speed, flexibility, and innovation, based on new forms of integration and coordination, and embodying not only new structures and tools, but a whole new way of thinking. Private, public, and social concerns ceased to be drivers of people, and had to become "drivers of learning" (Wriston 1992:119). They had to become learning organizations, based on new forms of alliances and partnerships rooted in more horizontal relationships and moral contracts.

While the dispersive forces have been played out in a number of dimensions (technical, social, etc.) they have been particularly evident in geographical space. Power, resources, and information have become dispersed over many sites, and this has substantially increased the difficulties of geo-governance.

This dispersive revolution crystallized into new network business organizations, into more subsidiarity-focused governments, and into increasingly virtual, elective, and malleable communities. Major governance challenges ensued: acquiring speed, flexibility, and innovativeness, while maintaining the necessary coordination, coherence, and integrity.

These forces have been at work for some time, but their impact has been considerably heightened by the digital revolution that has materialized over the last while.

Inter-networked technologies have transformed all levels of governance. As technology has made it possible, businesses, governments, and communities have been confronted with a greater demand for participation. Citizens have also become more active partners in the governance process. This has redefined the public space and triggered the emergence of distributed governance regimes based on a wider variety of more fluid and always evolving groups of stakeholders (Tapscottt and Agnew 1999).

A primer on geo-governance

By geo-governance, we refer to the ways in which effective coordination is effected in a world where resources, knowledge, and power are distributed through geographical space. The technologies of geo-governance refer to the many ways in which (1) individuals and institutions (public, private, and civic) manage their collective affairs in space, (2) diverse interests accommodate and resolve their differences, and (3) these many actors and organizations are involved in a continuing process of formal and informal competition, cooperation, and learning in space (Carlsson and Ramphal 1995).

Throughout the 20th century, geo-politics has attempted to make sense of the new complex, and at times seemingly chaotic, socio-political/economic realities, and to define a map of how power, resources, and information are allocated. This map has echoed the dominant power/knowledge infrastructures of the day. It was shaped by imperialism in the early part of the 20th century, by the East–West divide and the Cold War in the post-World War II period, and by globalization and the erosion of the powers of the Westphalian nation-state in the more recent past. Geo-politics has proposed different fault-lines of competition/cooperation, various linkages between the local/regional and the global realities, and different discourses to "rationalize" them for these different eras.

But, as the compilers of a recent reader in geo-politics boldly state, "geo-politics is not a science", it is "a field of contestation" (Ò Tuathail et al. 1998). It presents only partial images of the geo-governance process, and this has never been truer than after the fall of the Berlin wall. The extensive recent literature on geo-governance continues to define faultlines and interfaces in unduly simplistic ways. No one is entirely swayed by Luttwak's pronouncements that economic priorities and modalities are dominant; or by Luke's insistence that security and political issues continue to dominate the scene; or by Huntington's suggestion that clashes of civilization are the defining interfaces (Luttwak 1990; Luke 1991; Huntington 1993).

While each of these arguments has merits, each of these families of forces may be said to have at best dominated the scene only episodically. Strict geo-economic, geo-security/political and geo-civilizational/socio-cultural arguments therefore remain unpersuasive in accounting for the evolving pattern of geo-governance. These analyses remain unduly crippled by overly macroscopic and Manichean (either/or) interpretations that provide none of the nuances necessary to take into account the extraordinary diffraction of governance structures, and the new continental/regional/local division of labour that has ensued.

Contrary to the thrust that emerged from most of the recent analyses of geo-governance, no nexus of forces (private/economic, public/political, social/cultural) has had a dominant role in defining the fault-lines. The relationships among sectors have been *heterarchical*: there is no pecking order. Heterarchy introduces "*strange loops*" of authority "under conditions of time and place" very much like the "game of paper, rock, and scissors where paper covers rock, rock crushes scissors, and scissors cut paper" (Ogilvy 1986–7). Any sector may at times have dominion over the others: the three sectors co-evolve.

Indeed, the ecological concept of *co-evolution* provides an apt way to synthesize the links among these three universes. Co-evolution in biology refers to an evolutionary process based on reciprocal responses of closely interacting species, as in the co-evolution of the beaks of hummingbirds and the shape of the flowers they feed on. The concept can be generalized to encompass feedback processes among interacting systems (social, economic, political) going through a reciprocal process of change. The process of co-evolution becomes a form of *organizational learning*: joint learning and interadjustment of economy, society, and state (Perroux 1960; Boulding 1970; Laurent and Paquet 1998).

Necessarily hybrid models of global geo-governance

Despite the lack of agreement on a unique set of faultlines, there has been much time spent over the last while in developing mechanisms of global governance to complement the arrangements within and between nation states. The general thrust of this search for complementary global arrangements has been to elicit workable institutions and organizations, i.e., arrangements meeting the general principles of efficiency, legitimacy, resilience, transparency, etc.

This broad-ranging set of mechanisms (specialization of international institutions, political representation and responsibility of the nation states in the multilateral and global governing bodies, some balance between the relative priority of problem areas and the power of the institutions dealing with them, subsidiarity, etc.) does not, however, lead to a convergence of views about the best model of global governance.

4

A number of models in good currency (world government, cooperation among nations, network of independent technical authorities, cosmopolitical democracy, law without state and supranational courts and tribunals, private self-regulation) have their staunch defenders, but it is more likely that "hybrid forms" of governance (blending many such arrangements) will need to be designed to be most effective in different contexts (Jacquet et al. 2002; Archibugi 2003).

The reason why such institutional *metissage* is likely to emerge is that no simple univocal arrangement can be effective in meeting complex governance challenges in a world where an ever larger number of private, public, and social "interests" must be entitled to enter an ever expanding public forum to co-operate in multifaceted ways in resolving ever more complex evolving conflictive issues, and negotiating reasonable compromises.

Such a mammoth challenge can only be met through a partitioning of issues into "regional/sectoral" and "spatial/temporal" slices or clusters, which can be tackled separately but concurrently and coherently, through different instruments, norms, rules, and the like involving overlapping networks of stakeholders.

Such "partial" and "temporary" responses would be regarded by an omniscient external observer as quite an inefficient *tâtonnement* process (involving meso-level summits, task forces, clubs and partnerships, regime groupings, networks of cities, or mazes of structures and arrangements such as those evolved by the UN since the Second World War). Yet such arrangements based on soft power (incentives and persuasion) and soft laws (flexibility, evolving moral contracts, memoranda of understanding, etc.), that can meet only partially and imperfectly the imperatives of effectiveness, transparency, legitimacy, etc., may be the best that can be practically accomplished.

Indeed, in this world of "good governance", the best is often the enemy of the good (Paquet 1991–2b; Moreau Defarges 2003).

The important weaknesses of simplistic and overly ambitious responses have been that they have failed (1) in gauging the complexity of the task sufficiently well, (2) in acknowledging the facts that resources, knowledge, and power are inevitably distributed, (3) in accepting the harsh reality that no one is omniscient or omnipotent, (4) in factoring in that transnational, local, and non-state actors are bound to become more important, and (5) in understanding that collaboration is the new categorical imperative.

As a result, an unstated assumption has permeated most of the debates and dominated the various exercises of institutional architecture: the hope to design a set of state-centred arrangements defining precise rules, *ex ante*. This has led experts to indulge in much utopian thinking, and to maintain the view that one could count on an institutional and organizational architecture that would be capable of providing legitimacy, norms, implementation processes, and control mechanisms from the very start. This is a view I cannot share.

Rather, I hold the view that such a regime is always *en émergence* and that one can only work at helping such a regime to emerge as a gardener helps his garden to evolve (Côté 1991).

Resilience and social learning

In times of turbulent change, organizations (micro, meso, macro, and mega; economic, political, or civic) govern themselves by becoming capable of learning both what their goals are, and the means to reach them, *as they proceed*, by tapping into the knowledge and information that active citizens possess, and getting them to invent ways out of the predicaments they are in. This leads to a more distributed governance that deprives leaders of their monopoly on the governing of organizations. For the organization to learn quickly, everyone must take part in the *conversation*, and bring forward each bit of knowledge and wisdom and those capabilities that he or she has that have a bearing on the issue.

Distributed governance does not simply mean a process of the dispersion of power toward localized decision-making within each sector: it entails a dispersion of power over a wide variety of actors and groups within the economy, society, and polity. This diffraction of power has evolved because it triggers more effective learning in a context of rapid change, through decentralized and flexible teams, woven by moral contracts and reciprocal obligations, negotiated in the context of evolving partnerships (Nohria and Eccles 1992).

In the transition period from the present nation-state-dominated era to the emerging era of distributed governance and transversal coordination, there has been a tendency (1) for a great deal of devolution and decentralization of decision-making (i.e., for the meso-level units in polity, society, and economy to become prominent), (2) for the rules of the game of the emergent order to be couched in more informal terms, and (3) for the emergent properties of the new order to remain relatively unpredictable, as one might expect in a neural-net-type world (Ziman 1991; Norgaard 1994; Paquet 1993, 1995b, 1997d).

The new form of transversal coordination, now in the making, generates of necessity a loss of central control, and a weakening of the national state *imperium*. A different sort of *imperium*, adapted to the network age, is emergent: it is reminiscent of the Roman empire under Hadrian, where the institutional order was a loose web of agreements to ensure compatibility among open networks (Guéhenno 1993). We are entering an era where the governance process is becoming a game without a master, and, for many observers, this diffraction of power has raised the spectre of non-governability.

Governability is a measure of an organization's capability for effective coordination within the context within which it is nested. It corresponds to the organization's capacity to transform, its capacity to modify its structure, its process, and even its substantive guidance mechanism and orientation (Kooiman 1993:259–60). At any time, the gaps between governing *needs* and *capabilities* transform the governance pattern. This tends, over time, to trigger the emergence of a fitful degree of decentralization and differentiation, to bring forth a variety of partnerships and joint ventures to respond to the challenges posed by knowledge dispersion, motivation, and implementation problems, and by the need to correct some of the important side-effects of the existing governance structure.

The central thrusts of this evolving process are *resilience* (the capacity for the economy-polity-society nexus to spring back undamaged from pressure or shock, through some slight re-arrangements that do not modify the nature of the overall system), and *learning* (the capacity to transform in order to improve present performance, through a redefinition of the organization's objectives, and a modification of behaviour and structures) (Paquet 1999d). Resilience and learning would appear to point in contradictory directions (maintaining coherence versus structural transformation) and they do. They must be balanced because they are both necessary to underpin sustainability.

The governance system has evolved considerably over the past few decades, as a result of the important shocks emanating both from the internal milieu and the external context, and of the need to learn faster (Paquet 1999f). A number of rounds of adaptation have been necessary to provide the requisite flexibility and suppleness of action. The ultimate result of these changes is a composite governance system, built on unreliable control mechanisms in pursuit of ill-defined goals, in a universe that is chronically in a state of flux. This composite governance process has emerged as the result of cumulative efforts to harness complexity that have blended the different integrative mechanisms within organizations in a new way (Axelrod and Cohen 1999; Paquet 2000e).

Social learning, coordination failures, and the new ligatures

In a learning economy, wealth creation is rooted in the mobilization of knowledge: learning harnesses the collective intelligence of the team as a source of continuous improvement. This in turn commands new modes of production of knowledge, and new modes of collegiality, alliances, and sharing of knowledge, a degree of cooperation to take advantage of positive externalities, economies of scale and scope, and strong cumulative experience-learning processes. But these processes do not necessarily work perfectly (Argyris and Schön 1978; Gibbons et al. 1994; Lundvall and Johnson 1994).

While much know-what and know-why has been effectively codified, and can be produced and distributed as quasi-commodity, know-how and know-who have remained tacit and socially embedded (Foray and Lundvall 1996). Consequently, the production and the distribution of this latter form of knowledge have been more problematic: it depends a great deal on social cohesion and trust, on much trespassing and cross-fertilization between disciplinary fields, and on the development of networks capable of serving as two-way communication links between tacit and codified, private and shared knowledge, between passive efficiency-achieving learning and creative/destructive Schumpeterian learning (Boisot 1995). In this complex world, there are ample possibilities for the coordination failures that can slow down the process of learning.

Coordination failures are ascribable to a variety of problems (legal, organizational, etc.), and, as they materialize, they are bound to generate dysfunctions and some performance deterioration. This in turn puts pressure on the learning organization to modify its conventions and relational transactions, i.e., its functioning. When such adjustments in the functioning of the governance system prove insufficient to restore good performance, more serious modifications to the governance *structure* of the learning economy become necessary. However, neither modification is usually sufficient.

In addition to these plumbing-type repairs, new forms of social ligature must be put in place to forge a new dominant logic, capable of replacing the logic of centralization-cum-redistribution of the old nation-state. In lieu of the administrative territorial order imposed by the logic of top-down control (with its requirement that clearly delineated borders be respected, good fences be erected, inter-regional flows be regulated, and jurisdictions be enforced), one must invent a way of dealing with the new fluid order, still somewhat anchored in territorial proximities but to a much lesser degree than ever before.

This new logic is a "logic of flows", a dynamic logic of change through time that emphasizes cognition and learning. Flows are in some way the dynamic aspect of networks: the software that enables the hardware to run (Semprini 2003:99). It superimposes on geographical space a new sense of mobility and nimbleness: away from topographical coordinates to new topological dimensions—what Castells calls a "space of flows" (Castells 1989).

This "revenge of nomadism over the principle of territoriality and settlement" (Bauman 2000:13) is the result of (1) the "*révolution commutative*" that is allowing each individual to disconnect at will and reconnect differently (Guillaume 1999); (2) the revolution in connexity that has transformed the way we maintain and develop a community—from raising barriers and boundaries, to feeding relationships and networks (Mulgan 1997; Lévy 2000); and (3) the new diffuse "bridging capital" that has come to replace the old "bonding capital", tightly connected with the geography of proximity (Putnam 2000).

This new "soul", "*imaginaire*" or "north star" of the new governance system must construct nothing less than a new set of reference or focal points that will replace the fundamentally territorial and spatial coordinates of the nation-state. The old trinity of state–nation–territory is in question. The space does not correspond to homogeneous national territories, nor with their topographical sum, but with communities that have articulated a series of "reciprocal extraterritorialities in which the guiding concept would no longer be the *ius* (right) of the citizen, but the refugium (refuge) of the singular" (Agamben 2000:24).

The new "lightness and fluidity of the increasingly mobile, slippery, shifty, evasive and fugitive power" (Bauman 2000:14) is not completely a-territorial: it is characterized, however, by new forms of belonging that escape the control and regulation of the nation-state to a much higher degree than before, by virtual agoras, liquid networks: variegated and overlapping terrains where citizens may "land" temporarily.

The fabric of these new "worlds" is defined by the new dominant logic of subsidiarity in all dimensions: it welds together assets, skills, and capabilities into complex temporary communities that are as much *territories of the mind* as anything that can be represented by a grid map, and it does so on the basis of a bottom-up logic that assigns higher order institutions only those functions that cannot be accomplished effectively at the local level.

In the shorter run, coordination failures may be eliminated through *process redesign*, i.e., by eliminating obstacles to the collaboration of the different stakeholders within the learning cycle, and developing the relationships, conventions, or relational transactions required to define mutually coherent expectations and common guideposts. These conventions differ from sector to sector: they provide the requisite coherence for a common context of interpretation, and for some "cognitive routinization of relations between firms, their environments, and employees" (Storper 1996:259).

Such coherence must, however, remain somewhat loose: the ligatures should not be too strong or too routinized. A certain degree of heterogeneity, and therefore social distance, might foster a higher potentiality of innovation because the different parties bring to the "conversation" a more complementary body of knowledge (Granovetter 1973). More fruitful synergies ensue. But too much social distance and too much "noise" can prevent an effective harnessing of collective intelligence and sabotage the learning process. Modifying relational transactions transform the very nature of the power map. As collective intelligence comes to depend less on geographical proximity than on other proximities in cyberspace (Lévy 1994), the pattern of effective relational transactions is changed. This does not exorcise territoriality but it transmogrifies its role. "Smart communities" are a good illustration of the new comparative advantages derived from the compounding of these different types of proximity.

In the longer run, coordination failures may be eliminated more radically through *organizational architecture*, i.e., the transformation of the structural capital (networks and regimes) defining the capabilities of the learning economy.

Coherence and pluralism are crucial in the organizational architecture of a learning concern. This is what makes federal structures so attractive from a learning point of view: they provide coordination in a world where the "centre...is more a network than a place" (Handy 1995a; Petrella 1995). This is also the reason why federal-type organizational structures have emerged in so many sectors on most continents. Potentially, federalism represents a sort of fit or effective alignment between the different components of structural capital, in the sense of Saint-Onge (1996)—i.e., the systems (processes), structures (accountabilities and responsibilities), strategies, and culture (shared mindset, values, and norms). But since there is always a significant probability of misalignment between these components, there is often a need to intervene directly to modify the organizational architecture in order to ensure effective learning.

But social learning is unlikely to proceed apace (despite process and organizational repairs) unless the new dominant logic of the strategic state generates a new public philosophy and *outillage mental* capable of serving as a gyroscope in the learning process (Paquet 1996–7).

A framework and three broad terrains

In the rest of this volume, I will build on this basic perspective.

In Part 1, I present the *outillage mental* required to deal with the design task at hand. This is accomplished in four stages: (1) a look at the broad dynamics in the institutional order, (2) a note on what a distributed governance regime is, (3) a sketch of the sort of collaboration that will need to be put in place to support the distributed governance regime, and (4) a primer on ecologies of governance, chaords, and other generic types of organization likely to be suitable for the challenging tasks at hand.

The next three parts of the book apply this general conceptual framework to different "realities": territorial governance, ocean governance, and socio-technical stewardship.

The first two terrains are quite familiar: the governing of more and more diffracted territorial spaces, and of oceans where the conventional appropriation systems do not apply. The former is an easier terrain although we are still far from having achieved good governance. The latter is more complex, because of the transnational and common-property nature of the milieu, the migration of species, etc. The third terrain is more elusive. It focuses on the transformation of the institutional order itself, as a consequence and a most dramatic outcome of the dynamics in the other two terrains. This is the terrain of meta-governance.

In Part 2, I explore territorial connections at three levels. In chapter 5, I look at the emerging hemispheric governance regime in the Americas, and suggest that it can only be expected to evolve bottom–up, piecemeal, and progressively over the next few decades. In chapter 6, I examine the dynamics of meso-innovation systems in Canada, and the ways in which they have led to new definitions of milieux and proximities. In chapter 7, I delve into the inner dynamics of city-regions, as they are becoming the new cauldron in which the governance system is being redefined.

In Part 3, I deal with the world of common-pool resources or where commons abound—like oceans—where the traditional appropriation systems fail and therefore the governance challenges are even more daunting. In this world of natural frailty, sustainability is the dominant guidepost, but it is an essentially contested concept. I analyze this concept and put forward a few modest general propositions about the family of mechanisms that are likely to be necessary for effective governance to prevail (chapter 8). Then, I examine the foundations of a distributed governance regime for oceans (chapter 9)—constituting as they do 70% of the surface of the earth—and I review the mechanisms that might be useful in eliciting the emergence of this sort of regime (chapter 10).

It will become clear that both territorial governance and ocean governance are *emergent phenomena*. These phenomena may be influenced by wise and subtle interventions, but one cannot artificially impose an order on these realities, top-down.

Part 4 attempts to draw out the broader implications of this new geo-governance. It suggests that there are general trends that are worth exploring: first, the drift toward a form of *baroque* governance (chapter 11); second, the transformation of the notion of citizenship as "whatever communities" (*communautés quelconques*) emerge (chapter 12); and third, the evolution of the notion of federalism as the sort of social technology that has come to be regarded as the most likely candidate to become the workable instrument of sustainable stewardship in this new world (chapter 13).

In this world of greater diversity, of constant change, and of more diffuse and elusive groupings, where organizations in the private, public, and social sectors are more fluid, a new institutional order is *en émergence*. While one may not be able yet to fully identify its contours, one can at least identify a few of the new imperatives, and the likely new features of the coming geo-governance.

The conclusion reflects on the families of coordinating mechanisms that appear to be missing in order for effective geo-governance to prevail in an age of growing interdependence, international effervescence, and transnational terror.

PART I

A Framework

Chapter 1

Institutional Evolution in an Information Age

> "A map...does not 'solve' problems and does not 'explain' mysteries;
> it merely helps to identify them"
> E.F. Schumacher

Introduction

A socio-economy is an "instituted process", that is, a going concern held together and characterized by a certain number of rules, norms, principles, and conventions. Together, they make up the institutional order. Institutional orders differ from place to place, and evolve through time as circumstances and values change (Polanyi 1957).

As the production of material values, characteristic of the industrial age, has been progressively displaced as the driving force in the economy by the production of information values, the rules, norms, and conventions of the former age have been strained. This has triggered much institutional change (Masuda 1990:3). This chapter examines the ways in which the institutional order has been reconfigured, and the likely consequences of this mutation.

I look at what is meant by institutions, institutional order, and institutional change in section 1, and at some of the features of the information age in section 2. This enables me, in section 3, to identify some major institutional changes triggered by the information age, that have provoked the emergence of a new dynamic built on four pillars: a new centrality of cognition, new forms of regulation and network cooperation in the control of the forum, elements of a new world information order, and a new form of "neobiological" evolution of the institutional order. In section 4, I argue that there are, at the core of this new dynamic, new forms of transversal coordination across the different layers of the institutional order. In the conclusion, I speculate on the predictability of the routes through which the new context will institute itself.

Institutions, institutional order, and institutional change

Institutions are a world of "objective structures which are the products, not necessarily intentional, of minds or living creatures; but which, once produced, exist independently of them" (Magee 1973: 60). They are arrangements meant to reconcile the geotechnical constraints emerging from the world around us with the subjective world of minds, plans, and values. So if either of these realities changes, institutions are strained, and adapt more or less quickly and well.

These institutions are part of a loosely connected institutional order. This institutional order is reshaped throughout history (i) by the accretion or demise of layers of new specific institutions, (ii) by the adaptation of specific institutions to the overall institutional order (to fit better with the rest of the order), and (iii) by the evolving circumstances and organizations that are generating continuous pressure on institutions and the institutional order to evolve.

(a) Institutions and institutional order

Rules, norms, and conventions define what is and is not allowed. They "serve as orientation maps concerning future actions": they enable a large number of actors "to co-ordinate their actions by means of orientation to a common signpost" (Lachmann 1971:13, 49–50). Institutions are proteiform: they range from tacit and informal norms or conventions to explicit formal rules, from undesigned to designed entities, from wide-ranging framework institutions to secondary institutions that are more limited in scope. Taken as a whole, these institutions make up the institutional order.

Such an order may be loose or tight. Specific institutions do not necessarily aggregate into a tight institutional order with permanence, consistency, unity and gap-lessness like an ideal legal system (Lachmann 1971:75). Individual institutions may come and go, become stronger or be eroded without the system being imperiled. A tight institutional order embodies a *dominant logic* and influences the process of emergence of individual new institutions: it readily adopts some of these new institutions and considerably limits the influence of others. Specific institutions are more likely to adapt in certain directions if they belong to a particularly tight institutional order; a loose institutional order has limited adoptive power as well as limited power to elicit adaptive behaviour (Prahalad and Bettis 1986; Bettis and Prahalad 1995).

At any time, any specific institution may have a high or low degree of "goodness of fit" with the rest of the institutional order, and with the coordination needs of the socio-economic context. Specific institutions as social armistices do not necessarily correspond to an equilibrium situation (North 1990). At best, they embody a "workable tension" between coherence and flexibility, between the needed stability of the orientation points for coordination to occur, and the equally important need for flexibility to accommodate to the new circumstances. The institutional order is therefore not necessarily an equilibrium configuration. It corresponds to a "workable configuration" of the evolving "rules of operation and structure of institutions for the system as a whole" (Adelman 1973). The emergence, erosion, or dysfunctional evolution of individual institutions may at times throw the existing institutional order out of kilter and jeopardize its survival (Lachmann 1971:83).

(b) Institutions and organizations
Individual institutions often originate as a convention for the mutual convenience of purposive organizations. They may also emerge as the result of tough bargaining among powerful groups, or as the unintended consequences of endeavours by private or public concerns.

Institutions are both resilient and fragile. On the one hand, existing institutions that are inadequate arrangements (in the sense that they do not generate the best performance for the different organizations) may prove quite resilient, especially if some powerful forces benefit from them. On the other hand, even reasonably sound institutions, based on conventions of mutual convenience, may crumble, as circumstances change: pressures then tend to weaken the convention until it is no longer enforced and falls into disuse.

Once in place, specific institutions play a range of roles: they do much of our thinking for us, they confer identity, they classify, they remember and forget (Douglas 1986). On all these fronts, they serve the different interest groups more or less well. Organizational efforts by disgruntled groups may tend to erode informal institutions, or to modify formal framework institutions forming the outer structure of the institutional order (Lachmann 1971: 82–3). Depending on their importance, these pressures may even modify the dominant logic and threaten the institutional order. Such an erosion of the institutional order increases dramatically as the probability of adopting deviant institutions increases, and as organizations develop a propensity to adapt in what appear to be dysfunctional directions. This adaptation-adoption process is self-reinforcing (Arthur 1988).

(c) The cognitive dimension
Institutional orders, like other social systems, consist of a structure, a technology, and a theory. "The structure is the set of roles and relations among individual members. The theory consists of the views held within the social system about its

17

purposes, its operations, its environment and its future. Both reflect, and in turn influence, the prevailing technology of the system—that is, the set of procedures by which the game is played (Schön 1971; Ramos 1981). These dimensions are interdependent. Any change in one dimension leads to corresponding modifications in the others, and therefore in the whole system.

At first, scholars like Douglass North emphasized almost exclusively the importance of shocks originating from the environment to explain the modification in the structure or technology of the game. More recently, there has been a growing recognition that the "theory" may be the core dimension: when it is changed, critical disruption occurs. And the source of such disruption need not be anything more than a change in representations, in the symbolic space, in the cognitive process (North 1990, 1991, 1993). Indeed, change may result from a misrepresentation by organizations of the signposts the institution is putting forth: even if the real social space has remained unchanged, the representations of the social space, or the predispositions and inclinations of certain key actors, may be modified. Institutional change ensues.

This cognitive dimension of institutions and institutional change has become increasingly important with the emergence of the informational age. It has become also an ever more important feature of most models of the institutional order, as is illustrated by the contours of Douglass North's recent *problématique*. It emphasizes human learning as the foundation of both institution-building and institutional evolution. Mental models, ideologies, and belief systems are presented as the basis for *representational redescription,* and such cognitive dimensions are recognized as being fundamentally as important a source of learning (and therefore of institutional change) as any modification in environmental constraints (North 1993).

As will become clear in the following sections, the relative importance of the cognitive dimension, and of the impact of the symbolic space on the socio-economic-political space, have been heightened accordingly (Debray 1991; Abrahamson and Fombrun 1994).

The information society syndrome

The discontinuity triggered by the new telecommunications technology and the dawn of the information age has been epoch-making, and its impact will be on the scale of other information revolutions like the language revolution, the writing revolution, and the printing revolution. "In each case, these information epochs preceded the birth of a new system of societal technology that in turn became the basis for a transformation in human society" (Masuda 1982).

The information age and the new telecommunications have catalyzed a new dynamic, not unlike the one observed at the time of the Renaissance: changes in the social structure, new forms of entrepreneurship, new modes of thought, new lifestyles, and new modes of practical learning and expertise (Von Martin 1944).

There has been a transformation of the cognitive and socio-cultural fabric of our world.

(a) From energy to information dominance

The economic process has drifted from energy dominance to information dominance: the interaction between man and nature has become more extensively programmed by an ever more important knowledge-information component. The new employment has been generated in the knowledge development and transfer sectors, rather than in the manufacturing and transportation of material goods (McLaughlin 1966). And for various independent measurements of the size of the information-related segment of modern economies, indicators have shown a dramatic growth of that sector, especially since the 1960s (Parker 1975; Porat 1977).

One general point emerges from these analyses: the economy has become *more immaterial* (i.e., dematerialized) in the last half-century. The determinism (physical/technological/geographical), built on the framework of the material goods production system, has been considerably weakened. There are massive economies of scale in information processes (Wilson 1975) and those gains in information-transfer efficiency by large-scale flexible organizations underlie the oligopolization and the multinationalization processes which have been noted in recent years.

A number of corollaries follow. First, the dematerialization of economic activity has generated new forms of enterprise, and a *reconfiguration* of the manner in which the economy is instituted (Williamson 1975, 1985). Increasing returns have made it possible to construct "virtual organizations" based on instantaneous communication through global networks. Second, a certain *deterritorialization* of the economic process has been triggered: economic activity has become more footloose, that is, less dependent on the presence of not-easily-moveable physical resources. Formerly powerful places that had built their power on locational comparative advantages have been displaced by the new important placeless power of global networks. Third, these two processes have been self-reinforcing in a synergetic way: as information and knowledge become more central, increasing returns and network externalities become more important, and the dominance of placeless power increases (Graham 1994).

Such corollaries go a long way towards explaining the mutation in the structure and functioning of organizations like firms. The nineteenth century firm "was built around the notion of product". Its location was significantly dependent on proximate access to physical inputs and energy sources. Later, firms came to be defined less by the product itself than by the process that gave rise to the product. More recently, information processes, technological research and innovation have become more central to activities of firms, which have come to be defined by their information systems. While technology used to be transferred mostly through its embodiment in produced goods, or in the scope of the process, the increasing importance of information processes relative to energy processes has made the firm the *medium* of technology transfer: not just by the process that gives rise to the product, but through control over the information network or system necessary to produce it (Schön 1970). This has led some to suggest that a modern corporation is a "knowledge system" and its output "packaged knowledge" (Wikström and Normann 1994).

(b) Interconnectedness, turbulence, and accelerated change
Emery and Trist (1965) have analyzed the pattern of change in the transnational environment, and proposed a typology of environmental textures: placid-randomized, placid-clustered, disturbed-reactive, and turbulent. Supposedly, the transnational environment has evolved through these different stages, and can now be characterized as turbulent: the ground is in motion.

This turbulence is a result of the shift from energy to information dominance, and it is characterized by (i) a deepening interdependence of all facets of society: as interconnectedness grows with accelerating information transfers, complexity increases with the dimension of organizations, and synergies become ever more important; and by (ii) an increase in the degree of relevant uncertainty that affects organizations as complexity, interconnectedness, and the faster pace of change increase within the system. Even 25 years ago, a number of reports provided an impressive amount of data consistent with this hypothesis (Toffler 1975; Cairncross and McRae 1975; OECD 1979).

At the core of this turbulence are the new forms of transnational communication: new networks linking parts of the economic process in all countries. The firms and organizations that are well integrated transnationally have better access to information, and accordingly cope better with the heightened uncertainty. The firms or organizations excluded from such networks bear higher costs of adjustment. Hymer (1972) (at the international level) and Törnqvist (1968) (at the national level) have shown that differential patterns of information flows translate into changing patterns of location of economic activities and of methods of organization and coordination (Richardson 1960).

Finally, increasing returns become centrally important as learning effects and network externalities become relatively more prominent than in the previous age. This in turn leads to greater possibilities of path-dependence (i.e., that small chance events can determine which organization or institution prevails) and lock-in (i.e., that once an organizational or institutional "solution" is arrived at, it might be difficult to exit from it) (Arthur 1988).

(c)   A more distributed system of governance
The required speed, flexibility, and innovative adaptation characteristic of the information age can only be generated by a high degree of noncentralization, together with a high degree of integration. This has transformed the governance system, as the traditional hierarchical structures in the public, private, and social sectors have proved inadequate. The centralized power had to be diffused. In all sectors, organizations lost power outward to transnational networks, sideward through partnerships and alliances, and downward to regional/sectional fragments. Power has not dissipated, it has been diffused, and the system of governance has become more distributed.

Another important reason for this development has been the ongoing democratization resulting in, amongst other things, a proliferation of smaller organizations (private, public, and not-for-profit), and a multiplication of the number of players involved in the process of governance. This has triggered not only a breakdown of the old bureaucratic way of organizing and managing concerns, but also a "fuzzification" of the boundaries between the public and private sectors, between industries, and between organizations, as an ever larger number of planned non-permanent alliances and partnerships (that worked across organizational boundaries) materialized.

These arrangements depend much less for their effectiveness on "power over" or "power of the purse" and much more on "cooperation". Yet these new types of cooperative arrangements that have emerged as a result of "the dispersive revolution" are not necessarily "legitimate" in our institutional order (Genschel 1993; Hampden-Turner and Trompenaars 1993; Hollingsworth 1994).

Galaxy firms, federal governance systems, and a wide range of social "movements" have become what anthropologist Virginia Hine would call "segmented polycephalous networks" (SPN) held together by an "ideological bond" or "the power of a unifying idea", the sort of glue necessary to make the organization live and prosper. To underline this key dimension, Hine has labelled the new form of organization SP(I)N where I stands for ideology (Hine 1977). The organization chart of a SP(I)N would look "like a badly knotted fishnet with a multitude of nodes and cells of varying sizes, each linked to all the others directly or indirectly" such as it might be for the Audubon Society or the Sierra Club, or for a private firm like ABB (Asea Brown and Boveri), or the Confederaziun Helvetica (Hine 1977; Boisot 1987; O'Toole and Bennis 1992).

A central and critical feature of SP(I)Ns is the emphasis on voluntary adherence to norms. While this voluntary adherence does not necessarily appear to generate constraints per se on the size of the organization (as some of the examples mentioned above indicate), it is not always easy for a set of shared values to spread over massive disjointed transnational communities: free riding, high transaction costs, problems of accountability, etc. impose extra work. So the benefits in terms of leanness, agility, and flexibility are such that many important multinationals have chosen not to manage their affairs as a global production engine, but as a multitude of smaller quasi-independent units coordinated by a loose federal structure, because of the organizational diseconomies of scale in building a clan-type organization (O'Toole and Bennis 1992; Handy 1992).

The world of SP(I)N organizations is the world of the information age.

This new socio-economy is an evolving adaptive network of networks and has many characteristics that have been described graphically by John Holland: (i) it is composed of networks of agents acting in parallel, and its control tends to be highly dispersed; (ii) agents are acting on the basis of representations or mental models of the process; (iii) it has many building blocks and levels of organization, with all sorts of tangling interactions across levels; (iv) the building blocks are continually revised and recombined as the system accumulates experience; and (v) it is characterized by perpetual novelty (Holland 1988). This sort of information-age socioeconomy requires signposts and orientation maps that are quite different from those in good currency during the industrial era.

The institutional order likely to meet the coordination needs of this complex adaptive network world has to provide a guidance system made of *distributed, decentralized, collaborative and adaptative organizations* (Kelly 1994:189): they dwell in many places concurrently, strive to gain adaptability by delegating decision-making to the small group of persons closest to the task, are a loosely bound group of symbiotic partners, and are continually adjusting to new circumstances in order to generate knowledge value-addition.

Governance implies power, and distributed governance does not eliminate power. But one is forced not to rely solely on coordination by powerful vertical forces. Power may indeed be expressed as easily as *power with* or *power between* or *power around* than as *power over* (May 1972; Laurent and Paquet 1994). Such different notions of power have the great advantage of allowing one to focus on modes of coordination that make extensive use of all those forms of power.

In lieu of the dichotomy of *power over* versus *zero power,* of vertical coordination versus horizontal coordination, what is required in the information age of SP(I)Ns is a set of signposts likely to reach diagonally across levels, building blocks, and other such barriers, and based on all those forms of power is a mélange of technical, functional, social, ideological, and cultural synergies and competitions, where learning, consultation, negotiation and bargaining are ever present (Abrahamson and Fombrun 1994:736–7).

In a knowledge-based and innovation-driven economy, accumulation of knowledge is the name of the game. The choice of a governance structure does not aim simply at reducing *transaction costs*, but at ensuring dynamic efficiency, that is, at reducing transition costs from one technological situation, one process, one structure or one dominant logic to another, through learning. Since hierarchies have limited learning abilities and markets have limited capacities to process information effectively, network alliances are a way to counter these limitations; they reduce the uncertainty and adaptation costs arising from the complexity of the environment through an increase in the collective organizational capabilities of the partners (Ciborra 1992).

One powerful force fuelling effective transition is the meso-culture in which the network is embedded (Saxenian 1994). Another is the absorptive capacity of network organization—its capacity to learn, to adapt, and to innovate (Cohen and Levinthal, 1989, 1990). In our view, it is in the interaction between these "contextual" and "dispositional" dimensions that transversal coordination rests (Bourdieu 1994).

(d) The Gulliver effect
The joint impact of information dominance, accelerated change, and of distributed governance has made the socio-economy both more volatile and more malleable. But it has also put immense strain on "national institutions". "As the world integrates economically, the component parts are becoming more numerous and smaller, but also more important. All at once, the global economy is growing while the size of the parts are shrinking" (Naisbitt 1994:16). This has put much pressure on the institutional order to ensure a better capacity to coordinate transnationally in a shrinking world, while increasing its capacity to more finely coordinate subnational activities within a distributed governance system that has become more decentralized (Paquet 1994d).

In fact, the nation state, when confronted with the global adjustment processes and the demands of subnational groups, is not unlike Gulliver: unable to deal effectively either with the dwarfs of Lilliput or the giants of Brobdingnag (Sérieyx 1994). This creates a particularly difficult problem in an era when both the institutional order per se, and the mindset that underpins it, have to be transformed to meet the coordination needs of the network society in an information age.

In pre-modern society, the institutional order was primarily geared to reducing the risk of societal or individual disasters, subject to the constraint that some minimal economic surplus be extracted. It did not necessarily promote institutions geared to wealth-creation and economic growth. With the emergence of modern society (from the Renaissance to the Enlightenment, and culminating with the Industrial Revolution) the institutional order re-crystallized differently; it became geared to the imperative of maximizing value-added, subject to some loose, risk-minimization constraints.

The degree of turbulence that the world economy experienced during the middle of the twentieth century has triggered a switch back to a reemphasis on the importance of promoting institutions of risk avoidance. This has been the Welfare State era. While there are clear signs that the pendulum may again be swinging back to an institutional order geared to maximizing the economic surplus, in the twenty-first century, we are still very much trapped in a mid-20th century institutional order (Adelman 1973) and we are for the time being poorly served by such an institutional order not fully adjusted to the new realities (Paquet and Roy 1995a).

We are also badly served by the fact that the nation state is still being celebrated as the key instrument of risk-minimization or wealth-creation, at a time when it has lost much of its capacity to challenge, coordinate and lead business organizations. These organizations have become more and more distributed in order to ensure greater closeness to the market, to changes in society, to the opportunities for innovation, and have succeeded in eluding the reach of state control. But the "centralized mindset" that prevailed in the industrial age is still very much with us, and is stalling the adaptation of the institutional order to the new subnational coordination needs of the information age (Resnick 1994a).

Institutional learning in a network world: a new dynamic

Network organizations operate in the same manner as the brain. In the network world, adaptation and learning are the very same thing, for one cannot learn without changing. As new experience is sampled, learning occurs, parameters are changed, and the new recorded patterns are encoded in a distributed way.

The disadvantage of this form of storage is that it produces much interference: new patterns may crowd old ones, old patterns may distort new ones, congruent patterns may clump together. On the other hand, networks act as adaptive model-free estimators: they can store, recognize, and retrieve patterns on the basis of limited samples of fuzzy signals. This enables a network to be fairly resilient, and to recognize a pattern even if many components fail. The brain can recognize the Kanizsa square (see figure 1) even though technically it is not there (Kosko 1991).

In the same manner, the network organization is capable of recognizing patterns even if only a few nodes of the network register their presence, and even though some segments of the network have been destroyed, eroded, or rendered insensitive. Networks are fuzzy systems; they are not really rule-based (except in very limited domains), but rather principle-based. And the principles adapt

Figure 1: The Kanizsa Square

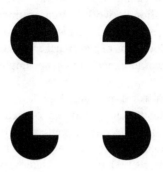

Source: Kosko 1991: 2.

continuously to novel circumstances. Courts cite principles to justify adopting certain rules. In the information age, where fuzziness is the new reality, the institutions are based on general principles that often work across layers and subsystems. Institutional learning and adaptation will therefore proceed at many levels concurrently.

To fix ideas, we have identified four basic components of this new dynamic.

(a) A cognitive institutional order
Markets handle commodities well; but they do not process information and knowledge as effectively, for information and knowledge cannot be reduced to the level of physical inputs, any more than management or entrepreneurship can be regarded as just another input. In both cases, we are referring to *enabling resources* that inform, shape, and catalyze other resources (Paquet 1994a).

Since cognition is conditioned and restricted by the mechanism of brain and mind, the institutional order and the coordination maps that are adapted to the information age must focus on the way in which people gain knowledge, on representations, on symbolic resources, on the whole process through which individuals and collectivities learn, because this is the central dimension that requires coordination in the new economy. Cognition-related institutions aim at developing a higher ratio of meaningful information to noise, through an improvement of the various information/communication enhancement mechanisms: more effective skills at extracting patterns, easier transformation of frames of reference, or of the dominant logic, as experience accumulates, reduction of cognitive dissonance, and so on.

Cognition does not occur only at the individual level. Creative individuals can rarely reach their goals in isolation. They operate in the context of organizations embodying communication networks. Organizations learn from experience (Hutchins 1991): changes in the informational environment, as a result of new circumstances or breakdown/loss of perceptual equipment generate new workable configurations. This is not unlike what is happening when a neuronal network is modified (Coward 1990).

As one moves from a world of material goods to a world of ideas, some of our most fundamental institutions pertaining to intellectual property (the most important new property) are becoming ineffective. In the industrial age, "the conceptual heart of a patent was the material result...it had to be a thing, and the thing had to work" (Barlow 1993). Institutions like the patents regimes were quite sufficient to protect the rights of the producer of new knowledge, and thereby to ensure that the appropriate amount of resources would continue to flow into inventive activity.

But it has become ever more difficult for copyright and patent institutions to deal with digitized property, ideas, and with information detached from the physical plane. Consequently, the ineffectiveness of existing laws is placing in peril the very process of production of new knowledge that is central to the information age, or so it would appear.

The new cognitive institutional order will specify the terms and conditions of enterprise in cyberspace: (i) the protections that will develop will depend much more on technology and ethics than on the law; (ii) knowledge and information will be experienced as perishable rather than possessed, and will be based on relationship and interaction rather than ownership, since access to the latest version of relevant information is desirable in a world of continuous and rapid change.

The technology of encryption will undoubtedly fill part of the gap left by copyright and patent laws, and allow much of the information flow to be privatized. This will have a major impact on the free flow of ideas. But most of the void will be filled by a new dependency on real-time performance and timely interactive service as privileges that users will be willing to pay for, even though some skeletal version of the information service of interest might be obtained for nothing.

The information age will trigger the growing importance of *relational exchange* (Goldberg 1989), and the need to develop institutional coordination devices based on appeal to solidaristic values, and collective goods to serve as signposts for them (Hollingsworth 1994). These are bound to generate governance mechanisms built more on complex collaborative ventures, partnerships, and "conversations", than on coercion or competition (Webber 1993).

The evolution in knowledge production is so dramatic in the information age that some have referred to it as "the new production of knowledge", labeled *Mode* 2, and is characterized as knowledge production (i) carried out in the context of application, and (ii) marked by transdisciplinarity, heterogeneity, organizational heterarchy and transience, and quality control which emphasizes context- and use-dependence (Gibbons et al, 1994). This is bound to call for a reconfiguring of the landscape of knowledge-producing, knowledge-mediating and knowledge-diffusing institutions as a more distributed knowledge production system emerges.

(b) A new key bargain

John R. Commons used to identify the different epochs in economic history by the dominion of key bargains: the rent bargain, the price bargain and the wage bargain as corresponding to the central nexus of the institutions of feudalism, commercial capitalism, and industrial capitalism (Commons 1934). In the information age, information has become the new crucial resource, and the key bargain is now over control of the forum.

Forum is used here "to refer not only to a particular place where speech and communication takes place, but to designate the whole range of institutions and situations of public communication. This usage is analogous to the way in which we speak of the 'market'—referring not merely to the supermarket on the corner, or to the stock exchange, but to the broad range of economic transactions at all sorts of other loci as well, and even to those that cannot be connected to any specific locus at all. The forum is essentially a system of opportunities and protections—opportunities to enter into communication and protection against some of the consequences of doing so" (Tussman 1977:95). Key bargains are central nexuses of arrangements having an asymmetric and determining impact on the shape of other institutional arrangements because of the centrality of the bargain in question.

Information is expandable without any obvious limits; it is also compressible— it can be concentrated, summarized, miniaturized. It is also a substitute for labour, capital, or physical materials, transportable at the speed of light, and diffusive like a virus. Most importantly, information is *shareable:* "if I give you a flower or sell you my automobile, you have it and I don't. But if I sell you an idea, we both have it. And if I give you a fact or tell you a story, it's like a good kiss: in sharing the thrill, you enhance it" (Cleveland 1982). Yet this new kind of shareable resource is in the nature of a collective good, and is not easily allocated by markets.

Coordination is therefore likely to depend on the building of alliances, partnerships, and collaborative relationships, bringing together partners from all sectors through a variety of non-market mechanisms. In turn this means that a great premium is put on networking, if one is to engineer the requisite capacity to transform in order to ensure dynamic efficiency.

The new institutional regulation of the forum will resemble what Richard Schultz was hinting at in the title of a paper published a few years ago: *Partners in a Game WithoutMasters* (Schultz 1982). These sorts of institutions are based on new forms of governance, demanding co-decisions, concertations or harmonizations for there is no other way one can hope to gain control of the forum. But such forms of governance cannot evolve without the requisite infrastructure of collective institutions, based on solidaristic values leading one to promote and adopt such practices (Hollingsworth 1994). And, in turn, we know that this sort of macroculture is not emerging naturally in the North American environment and in the Anglo-American economic space (Canada, United States, U.K., Australia, New Zealand, South Africa) that is built on the primacy of competitive values (Choate and Linger 1988). Therefore, one could expect that North America may be somewhat at a disadvantage vis-à-vis the other two economic blocks of the Triad (Asia and Europe) that have developed a more robust infrastructure of institutions capable of adopting arrangements based on collaboration and cooperation.

(c)   The NWIO and fair bargain
In the information age regulation of the forum cannot be a strictly national affair. The new telecommunications create a "global village", so there is a need for some form of joint accord on forum regulation. This has found its way into the expression "The New World Information Order" (NWIO). This is nothing more than a reference to an "evolutionary process of seeking a more just and equitable balance in the flow and content of information, a right to national self-determination of domestic communication policies, and finally, at the international level, a two-way information flow, reflecting more accurately the aspirations and activities of the less developed countries" (McPhail 1981).

This is a crucial pillar of the new institutional order because of the emergence of the computer-mediated global economic system in which the global financial and trading systems are dependent on a transnational information infrastructure that eliminates geographical, functional, and jurisdictional boundaries. The many colloquies around the world are the forerunners of a new set of institutions that may take us in any number of directions: either in the direction of lesser interdependency among nations at one extreme, to global government at the other, with intermediate positions occupied by a market-driven global computer-mediated society, or by "some form of limited but cooperative control, regulation and guidance over the global economy" (Estabrooks 1988).

The NWIO is a fuzzy version of the last option: an alternative regulatory framework, a way to replace the "colonialism" and the "imperialism" of the market-driven option by a framework that would aim at fairness.

This new regulatory framework has become necessary because international transactions have been transformed dramatically in the information age. Asymmetries in information and "reasonable" constraints on data flows may amount to nothing less than a substantial non-tariff barrier. As John Diebold (1985) puts it, "whether a case involves Brazilian procurement preferences, or Japan's requirement that data be transmitted in a batch instead of an on-line mode, or French reporting requirements concerning data banks, the net result is a competitive edge for domestic industry" (88). The same may be said about national information policies designed to promote political and social goals like the protection of privacy, national security, cultural sovereignty, or the like.

The foundation of the new order has been widely discussed in terms of rights—rights of individuals and collectivities—to ensure a *fair bargain* regime in the information age. Yet we do not know what sort of legal, institutional, or ethical structures are likely to generate the requisite progressivity (i.e., a capacity to adjust optimally) as change occurs. The new order is rooted in negotiated access to the particular world networks that are at the source of the wealth of nations.

Some principles might help to define the contours of a fairness regime in the information age:

- the principle of minimal entitlements (to provide the maximum margin of manoeuvrability for co-decision, concertation, and harmonization);
- the principle of requisite variety (to emphasize the degree to which one must count on variety to control variety);
- the principle of generalized recontracting (to underline that arrangements should be open for continuous renegotiation as circumstances change);
- the principle of progressivity (to define the meta-vision of continuous capacity to transform in the direction of dynamic efficiency).

These design guidelines are preferable to the strict reliance on rights and markets on the one hand, or to the emergence of warring blocs on the other.

But such principles require forums where deliberations on such issues can be carried out. And such forums are not readily available at the transnational level. GATT served as an unconstrained forum for some 50 years, but it may have outrun its usefulness. Indeed, the formalization of the World Trade Organization (WTO) may have deprived the GATT roundtable of much of its fluidity.

In any case, in a world where finance, and not trade, is the prime mover, the WTO will not suffice. The financial coordination agencies have to be brought in for modernization. The development of the open, integrated, and interactive global economic system is now translating into an extremely volatile global financial economy.

What is required now is a coordinated system of "circuit-breakers" operating across the major markets when the situation in one locale threatens to get out of control (Estabrooks 1988:167). But we have not yet found a way to introduce such a form of soft co-regulation in the institutional order.

(d) Neobiological evolution of the institutional order

In the information age, the butterfly effect prevails: small variations in input can translate into huge variations in output. Strange loops are ever present. Evolution is therefore not necessarily gradual and continuous. Indeed, one of the great weaknesses of Darwinian explanations is the lack of evidence about intermediate evolutionary stages in the fossil records. Darwin did not know what triggered mutation, or how evolution developed. He assumed that it emerged randomly and proceeded continuously as if managed by a bureaucracy of genes overviewing the lives of other genes (Kelly 1994).

In a paradoxical way, the information age has modified the evolutionary character of the socio-economy and the institutional order in a way that has brought it closer to what happens in natural systems and vivisystems.

"Natural systems" and vivisystems are instituted according to principles that run against the grain of the sort of gradualness implied by Darwinism. Evolution proceeds in a much more discontinuous and synergetic way. In the same way, "human institution clumps...find it easier to grow than to evolve, required to adapt too far from their origins, most institutions will die" (Kelly 1994:381). Life and information age institutions do not evolve as much as they *crystallize* into a new form, as if they were switching to a new dominant logic.

Stuart Kauffman (1993) has shown that order emerges spontaneously and inevitably from rich and complex networks, and that such evolutionary systems tend to evolve towards a state where each node has very few connections. Sparsely connected networks are stagnant and overly connected networks are frozen; maximal nimbleness would appear to be achieved at low connectivity especially diagonal interdependence across boundaries for they are more likely to stimulate innovation (Abrahamson and Fombrun 1994:735–7).

Thus, the new institutional order will crystallize into new orientation maps in a discontinuous manner.

While we do not know what will trigger the discontinuity, Kevin Kelly has suggested a composite portrait of the *emerging new institutional order* if, as suggested, it were to evolve in a neobiological way:

- distributed intelligence;
- bottom-up control;
- omnipresence of increasing returns;
- growth by creating multiple layers of simplicity and chunking;
- encouraging diversity;
- eccentricity and instability;
- seeking persistent disequilibrium; and
- organizing around self-changing rules (Kelly 1994; Taylor 1994).

This mutation to the new institutional order has to overcome the major hurdle generated by the need to reframe most of our institutions, from patents to money, in order to ensure coordination in the network world of virtual organizations.

In such a world, successful organizations are those that find ways to accommodate and resolve the contradictory needs of promoting competitive pressure and network cooperation at the same time. These countervailing pressures raise the question of the source of the requisite amount of trust, unrequited transfers, and the like that are necessary for such islands of cooperation to be built in a sea of competition. This calls for an institutional order that promotes and adopts clan-type governance systems (Boisot 1987).

The road to this new pattern of governance (less heavy-handed and more flexible, less directive and more participative, less technocratic and more diffuse) may appear at best somewhat utopian, and at worst as a hybrid form of organization that might unleash the dominance of the most ungodly exclusive coalitions.

These two objections have been voiced in very articulate ways, yet they are not warranted.

Clan-type networks exist both in the private and the public sector: this should answer the charge of impractical idealism; moreover, the successful clan-type networks are open, inclusive, pluralist, and coherent. This should dispel the fear that clans must degenerate into conspiracies (Hine 1977; O'Toole and Bennis 1992; Paquet 1994d).

First, the new institutional order will be more cognition-oriented and provide signposts geared to relational exchange to better coordinate *Mode 2* systems of production of knowledge. Second, it will be built around a new institutional regulatory regime (to control the forum) that is based on much harmonization, concertation, and many co-decisions to help partners cooperate in a game without masters. Third, it will be spread over many layers of orientation maps pertaining to different dimensions of the institutional order (international, national, subnational, and so on, but also financial, informational, etc.) and will aim at providing the necessary signposts to ensure fairness. And finally, in the name of progressivity, it will ensure maximal nimbleness through low connectivity across boundaries.

The precise characteristics of the new institutional order remain unclear, but it is likely that, on the occasion of the emergence of some key feature of the new order (like electronic money, or a new regime of patent and copyright arrangements) there may be a quick crystallization of the new order around such new key central bargains. This is why the debates about encryption or the information highway are so acrimonious. The outcomes of some of the ongoing debates may indeed determine who would be allowed to hijack the forum.

One encouraging preliminary result of this analysis is that the required form of coordination may be neither simple vertical nor horizontal ligatures, but may not be as complex as might have been presumed; it will depend on fuzzy principles rather than rigid rules, but the number of principles and the optimal degree of connectivity for the maximal nimbleness of networks need not be large (Resnick 1994a). Finally, to promote innovation in network organizations that are distributed, decentralized, collaborative, and adaptative, the institutional order requires signposts and orientation maps that cut diagonally across layers of organizations. One may now turn to an examination of this transversal form of coordination.

Transversal coordination

The coordination maps of use in the complex networks of conversations characteristic of the information age must provide the requisite guidance system for the cognitive economy to be as dynamically effective as it can be. But one cannot ascertain what mechanisms of coordination are required until one prospects the nature of the terrain. We have underlined three major characteristics of the new environment in the information age that will constrain the nature of the required coordination.

(a) Spectrality and anonymity
One of the most important impacts of the information age on society has been what Marc Guillaume has called *spectralité*. The omnipresence of information and technical change has generated the emergence of multiple networks which have generated a new form of sociality where "spectres who do not know one another meet" and where, in an anonymous way, a new type of relationships, freed from the usual ritual of identification and of the rules of civility, has emerged (Baudrillard and Guillaume 1994). This is already the world of the Citizen's Band, of "*messageries roses*", of "virtual communities" and "smart mobs" (Kelly 1993, 1994; Rheingold 1993, 2002).

Spectralité does not only connote phantom-like existence but also a prismatic reality, that is, a reality deconstructed into many elements. To be spectral is to have many faces and to engage only one of them in any communication interface. In this context, everyone can disconnect and avoid a well-defined identity. Many have already inferred that the information age will generate a society of phantom-like nomads, where partnerships and alliances would appear unlikely and precarious.

Spectralité does not mean loss of identity, but a *dispersion of identity* and the possibility of getting involved in a variety of networks and virtual relationships. While this may signal the demise of the traditional community and neighbourhood as we have known it, it opens the door to a multitude of "cyberhoods" and new ligatures. These new groupings and networks are bound to generate new forms of relationships which, though partial and somewhat "disembodied", could forge strong community bonds (Rheingold 1993, 2002; Barlow 1995). In this spectral world of anonymity, coordination is difficult. Some pessimistic observers have been led to suggest that anonymous market-type ligatures are the only viable ones; the social contract becomes a commercial contract and the citizen is reduced to the role of client. Others are more optimistic and see the spectral society evolve into non-centralized networks, into a cognitive economy and a learning society where new ligatures and new rules can and will emerge (Paquet 1994c).

What those new ligatures might be is not entirely clear, but since every individual is partially connected to many others via all sorts of networks in cyberspace, coordination requires that we find ways to somewhat *integrate those overlapping networks* in order to allow the individual to adjust and adapt in many different dimensions simultaneously. Indeed, the flip side of multiple limited identities might well be a greater flexibility and adaptability.

The coordination maps likely to be of use in providing guidance for such multidimensional adjustments must obviously be transversal to all those different overlapping networks in cyberspace; they must provide the necessary signposts to ensure that those vertical layers of organizations, the many different horizontal meso-forums and the diagonal ligatures across boundaries are loosely integrated to ensure nimbleness. This can only be engineered through transversal coordinating institutions.

(b) Distributed governance and tangled hierarchies

In the network society of the information age, governance must be distributed. This calls for a reconfiguration of the forms of governance according to a dominant logic like the principle of subsidiarity (with its multiplicity of levels of governing) but also for a reconstruction of society around meso-forums dedicated to discussions about different sub-worlds.

33

Although the usual way of dealing with governance is to identify the top-down vertical centralized links that provide the integrative forces for the society as a whole, this is not workable in the information age. In a world where each agent has a multiplicity of limited identities and belongs to a vast array of networks, private, public, and social organizations have to become distributed to reach out to those spectral actors.

In this complex and fluid informational environment, effective coordination can occur neither by threat of coercion (i.e., via power systems) nor by the operations of the market exchanges *stricto sensu* (i.e., via transaction systems). One has to count on consensus and inducement-oriented arrangements (Kumon 1992). This new form of governance, deliberately distributed, dispersed, non-centralized, is built on "vigilant trust" and "negotiated loyalty" (Sabel 1993; Paquet 1994b, 1994d).

In societies like Japan, where the shared "contextualist" culture is strong, such a distributed networked governance system works rather well. The "network state" is nothing but a transversal process of consensus formation and inducement going through the multiple layers of societal and organizational networks that are either formally or semi-formally institutionalized (Kumon 1992). But in societies that do not have this strong contextualist culture, coordination is more complex. It requires new ways of linking the different layers of private, public, and social organizations to ensure nimbleness and progressivity.

This coordination is often provided by informal administrative arrangements and conventions that are not always a strong enabling glue, and may not trigger the required social learning (Orléan 1994).

The most basic challenge is to effect coordination in the presence of strange loops and tangled hierarchies. Strange loops are aptly illustrated in many drawings of Escher, and are defined by Douglas Hofstadter as a phenomenon that "occurs whenever, by moving upwards (or downwards) through the level of some hierarchical system, we unexpectedly find ourselves right back where we started" (Hofstadter 1979:10).

In such a context, co-evolution (i.e., organizational and institutional co-learning) in society, polity and economy, but also among the different layers of networks, and among the different meso-forums, occurs in loci where there are overlapping jurisdictions or interests, and where paramountcy may depend on circumstances. This is the locus for transversal integration.

In federal-provincial affairs in Canada, where jurisdictional concurrency with paramountcy of one sort or another prevails, we have the basis for co-evolution of the rules of the game. Under conditions of time and place, negotiated consensus evolves, but it may evolve in many different ways. One of the merits of Burelle's 1995 book is that it paints a rainbow of institutional arrangements covering the whole range of fields—from complete federal jurisdiction to complete provincial jurisdiction through different terrains demanding harmonization, coordination, or co-decision, with paramountcy belonging to one or another level—but it also underlines the lack of adequate forums in which to debate many of these issues and the gaping holes in the institutional order in place (Burelle 1995).

Co-evolution thrives on the symbiosis among the political, social, and economic spheres, on alliances and partnerships across borders and boundaries. Consequently, the emerging consensus or compromise may take root in any portion of the terrain and constrain other portions of the institutional order. Any tight compartmentalization of the three families of institutions is bound to be counterproductive, for they are in a process of co-evolution (Norgaard 1994). Co-evolution entails a focus on transversal relations as the relevant unit of analysis, and a forging of coordination built on trespassing (Paquet 1993).

In the rapport between government and business, for instance, this approach stands in sharp contrast to the cut-and-dried position of Jane Jacobs. She has denounced any mixing of the guardian moral syndrome (underpinning the power system) and the commercial moral syndrome (underpinning the transaction system). For Jacobs, the first syndrome (the guardian syndrome) translates into imperatives like "shun trading", "exert prowess", "adhere to tradition", hierarchy, discipline, ostentation, largesse, honour, fortitude, and deception. The second syndrome (the commercial syndrome) translates into imperatives like "shun force", "celebrate voluntary agreements", "collaborate", "compete", "be industrious and thrifty" and "dissent". Any attempt to mix the two syndromes can only lead to "monstrous hybrids" (Jacobs 1992).

In the informational age of networking, symbiosis between syndromes cannot but occur, does occur, and one does not find that "crazy things happen", as Jane Jacobs suggests. Indeed, networks require a system of governance that combines many appreciative systems or syndromes, and the role of *transversal* coordination is to weave them together.

(c) Fuzzy systems and switching mechanisms
In a complex information world, one cannot rely on rigid permanent rules. The governance system becomes a fuzzy system. And yet key decisions, reorientation decisions have to be made in keeping with changing and turbulent circumstances, but also in keeping with some strategically imprecise guiding principles.

In the absence of an animal instinct, providing a switching mechanism from one regime of action to another as required, or of a most effective "contextualist" culture as in the case of Japan, a fuzzy syncretic meta-vision is necessary (Vertinsky 1987; Lenihan et al. 1994).

The reason for this is rather simple. If one is intent on changing rules, one must be in a position to discuss the principles involved. In a legal framework, laws, rules, and regulations are established. The principles and rules about defining rules are outlined in the constitution—the constitution being a meta-rule. In the same manner, if one wishes to change the constitution (i.e., the rules about changing rules) one must shift the debate to a higher plane: the rules about changing rules about changing rules. In many countries, this requires a referendum. In the information age, basic values and fuzzy principles will act as meta-rules in decisions about activating the switching mechanism between regimes (Orgogozo and Sérieyx 1989).

The search for such a meta-vision is at the core of the current discussions about governance in Canada. This is one of the merits of the recent book by André Burelle (1995) but also of the book by Lenihan, Robertson and Tassé (1994), and of the program review mandate proposed by the Chrétien government in 1994. They provide, each in its own way, hints of what might be called a *workable meta-vision* that puts forward a public philosophy capable (1) in Burelle's case, of inspiring a dramatic jurisdictional reallocation of duties over a whole range of fields coordinated by an array of new institutions; (2) in Lenihan et al.'s case, of suggesting a new orientation for the constitutional debate; and (3) in the case of the program review mandate, of guiding the process of rethinking the Canadian governance system that might have made it possible for Canada to accomplish through the administrative route what could not be accomplished through constitutional ordeals (Paquet 1995a; Paquet and Roy 1995b).

This sort of meta-vision (with the principle of subsidiarity at its core in many cases) signals the emergence of a new dominant logic.

This adaptive emergent property already permeates the disparate arrangements under construction, and underpins the transversal coordinating mechanism across layers of network boundaries and organizations. Whether this new dominant logic will simply supersede or revise the one in place, or whether, in order to tackle our complex evolving realities, there will be a need for a multiplicity of dominant logics operating selectively, depending on time, place, and circumstances, remains an open question.

This sort of selective operation of a plurality of dominant logics may express itself through a set of principles for "normal times" and another set for "crisis situations", or may lead to different logics applied in different loci. These challenges impact daily life. For instance, top management draw on different sources of strategic variety when firms diversify and must add new business lines that are very dissimilar to previous operations. This often forces the firm to operate with multiple logics simultaneously. The variegated world brought forth by the information age will require learning to live with multiple dominant and partially contradictory logics (Prahalad and Bettis 1986:495–6).

Switching to multiple dominant logics is one of the main challenges facing Canada's governance system. But it is not easy to modify mental maps. Usually, only substantial problems or crises can provoke an acceptance of the need to change, and this opportunity can only be seized if concurrently there is a significant amount of unlearning to make way for new mental maps. This is even more difficult when the information age would appear to force organizations to learn to use multiple, partially contradictory cognitive maps (Prahalad and Bettis 1986:499).

Conclusion

The institutional order is an *emergent phenomenon:* it is adaptable, evolvable, resilient, boundless, and it breeds novelty; but it is also, most of the time, non-optimal, non-controllable, non-predictable and even fundamentally non-understandable (Kelly 1994:22–3). This explains why the discourses about social transformation of the institutional order are so vague and non-committal (Drucker 1994). We have to be satisfied with observing the "emergent properties" of the new order as they materialize.

In the transition period, one may expect a strong affirmation of "limited identities", much disconnection, and challenges to most of the rigid and centralized institutions. There will also be a tendency for the emergent order to get anchored at the meso-level, and to be couched in informal rules of the game agreed to by persons who share a "web of trust". One may expect that, at a given point in time, one key signpost or standard will mutate—the minting and issuing of currency, for instance; this may be the signal that the institutional order is about to crystallize differently as "para-currencies can pop up anywhere there is trust" (Kelly 1993:58).

But it may well be that the main challenge will not be in mastering the switching from one dominant logic to another, but in learning to cope with multiple dominant logics, and therefore with concurrent distributed institutional orders.

The new "coordination" *en chantier* will *loosely* intermediate the spectral and distributed network world generated by the information age, and its dynamic will probably depend on multiple meta-visions built on very few principles. Many suggest that this spells not only the end of the nation state but also the end of politics and parliamentary democracy.

In the network age, fluidity is the foundation of dynamism and survival, and institutional stability imposes constraints to relational fluidity. Some predict the emergence of an "imperial age" reminiscent of the Roman empire under Hadrian, where the "institutional order" will not aspire to being more than a loose web of agreements to ensure compatibility among open networks (Guéhenno 1993).

What is most troublesome is that the "emergent properties" (Wheeler 1928) of this new "imperial age" are not discernible and predictable at this time. But one need not await the new age inactively. One should monitor carefully the emergent properties of the new order, attempt to identify its dominant logic or logics, and modestly interfere to improve ever so slightly the goodness of fit with the coordination needs of the economy, society, and polity.

This is a modest role in keeping with our abilities. Indeed, one is reminded of the role played by the Stoics after the demise of *polis*. At the time, a wisdom rooted in robust intellectual independence gave freedom a new meaning that was more philosophical than political. This could only lead to questions about the conformity demanded by the institutional order, and the *naiveté* of those who had come to expect too much from social and political mechanical contraptions. It is from those local ethical debates that a new sense of solidarity could emerge bottom-up, as it did in Antiquity. In this sort of world, granting much space to freedom, tact, civility, and solidarity, one may expect politics to rise from the ashes like the Phoenix.

Chapter 2

States, Communities, and Markets:
The Distributed Governance Scenario

<blockquote>
"...the creation of risks
has outpaced the development of trust ..."
M. Horsman and A. Marshall (1994:212)
</blockquote>

Introduction

According to Richard Cooper (1997), our era marks the "beginning of the end of the Westphalian state system". This conclusion echoes many other recent diagnoses of the demise of the nation state (Kaplan 1994; Drucker 1994; Ohmae 1995; Huntington 1996). What is particularly interesting in Cooper's analysis is his ruthless use of Ockham's razor. He focuses on three rather simple factors that are, in his estimation, sufficient to explain the erosion of this dominant jurisdiction.

The first two (population pressure and higher standards of living) explain the growing demand pressures put on the state as an echo of the expectations of this larger and richer population. The third factor (the greater mobility of the factors of production) underpins the state's considerably weaker capacity to extract from footloose factors of production any additional resources at the very moment when the nation state requires them to meet the growing demands for public goods.

This is not the first time that the nation-state has been pronounced dead or dying. Even some twenty years ago, many observers had already declared that it had become too small to deal effectively with important transnational issues, and too large to deal effectively with smallish local issues (Bell 1976). But this argument is persuasive only if one focuses on the state component of the nation state.

It is easy to show that demographic movements and technology, financial and communication flows have transformed the borders of the national state into rather porous boundaries, and that the political territory of the national state is becoming less and less congruent with meaningful contemporary economic realities. This is the case even though the borders of the national state would still appear to be significant and to matter (The Economist 1990; McCallum 1995). One may explain this residual meaningfulness by the fact that the socio-economic outcomes are still mediated to a certain extent by the national state context (i.e., by resilient modes of regulation that remain national in scope, and engender principles of cooperation and competition shaped by national regimes) (Ettlinger 1994).

But this insistence on national state structures leaves too much out of the equation: the central concern is not structures but *the process of governance* (Paquet 1994b). Consequently, even though one might go along with the thrust of Cooper's argument about the traditional state, there is much to be gained from developing a heuristically more robust alternative *problématique*, based on governance. It should be capable of providing not only an explanation for the faltering of the national state, but also some sense of what governance system is emerging in its place.

In the next sections, I first suggest an analytical framework to examine the process of governance. Then I show that governance has evolved away from state-centred, bureaucratic and hierarchical regimes toward a more distributed pattern of authority dispersed over economy, society, and polity. This leads, in section 3, to an exploration of the consequences of this *de facto* decoupling of nation and state on the emerging governance system. In conclusion, I suggest that the new distributed governance will generate not only a more diffused pattern of power, but that it will also tend to vest communities, networks, and meso innovation systems with new and greater valence.

The governance *problématique*

Governance is about guiding: it is the process through which an organization is steered, through which effective coordination is engineered when power, resources, and information are widely distributed.

(a) From a Newtonian to a Quantum world
Fifty years ago, in Canada, governance was debated in the language of management science. It was presumed that public, private and social organizations were strongly directed by leaders who had a good understanding of their environment, of the future trends in the environment if nothing were done to modify it, of the inexorable rules of the game they had to put up with,

and of the goals pursued by their own organization. Those were the days when the social sciences were still Newtonian: a world of deterministic, well-behaved mechanical processes, where causality was simple because the whole was the sum of the parts. The challenge was relatively simple: building on the well-defined goals of the organization to design the control mechanisms likely to get the organization where it wanted to be.

Many issues were clearly amenable to this approach, and many still are. But as the pace of change accelerated, and as the issues grew more complex, private, public, and social organizations came to be confronted more and more with "wicked problems", that is, issues in which the goals either are not known or are very ambiguous, *and* in which the means-ends relationships are highly uncertain and poorly understood (Rittel and Webber 1973). In dealing with such problems, inquiry (in the Deweyan sense) can only mean "thinking and acting that originates in and aims at resolving a situation of uncertainty, doubt and puzzlement" (Schön 1995:82).

This calls for a new way of thinking about governance. At best, one could hope for pattern causality: the gradual construction of a "causal" story on the basis of a background knowledge of the system that is often tacit and "working back", so to speak, as plumbers do when tracing a leak to its source. In this Quantum world, there is no objective reality, the uncertainty principle looms large, events are at best probable, and the whole is a network of synergies and interactions that is quite different from the sum of the parts (Becker 1991).

Three important forces have played a central role in generating this Quantum world: the rise of the international flexible production system, the accelerating pace of technological change, and the new global financial structure. As a result, governments and state authorities have lost much of their dominion over national economies and societies, and there has been a decline in state legitimacy (Strange 1996).

(b) The Boulding triangle
The erosion of the state's power and legitimacy has shifted attention to the non-state authority in the governance of the nation state, to the other loci or sources of power and authority. Recently, a number of important studies have explored these different sites of power and tracked down the ways in which much of the state authority has become diffused to non-state agents, in both economy and society (Horsman and Marshall 1994; Held 1995; Strange 1996).

Even in the old world of governance, the boundaries between the economic, political, and social spheres were never either well-defined conceptually, or well-delineated statistically: they did not correspond to a rigid frontier, but rather to a wavering and evolving fracture zone between subsets of organizations and institutions integrated by different mechanisms. This has become even more true in the new world of governance.

Economists have explored this terrain for quite some time. François Perroux and Kenneth Boulding have proposed a simple conceptual scheme to map out this terrain (Perroux 1960; Boulding 1970). Both identified three generic ensembles of organizations more or less dominated by a different mechanism of integration: *quid pro quo exchange* (market economy), *coercion* (polity), and *gift or solidarity* (community and society). These mechanisms had been explored by Karl Polanyi (1957) as dominant features of the concrete socio-economies of the past. Perroux and Boulding fleshed out the idea and applied it to the modern context.

To map out this terrain, Boulding used various stylizations of a simple triangle, with each of these mechanisms of integration in its purest form at one of the apexes; all the inner territory represented organizations and institutions embodying different mixes of these integrative mechanisms. A slightly modified version of this sort of triangle is presented in Figure 2.

This approach provides a rough cartography of the organizational terrain into three domains where the rules, arrangements, or mechanisms of coordination are based on different principles: the economic/market domain (B) where supply and demand forces and price mechanism are the norms; the state domain (C) where coercion and redistribution are the rules; and the civil society domain (A) where cooperation, reciprocity, and solidarity are the integrating principles. This corresponds roughly to the standard partitioning of human organizations into economy, polity, and society (Wolfe 1989).

A careful survey of the organizational terrain of many advanced socio-political economies would reveal that society (A), economy (B), and polity (C) each occupy roughly one third of the organizational territory, and that the central point is a rough approximation of the centre of gravity of the organizational

Figure 2: The Boulding triangle

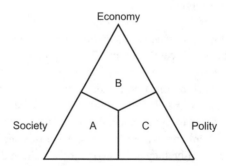

Source: Adapted from Boulding 1970:31.

triangle. This does not correspond to the statistical portrait emerging from official agencies. Zone A activities are under-reported, and little effort has been made to measure them better.

These three sectors have not always had equal valence, and need not carry a similar weight in every socio-political economy. A century ago, the state portion was quite limited, and the Canadian scene was dominated by the other two sets of organizations. From the late 19th century to the 1970s, government grew in importance to the point where probably half of the *measured* activities fell into the general ambit of state and state-related activities. The boundaries have been displaced accordingly over time. More recently, there has been a vigorous counter-movement of privatization and deregulation that has caused a reduction of the state sector, and a reverse shift of the boundaries (Paquet 1996–7).

There has been, in parallel with these swings (giving more valence to one or another of the family of integration mechanisms), a tendency for the new socio-economy to trigger the development of an ever larger number of *mixed* institutions, blending these different mechanisms to some extent (market-based public regulation, public-private-social partnering, etc.) in order to provide the necessary signposts and orientation maps. This has translated in the recent past into a much denser filling-in of the Boulding triangle. A variety of arrangements now exist that provide for compromises between the different pure principles of integration. Mixed institutions have been designed that are capable of providing the basis for cooperation, harmonization, concertation, and even co-decision mechanisms involving elements from all three sectors (Leroy 1990; Burelle 1995; Laurent and Paquet 1998).

Toward a distributed governance

Over the past decades, the governance system has evolved considerably as a result of the important shocks emanating from demographic, financial, and technological change.

(a)   The Boisot information space
In earlier times, when organizations were relatively small and under the direction of autocratic leaders, governance had a fiefdom quality: information flows were very informal, and they were strongly focused on a small group around the leader. But as problems grew more complex, this pattern of governance faltered. More elaborate structures and more formal rules had to evolve to meet the organization's changing needs. But these formal rules remained the preserve of those at the top of the hierarchies. From these emerged the more or less standardized bureaucratic forms of organization that played an important role during *les trentes glorieuses années* from the 1940s to the 1970s.

As the pace of change accelerated, problems became ever more complex, more un-structured, and ever-changing, and the bureaucratic system, with its slow capacity to transform, began to show signs of dysfunction. This led to efforts to partition private, public, and social bureaucracies into smaller, self-contained, and more flexible units that were likely to be more responsive to clients. This market-type governance, built on the price system, had the benefit of being more inclusive, since price information is widely shared.

In the private sector, large companies went into a process of segmentation, creating a multiplicity of more or less independent profit-centred organizations likely to be more attentive to the changing needs of clients, and more adaptable to evolving circumstances. With a lag, public bureaucracies have gone the same route with, for instance, the creation of Executive Agencies in the United Kingdom, or Special Operating Agencies in Canada. Organizations came to be governed—to a much greater extent than before—by the "invisible hand" of the market.

However, information flows in market-type organizations are anonymous and highly stylized. The price-driven steering mechanism within organizations often proved, therefore, less than perfect. For instance, it was insensitive to third-party effects and external economies, and was incapable of appreciating either the synergies within the organization, or the various forces at work in the external environment. More importantly, the myopia of the market led to short-term opportunistic competitive behaviour that proved disastrous for organizations.

As a result, an effort was made to establish or re-establish within their decentralized units the informal cooperative links—*les liens moraux*—that might give an organization a sense of shared values and commitments. Corporate culture acquired a new importance as the sort of social glue that enabled organizations to steer themselves better through a greater use of informal moral contracts based on shared values.

This shift in the governance system's centre of gravity of the governance system is captured well by Max Boisot's information space (Figure 3), in which he identifies the different types of governance schemes that correspond to more or less codified and more or less diffused information flows (Boisot 1987).

While earlier forms of governance continue to persist and endure, the whole organizational architecture has come to be dominated less and less by the sort of centralized formal decision-making and hierarchical control that characterize the governance of fiefdoms and bureaucracies, and more and more by informal and distributed governance systems, such as those that characterize markets and clans. Within a complex and multifaceted governance process, the centre of gravity of Boisot's information space has been shifting broadly from a bureaucratic focus to a market-cum-clan focus over the past few decades.

Figure 3: Boisot's Information Space

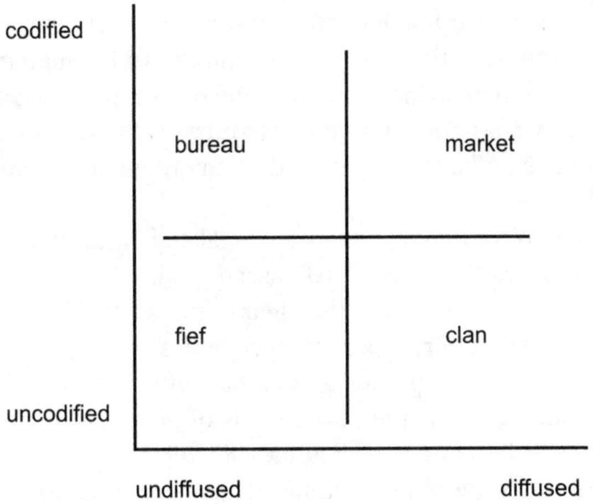

Source: Boisot 1987: 178.

(b) Glocalization and dispersion

Numerous forces have brought about this drift in the governance process of organizations from all three broad sectors. But the acceleration of technical change, the globalization of the finance, investment, and production processes, and the information/communication revolution have been central. They have set the stage for globalization and the breaking down of borders (Horsman and Marshall 1994). As a result, the centralized and hierarchical governance structures have been under stress because of their poor capacity to respond quickly and effectively to fast-changing circumstances.

In times of change, organizations can only govern themselves by becoming capable of learning both what their goals are, and the means to reach them *as they proceed*. This is done by tapping into the knowledge and information that active citizens possess, and getting them to invent ways out of the predicaments they are in. That leads to a more distributed governance, which deprives the leader of his or her monopoly on the governing of the organization. For the organization to learn quickly, everyone must take part in the *conversation*, and bring forward each bit of knowledge and wisdom that he or she has that has a bearing on the issue (Paquet 1992b; Webber 1993; Piore 1995).

To cope with a turbulent environment, organizations must use the environment strategically, in the manner in which the surfer uses the wave, to learn faster, to adapt more quickly. This calls for non-centralization, for an expropriation of the

45

power to steer held by the top managers of the organization. We have moved very far from a unilateral decentralization that can be rescinded. There must be a constant negotiation and bargaining with partners. Managers must exploit all the favourable environmental circumstances, and the full complement of imagination and resourcefulness in the heart and mind of each team player; they must become team leaders in taskforce-type projects, quasi-entrepreneurs capable of cautious sub-optimizing in the face of a turbulent environment (Leblond and Paquet 1988).

This sort of strategy calls for lighter, more horizontal and modular structures, networks, and informal clan-like rapports (Bressand et al. 1989) in units free from procedural morass, empowered to define their mission and their clienteles more precisely, and to invent different performance indicators. This is the case not only in the public sector: in the private sector, the "virtual corporation" and the "modular corporation" are now the new models of governance (Business Week February 8, 1993; Tully in *Fortune* February 8, 1993).

These new modularized private, public, and social organizations cannot impose their views on clients or citizens in a Taylorian way. The firm, very much like the state, must consult. Deliberation and negotiation are everywhere: moving away from goals and controls and into intelligence and innovation. A society based on participation, negotiation, and bargaining more and more replaces one based on universal rights. The strategic organization has to become a broker, a negotiator, an animateur: in this network a consultative and participative mode obtains among the socio-economy, the firm, the state, and communities (Paquet 1992b, 1994e; Castells 1996).

All this triggers a paradoxical outcome that has been analyzed by Naisbitt (1994) and christened *glocalization* by Courchene (1995). As globalization proceeds, economic integration increases, and the component parts of the system become more numerous. The central question is how to organize for faster learning. And it would appear, according to Naisbitt, that the game of learning is going to generate innovation and speed if those components confronted with different local realities are empowered to take decisions on the spot. This is why globalization has led to localization of decision-making, to empowerment, to the dispersion of power, and to a more distributed triangle-wide governance process.

Decoupling nation and state

A decoupling of the nation from the state is indeed one of the central features of the recent evolution. The realignment between state and nation may well translate into a weakening of the state at the national level, while the nation or tribe may acquire a greater presence in the governance system, and fuel a new prominence of national and subnational communities. In the world of glocalization, the community's culture and ethos, together with the sort of partnerships enterprise may construct with local government and third sector organizations, may hold the key to regional or subnational success (Saxenian 1994). So it may well be that the national state is losing power, while the power and authority of the national communities is growing.

(a) More nation and less state

Observers of the 1980s forcefully made the point that "new realities" had been emerging, which had created a dual crisis for the national state: a crisis of performance as the state proved more and more clearly that it could not adequately perform its traditional functions, and a crisis of legitimacy as it became obvious that it could no longer count on mass loyalty to perform its duties (Horsman and Marshall 1994:219).

In Peter Drucker's "new realities" (1989), the questions: who has the authority? who has the power? to whom are the institutions accountable? have become more complex as the power and authority became dispersed in a mutiplicity of sites, and as an array of allegiances ensued. While it has been said that much of that dispersion was possible only because of the modern state, and its capacity to act as a container that shapes all these other allegiances (Walker 1991), the sheer diffraction that this dispersion of power generated led quickly to the modern state's becoming only one form of collective action among many, and one that could no longer claim to be the repository of sovereignty. Sovereignty had become distributed among many sites, and the new citizen had to develop multiple allegiances, as bodies other than the nation state came to be the legitimate repository of much authority. The state was left with only limited brokerage power in this new setting.

The nature of this diffusion of power, and the consequent quantity and quality of authority exercised by the different sites, is a matter on which consensus is not yet established. But there is a broad agreement that non-state authorities exist not only all over the terrain covered by the Boulding triangle, but at all territorial levels (i.e., at all levels of governance: global, regional, continental, national, sub-national, and local). Some have argued that the weakening of states' authorities has led to their failure to discharge their former responsibilities, and that some *ungovernance* has ensued (Strange 1996:14).

This proposition is on the whole correct in the short run. In the longer haul, however, the pattern of power changes, but the lesser authority of the national states and polities leads to other actors in the economy and society taking on these new responsibilities.

This co-evolutionary nature of the pattern of authority does not presume that there is a given quantity-cum-quality of authority that is always retained by someone. Rather, it suggests that any vacuum left by the weakening of the national state leads to some reaction in the other two sectors of the Boulding triangle, and to some reaction at the other levels of governance as well (global, continental, regional, sub-national, and local) and that tends to generate other sites of authority to fill the vacuum.

This process may obviously be derailed by major changes in the fluidity of the system. Broad sweeping civilizational moves à la Huntington (1996) on the global scale, or the development of new corporatist single-issue "identity groups" defined by a total allegiance to a single club at the national or sub-national level (Piore 1995) may prevent the sort of on-going conversation that will lead to social learning and to the emergence of compensatory institutions in other sectors, or at other levels, when the state weakens. But these are unlikely to prevent the dispersion of power (outward, sideways, and downward) toward new sites of authority.

One should not infer from these trends that the national state is about to disappear. At this time, there are still "no substitute structures that can perform all the functions traditionally associated with the nation-state"; one may only say that people "are prepared increasingly to divide their loyalties...and multiple loyalties will be the inevitable result" (Horsman and Marshall 1994:264; Strange 1996:86). The national state is simply losing its privileged position. What is less clear is the way in which the new pattern of loyalties and allegiances will crystallize.

(b) Transversal governance and meso-innovation systems
Our exploration of the evolution of the governance process suggests that this new pattern tends to evolve in two very well-defined directions: (1) its centre of gravity shifting downward toward the sub-national level, with a pattern of power distributed more broadly along the supra-nation-state / infra-nation-state axis, and (2) its diffusion not only reducing the valence of the national government in the governance process, but spanning a broader terrain involving institutions and coordinating maps from the private and social sectors. This new, more devolved and more distributed governance process will be transversal, and built on a multifunctional *esprit de corps* that provides a most fertile ground for social learning, and underpins the sound functioning of economy, society, and polity.

The fact that the national state loses its prominence does not mean that the governance process loses its integrity. What it means is that the governance system comes to be built on a different logic, and becomes coordinated much less by coercive and hierarchical top-down pressures than by associative networks of cooperation built on a *quid pro quo* exchange and on consensus and inducement-oriented systems. Moreover, it means that the governance system's centre of gravity is going to shift downward to the sub-national level from its former focal point on the nation-state.

The transversal governance system will therefore blend components at the transnational, national, and sub-national levels across the three zones of the Boulding triangle.

The addition of a major component of *associative governance* to the more traditional state and market governance mechanisms triggers a major qualitative change. It introduces the network paradigm within the governance process (Cooke and Morgan 1993). And this paradigm not only dominates the transactions of the social sector, but permeates the operations of both the state and market sectors (Amin and Thrift 1995). For the network is not, as is usually assumed, a mixed form of organization existing halfway on a continuum ranging from market to hierarchy. Rather, it is a generic name for a third type of arrangement, built on very different integrating mechanisms: networks are consensus/inducement-oriented organizations and institutions (Kumon 1992).

Networks have two sets of characteristics: those derived from their dominant logic (consensus and inducement-oriented systems) and those derived from their structure.

The consensus dominant logic does not abolish power, but it means that power is distributed. A central and critical feature of networks is the emphasis on voluntary adherence to norms. While this voluntary adherence does not necessarily appear to generate constraints per se on the size of the organization, it is not always easy for a set of shared values to spread over massive disjointed transnational communities. Free riding, high transaction costs, problems of accountability, etc. impose extra work. So the benefits in terms of leanness, agility, and flexibility are such that many important multinationals have chosen not to manage their affairs as a global production engine, but as a multitude of smaller quasi-independent units coordinated by a loose confederated structure, because of the organizational diseconomies of scale in building a clan-type organization (O'Toole and Bennis 1992; Handy 1992).

As for the structural characteristics of the network, they complement nicely the distributed, decentralized, collaborative, and adaptive network intelligence (Kelly 1994:189). The network externalities and spillovers are not spreading in a frictionless world. Networking casts much more of a local shadow than is usually presumed: "space becomes ever more variegated, heterogeneous and finely textured in part because the processes of spatial reorganization...have the power to exploit relatively minute spatial differences to good effect (Harvey 1988). Consequently, a network does not extend boundlessly, but tends instead to crystallize around a unifying purpose, mobilizing independent members through voluntary links, around multiple leaders in integrated levels of overlapping and superimposed webs of solidarity. This underscores the enormous importance of "regional business cultures", and explains the relative importance of small and medium-sized enterprises networks in generating new ideas (Putnam 1993; Lipnack and Stamps 1994).

Reciprocity based on voluntary adherence generates lower costs of cooperation, and therefore stimulates more networking as social capital accumulates with trust.

Not only are the networks generating social capital and wealth, but they have also been closely associated with an increasing degree of progressivity in the economy: that is, with a higher degree of innovativeness and capacity to transform due to the crossing of network boundaries. Indeed, boundary-crossing networks are likely to ignite much innovativeness because they provide an opportunity for reframing and recasting perspectives, and for questioning the assumptions that have been in good currency. One might suggest a parallel between boundary-crossing and migration into another world in which one's home experience serves as a useful contrast to the new realities. Much of the buoyant immigrant entrepreneurship is rooted in this dual capacity to see things differently, and to network within and across boundaries. In the face of placeless power in a globalized economy, seemingly powerless places, with their own communication code on a historically specific territory, are particularly suitable terrains for local collaborative innovation networks.

(c) Renaissance-style interdependency
In the last chapter, we have explained that co-evolution (i.e., organizational and institutional co-learning among society, polity, and economy, but also among the different layers of networks, and among the different meso-forums) occurs in loci where there are overlapping jurisdictions or interests, and where paramountcy may depend on circumstances. This is the locus for transversal integration.

Co-evolution thrives on the symbiosis among the political, social, and economic spheres, on alliances and partnerships across borders and boundaries. Consequently, the emerging consensus or compromise may take root in any portion of the terrain, and importantly constrain other portions of the institutional order. Any tight compartmentalization of the three families of institutions is bound to be counterproductive, for they are in a process of co-evolution (Norgaard 1994). Co-evolution entails a focus on transversal relations as the relevant unit of analysis, and a forging of coordination built on trespassing (Paquet 1993, 1996a).

In the transition period from the present nation state dominated era to the emergent new era of distributed governance and transversal coordination, there will be a tendency for much devolution and decentralization of decision-making, for the meso-level units in polity, society, and economy to become prominent, and

50

for the rules of the game of the emergent order to be couched in informal terms. Moreover, the emergent properties of the new order (be it a public philosophy of subsidiarity or another set of workable guiding principles) are likely to remain relatively unpredictable as one might expect in a neural net type model (Ziman 1991).

The multi-layered structure is something very like a neural net of the kind found in a living brain. Such a layered system of many signal-processing units, interacting in parallel within and between layers, has remarkable properties. It can learn and transform in reaction to external stimuli, and develop a capacity for pattern recognition and for adaptation through experience. Indeed, if the metaphor can be used, the resiliency of the neural net (in the brain or in an organization) is due to the redundancy of connections which allow the information flow to circumvent a hole or a lesion.

It is our view that the new form of transversal coordination now in the making may not suffer as much as some fear from the loss of central control and the weakening of the national state *imperium*. One may indeed expect, as we suggested in the last chapter, the emergence of a different sort of *imperium*, better adapted to the network age: an "imperial" age, reminiscent of the Roman empire under Hadrian, where the institutional order did not aspire to be more than a loose web of agreements to ensure compatibility among open networks (Guéhenno 1993).

Conclusion

In the face of this new emerging institutional order, the whole difference between the perspectives of the optimist and the pessimist hinges on the extent to which one believes in the effectiveness of the self-regulation of neural net-type networks. A large number of observers have developed a "centralized mindset" in the discussions about issues of governance. They assume that any effective organization requires a central authority. They focus on "centralized solutions even when decentralized approaches might be more appropriate, robust and reliable" (Resnick 1994a:36). For them, decentralization is a sign of ungovernance. It is clear that for such observers the demise of the national state is perceived as a catastrophe. But there are others, for whom this very centralized mindset is the source of much misapprehension, and they believe the new emerging distributed governance system is likely to be more resilient for the very reason that it is distributed. For this second group, the new distributed governance is likely to generate a much more effective guidance system and a much more progressive socio-economy than the old national state.

If indeed there is a danger looming large on the horizon, it is that the "dynamic conservative" forces, at work in defense of the refurbishment of the nation state, may find it convenient, as a second-best solution designed to allay their basic fear of devolution, to set their sights on the region-state, instead of focusing on a much more massive devolution in line with the philosophy of subsidiarity that suggests that no authority should be allowed to flow to a higher level of governance if it can be exercised economically, efficiently, and effectively at a lower level. Such a second-best strategy might prevent the highest and best use of networking by freezing whole regions that are deprived of the requisite common culture, governance nimbleness, and economic development block into a role for which they are unsuited (Ohmae 1995). There may be meaningful "learning regions" (Florida 1995), but these will probably be much smaller than the units generally associated with such labels. For instance, it is unlikely that Ontario as a region state can do more than replicate at somewhat less undesirable levels many of the traits of the Canadian nation state.

A strategy based on city regions might be much more promising.

Chapter 3

Social Learning, Collaborative Governance, and the Strategic State

"Anchor new solutions
in stand-alone principles"
A. J. MacEachen

Introduction

Coordination failures and crippling disconcertation in the learning economy are an important source of inefficiency and lack of progressivity. They cannot be eliminated by the conventional panoply of nation-state policy instruments based on fence-keeping, centralization, and redistribution. It requires a new governance, focused on enabling effective social learning. We must develop the required new instruments by effecting a significant reframing of the vocation of the state—away from tinkering with static resource allocation and redistribution, and toward a significant involvement in fostering dynamic Schumpeterian efficiency, by inventing new ways of enhancing the collective learning power of the socio-economy as a collaborative venture.

We must also find ways to fully engage the private and civic sectors as partners with the state in genuinely innovative collaboration. How can this be done in line with the broad directions defined in the last chapters?

In this chapter, I suggest that two major challenges must be met. First, one must probe the foundation of social learning to be able to intervene effectively in making it dynamic; second, one must also better understand the foundation of collaborative e-governance in order to be able to ensure that the pattern of assets, skills, and capabilities are in place.

Social learning: process, organization, and public philosophy

Collective intelligence is defined by Pierre Lévy as "*une intelligence partout distribuée, sans cesse valorisée, coordonnée en temps réel, qui aboutit à une mobilisation effective des compétences*" (Lévy 1994:29). Such intelligence is continuously producing new knowledge and sharing it with all the partners, for its main purpose is social learning and the effective mobilization and coordination of the continually growing competencies of all the partners.

(a)   Catalyzing the social learning process

To catalyze social learning, one must have some view about the ways in which collective intelligence works, and be in a position to intervene to remove any obstacles likely to hinder social learning. In an effort to identify the major obstacles to social learning (and therefore to guide the process architecture interventions), Max Boisot has suggested a simple mapping of the social learning cycle in a three-dimensional space—*an expanded information space*—which identifies an organizational system in terms of the degree of *abstraction, codification,* and *diffusion* of the information flows within it. (See Figure 4.) This three-dimensional space defines three continua: the farther away from the origin on the vertical axis, the more the information is codified (i.e., the more its form is clarified, stylized, and simplified); the farther away from the origin laterally eastward, the more widely the information is diffused and shared; and the farther away from the origin laterally westward, the more abstract the information is (i.e., the more general the categories in use) (Boisot 1995).

The social learning cycle is presented in two phases with three steps in each phase: phase I emphasizes the cognitive dimensions of the cycle, phase II the diffusion of the new information.

In phase I, learning begins with some scanning of the environment, and of the concrete information widely diffused and known, in order to detect anomalies and paradoxes. Following this first step, one is led in step 2 to stylize the problem (p) posed by the anomalies and paradoxes in a language of problem solution; the third step of phase I purports to generalize the solution found to the more specific issue to a broader family of problems through a process of abstraction (at). In phase II, the new knowledge is diffused (d) to a larger community of persons or groups in step 4. Then there is a process of absorption (ar) of this new knowledge by the population, and its assimilation so as to become part of the tacit stock of knowledge in step 5. In step 6, the new knowledge is not only absorbed, but has an impact (i) on the concrete practices and artefacts of the group or community.

In Figure 4, one may identify the different blockages through the learning cycle. In phase I, cognitive dissonance in (s) may prevent the anomalies from being

Figure 4: Learning cycle and potential blockages

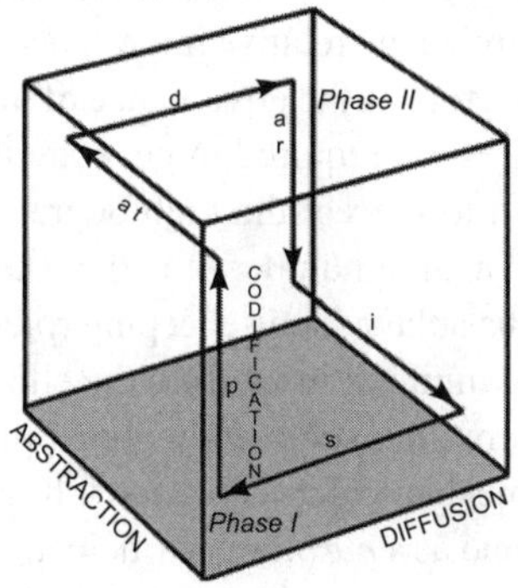

Source: Max Boisot 1995:237,190.

noted, epistemic inhibitions of all sorts in (p) may stop the process of translation into a language of problem solution, and blockages preventing the generalization of the new knowledge because of the problem definition being encapsulated within the *hic et nunc* (at) may keep the new knowledge from acquiring the most effective degree of generality. In phase II, the new knowledge may not get the appropriate diffusion because of property rights (d), or because of certain values or very strong dynamic conservatism which may generate a refusal to listen by those most likely to profit from the new knowledge (ar), or because of difficulties in finding ways to incorporate the new knowledge (i).

Interventions to remove or attenuate the negative effects of such blockages always entail some degree of interference with the mechanisms of collective intelligence. In some cases, like the modification of property rights, the changes in the rules appear relatively innocuous, but government interferes with the affairs of the mind: correcting social learning blockages modifies relational transactions and therefore the psycho-social fabric of the organization.

These interventions at the cognitive level often have unintended consequences, and may even aggravate the dysfunctions. At the core of these difficulties is the illegitimacy that is still attached to government being involved in the "politics of cognition", or in general in the realm of the mind (Tussman 1977). This has led to very costly delays in the process through which the state has agreed to shoulder these new fundamental responsibilities in a knowledge-based and learning socio-economy, and has invested in discovering effective ways of intervening.

(b) Redesigning the organizational architecture

But eliminating the blockages in the social learning cycle cannot suffice, and one should not be led to minimize the relative importance of the required changes to the organizational architecture of the governance of the learning economy in the longer run. New structures are required to generate the requisite collaboration among stakeholders, and to correct the high degree of disconcertion that has marred the operations of a large number of nation states (Paquet 1997e).

The state, in the past, has played housekeeping roles and offsetting functions. These functions required minimal input from the citizenry. The state must now, in complex advanced capitalist socio-economies, play new central roles that go much beyond these mechanical interventions. It must become involved as a *broker*, as an *animateur* and as a *partner* in participatory planning, if the requisite amount of *organizational learning*, co-evolution and cooperation with economy and society is to materialize.

In order to be able to learn, the state must develop a new interactive regime with the citizenry, to promote the emergence of a *participation-society* (where freedom and efficacy come from the fact that the individual has a recognized voice in the forum on matters of substance and procedures in the public realm, and more importantly, an *obligation to participate* in the definition of such matters). The citizen should not be confined to living in a rights-society, where the dignity of individuals resides exclusively in the fact that they have claims. (Taylor 1985).

The design principles for a social architecture in keeping with this mandate are clear.

First, there is the principle of *subsidiarity*, according to which "power should devolve on the lowest, most local level at which decisions can reasonably be made, with the function of the larger unit being to support and assist the local body in carrying out its tasks" (Bellah et al. 1991:135–6; Millon-Delsol 1992). This applies in the three realms (private, public, and civic), and the level of empowerment and decentralization may call for the individual or the family or a minute constituency in the market, the society or the polity to take charge.

The rationale for this principle is that the institutions that are closest to the citizen are those likely to be the closest approximation to organic institutions, i.e., to institutions that are likely to emerge *"undesigned"*, to emerge from the sheer pressure of well-articulated needs, and likely to require minimal yearly redesigning. While subsidiarity reduces the vertical hierarchical power, it increases the potential for participation in a meaningful way.

This is not the death of central government, but the demise of big government as the morphological assurance of resilience. When the ground is in motion, the bulkier and more centralized the government, the more it will flounder. The lean new central strategic state must deal with norms, standards, general directions, and values. The process of ministering to the public, and delivering a service well-adapted to its needs, must be devolved to the local level.

The second design principle is that of an *effective citizen-based evaluation feedback* to ensure that the services produced, financed, or regulated by the public realm meet with the required standards of efficiency, economy and effectiveness, and are consonant with the spirit of the agreed standards or norms. Some may argue that this is essentially what democracy is all about. However the democratic political process is hardly a fast and always-effective piece of machinery. The intent here is to strengthen considerably the cybernetic learning loop feature at the core of the refurbished state. It is essential if organizational learning is to proceed as quickly as possible (Crozier 1987).

This sort of evaluation (rooted in collective reporting and a recognition of the necessity of collaborative governance) ensures that the process of participation is significantly strengthened. It partially provides some content to the *silent relation* or *implicit contract* that obtains between the state and the citizenry. This sort of feedback cannot be presumed to materialize organically. Its objective would be to ensure that the state activities, standards, and rules have legitimacy in the beneficiaries' eyes, and that they are compatible with everyday morality, rather than incentives to lie or misrepresent their situations. It would allow the ordinary citizen to be heard better, because "politics is not only the art of representing the needs of strangers; it is also the perilous business of speaking on behalf of needs which strangers have had no chance to articulate on their own" (Ignatieff 1985).

These sensible principles may entail a somewhat *decoupled organizational form* of social architecture. Since the centre focuses on norms and the periphery on delivery, there is the serious possibility of lack of coordination unless (1) a clear sense of public purpose materializes; (2) new partnerships, new skills (strategic management, consultancy and advice, evaluation, etc.) along with new moral contracts binding the partners, are developed to weave this whole enterprise together; and (3) the agencies are granted the necessary powers to organize activities in a way consonant with the principle of subsidiarity, and become *negotiating arenas* in which there is (i) significant space for interaction between the agency and the citizens, (ii) scope for defining and redefining activities, and for re-orienting them "under conditions of time and place", and (iii) ample provision for dynamic monitoring from above, and for continuing feedback from below.

Centrally important in this context is what Charles Lindblom has labeled "preceptoral politics": leaders become educators, animateurs, persons called upon to *reframe* our views of the public realm, to design the organization of mutual education, and to "set off the learning process" necessary to elicit, if possible, a latent consensus (Marquand 1988). Such learning is unlikely to occur easily and well in a postmodern society through a forum organized exclusively through national institutions. The requisite institutions will have to be *middle-range* or *meso* institutions, networks designed to promote communication and cooperation on a scale of issues that mobilizes existing communities, and meso-forums (regional and sectional) likely to remobilize the commitment of the citizenry in organizations "*à leur mesure*".

The strategic state must bet on the flexible exercise of control, and on extremely effective organizational learning through such meso-forums. Their triple role—as mediating structures, as setting patterns for the provision of services, and as educating individuals in their mutual and civil commitments—needs to be revitalized accordingly (Etzioni 1983).

Many officials have expressed great concern about the improper devolution of authority from elected officials to bureaucrats and citizens (Schaffer 1988; Auditor General of Canada 1991). Such complaints are ill-founded. This exercise of power is neither improper, nor illegitimate, nor inefficient. In fact, cumulative decision-making by bureaucrats and citizens, *working within and with a public philosophy appropriately defined*, enables the postmodern state to learn faster through decisions based on the particulars of the case, while maintaining basic standards. Clinging rigidly to the old "parliamentary control framework" of the Westminster model years is not necessarily enlightened. What is essential is the development of a *modified* framework, better adapted to the needs of a strategic state.

The new kind of institutions requires the government to be satisfied with providing a problem setting, with framing the context of the situation and the boundaries of public attention, while allowing the bureaucrats and the citizens to use a lot of their tacit knowledge and connoisseurship to deal with specific situations, and to arrive at decisions on the basis of a "reflective conversation with the situation" (Schön 1983; Argyris et al. 1985). This in turn calls not only for a very decentralized structure but also for new forms of horizontal accountability for the system of governance to be effective.

(c) Rethinking foundational values

It is not sufficient to remove obstacles to social learning or to improve organizational architecture; one must also provide the dominant logic (requisite infrastructure + public philosophy) to ensure that the new centrality of social learning is a permanent feature of the new governance. These guiding values and design principles, and the language to articulate them, are not hewn in stone. Any ideal can be dropped as learning proceeds: our desires and ideals "are not like our limbs: they are not a fixed part of us" (Schick 1984).

The challenge is that of producing a language adequate for our times, a language of belonging and common citizenship, a language of problem definition that provides the citizen with a translation of his needs, usually expressed in unspecialized language, into categories that are both relevant and inspiring. This would be a language of human good that would serve as an arena, "in which citizens can learn from each other and discover an "enlightened self-interest" in common" (Dionne 1991).

The new dominant logic of the strategic state is a response to the failures of the Keynesian state. The main critiques of the Keynesian state that emerged in the post-World War II period have been well documented. They may be subsumed under a few headings (Duncan 1985): (1) *overgovernment and government overload*: the state is presented as "a kind of arthritic octopus, an inept leviathan" unable, despite massive growth, to do much to meet the demands of the citizenry; as a result, it has triggered weakened citizen compliance, growing civic indifference, and much disillusionment (King 1975); (2) *a legitimation deficit*: the depoliticized public has by now ceased to believe that the state has any moral authority or technical ability to deal with the issues at hand; this would explain the disaffection and the citizenry's withdrawal of support (Habermas 1973); (3) *a fiscal crisis*: revealing the incapacity of the state to reconcile its dual obligation to attenuate social difficulties, and to foster the process of capital accumulation without generating fiscal deficits that are in the long run unbearable (O'Connor 1973); (4) *social limits to growth*: the three crucial dimensions of our social organization (liberal capitalism, mass democracy, and a very unequal distribution of both material and symbolic resources) cannot coexist easily; democratic egalitarianism (in society) generates compulsive centralism (in the polity) to redistribute more and more resources with little success in reducing inequality, but growing shackles on the economic system's productive capacity (Hirsch 1976).

This overall crisis of the Keynesian state has been analyzed historically as a two-stage process: (1) it evolved first as a crisis in the *economic realm*: coordination failures became more and more important in advanced market-type economies, thereby creating a demand for intervention and regulation by the state; the economic crisis was therefore shifted to the state; (2) the *state crisis* developed as the legitimation deficit grew: the state was failing to mobilize the requisite commitment of citizens to be able to do the job; in despair, the state made an attempt to effect an "epistemological coup", to obtain a "blank cheque" from the citizenry. The argument was that since the management problems were so technically complex, the citizenry should pay its taxes and demand no accountability from the professional experts. This coup has failed, and "cognitive despotism" has not succeeded in suppressing the autonomous power of the community to grant or withold legitimacy (Habermas 1973; Wiley 1977; Paquet 1977a). The polls have recorded this story line. Why has such a situation developed?

The central reason would appear to be that the public institutional framework built by the Keynesians in the post World War II era was presented to the citizenry as designed for *instrumental purposes*: to combat a depression, raise standards of living, provide public goods not otherwise produced, assist the needy, etc. As a result, citizens have come to define the state in terms of *claims* they could make on it: "claimant politics began to overshadow civic politics". By comparison, "the activities of the private sphere were seen as ends pursued for their own sake". It is hardly surprising that the instrumental goods of the public sphere were regarded as subordinate to the intrinsic goods of private life (Bellah et al. 1991).

Even though the governments were major funders, underwriters and regulators, and therefore the fundamental bedrock on which the economy and society prospered from the 40s to the 70s, a number of countries have continued to occlude the importance of the state. This ideology of Lockean individualism has continued to prevail, despite the fact that government activities had grown so much by 1980 that very little remained absolutely private in a meaningful sense.

In a more and more globalized context, the private sector made ever greater demands on public institutions, at a time when the capacity to supply services from the public sphere could not expand further. This was due to the fact that participation, trust, and creative interaction (on which politics and the public sphere are built) had all but disappeared, as had the sense of community that underpinned civil society and the collective/private ways of meeting the needs of strangers.

In the current world of rugged individualism where most citizens are strangely unaware that the government has been the prime mover in the postwar period of prosperity, *private enterprise at public expense has become the rule.* The lack of commitment of emotional, intellectual, and financial resources to refurbish the public infrastructure could only lead to demand overload, and the frustration generated by the policy failures of the 1970s set the stage for citizens to suggest that the best way to strengthen democracy and the economy was to weaken government.

At the core of our difficulties is a *moral vacuum*. The notion of public purpose is alien to us. We need first and foremost a *philosophy of public intervention*, a *philosophy of the public realm* (Marquand 1988): the recognition that despite statements from social scientists, and the fact that it is not fashionable to say so, *the state is a moral agent*, and not a morally neutral administrative instrument. Both on the left and on the right, there is a longing for civil society to organically provide the well-defined codes of moral obligations that underpin the realization of the good society. However, the "built-in restraint derived from morals, religion, custom, and education", that were considered by Adam Smith as a prerequisite before one could safely trust men to "their own self-interest without undue harm to the community", are no longer there (Hirsch 1976).

The disappearance of this socio-cultural foundation has been noted and deplored, and much has been written about the need to rebuild it, but it has also become clear that it is futile to hope for some replacement for these values to come about by "immaculate conception" in civil society. And thus many have called on the state and on political leaders to accept their responsibility as second-best moral agents (Mead 1986; Wolfe 1989). Political leaders are called upon to provide a *vision*, to propose a *sense of direction*, a commitment to ideals, together with the *public philosophy* to realize them.

Such a public philosophy is both *constraining* (in the sense that it echoes some fundamental choices and therefore excludes many possibilities) and *enabling* (in the sense that it provides a foundation on which to build a coherent pattern of institutions and decisions in the public realm).

The choice of a public philosophy must be rooted in the basic values of civil society, and on the criterion of *enlightened understanding*. This calls not for the least constraining public philosophy, but for one recognizing that the optimal amount of coercion is not zero. Such a position would be the choice of citizens if they had "the fullest attainable understanding of the experience resulting from that choice and its most relevant alternatives" (Dahl 1989). The challenge is to bring about that sort of "fullest understanding" in the population. It means that government can no longer operate in a top-down mode, but has a duty to institute a continuing dialogue with the citizenry.

This will require a language of common citizenship, deeply rooted in civil society: the citizens have goals, commitments, and values that the state must take into account. But the citizens must also insist that they want an active role in the formation of these values, goals, and commitments, and in the making of policies supposedly generated to respond to their presumed needs (Sen 1987). Only through a rich forum, and institutions that enhance citizens' competence as producers of governance, can an *enlightened understanding* be likely to prevail—both as a result of, and as the basis for, a reasonable armistice between the state and the citizenry.

The fluid and seemingly scattered—baroque—system of governance (Paquet 2003b) likely to ensue, must, however, be anchored in a clear sense of direction. So there must be a plan. Most state leaders in advanced socio-economies outside of North America have such a plan, a direction for strategic intervention, and a public philosophy that will articulate and rationalize it; "they do not publish their plan because it would never gain consent. Yet it is not what one ought to call a conspiracy...The plan is not entirely conscious or systematic, and it cannot be as long as it is not written, published, debated, revised and so on. But it is not what you could call a secret" (Lowi 1975).

The importance of this *unwritten plan* is that it serves as a gyroscope in the definition of actions taken by the personnel of agencies and ministries. It serves as the basis for a double-looped learning process, as organizational learning must be (i.e., not only finding better means of learning to do what we do better, but also, and more importantly, finding the right goals, learning whether the objectives we pursue are the right ones).

Such learning cannot be done by elected officials alone. Elected officials, bureaucrats and citizens must work symbiotically, and elected officials must learn to devolve a greater amount of discretion to bureaucrats and citizens, not only in the delivery process, but in the governance process itself. Moreover, it must be recognized by all those who take on public service that the world is changing around them, that they need to continually refurbish their *outillage mental* in order to be equipped and able to develop new ways of getting things done—without running into political walls.

The ecology of collaborative governance

Whether one wishes to emphasize process architecture, organizational redesign, or the distillation of a new dominant logic, it is unlikely that anything will be accomplished without the development of new collaborative governance capabilities. But to foster the development of these new capabilities, one has to understand the ecosystem within which they blossom, and to optimize the ways in which organizations can capture the imagination of all the relevant players in order to make the highest and best use of collective intelligence.

As Dalum et al. suggest (1992), this entails intervening to improve the means to learn (and this goes much beyond the formal education and training systems), the incentive to learn (supporting projects of cooperation and networks), the capability to learn (promoting organizations supporting interactive learning, i.e., more decentralized organizations), the access to relevant knowledge (through bridging the relationships between agents and sources of knowledge, both through infrastructure and mediating structures), but also fostering the requisite amount of remembering and forgetting (act to preserve competencies and capabilities, but also compensate the victims of change and make it easier for them to move ahead). This in turn requires a well-aligned nexus of relations, networks, and regimes.

States can be important catalysts in the construction of the new "loose intermediation" social capital: improving relationships here, fostering networks there, developing more or less encompassing formal or informal regimes at other places, and ensuring that the new dominant logic of the strategic state unfolds. This is the central role of what some have called the *catalytic state* (Lind 1992).

(a) Collaborative capabilities: relations, networks, regimes

Managers in the private, public, and civic sectors have to exploit not only the favourable environmental circumstances but also the full complement of imagination and resourcefulness in the heart and mind of each team player. They have to become team leaders in task force-type projects, quasi-entrepreneurs, capable of cautious sub-optimizing in the face of a turbulent environment. This sort of challenge has pressed public, private, and civic organizations to design lighter, more horizontal and modular structures, to create networks and informal clan-like rapports, and to develop new rules of the game. In general, this has generated pressure for non-centralization, for an expropriation of the power to steer that was held by the top managers.

These new modularized organizations cannot impose their views on their clients, citizens, or members: they must consult, and they must move toward a greater use of the distributed intelligence and ingenuity of the members. The strategic organization is becoming a broker, an animateur; and, in this network, a consultative and participative mode obtains among the firm, the state, and the communities (Paquet 1994b, 1995a, 1996–7, 1997a).

This entails a major qualitative change. It introduces the network paradigm within the governance process (Cooke and Morgan 1993; Castells 1996, 1997, 1998). This paradigm not only dominates the transactions of the civic sector, but permeates the operations of both the state and market sectors. For the network is not, as is usually assumed, a mixed form of organization existing halfway along a continuum ranging from market to hierarchy. Rather, it is a generic name for a third type of arrangement, built on very different integrating mechanisms. Networks are consensus/inducement-oriented organizations and institutions.

In the best of all worlds, learning relationships, networks, and regimes would be in place as a response to the need for nimbleness in the face of increasing diversity, greater complexity, and the new imperative of constant learning. Moreover, in such a world, organizational culture would have become an important bond that makes these networks and regimes operative and effective at collective learning.

Organizational culture refers to unwritten principles, meant to generate a relatively high level of coordination at low cost, by bestowing identity and membership through stories of flexible generality about events of practice that act as repositories of accumulated wisdom. The evolution of these stories constitutes collective learning, an evolving way to interpret conflicting and often confusing data, but also the social construction of a community of interpretation.

Unfortunately, we do not live in the best of all worlds. The requisite relationships, networks, and regimes do not necessarily fall into place organically. Moreover, at any time, the organizational culture may not serve as the best catalyst to make the highest and best use of relationships, networks, and regimes.

Arie de Geus uses an analogy from evolutionary biology to explain the foundations and different phases of collective learning and collaboration, and to identify the loci for action in correcting learning failures. The ability of individuals to move around and to be exposed to different challenges (new relations), the capacity of individuals to invent new ways to cope creatively in the face of new circumstances (new networks), and the process of communication of the new ways from the individual to the entire community (new regimes) (de Geus 1997).

First, a certain measure of heterogeneity is an important source of learning, since a community composed of identical individuals with similar history or experiences, is less likely to extract as much new insight from a given environment. However, there must be a sufficient degree of trust to sustain learning. This in turn requires a cultural basis of differences that members recognize and share (Drummond 1981–2). This "cultural" basis of heterogeneity and trust, and the mastery of weak ties (i.e., the capacity to build strong relations on weak ties), are obviously dimensions that can be nurtured and represent a critical capability (Laurent and Paquet 1998).

Second, learning is not about transmission of abstract knowledge from one person's head to another's: it is about the "embodied ability to behave as community members". It is fostered by contacts with the outside, by facilitating access to and membership in the community-of-practice. Trust is at the core of the fabric of such networks and communities of practice that transform "labourers into members", an employment contract into a membership contract (Handy 1995b).

Third, belonging is one of the most powerful agents of mobilization. So what is required is an important "moral" component to the new membership contract, to make it less contractual and more interactive. This *new refurbished moral contract* is "a network of civic engagement...which can serve as a cultural template for future collaboration...and broaden the participants' sense of self... enhancing the participants' 'taste' for collective benefits"(Putnam 1995, 2000).

These loose arrangements or regimes require a certain degree of interaction and proximity. These are important features of the learning process. Regime institutions facilitate the adjustment of the group to external shocks through policy coordination, enabling the group to define more effective ways either to prevent a shock or at least to attenuate the impact through compensatory mechanisms, and collaboration capable of providing adequate forums for consultation and co-decision (Preston and Windsor 1992).

Relations, networks, and regimes constitute layers of the collaborative capabilities of the process of governance. They evolve as the socio-economy is transubstantiated, but neither fast enough nor in an integrated way: the process is evolving *lentement et par morceau*. As a result, the emerging governance process is much like a patchwork quilt, becoming ever more complex as the environment evolves from being more placid to being more turbulent (Emery and Trist 1965).

(b)   Assets, skills and styles behind these collaborative capabilities
In our new turbulent environment, strategic management is no longer sufficient. What is required is the development of capacities for collaborative action in managing large-scale re-organizations and structural changes at the macro level. The ground is in motion: acting independently not only may not ensure effectiveness, it may even make things worse and amplify disintegrative tendencies. What is required is collective action by "dissimilar organizations whose fates are, basically, positively correlated". This requires trust-enhancing mechanisms like stronger relationships, networks, and regimes.

The challenge is to succeed in finding ways to pragmatically resolve the sort of reconciliation that is possible between different but somewhat compatible perspectives or frameworks. This is the sort of compromise promised by *design rationality*—"the kind of limited reason that is feasible and appropriate in policy-making" (Schön and Rein 1994). It is a pragmatic approach, based on the assumption that there is no frame-neutral position in policy analysis.

Consequently, the only way to resolve these framework differences is to seek a "situated resolution", by efforts at reframing the debates in such a way as to make the differences manageable, and agreement combining antagonism and cooperation reacheable.

But this requires some probing into the assets, skills, and styles of coordination that underpin governance capabilities.

First, in order for these collaborative capabilities (relationships, networks, regimes) to be created, and maintained, there are some requirements: a mix of different sorts of (1) rights and authorities enshrined in rules; (2) resources, i.e., the array of assets made available to individuals and institutions such as money, time, information, and facilities; (3) competencies and knowledge, i.e., education, training, experience, and expertise; and (4) organizational capital, i.e., the capacity to mobilize attention, and to make effective use of the first three types of resources (March and Olsen 1995).

These various resources are obviously related in a dynamic fashion. Governance through organizational capital both reflects the tensions between the rights and rules in place, the resources available, and the competencies and knowledge defining other possible configurations, but it also affects the evolution of the system through an erosion of existing rules, and the distillation of new patterns of authority, asset-holding, and different sorts of expertise.

Second, Spinosa, Flores, and Dreyfus (1997) have shown that the engines of entrepreneurship (private sector), democratic action (public sphere), and cultivation of solidarity (civil society), are quite similar. They are based on a particular skill that Spinosa et al. call "history-making" and that can be decomposed into three sub-skills: (1) acts of articulation—attempts at "*définition de situation*" or new ways to make sense of the situation; (2) acts of cross-appropriation—to bring new practices into a context that would not naturally generate them; and (3) acts of reconfiguration—to reframe the whole perception of the way of life. Such individual actions are necessary but not sufficient, to generate new capabilities nor to trigger the required *bricolage* in the different worlds. As Putnam (2000) puts it, the renewal of the stock of social capital (relationships, networks, regimes) is a task that requires the mobilization of communities. This in turn means that we must be able to ensure that these actions resonate with communities of interpretation and practice—what Spinosa et al. call "worlds".

This is at the core of the notion of institutional governance proposed by March and Olsen. For them, the craft of governance is organized around four tasks: developing identities, developing capabilities, developing accounts and procedures for interpretation that improve the transmission and retention of lessons from history, and developing a capacity to learn and transform by experiments and by reframing and redefining the governance style (March and Olsen 1995:45–6). In a turbulent environment, the styles of the different worlds but also the very nature of the equipment, tasks, and identities, are modified. This transforms the organizational capital, but also the rest of the assets base of the system, and stimulates a different degree of re-articulation and reconfiguration, as well as enriching the possibilities of cross-appropriation.

(c) Disclosing new worlds
There is no way one can hope to transform these "worlds" (in the private, public, and civic spheres) unless one can first disclose these "worlds" (in the sense that we use the word when we speak of the "world of business" or the "world of medicine"). By "world", we mean a "totality of interrelated pieces of *equipment*, each used to carry out a specific task, such as hammering a nail. These *tasks* are undertaken to achieve certain *purposes*, such as building a house. This activity

enables those performing it to have *identities*, such as being a carpenter". Finally, one may refer to the way in which this world is organized and coordinated as its *style* (Spinosa et al. 1997:17). Articulation, cross-appropriation, and reconfiguration are kinds of style change (making explicit what was implicit or lost, gaining wider horizons, reframing).

The distinctiveness of any territorial governance system is this ensemble of components: the way the system adopts certain patterns of assets and skills, distills capabilities, and constitutes a particular variety of partly overlapping and interconnected "worlds", corresponding to different games being played (political, bureaucratic, interest groups, media, electorate, etc.). All these worlds cast some sort of "territorial shadow", and disclose a particular space. The market economy space may not fit well with the political formation space or the contours of the civil society. Indeed, the disconnectedness among these three spaces has been amply noted in the recent past.

The intermingling of all these worlds (with their infrastructures/equipment, their particular tasks or purposes, the variety of identities they bestow on individuals and groups, and the various styles they allow to evolve) adds up to a variety of spatial coordinates lending themselves to some extent to some sort of design. They all reflect frame differences (i.e., different notions of actors, criteria of effectiveness, etc.) and frame conflicts (when these perspectives clash). Indeed, the existence of the different frames corresponding to the different "worlds" or "styles of worlds" cause participants to notice different facts and make different arguments. The outcome of this cumulation of "worlds" is indeed what generates the territorial fabric that ensues. But these contours are truly unpredictable.

This is especially clear when one realizes that those "worlds" are not disclosed only by reference to some underlying realities or facts, but may be contrived by perceptions and imagination. There are as many "imagined" economies, polities, and communities as one may wish, with corresponding purposes, identities, styles, and territorial imprints. In that sense, any entrepreneur, theorist, or fanatic is a discloser of a new space that may or may not leave a scar on the territorial realities. But these in turn always have an impact (important or minute) on the world of assets, skills, and capabilities.

We have synthesized this dynamic in the graph below. It depicts the political socio-economy as an "instituted process", characterized by a particular amalgam of assets, adroitly used and enriched by political, economic, and civic entrepreneurs, through skillful articulation, cross-appropriation, and reframing activities, and woven into a fabric of relations, networks, and regimes, defining the distinctive habitus of a political economy as a complex adaptive system.

Such a complex world is disclosed by multiple examinations of its equipment, tasks, and identities, organized and coordinated in a variety of ways with

Figure 5: Radiography of the Governance Process

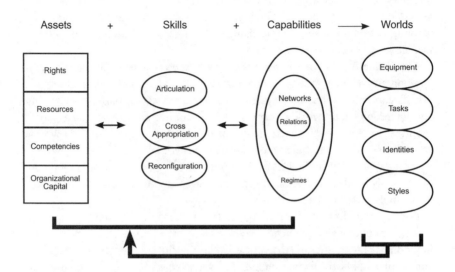

particular styles. Modification in the structure of assets, skills, and capabilities are echoed in a transformation of the "particular integrated world" that emerges as the synthesis of all these disclosed "worlds": a transformation that impacts back on the pattern of assets, skills, and capabilities.

These various forces contribute to the shaping of the territorial connections that ensue, but it is impossible to state *ex ante* which one will turn out to be the defining one.

Conclusion

The strategic state undoubtedly has a role to play in jump-starting, catalyzing, and steering the process of social learning, while allowing the other two domains (the private and civic sectors) to occupy their own terrains as fully as possible. It should obviously be remembered that the new bottom-up and distributed governance elevates the citizen to the inescapable role of producer of governance, and imposes on the citizenry *in toto* a key role in the transformation of the overall capacity to make and implement the decisions. But there is still some margin of maneuverability left for creative initiatives. Indeed, one may envisage two broad avenues that might deserve to be considered: one that is modest, and one more ambitious.

In the modest agenda, the strategic state does not aim at the *optimum optimorum,* in this context, but only strives for ways of avoiding excesses, for a loose codifying of a sense of *limits*, for some reframing likely to lead to some workable agreement. This modesty stems from the fact that very few political questions can be handled by simple rules. Therefore, even a wise public philosophy, and an efficient process of organizational learning, is regarded as at best capable of establishing by negotiation nothing more than an agreement on what is *not* moral, what is *not* acceptable. Since we understand intuitively what is unjust more easily than what is just, the challenge is to find the path of minimum regret, for that corresponds to the only hope a leader may reasonably entertain in a postmodern state (Shklar 1989).

In the more ambitious agenda, the challenge is somewhat more daunting: the objective is not to seek the utopian just society of yesteryear, but to develop an active citizenship. This agenda is built on the following premises: (1) the *Tocqueville lament* about the peril of democracy is warranted: "not only does democracy induce to make every man forget his ancestors, it hides his descendants and separates his contemporaries from him; it throws him back forever upon himself alone, and threatens in the end to confine him utterly within the solitude of his own heart"; and (2) the *John Stuart Mill statement* about social obligations is also warranted: "every one who receives the protection of society owes a return for the benefit" (Buckley 1990).

From these premises, three sets of actions follow:

- the search for a way to frame a public philosophy aiming at nothing less than a change in the national ethos;
- the citizen needs to become an "official", i.e., "a person with duties and obligations", not only of foregoing private interests in the name of public duty, but also being capable of "getting the ruled to do what they don't want to do" because what the public wants, or thinks it wants, or thinks is good for it, may not be what the public good requires; this entails a "*devoir d'ingérence*";
- the citizen needs to be persuaded that he/she may act unjustly, not only by breaking a law, but also by remaining passive in the face of a public wrong; this means that the citizen has to be educated into an active citizenship that entails a "*devoir de solidarité*" (Tussman 1977, 1989).

The public philosophy in good currency suggests that the modest agenda is the only viable one. Dwight Waldo, one of the foremost observers of the public administration scene over the past 40 years, has reminded us recently that "we simply do not know how to solve some of the problems government has been asked to solve" (Waldo 1985). For Waldo, the central feature in the discussion of the boundaries between the private and public spheres is the "growth of the 'gray area'...the fading distinction between public and private, caused and accompanied by the increasing complexity of organizational arrangements where what is—or was—government meets and interacts with what is—or was—private, usually but by no means exclusively 'business'". And Waldo added somewhat sharply that any person who claims to have clear ideas about this "gray area" is "suspect as ideologue, scenario writer, or a con artist".

Yet the times may call for initiatives envisaging a real attempt at a somewhat immodest agenda: enlightened pragmatism, an emphasis on practice guided by a modest public philosophy, an on-going and somewhat directed conversation with the situation, "under conditions of time and place", which would be the bedrock of the new modern and modest strategic state. But this enlightened pragmatism need not be amnesic and myopic; it must forge new concepts and new symbols, new options, and as "options are thus changed or expanded, it is to be expected that choice behaviour will change too, and changed choice behaviour can in turn be expected, given appropriate time lags, to be conceptualized or 'habitualized' into a changed set of values" (Mesthene 1970).

This hemi/semi/quasi-immodest agenda is not echoed in the triumphant "politics of principle" developed by supposedly "great" political leaders, and likely to convulse society, but in the solution of "particular cases" in an innovative way. There is already an agreement on the profile of the new type of leader that the times call for, and its key features are (1) a capacity to listen, to learn, and to entice others to learn, to change and adapt to change, and to inform the public clearly and serenely about the general orientation of the guiding public philosophy, (2) the courage to rethink when circumstances and problems demand it, but above all (3) an "ethical attitude" acting as a gyroscope and permitting no concession to opportunism (King and Schneider 1991).

It is not clear whether what is needed to kickstart this transformation is a fully worked out "*projet de société*", an *avventura comune*, or nothing more than what Aristotle identified as "concord" (homonoia "a relationship between people who... are not strangers, between whom goodwill is possible, but not friendship...a relationship based on respect for...differences" (Oldfield 1990). What is clear is that the leader of the strategic state needs to find a way to energize the nervous systems of the economy, society, and polity, for, as Joseph Tussman would put it, a modern democracy is committed to "governance not by the best *among* all of us but by the best *within* each of us" (Tussman 1989:11).

Chapter 4

Ecologies of Governance as Social Technologies*

"adhocery… is a practice that need not be urged
because it is the only one available to us"
Stanley Fish (1999:72)

Introduction

It is not quite sufficient to disclose new worlds and to reflect on the requisite capabilities, skills, and assets for better concertation and governance. This has to be translated into particular arrangements capable of handling the governance challenges *hic et nunc*.

As mentioned earlier, it is most effective to partition the problem into compartments, and to put in place ecologies of governance making the highest and best use—in an eclectic way—of all the possible instrumentation available. This poses "wicked" design problems.

Gérard Bélanger (2002) used the occasion of the current debates on the dilemmas posed by various proposed reforms for the governance of health care—many of which suggest some form of demonopolization, deconcentration, and decentralization—to suggest that one may not have as much margin of maneuverability as one might wish to have in such design work, and to argue that it is futile, for instance, to try to decentralize a centralized system. It is like trying to get a cat to bark.

Bélanger adopts Jane Jacobs's point of view (Jacobs 1992) that there is no meaningful middle ground between centralization and decentralization, that

* In collaboration with Ruth Hubbard.

they represent two different and self-contained syndromes of moral principles, that they embody dominant logics that are impermeable. In Jacobs's words, any attempt at commingling can only lead to "monstrous hybrids". Bélanger's position—if one were to accept it *holus bolus*—entails that any reasonable person or group is always forced in all circumstances to make a Manichean choice and to bet either on a decentralized or on a centralized system.

Bélanger is aware of the starkness of the choice he proposes, and he suggests that some may well try to find ways to correct some of the most unfortunate consequences of such choices by adjustments in the management and governance structures of the system. But such flats and sharps, he contends, cannot modify the dominant logic: it would simply attenuate, ever so slightly, some of the malefits.

This approach, based on pure dominant logics, is both overstated and counterproductive because it fails to explain the real-life situations and to provide for the real-time choices that we know exist. Bélanger dramatically underestimates the possibility of designing systems, and of systems emerging, that truly embody multiple logics, and the possibility of taking advantage of the benefits of both centralization and decentralization.

In the next section, I provide a general critique of Bélanger's argument, based on our daily observation of effective mixed organizational forms, both in nature and in society. In the following section, I show that "ecologies of governance" combine top-down and bottom-up logics very effectively, and I use the example of VISA in the private sector, and of regime-based federalism in the public sector, as illustrations of effective ecologies of governance. Finally, I identify some principles of design that might help interested parties in engineering an effective third way, avoiding the malefits of both hyper-centralization and hyper-decentralization.

The single dominant logic syndrome as ideology

At the centre of Bélanger's argument is the idea that one cannot tinker with an institutional order that is fundamentally centralized with any hope of success due to the fact that the "single dominant logic" that inhabits any socio-technical system is overpowering. Any attempt to change the style of the socio-technical system is futile: the single dominant logic will ensure that these add-ons are absorbed, integrated, and transmogrified in the dominant direction.

This either-or dynamic has some attraction. It emphasizes the integrity of socio-technical systems, and underlines the importance of acknowledging the power of this logic. Lachmann has indeed shown that the institutional order has some capacity to thwart efforts at modifying it, and that there is a Darwinian selection mechanism at work that often leads the system to reject alien accretions or transplants (Lachmann 1971).

However, this rigid perspective imposes an either-or framework on situations that could be classified as more-or-less situations most of the time. In fact, real-time systems are much less rigid and much less *"intégristes"* than Bélanger postulates. They are constantly evolving and have to adapt and adjust to ever changing circumstances. As a result, institutional *métissage* is a fact of life.

Such a *métissage* may take many forms.

For instance, Vertinski has shown that natural systems, like colonies of slugs, reveal a capacity for cohabitation of both centralized and decentralized modes of operation. They switch from one mode to the other depending on circumstances: in placid times, a leisurely decentralized system prevails, where every individual slug pursues its own activities, but this system is "instantaneously" transformed to an army-like centralized system when the colony is under attack. As soon as the threat has gone, the system reverts back to its decentralized state. Vertinski has shown that there are similarities between this sort of switching strategy and certain Japanese management strategies (Vertinski 1987).

Institutional and organizational *métissage* may also lead to a true coupling of top-down and bottom-up dynamics. This may be said to exist in systems like common law, in which there is a learning loop: decentralized bottom-up experiments and decisions in the local environments cumulatively putting pressure on the institutional order, and leading to changes in it. Such changes, in turn, modify the institutional order and, top-down so to speak, lead to certain types of experiments being adopted, i.e., gaining a higher probability of success.

As long as the bottom-up experiments do not push the system outside of a certain corridor of acceptable performance, the system remains self-regulating. However, if and when the system drifts out of the corridor and enters a danger zone for its stability, some form of top-down regulatory power kicks in. This is the moment when Delta organizations à la Dror, (i.e., organizations standing above the fray, like the Supreme Court, e.g.) get into the act (Dror 1997).

In yet other instances, truly different dominant logics routinely prevail in an intermingled way, and do so quite effectively. An example is the After Action Program of the U.S. Armed Forces—a programme that entails planned temporary hiatuses in the hierarchical operations of the forces, when horizontal and rank-free discussions are allowed to prevail among the troops and their officers on what went right or wrong in certain recent operations. The old hierarchical order is re-instated as soon as this after-action, planned non-permanent debate has concluded (Pascale et al. 1997).

Finally, there are organizations where neither the vertical/hierarchical top-down links nor horizontal/bazaar like links predominate. These are truly ambivalent organizations, where transversal or cross-functional collaboration prevails, as it does in a well-working matrix-form or federal-type organization. In such cases, the organization coalesces in all sorts of ways, as needs require:

vertically, horizontally, or in transversal task-force clusters involving various sub-sets of actors for planned and yet non-permanent periods (Tarondeau and Wright 1995).

Ecologies of governance

The prime challenge for managers is not to design a socio-technical system that has integrity, but one that works. This practical imperative calls for a governance that will succeed in squaring the circle, i.e., in finding effective ways to have most of the advantages of a centralized system, while also obtaining all the advantages of a decentralized system.

This entails avoiding two pitfalls: the illusion of control (for one is rarely faced in the real world with a complex socio-technical system that has a fixed shape and predictable behaviour, and therefore that one can fully control), and the illusion of Candide (for it is equally naïve to believe that the appropriate institutional and organizational arrangements will always emerge organically in the best way).

Avoiding these pitfalls is at the core of the work of governance experts. They try to nurture the sort of basic architecture that ensures effective social learning through interventions at both the strategic and operational levels. In so doing, many assume that strategic choices can shape the system top-down as if it were an integrated whole. This is rather naïve. Most of the time, one faces a set of interdependent systems that can neither be fully brought under the same logic, nor even handled in congruent ways. And yet *laissez-faire* is not an option either, for the costs of unsatisfactory governance or governance failures are too high.

The best one may hope for is a new fluid form of governance—something called "ecology of governance" by Walt Anderson. He describes it as "many different systems and different kinds of systems interacting with one another, like the multiple organisms in an ecosystem" (Anderson 2001:252). Such arrangements are not necessarily "neat, peaceful, stable or efficient...but in a continual process of learning and changing and responding to feedback". Their main objective is to ensure resilience.

An ecology of governance amounts to a group of loosely integrated "uncentralized networks", each focused on an issue-domain. Two examples might help flesh out what is meant by such an arrangement that yields most of the benefits of centralized and decentralized organizations: VISA and subsidiarity-based federalism.

(a)   VISA as chaord

Dee Hock has described in great detail the saga that led to the creation of VISA, the credit card empire (1995, 1999). VISA is presented as the result of a process through which deliberation about purpose and principles led to the creation of a new organizational structure that Hock calls chaord. Chaord is a combination of chaos and order. It is defined by Hock as "any self-organizing, adaptive, non-linear, complex system, whether physical, biological or social, the behaviour of which exhibits characteristics of both order and chaos or, loosely translated to business terminology, cooperation and competition" (Hock 1995:4).

Hock has shown that in attempting to govern something as complex as VISA's financial empire, for instance, the design problem was so momentous that they had to create a new form of uncentralized organization. This was seen as the only way to ensure durability and resilience in such a complex organization, exposed to a vast array of turbulent contextual circumstances, but also having to face the immense coordination challenge involved in orchestrating the work of over 20,000 financial institutions, in more than 200 countries, trying to serve hundreds of millions of users.

In such circumstances, neither a fully centralized system nor a completely decentralized one would appear to be capable of providing the sort of arrangement likely to ensure the requisite resilience. Consequently, a new form of organization had to be designed, that would provide both the "main purpose" and the mix of norms and mechanisms likely to underpin its realization through bottom-up effervescence, within the context of some loose framework of guiding principles agreed to by all.

Hock has given some examples of the principles defining the sort of organization used to cope with these challenges in the construction and design of VISA:

- it must be equitably owned by all participants; no member should have an intrinsic advantage; all advantages should result from ability and initiative;
- power and function must be maximally distributed; no function and no power should be vested with any part that might be reasonably exercised by any lesser part;
- governance must be distributed; no individual or group of individuals should be able to dominate deliberations or control decisions;
- to the highest degree possible, everything should be voluntary;
- it must be infinitely malleable, yet extremely durable; it should be capable of constant, self-generated modification without sacrificing its essential nature;
- it must embrace diversity and change; it must attract people comfortable with such an environment, and provide an environment in which they can thrive (Hock 1995, 1999:137–9).

Such norms and rules cannot be simply dichotomized.

There is an "essential nature" in VISA as an organization, but there are also many dimensions and categories in the architecture and operations of this socio-technical system that do not fall necessarily into a centralization or decentralization box, because they correspond to both.

(b) Subsidiarity-based federalism

The traditional concept of federalism is territorial. It delegates the responsibilities of the organization (private, public, or civic) among different layers of the organization, more or less firmly based on a certain geographical area. This is the case for American federalism (Carter 1998) but also for some firms that have adopted a federal structure, like Shell, Unilever, etc. (Handy 1992). But it would be unwise to restrict the application of federalism to territorial federalism.

Diversity has many faces, and federalism is an extraordinarily effective way to deal with diversity. One can easily see the possibilities of federalism as an agency of reconciliation of various sets of purposes: a social architecture providing for multiple logics to cohabit.

As Handy put it, federalism is "a well-recognized way to deal with paradoxes of power and control: the need to make things big by keeping them small; to encourage autonomy but within bounds; to combine variety and shared purpose, individuality and partnership, local and global" (Handy 1992).

Subsidiarity is a key principle of federalism. It establishes that no higher order body should take unto itself responsibilities that can be despatched properly by a lower order body.

In territorial terms, this means that only if the local or state levels cannot effectively shoulder some responsibilities should they be taken over by the federal government. The same logic would lead the head office of a company to provide subsidiaries with as much autonomy as they can properly exercise.

However, organizations are not limited to territorial partitions. They are composed of a multitude of communities of meaning. For instance, a health care system integrates more or less fitfully a goodly number of communities of practice (doctors, nurses, etc.). IBM contains communities of researchers, of production engineers, and financial artists. A country contains diverse communities—political groups, religious groups, gender groups, etc.

Very often, in the absence of a higher order authority (as in the case of the transnational scene, because of the void at the level of world government) networks emerge to deal with issues like weather, environment, racism, etc.: such networks correspond roughly to both issue-domains and "communities of meaning", while taking into account territorial and national dimensions. Such specific forums are created on the global scene to handle critical issues (management of oceans, for instance), and accords or agreements of all sorts (the Kyoto protocol, for instance), are arrived at in such agoras.

Such arrangements are referred to as "regimes".

Stephen Krasner has defined regimes in the international context as "sets of implicit and explicit principles, norms, rules and decision-making procedures around which actors' expectations converge in a given area of international relations" (Krasner 1993:2). This definition has been refined and expanded by Hasenclever et al., who have made more explicit the different conceptual elements of the definition: "Principles are beliefs of fact, causation and rectitude. Norms are standards of behavior defined in terms of rights and obligation. Rules are specific prescriptions or proscriptions for action. Decision-making procedures are prevailing practices for making and implementing collective choice" (Hasenclever et al. 1997:9).

Federalism is a way of thinking. It is not simply a geographical divisionalization. It is a way to embody the motto, "as much decentralization as possible and as much centralization as necessary". And the optimal degree of centralization/ decentralization changes through time, depending on circumstances. Indeed, it is the very advantage of federalism that it can choose to move either way in response to the particular circumstances and challenges of the day. This leads most federal organizations to develop regimes of all sorts to deal with certain portions of the terrain, and to work constantly at articulating and somewhat reconciling those different regimes that are always only partially compatible.

One may argue that any private, public, or civic organization, adopting a federal structure, is choosing that very flexibility as an important asset, because federalism matches the complexity of the environment with the complexity of the organizational form.

One can show that in many sectors the only effective way to manage complex socio-technical systems—like hospital systems for instance—is indeed to adopt a federal structure, allowing for the appropriate mix of centralization and decentralization.

It is not surprising that, very much as in the case of the VISA chaord, federalism as a way of thinking and as a way of governing organizations has been echoed in a variety of guiding maxims that provide the culture of the organization. Charles Handy has identified a few such principles:

- authority must be earned from those over whom it is exercised;
- people have both the right and the duty to sign their work;
- autonomy means managing empty spaces;
- twin (status and task) hierarchies are necessary and useful;
- what is good for me should be good for the corporation (Handy 1992).

No single template is likely to become a rigid recipe in the use of a mixed regime-based organization, but both chaords and federal systems are interesting illustrations of plausible and credible experiments. Both organizational forms are examples of institutional and organizational *métissage*, and have revealed through multiple instances of effective use that one need not fall into the either-or trap set by Bélanger's unidimensional world. In a multidimensional world, there is always some scope for modification of the parameters, and for forging an organization that can be said to be both centralized and decentralized at the same time.

Some principles of design

The design of governance systems, very much like the design of a building, must remain closely linked with circumstances, and with the priorities of ultimate users. Moreover, much in the real experience of governance systems emerges unplanned as unintended consequences, or as the result of the sheer creativity of the users of the systems. Social architects are never fully in control. But it is extraordinarily simplistic to presume that they can be only sorcerer's apprentices, and that their design efforts are condemned to generate "monstrous hybrids", when they attempt to bring forth organizational and institutional designs that blend centralization and decentralization, as Jane Jacobs suggests.

The vast array of principles and mechanisms of governance that have proved helpful in dealing with the challenges generated by the new turbulent environment in a variety of contexts have been explored elsewhere (Paquet 2005b): principles like true price-cost relations, competition, subsidiarity, maximum participation, multistability; and mechanisms like dialogue, moral contracts, reframing, and belief-action relations.

I would not pretend that this provisional list is comprehensive, nor that it has necessarily underlined the most important principles and mechanisms of good governance. However, it has underlined the usefulness of identifying some such generic guideposts.

In fact, in reflections on governance, one is almost automatically driven back to the same set of guideposts that appear to be promising when one is intent on nurturing the emergence of (1) an effective sense of direction for the organization or socio-technical system, together with (2) the required sorts of conduct by stakeholders in achieving the purpose, and (3) the kind of congruence of behaviour by all stakeholders and partners that will gradually build the requisite trust needed for the organization to thrive.

These guideposts do not provide recipes or models, but they draw attention to certain dimensions of effective governance regimes that are likely to increase system resilience.

(a) Participation, transparency, deception, and fail-safe mechanisms

One of the saddest and most unhelpful assumptions that can be made by organization or system designers or nurturers is the assumption of the passive nature of human beings, the postulate that citizens, partners, employees, etc. are passive holders of rights—"forgetting that those rights are the flip side of others' duties". This passive culture of human rights suggests that one can sit back and wait for others to deliver what is one entitled to (O'Neill 2002:35–9).

A more useful assumption is that human beings are active, and want to participate in the construction of their organizations and institutions. This entails a need to engage citizens, partners, employees, etc., and build and count on trust to provide the social glue to generate the requisite collaboration.

Some have been suggesting that transparency might be some sort of panacea, since it has the great advantage of providing all participants with a clear view of both issues and outcomes. But one should not develop a fixation on transparency. Often, as O'Neill suggests, "increasing transparency can produce a flood of unsorted information that provides little but confusion" (O'Neill 2002:73). Combined with the wrong sorts of accountability that imposes targets and all sorts of other phony performance indicators, mainly chosen for ease of measurement, transparency entails mainly quantophrenia and not much intelligent accountability (Paquet 1997b).

Indeed, demands for "universal transparency" are "likely to encourage the evasions, hypocrisies, and half-truths that we usually refer to as 'political correctness', but which might more forthrightly be called 'self-censorship' or 'deception'" (73). And total transparency may not do much to reduce deception (Bennis 1976; Juillet and Paquet 2002).

Formal, accessible, and useful technology-based information management systems that interconnect all the stakeholders are likely to be useful, but they must not be designed to eliminate secrecy, but rather to discourage deception, and they must be geared to intelligent accountabilities. However, these internal mechanisms may not suffice. Real-time systems (that need to evolve, adapt, and adjust to changing circumstances) cannot be assumed to always do so in a smooth way. Consequently, there must be provisions for both active trust and some kind of built-in "fail safe" system that kicks in if the system drifts out of the corridor of acceptable performance and enters a danger zone in terms of its integrity and stability.

For the polity, such a "fail safe" mechanism is made of both formal and informal checks and balances. Examples would be the existence of the Constitution and the Charter, together with a judiciary that is independent of the legislature and the executive, a healthy free press along with fundamental freedoms of speech and assembly, etc.

In private organizations, much of this fail-safe system depends on external restraints such as the criminal code, or the values in good currency in a society, that complement internal mechanisms built into the corporate culture like robust corporate governance standards, strong audit committees, and well-defined procedures and protocols, to be put in place in extraordinary circumstances.

The co-existence of (1) much stakeholder activism with (2) "border controls"/a "sense of limits" would appear to be one of the most important underpinnings for a self-organizing and self-regulating system. A true liberal pluralist system cannot exist without both of these components.

(b) Intelligent acccountability

Active human beings need not only a sense of limits, but also intelligent accountability structures. But, as O'Neill wisely points out, intelligent accountability requires good governance, and good governance is possible only if institutions and organizations are allowed some margin of self-governance (O'Neill 2002:58).

One must therefore have in place a network of accountability links to ensure the viability of self-organized structures. Such accountabilities are geared to providing the sort of interactions likely to generate both a modicum of coordination in the short term, and a sort of radar to guide social learning in the longer haul.

These coordination guideposts need to solve four important accountability challenges.

First, one must ensure maximum participation of all the stakeholders, since knowledge, power, and resources are widely distributed. Wide participation has the additional advantage that it brings forth the kind of skill sets that are most likely to produce the most imaginative and creative solutions to problems.

Second, the designer must commit to a minimum of rules, so as to make the system as flexible and adaptable as possible. Consequently, much has to depend on voluntary agreements and conventions.

Third, there must be an agreement to delegate to the front line all the decision-making that can be done there. The principle of subsidiarity is built on a sense of responsibility at the most local level, but it must be nested in a nexus of integrative moral contracts providing broader values to serve as a guiding framework. Such moral contracts, based on broadly based values underpinning more local principles, serve as an assurance that local decision-making will be made in a manner taking into account broader values. Such a setting both enables the kind of proximity that generates ideas that meet local circumstances, and at the same time allows for the things that need to be discussed and agreed to at a broader level to take place (Paquet and Wilkins 2002).

Fourth, to ensure lateral accountability, one must build in an element of competition as a safeguard against the tyranny of monopoly or of the state.

(c) Multistability

The mix of active human beings, a basis for organizations' self-governance, and intelligent accountability leads to another important design principle: the recognition that the illusion of control must be tempered by a good dose of awareness that circumstances being rather diverse in dealing with complex systems, it is preferable, both for external and internal reasons, that the socio-technical system be partitioned into sub-systems allowed to operate somewhat independently.

A socio-technical system is both more resilient and more likely to be innovative if (1) it is partitioned in such a way that it can avoid being totally destroyed or "crashed" by external shocks; in systems design parlance, a system is said to be multistable when it has the requisite degree of balkanization necessary to react *"par morceau"*, allowing the delegation of the job of reacting to and managing these external shocks to the best-prepared sub-system, and of doing so in a manner that preserves the system from totally crashing (Ashby 1960); (2) it allows parallel lines of reasoning and logics to thrive, to interact and to generate the most creative synergies.

Such partitioning of large systems (of which both chaords and federal systems are examples) also has the merit of not only allowing the socio-technical system to adjust more easily to external shocks in turbulent times, and to improve social learning by ensuring a modicum of diversity regarding points of view, but also of immunizing the system against hijacking by central powers, or sabotage by marginal groups.

Neither of these threats is unimportant in difficult times: on the one hand, when the central powers—experiencing loss of control and being accused of not being able to maintain a modicum of effectiveness and stability—are under attack, they are normally tempted to re-establish a form of centralized control, be it only by reason of expediency; on the other hand, while chaords and federal systems are often difficult to govern—some would say it is like herding cats—they are easily sabotaged or "flamed" by well-organized disgruntled groups especially in the era of new technologies of information and communication (Paquet 2001b).

Conclusion

These principles of design do not ensure that the appropriate mix of centralization and decentralization will materialize. They simply provide help in preventing centralization from triggering the generation of a rigid order, deception and abuse of power, and in ensuring that certain basic features of a mixed centralized/ decentralized arrangement are built into the original organizational design.

These principles are most effective in preventing a cumulative causation process from generating a drift toward either pole—pure centralization or pure decentralization—because they help to throw some light on the malefits of both extreme rigidity and limited learning on the one hand, and lack of both focus and resilience on the other.

The fact that there may be a tendency for a single dominant logic to prevail requires that safeguards be put in place, and that ideological blinkers be exposed. For the propensity to elect pure centralization or pure decentralization is much less a result of real constraints than the consequence of ill-founded ideological assumptions the decision-makers are often not even aware they are making. Consequently, one should be equally suspicious of prophets claiming that the answer is totally in an act of faith in the "invisible hand" of decentralization, or in the "visible hand" of centralization.

The primacy of pragmatism calls for no act of faith, but rather for an act of hope that cleverly designed checks and balances will succeed in leaving as little space as possible for the "invisible foot" of inefficiency.

PART II

Territorial Connections

Chapter 5

On Hemispheric Governance

> "We kick against the pricks of our necessity.
> Yet, strangely, we are in love with this necessity.
> Our natural mode is therefore not compromise
> but 'irony', the inescapable response to the presence
> and pressures of *opposites in tension*"
> Malcolm Ross (1954)

Introduction

Canadians have a distorted view of the world system and their own place in it. This is inherited both from the post-World War II experience, when Canada stood tall among nations because of the fact that so many of them had been badly damaged during the 1939–45 war period, and from the activist Pearson era, when Canada played a leadership role in world affairs. One can get a visual sense of this aggrandized self-portrait in the maps of the world as presented in Air Canada in-flight magazines. In these maps, Toronto, Montréal, and Vancouver are nodes toward which every portion of the world appears to converge.

A less parochial perspective would reveal that Canada, as a middle-power country, is a relatively minor actor on the world scene, and that it is increasingly losing power to transnational institutions. Canada still represents a small if not insignificant portion of world production and trade. But over the past 40 years, the relative importance both of Canada's government and of its banks has declined considerably on the world scene. Canada has had to make a number of adjustments to external constraints.

Consequently, Canada has had to increase its capacity to adapt to external exigencies. Therefore, a keener appreciation of the causal texture of Canada's environment has become quite crucial, if one is to venture a diagnosis about the prospects for the country in the next century. Indeed, the sort of effective governance likely to evolve in Canada will be dictated to a large extent by this context.

In this chapter, there will be no attempt to reconstruct the entire web of connections linking Canada to every other actor on the world scene. Rather, the focus will be on Canada's hemispheric circumstances. The rationale for this choice is that Canada is embedded in the Americas. The geopolitical context of the country is obviously broader than Pan-America. Canada is a member of many international clubs (OECD, G-7, the Commonwealth, la Francophonie, etc.); it is linked historically, culturally, and politically to European powers; it is connected through immigration and increasing trade flows with Asia; and it is having some impact on Africa through its aid programmes. But mostly, Canada's reality is dominated by its embeddedness in the Americas.

This makes the hemispheric governance system a matter of crucial interest for Canadians, for the governance regime that is likely to evolve in the Americas will not only be an important echo chamber through which global forces will reach Canada, but also an instrument through which Canada may be able to participate actively in global governance issues, and to exercise more influence over its circumstances in the next century.

The first two sections of the chapter briefly sketch Canada's position within the six Americas, and examine the hemispheric dynamics as they unfold. The next two sections review some of the challenges and choices generated by hemispheric governance issues, outline the most likely scenario, "a distributed governance scenario through flexible regimes for the Americas", examine the impact of this prospective scenario on Canadian governance, and the action agenda it calls for. The conclusion underlines the reasons why the process of emerging hemispheric governance is bound to be slow, and requires considerable creative politics.

Canada and the six Americas

Canada is nested in a broad ensemble that is usually partitioned into three portions (North America, Central America and the Caribbean, and South America). But this is an ensemble of some forty countries which can be partitioned more usefully from our point of view into six families:

1. North America:	Canada, United States of America, Mexico;
2. the Caribbean:	Jamaica, Trinidad and Tobago, Barbados, Dominican Republic, Haiti, Guyana, Suriname, French Guyana, Antigua and Barbuda, the Bahamas, Belize, Dominica, Grenada, Montserrat, St Christopher-Nieves, Saint Lucia, St Vincent and the Grenadines;

3. Central America: El Salvador, Guatemala, Honduras, Costa Rica, Panama, Nicaragua;

4. Andean community: Venezuela, Colombia, Ecuador, Peru, Bolivia, Chile;

5. Mercosur: Brazil, Argentina, Paraguay, Uruguay; and

6. Cuba

Figure 6: a snapshot of the southern portion of the Americas

Source: RSC 2000.

These countries have evolved a variety of integrative arrangements over the past 40 years: the Canada–USA Free Trade Area (FTA), the North American Free Trade Area (NAFTA), the Latin American Free Trade Association which became the Latin American Integration Association (LAFTA/LAIA), the Central American Common Market (CACM), the Caribbean Common Market (CARICOM), the Andean Community, and the Common Market of the Southern Cone (Mercosur). All of these arrangements have generated some "regional" integration of the Americas, but these arrangements have all been sub-hemispheric, and many small countries have been left out of these diverse schemes.

Thirty-four of these countries (including Canada) are members of the Organization of American States (OAS). The melodramatic history of the OAS has registered the different phases of optimism and pessimism, ebullience and suspicion that marked the evolution of the web of cooperation within the Americas. Another important forum for Canada is the Association of Caribbean States (ACS), consisting of a group of 25 countries around the Caribbean Sea (including Cuba), founded in 1994 and designed to "develop the potential of the Caribbean Sea through interaction with Member States and third parties". Canada has observer status in the ACS.

In the last decade, Canada and the USA have "rediscovered" the Americas, and there have been sustained American and Canadian strategies to engage with the Americas. The 1990 Bush's Enterprise for the Americas Initiative has given a great deal of importance to the idea of a free trade area for the Americas. Canada has actively pursued its strategy through summit meetings (Miami 1994, Santiago 1998) and negotiated treaties or agreements of all sorts. But this interest in the rest of the hemisphere has not translated into a significant increase in Canadian trade and investment in the Americas outside of the Northern cone (Daudelin and Dosman 1998).

(a)   Trade between Canada and Latin America/the Caribbean (LAC)
Over the past decade, Canada's trade with LAC has remained a little under 2% of its total trade, but the relative importance of the stock of Canadian direct investment abroad vested in LAC has doubled over the last decade: from 8.3% in 1989 to 17.2% in 1998 (see Table 1). This is a harbinger of foreign trade to come, since foreign trade usually follows foreign investment. However, it is important to note that Bermuda and the Caribbean are the beneficiaries of two-thirds of this direct investment, whereas the pace at which Canada appears to invest in Latin America is relatively slow compared to the pace of the European invasion.

Almost half of Canada's total merchandise trade with LAC is with Mercosur (43%) if one includes Chile—an associate member of Mercosur—and over one-

Table 1: The Stock of Canadian Direct Investment Abroad (CDIA)
($Cdn mil)

	1989	% of Total CDIA	1992	% of Total CDIA	1995	% of Total CDIA	1998	% of Total CDIA
North America								
United States	56,578	63.0	64,502	57.8	87,596	53.3	126,005	52.6
Mexico	237	0.3	451	0.4	948	0.6	2,246	0.9
Total North America	56,815	63.2	64,953	58.2	88,544	53.9	128,251	53.5
Latin America and the Caribbean								
Caribbean								
Bahamas	1,820	2.0	2,149	1.9	2,313	1.4	6,098	2.5
Barbados	1,144	1.3	4,115	3.7	5,736	3.5	14,328	6.0
Bermuda	1,495	1.7	2,619	2.3	3,006	1.8	4,690	2.0
Nertherlands Antilles	82	0.1	36	0.0	657	0.4	134	0.1
Other Caribbean*	722	0.8	790	0.7	1,511	0.9	2,416	1.0
Total Caribbean	5,263	5.9	9,709	8.7	13,223	8.1	27,666	11.5
Central and South America								
Argentina	115	0.1	225	0.2	1,335	0.8	2,239	0.9
Brazil	1,679	1.9	1,880	1.7	2,458	1.5	2,827	1.2
Chile	211	0.2	482	0.4	2,673	1.6	4,221	1.8
Columbia	25	0.0	32	0.0	272	0.2	796	0.3
Panama	19	0.0	18	0.0	101	0.1	160	0.1
Venezuala	56	0.1	168	0.2	355	0.2	401	0.2
Other Central and South America**	121	0.1	288	0.3	661	0.4	2,859	1.2
Total Central and South America	2,226	2.5	3,093	2.8	7,855	4.8	13,503	5.6
Total Latin America & Caribbean	7,489	8.3	12,802	11.5	21,078	12.8	41,169	17.2
Total Europe	18,626	20.7	22,874	20.5	37,206	22.7	49,611	20.7
Total Africa	233	0.3	301	0.3	632	0.4	1,541	0.6
Total Asia and Oceania	6,689	7.4	10,760	9.6	16,744	10.2	19,181	8.0
Total CDIA	89,851	100.0	111,691	100.0	164,205	100.0	239,754	100.0

* Antigua and Barbuda, Cayman Islands, Dominica, Grenada, Jamaica, British Virgin Islands, St. Lucia, Trinidad and Tobago, Cuba, Dominican Republic, French West Indies, Haiti, and Guadeloupe.
* Belize, Guyana, Bolivia, Costa Rica, Ecuador, El Salvador, French Guiana, Guatemala, Honduras, Nicaragua, Peru, Suriname, and Uruguay.
Source: Statistics Canada.

quarter (28%) is with the countries of the Andean Community, while trade with the Caribbean accounts for just under one-fifth (18%) of total merchandise trade. Trade with Central America (CACM countries) makes up only 7% of total trade between Canada and LAC.

In LAC, Brazil is the main recipient of Canadian exports (adding up to well over US$1 billion), with Venezuela and Cuba well below this level (approximately 40% of the level of exports to Brazil), and Colombia, Chile, and Argentina roughly at 30% of the level of exports to Brazil. Canada also imports primarily from Brazil (again well over US$ 1 billion), followed by Venezuela (at some 60% of that level), and Chile, Colombia, Argentina, and Jamaica (in the 20–25% range of the Brazilian level).

Canada's export structure is fairly distinct from that of LAC, with manufactured goods comprising almost two-thirds (63%) of the country's exports (machinery and transportation equipment account for 40% of the country's total exports). Following manufactured goods, fuels, agricultural materials, and food items make up 10%, 8%, and 8% of Canada's exports, respectively. Overall, Canada is much more active in exporting manufactured goods than LAC, although the Dominican Republic, Jamaica, and Brazil also export a large percentage of manufactured goods (77%, 69%, and 54%, respectively). It is noteworthy, however, that of these three countries, only Brazil exports a substantial amount of machinery and transportation equipment (20% of Brazil's total exports fall into this category).

In contrast to Canada's focus on manufactured goods, the LAC countries show a greater reliance on food items, with, for example, 90% of Cuba's exports falling into this category, and food items accounting for over half of the exports in the CACM and most Mercosur countries (excluding Brazil). Fuels and ores/metals are also significant export items for some countries, particularly Venezuela, which derives 82% of its export revenues from fuel, and Chile, for whom almost half (46%) of its export income can be attributed to ores and metals.

(b) Foreign Direct Investment in LAC
Data on FDI to LAC from Canada is limited. Some fragmented data from the late 1980s and early 1990s assembled by Sáez (1997) shows that Canada's FDI stock in South America was primarily to be found in Brazil (US$2.3 trillion), although Canadian FDI stocks in Argentina, Venezuela, Colombia, Bolivia, and Peru were also listed as being substantial ($220 billion, $85 billion, $72 billion, $66 billion, and $51 billion, respectively). In the 1990–2 period, the Canadian FDI in Chile was no less than US$552 million according to the data set compiled by Sáez. This presaged an extraordinary increase in the Canadian FDI stock in Chile in the 1990s.

The following table (Table 1) provides a snapshot of the stock of Canadian Direct Investment Abroad (CDIA) at different dates over the last decade (given in Canadian dollars).

It reveals the relatively limited importance of the rest of the hemisphere (except for the USA) for Canada's capital export. However, it shows that there has been a decided shift over the last while.

While the absolute value of the stock of CDIA has almost trebled from 1989 to 1998, the percentage distribution of Canadian direct foreign investment on other continents has remained rather stable. But there has been a shift within the Americas: the percentage moving within the North American economic sphere has declined by some ten percentage points (63.2% to 53.5%) while the percentage going to Latin America and the Caribbean has increased by the same number of percentage points (8.3% to 17.2%).

Even though this is the most complete data set we have been able to compile on Canadian FDI stock in LAC countries, it should be clear that it is not as exhaustive as one would like. The Sáez (1997) data set, taken from research done by the Economic Commission for Latin America and the Caribbean (CEPAL), would appear to be more exhaustive than the one we were able to compile from Statistics Canada sources. However, there is no reason to believe that the trends shown in Table 1 are not reliable.

But when one is reminded not only that in 1997 Brazil attracted one-third of the foreign capital inflows to LAC from the rest of the world, which amounted to some US$20 billion, but also that Argentina, Columbia, Chile and Venezuela received over US5 billion in FDI in that year alone, one is forced to realize that Canadian investment in LAC has not grown anything like as rapidly as the investment flows from other parts of the world into LAC (World Bank 1999).

Hemispheric dynamics: *intégration par morceau et lentement*

The central economic pillar of the Americas is obviously the United States, which serves as a magnet for all the countries of the hemisphere. The main interest of these countries is the possibility of access to the profitable US market by means of some liberalization of the trade and capital movements in the Americas. Yet very much as in the story of the Canadian mouse and the US elephant, each country in the hemisphere has a "fatal attraction" toward greater integration with the USA, in spite of what it may mean in terms of loss of sovereignty.

This is all the more important because (1) US trade policy is a mix of multilateralism, preferential bilateralism, preferential regionalism, and unilateral action when it suits its purposes (Weintraub 1993); and (2) even though the LAC countries shifted from defensive to positive nationalism during the 1980s, a certain degree of protectionism and insistence on managed trade remains, largely as a result of the old experience of sub-regional integration, which served as protection against imports from non-member countries.

Simple tariff reductions are only the beginning of what hemispheric integration will entail. As Sidney Weintraub suggests, hemispheric free trade will amount to nothing less than "a redefinition of sovereignty" (Weintraub 1993:19). It will redefine the "philosophical framework" within which the countries of the Americas have been accustomed to operating. Free trade negotiations in the Americas are bound to lead to a redefinition of how nationals deal with each other both in their own country and across borders, and this in turn is bound to transform the institutional order. Canadians have gone through this rather painful process of redefinition vis-à-vis the United States, and it is often said that, after more than a decade of experience within the free trade area, this process of redefinition remains incomplete.

(a)   The necessary sequence of integration

The scope of instantaneous integration is rather limited everywhere in the world, except where security concerns predominate, such as in Korea or the Balkans. Elsewhere, economic integration is bound to evolve slowly, as it has done in the last 50 years wherever it materialized. In the North American case it took twenty years from the Auto Pact to the Free Trade Agreement of 1988; there was a fifty-year span between the European Payments Union in 1950 (through the Treaty of Rome in 1957 and the Maastricht Treaty in 1993) and the European Monetary Union by the year 2000. It would be expected that hemispheric integration will proceed equally slowly.

This foot-dragging is due not only to a reluctance or unreadiness to proceed shown by countries in all parts of the hemispheric economic space, but also to the unwillingness of the have-portion of the hemisphere to share with the have-not portion to the extent that has been the case in Europe. In Europe, the important social disparities among regions have been addressed through social transfers in the manner also done within the Canadian federation. These transfers constituted a way to catalyze the process through which the economic infrastructure of the less affluent countries could be refurbished, and eased the way to integration. But this sort of arrangement is unlikely to evolve in the Americas where the tradition of equal and sovereign trading partners, responsible for the management of their own socio-political affairs, is so deeply rooted.

It should not be presumed, however, that the reluctance to proceed is due to an across-the-board lack of readiness everywhere in the hemisphere. Huffbauer and Schott (1994) have examined the readiness indicators of the major countries of the hemisphere (price stability, budget discipline, external debt, currency stability, market-oriented policies, reliance on trade taxes, and functioning democracy). Overall, the NAFTA region received very high scores (around 4.4 on 5 on average) except where budget discipline was concerned, and we know that this has been remedied since 1994. Mexico scored significantly lower (3.9) than Canada and the USA. Chile also drew a high score (4.4) comparable to the NAFTA countries rather than to other Latin American countries.

The Mercosur countries received a score of 3.1 on average, with the smaller countries (Paraguay and Uruguay) scoring 3.7—a full point more than the larger countries (Argentina and Brazil). In this part of the hemisphere, problems with price stability, external debt, and reliance on trade taxes remain important. The Andean Community has experienced important market-oriented reforms over the past decade, and therefore would appear to not fare too badly except for price stability and external debt, but the serious problems of drug trafficking and guerrilla violence are generating significant instability. Central America is somewhat splintered: El Salvador and Costa Rica can be rated in the mid-3 category, Honduras and Guatemala a full point below, and Nicaragua another full point below still. As for the Caribbean, at least the larger countries within the Caribbean, they appear to be relatively well-positioned, but the smaller countries are actively slowing down the pace of an integration they fear.

This brief survey reveals a great variety among these different corners of the Americas in terms of readiness for hemisphere integration. In the absence of what can be regarded as a most unlikely equalization payment scheme, it would seem that the "big bang" model is most unlikely to be workable. This is the basic reason why an *intégration par morceau et lentement* is the most plausible scenario. One of the advantages of this approach is that regional initiatives are more likely to progress faster than broader schemes, and that this approach, complemented by sector-by-sector regime negotiations, this approach may indeed provide an easier way to ensure progress without the risks of blockage generated by the all-or-nothing approach.

(b) Piecemeal integration, multistability and dispersion of authority
Some have claimed that the multiplication of such regional/sectoral groupings has resulted in a loss of allocative efficiency as a consequence of the impediments to trade and investment flows that have been erected for countries outside the different groups. However, a compensating factor is that there has been an increase in the *multistability* of the overall system as a result of the partitioning of the world system in a multiplicity of these semi-disconnected zones.

A multistable system is one in which a greater ability to adapt is ensured through a certain disconnect among sub-systems. An adjustment called for by a shift in some essential variables is delegated, so to speak, to a partial system enabling the overall process to adjust more smoothly to important shocks in the environment, in a manner that would have been either impossible or very time-consuming had the overall process been forced to adjust in toto (Ashby 1960; Paquet 1978). More multistability considerably reduces the probability of the whole system crashing as the result of a systemic crisis. A comparison of the impact of the 1930s crash, and its propagation throughout the world, with the impact of the Japanese crash of the early 1990s, shows that the latter was much more contained, and was resolved faster because of the higher degree of multistability in the world economy today (Emmott 1999:17).

The regional zone/regime strategy amounts to a limitation of the market place's dominion over the world economy, through governance mechanisms imposing restraints on flows of commerce and capital across borders, *and* the ensuring of some collaborative action on the part of clutches of countries vis-à-vis the rest of the world.

Canada has joined one such regional grouping in North America over the last decade, and this has generated an increase in the concentration of Canada's trade with the USA. This increased Canada–USA trade has undoubtedly had a dampening effect on the pains of labour market restructuring that were triggered by shocks elsewhere in the world system. But it has not increased (and might even have decreased) Canada's geo-political power over its own future, since Canada and Mexico have remained "satellite economies" vis-à-vis the United States, in a hub-and-spoke type arrangement.

One way for Canada to gain more influence over its own future is to ensure the construction of a broader regional economic zone including all of the Americas. In such a club, Canada might be able to develop alliances with other significant middle-range economies of the Americas to ensure that the "regional zone" does not serve only the interests of the dominant economies (the United States in the North, and Brazil in the South), but also serves those of the other partners. According to Daudelin and Dosman (1998), this is the only way (if indirect) in which Canada can increase its geo-political importance on the world stage.

This "hemispheric governance strategy" was articulated in Canada in 1989 when Canada joined the Organization of American States. Since then Canada has participated in many summits where this strategy has been slowly unfolding. By 2005, it is expected that the 34 countries of the Americas will become members of a free trade area. However, Canada may not have been promoting this strategy in the right way.

A sensitive and effective promotion of hemispheric governance does not simply mean an extension of the North American free trade agreement to the rest of the Americas. This approach is unlikely to succeed, as the larger economies in the South, notably Brazil, are less willing than Canada and Mexico to become a spoke to the USA's hub. Rather, what is more likely to generate a consensus is a proliferation of ad hoc functional arrangements, negotiated in a variety of arenas, as a "disaggregating response of sovereign states to the complexity of a highly interconnected world" (Falk 1999).

These arrangements would entail a devolution and dispersion of authority, and the participation of private, public, and civic sector representatives in rule-making. While it may not square well with the promotion of a single agreement, as per the United States' wishes for the 2005 process, the progress via this piecemeal approach might serve to test whether middle-power countries like Canada (in alliance with other middle-power countries) might be able to gain some influence within the Americas. Influencing the process itself would be a meaningful test case.

(c)   The next steps: negotiation by sub-regions
One of the important implications of our relative inertia on the hemispheric governance front is that in the meantime the situation is evolving: the European Union (EU), building on some traditional economic, trade, and cultural links with many South American countries, has already signed a trade agreement with Mercosur. And since many South American countries trade more with the EU than with the US, it has been suggested that a free trade agreement with the EU might be more beneficial to Latin America than one with the US (Bhalla and Bhalla 1997:156).

If a global approach is premature, and most certainly feared by many Latin American countries (for which US domination in such a scheme is ominous), the only other viable strategy would appear to be the one adopted by the EU: negotiation by sub-region. This sort of meso-economic approach, when combined with the development of sectoral regimes at the hemispheric level, might indeed provide a transition to a loosely coupled hemispheric "federation" of more or less free trade areas. While this detour on the road to hemispheric integration may appear to be wasteful (in a static efficiency sense), it is probably necessary, given Argentina's and Brazil's political decision to push Mercosur.

However, this detour cannot be improvised. If any sub-component of any group were to negotiate special arrangements with any other sub-group of countries, considerable systemic damage could be done. Mexico's bilateral agreements with certain countries and groups in Latin America has already damaged the substantial trade (existing and potential) between Canada and these countries (Wonnacott 1996).

In other words, Canada needs to develop a strategy to ensure that it is not walled out by a multiplication of regional agreements within the Americas: for Canada, the architecture of the trading system is not inconsequential. Although a generalized FTA throughout the Americas would be simpler, it is not plausible at this time, and therefore it is crucial for Canada to think through the different stages through which the hemispheric integration will proceed, and to design a proactive strategy to increase the probability of some of the less undesirable scenarios. Once trading and investment patterns have crystallized, it may be very difficult to negotiate substantial transformations to the trading system.

And yet, as Daudelin and Dosman (1998) suggest, there is no functional necessity pertaining to Canada's option for the Americas. Indeed, its very complexity may be an additional reason not to bother. Only a robust policy initiative would appear to be capable of generating some effort in this direction. But this policy initiative would have to be more sophisticated than the simple suggestion of quick trade liberalization and elimination of capital controls, or the negotiation of an all-countries agreement, where the USA would be eminently first among equals. Such simplistic approaches are bound to fail, for Latin American countries have more to fear from United States unilateralism than does Canada. A soft, slow, multifaceted, and sophisticated regime-type approach is called for (Paquet 2000b).

Distributed governance through flexible regimes

Canada, like most other advanced economies, has been subjected to a variety of pressures over the last twenty years as a result of dramatic changes in its economic environment. These pressures have been ascribable mainly to globalization and accelerated technical change. As a result of these changes, the environment has become more complex and more turbulent, and concerns from the private, public, and civic sectors have been forced to acquire a greater capacity to transform, and to develop a philosophy of continuous improvement and innovation in order to survive. In the face of the "new competition", these concerns have had to become "learning organizations" (Best 1990; Paquet 1999a, 1999d).

(a)   The learning economy

Learning organizations must be capable of redefining goals and means *as they proceed* through tapping into knowledge and information that other agents and groups possess, i.e., through cooperation with other stakeholders. This has triggered a drift in the governance process: the governance pattern has evolved from the more exclusive, hierarchical, and paternalistic forms of the 1970s, toward more inclusive, horizontal, distributed, and participative forms in the 1990s, and from a pattern where the national leader was in charge to what would appear to be a game without a master.

To be effective, the new distributed governance through social learning requires not only a new regime in its interactions with the rest of the world, but also new

96

structures (more modular and network-like), new strategies (based on dynamic efficiency and learning), and new forms of coordination (more decentralized and more dependent on moral contracts and trust) (Paquet 1999f).

These moral contracts, and the alliances they embody, would work in a variety of ways on the hemispheric front: through some constraints on the flows of commerce and investment to somewhat insulate a region or a group from catastrophes elsewhere; through the development of zone or regime institutions to facilitate the adjustment of the group to external shocks; through policy coordination, enabling the group to define more effective ways either to prevent the shock or at least to attenuate the impact; through compensatory mechanisms put in place to ensure that those most seriously hit by these shocks are somewhat compensated through some sort of redistribution scheme; and through collaborative mechanisms capable of providing adequate forums for consultation and co-decision (Preston and Windsor 1992). The important cooperative work done by the Cairns group of medium-sized agricultural exporters provides a valuable lesson. Canada, Australia, New Zealand, and some Latin American and South East Asian exporting countries were able to form a reasonably cohesive group that was able to raise a strong voice at the multinational trade negotiations table (Christie 1993).

Although some have come to believe that the only alternative to the hub-and-spoke model is a "mishmash of overlapping agreements" (R. G. Lipsey in Lipsey and Meller 1997:254) that can only lead to chaos, this is not the case.

The required speed, flexibility and innovative adaptation necessary in the new globalized socio-economy can only be generated by non-centralization and sectional networking. Hierarchical structures have proved inadequate. The reason the guidance system has to be decentralized, collaborative, and adaptative is that this is the best sort of arrangement to serve the continual need to adjust to new circumstances in order to generate knowledge value-addition.

This is also the recipe for productivity gains in a world of alliances and partnerships across borders, and among different layers of networks. Hierarchies have limited learning abilities, and markets have limited capacities to process information effectively. Network alliances are a way to counter these failures: they reduce uncertainty and adaptation costs arising from the environment's complexity through an increase of the partners' collective organizational capabilities (Paquet 1999a, 1999c).

(b) The catalytic state

These collaborative arrangements through networks foster faster and more effective learning, but the development of such arrangements calls on the state to recognize that it cannot achieve its goals by simply relying on its resources and coercive power. The state must assume a dominant role in coalition-building, both internationally and domestically. This is what Michael Lind (1992) has called "the catalytic state".

The proliferation of regional/functional regime agreements, and the evolving character of close government–business–society relations in Japan, Germany, etc. are manifestations of the new importance of the catalytic state (Weiss 1998:210). Not all states have the same catalytic capabilities, however. Some, like the US, have the clout necessary to exploit international leverages; others, like Germany and Japan, have both domestic and international clout in coalition building; still others, like Canada, would appear to lack both capacities.

It may well be that the sort of consensus required among private, public, and civic partners for such networks to be effective is not possible in a large fractured country like Canada; that the only way to generate catalytic action is at the level of region-states, through the empowerment of sub-national units (Courchene and Telmer 1998). This is a pattern that has developed in the European Union, where sub-national segments of country A may enter into agreements or treaties with sub-national segments of country B, without asking permission from higher order governments. Perhaps in Canada such decentralization-cum- distributed-governance is the only way to ensure that the socio-economy *in toto* can evolve faster toward a less ineffective governance.

Despite the fact that an extensive literature has shown that, both internationally and nationally, the new distributed governance system is most effective in coping with globalization and productivity slowdown (Naisbitt 1994; Whitman 1999; Leadbeater 1999), the degree of cognitive dissonance remains high in Canada. The cumulative effect of a certain degree of glibness, blindness, and denial, and a pervasive centralized mindset that prevents the engineering of the requisite degree of decentralization, has meant accepting many broad world trends somewhat fatalistically, but has also fed an attitude suggesting that we need not worry about the required governance overhaul (Paquet 1999c, 1999d, 1999f).

Consequently, Canada is not taking action domestically to capitalize on its own potentially greater valence in the free trade scheme of the Americas. The Canadian knowledge and competence base about Latin America is limited, and the "winning conditions" for greater penetration of LAC markets have not been analyzed extensively enough. Indeed, hemispherically distributed governance is neither promoted nor even discussed openly, so Canada is currently unlikely to be in a position to take full advantage of this new distributed governance scheme when it materializes.

Yet the integration of the Americas *par morceau* (around Brazil in Latin America, as it has proceeded around the USA in North America) is promising in the long run. As the United States' valence in the world economy diminishes with the strengthening of other regional groupings such as the European Union, and as Latin American countries become much more sizable economic powers than Canada in the next decades, Brazil, Argentina, and other LAC countries are likely to remain, throughout this slow process of integration, the natural allies of Canada against the protectionist and unilateralist forces of the United States (Lipsey and Meller 1997).

A realistic Canadian strategy

There are many scenarios envisaged about the nature of the new institutional order and about the ways in which the transition toward it will materialize. The United States favours either a hemisphere-wide agreement, or a US-centred hub-and-spoke series of bilateral or multilateral free trade agreements. Neither of these scenarios appears plausible or realistic at this time. This is due to the deep fear of US dominance and the concern about loss of sovereignty exhibited by countries throughout the hemisphere in question. A more likely scenario is the intregration *par morceau et lentement* of a set of subregional free trade agreements into a loose federal-type system more or less governed by reconstituted existing OAS agencies, in coordination with the Inter-American Development Bank and other inter-American bodies or sub-hemispheric regional associations. This scenario may appear unwieldy, but is more likely to materialize than either of the other two (Atkins 1993).

It is not sufficient, however, to suggest that distributed governance and flexible regimes are the way out of the present predicament. These general concepts provide no true guidance: they are like 16th-century maps, elegant but not helpful to navigation.

What is required is a translation of this general scenario into a strategy indicating the way in which Canada might operate to make the highest and best use of the opportunities offered by the emerging hemispheric integration. Such an action plan must be based on reasonable assumptions about the environment, and on a good appreciation of the dynamics within the world economy and within the hemisphere. It must also realistically take into account the strategies of the other partners.

(a) Some perspectives
It must be stated clearly from the start that there is no consensus on the priority to be given to hemispheric integration. Some Canadians (like many Americans) consider that not only are there slim pickings to be expected from the extension

of the free trade area from North to Central and South America (given the very limited trade links between these three portions of the Americas) but that it might even be counterproductive since it might well undermine the construction of a global trade regime by making other mega-regions react defensively to this initiative (Bhagwati 1997; Gordon 1998). On the other hand, a number of observers are more optimistic. They do not minimize the difficulties for Canada in taking advantage of these new markets, but suggest that it would be a matter of appropriately supported entrepreneurship (Berry, Waverman, and Weston 1992; Purvis 1999). These more optimistic observers insist on the fact that in a multilateral initiative of this sort, smaller economic powers stand to gain the most, and that Canada therefore has much to gain.

If there is no consensus on hemispheric integration per se, neither is there consensus, even among those favouring integration, about the form of and the route to this integration, or about the "deep" or "shallow" integration outcome of these processes (Ostry 1997).

The United States tends in general to favour fast-track global agreements. In this case, however, this strategy was derailed by the refusal of Congress to grant President Clinton the authority for fast-track negotiation, but the global integrative accord remains the preferred way for the US.

Others see the hemispheric integration following the path of the European integration. This would mean a process in three stages or generations: first, trade liberalization plus cooperation; second, limited preferential trade, plus deeper cooperation and harmonization; third, community-level trade liberalization, plus normative supranationalism. This plan for a progressive construction of trade arrangements, mechanisms for coordinated decision-making, commitment for cooperation, and adherence to some fundamental principles, has been sketched by Frank Garcia in what he calls "Americas Agreements"—a blueprint for an interim stage in building an integrated hemisphere (Garcia 1997). This process might take 10 to 15 years to become operational.

Others still see the process of integration proceeding on the basis of the regional blocs already in place, building on inter-bloc regimes, on a piecemeal basis, as the most promising path. This sequential programme is based on a realistic assessment of the varying degrees of readiness of different actors within the LAC. This has already been proposed as a second-best strategy, when it became clear that the single global hemispheric order sought through the fast track might not materialize.

Finally, others suggest that even this integration *par gros morceaux* is unduly optimistic: they put forward the possibility that the only viable strategy is a strategy of *petits pas* via the proliferation of bilateral arrangements within the

Americas, probably through the travails of the Latin American Integration Association (ALADI) with some key countries like Mexico and Brazil playing crucial roles as southern hubs (Axline 1997).

In the absence of a fast-track negotiating strategy by the United States, and given the "managed trade" approach favoured by Brazil, it is unlikely that the US global neo-liberal scheme will prevail, or even that the ordered process of "Americas Agreements" will materialize. It is much more likely that the latter two scenarios will ordain the integration of the Americas, and that what can reasonably be expected over the next decade is a "shallow" rather than "deep" integration of the Americas.

In order for Canada to develop the will for an action plan in the face of such fuzzy and unpromising circumstances, especially when the political actors have such a fixation on short-term results, the Canadian citizenry needs to come to the stark realization that the Canadian socio-economy is falling significantly behind its competitors. The stagnation of productivity growth is troublesome, and so is the failure of Canada's service sector to generate adequate exports. This is an indirect indictment of our health and education sectors, which in spite of being such important components of the service sector are badly in need of improvements (Paquet 1998).

The rapid progress of the digital economy is also rendering most of the traditional protective techniques rather ineffective, and calls for ever more flexibility, openness, and decentralization. This should act as an additional force, driving the Canadian government to spearhead initiatives to educate the citizenry and in so doing help quash what Bob Rae has cleverly labeled "the comfortable immaturity of permanent opposition" (Time, June 28, 1999). For hemispheric integration is not so much about tariffs as it is about a transformation of structures and attitudes.

Whether Canadians will be driven to press their governments to action as a result of fear for their standard of living, or whether governments will be pressed by Canadian "entrepreneurs, executives and government trade mavens" (Purvis 1999) into taking advantage of this new frontier, is no longer relevant as both forces are already at work.

What is less clear is how the Canadian catalytic state should develop its strategy. This process, of necessity, involves the Organization of American States (OAS) and other associations of the sort, to serve as deliberative forums through which governments, business communities, and civil societies might be able to shape different regional consensi. Such consensi are unlikely to be constructed except on a piecemeal basis, through some regime-building in different areas until the time is ripe for more universal rules. But this will require creative leadership on the part of the Canadian government in order to ensure that both the Canadian business and non-governmental communities are mobilized, and the requisite resources for capacity-building in Canada are found.

With the requisite mobilization and capacity building, one can expect the Canadian government to be able to take on a leadership role in the development of an organized system of cooperation with Brazil, Argentina, Venezuela, Peru, Chile, etc. It will require that trust be recognized as a foundational capability, and as something which can lend itself to design only up to a point (Paquet 1999e). Building cooperative relations will require much imagination, especially when it involves countries like Brazil and Argentina that might be seen as competing with Canada in a number of key areas, but this also provides opportunities for joint ventures, alliances, and strategies. This is a major reason for pursuing such objectives in the longer run, while focusing maybe in the shorter term on the Caribbean Sea as a region of choice, where Canada already has affixed roots that are likely to help immensely in the construction of alliances built on trust.

(b) A long-range strategy

It is important to explain to the Canadian citizenry that, for a middle-power country like Canada, being part of the hemispheric zone is *an insurance* against the uncertainties of the new global order, but also *a way to gain some leverage* in dealing with the USA through the possibility of selective alliances with other middle-power countries like Mexico and Brazil. This is a matter that needs to be explored more fully, but it should be clear that in this game, Canada starts as a dominant player in the hemisphere—obviously not as powerful as the United States, but often regarded as "Big Guy No. 2" (Purvis 1999).

Second, one cannot explore these possibilities without a much better understanding and a much more realistic assessment of Canada's circumstances within the world economy. An occasion for such a re-evaluation might be serious parliamentary hearings on the Free Trade Area of the Americas, or another meaningful hemispheric strategy. These might provide opportunities to gauge the nature of the risks and uncertainties Canada is likely to face, and the nature of the sort of insurance and new capacities it may need. For one of the extraordinary impediments to the development of hemispheric integration is Canadians' abysmal ignorance about Latin America. One might have expected that the migration flows from Latin America to Canada in recent decades would have helped bridge the chasm. That may have been the case in Quebec to a certain extent, but most certainly this has not been the case for Canada in general.

Third, in designing new coordinating forums and institutions, there is an urgent need to recognize *the limits imposed by the faultlines* underlined by Luke,

Luttwack, and Huntington. Cultural, security and economic divides must be taken into account. There is much naïveté in the neo-liberal shotgun approach adopted by Canada, when it showers a multitude of trade missions over the different continents without paying much attention to these factors. The determination to seek multilateral liberalization and to single-mindedly pursue the elimination of trade and investment barriers, without sufficient attention to the non-economic costs of such initiatives (the MAI initiative is a good example), often reveals a less than adequate appreciation of cultural and civilizational faultlines. On the other hand, it is also the same lack of appreciation of cultural factors that leads Canada to imitate US trade activism and methods, when very different foci and very different methods might be much more potent.

Fourth, Canada's relative importance in the world economy is declining, even though Canadians find that difficult to accept. This translates into the unlikelihood that Canada's preferences will carry much weight in an economic confrontation, and is forcing the country into *a mode of oblique action and soft diplomacy*. Such an approach is illustrated by Canada's insistence on the involvement of civil society in the Americas. But this in turn requires that the Canadian population be much better informed about the nature of these international initiatives, and that Canadian business and Canadian civil society be made aware of the role they must play, in order for the outcome of the hemispheric governance model to be most profitable for Canada (economically, politically, and socially). A number of negotiating groups are already at work, and a committee on the participation of civil society (a Canadian initiative) is in operation.

While there is a consensus on the fact that Canada has lost its place in the world (Cohen 2003), there has been no consensus on how Canada might be able to forge a new internationalism capable of helping it regain a greater role abroad. Rebuilding our military, replenishing our foreign aid, reviewing our foreign policy framework, renewing our foreign service, etc. (all things that Cohen calls for) may be necessary but it must also be recognized that Canada's relative weight in the world has diminished, not only because Canada was sleeping at the switch but also because of the emergence of many powerful players. Pretending that we can be the powerhouse we were at a time when Europe and Japan were devastated, and China and India still crippled giants is unrealistic. Our strategy must be based on the recognition that we are a small player on the world stage, and that this calls for oblique action and soft diplomacy. Nothing can better illustrate the power of soft diplomacy than the First Spouses Summit in the fall of 1999. Canada chose to be a continental "master of ceremonies", and in so doing has defined an agenda that even the United States had to adjust to (Time Magazine 1999). But such oblique action and soft diplomacy must be sustained and designed in a very creative and imaginative way. While a new wind of interest in international affairs has blown over Canada recently, and the latter period of the Chrétien government and the Martin government have given more importance to international affairs, it is not clear that this has been done in a forceful and coherent manner, and it is evident that the relative importance of the hemisphere in all this has been very limited.

(c) Building governance capabilities

To bring about a robust and coherent strategy to build Canada's presence in the hemisphere requires the mobilization of Canadian groups' interest and imagination. If the hemispheric integration movement is to succeed, from Canada's point of view, some blueprint for governance and management capacity-building needs to be put in place.

In our new high-risk and turbulent environment (type 4, in the language of Emery and Trist 1965) strategic management is no longer sufficient: what is required is the development of capacities for collaborative action in managing large-scale re-organizations and structural changes at the macro level (Metcalfe 1998). In environments of type 1, 2, or 3 (corresponding crudely to the world of perfect competition, imperfect competition, and oligopolies, respectively), operational, tactical, and strategic management suffice. In turbulent type-4 environments, acting independently not only may not ensure effectiveness, but may make things worse and amplify disintegrative tendencies. What is required is collective action by "dissimilar organizations whose fates are, basically, positively correlated". In particular, this requires trust-enhancing mechanisms.

Metcalfe has synthesized this sort of predicament in a catastrophe theory type graph (below) depicting the major aspects of the issue in three dimensions: the environment's degree of complexity, the degree of management/governance capacities, and the degree of governance effectiveness. He shows that, as complexity increases, management capacities must improve to avoid disintegration. If these capacities already exist, they must be brought into use (a–b); if they do not exist, they must be developed (e–b). If they do not exist and no development effort is made (e–f), or if the capacity building is inadequate (e–c–d), disintegration ensues. Type 4-environment requires innovations which strengthen the capacity for collaborative relationships (Metcalfe 1998:29–30).

This framework shows how the dual task of group mobilization and building management and governance capabilities are integrally related, since the driving force behind the new governance effectiveness is collaboration. It puts the emphasis on the need for creative politics, and for innovative institutions. In particular, it underlines the challenges generated by the "new complexity" of the cognitive division of labour, which calls for new forms of collaboration, not only at the level of trade and exchange, but at the very core of the production process (Moati and Mouhoud 1994), and the need for new modes of coordination.

There are four broad types of capabilities to be created, distributed, and maintained, that are particularly relevant to governance: *rights and authorities*, i.e., capabilities enshrined in formal rules; *resources*, i.e., the array of assets made available to individuals and institutions like money, time, information, facilities; *competencies and knowledge*, i.e., education, training, experience and expertise; and an *organizing capacity*, i.e., the capacity to mobilize attention, and to make effective use of the first three types of capabilities (March and Olsen 1995).

It may appear somewhat impetuous to say that there is at present a deficit on many of these fronts, but this is what a rapid survey seems to reveal. The catalytic state cannot be expected to resolve these deficits in isolation, but it is expected to generate an awareness of these gaps, and to lead the process through which they will be filled.

For the time being, the most glaring gap is on the competencies and knowledge front: the mutual ignorance on both sides of the Canada–LAC chasm is a major stumbling block when it comes to constructing new governance capabilities. Yet the resources allotted to the process of hemispheric governance (in the broadest sense) are not inconsequential. However, since we do not have a fair appreciation of what they are, they are probably not well coordinated.

Indeed, little is known about the network of initiatives, sponsored by individuals and private or civic organizations, that link Canada and the southern part of the hemisphere. Without a complete inventory of these initiatives and the immense capital of trust accumulated through them, it is difficult to identify the best opportunities facing Canada, as well as critical blockages that might be resolved by negotiating new rules or agreements. Another important gap is the lack of "organizational capital". This is likely to be even more determinant when creative politics become *de rigueur*, and much must be done in an informal way. Again, the vital importance of trust-building as a base for a new, workable organizing capacity needs much attention in the choice of focal points for action (Keen 1999).

(d) A three-pronged action plan

From our analysis to this point, it should be clear that no simple fix will do. The Canadian strategy must be multifaceted, and build on a variety of potential pressure points on which it might have an impact. It should proceed simultaneously at three levels.

Figure 7: Les Metcalfe's catastrophe theory framework

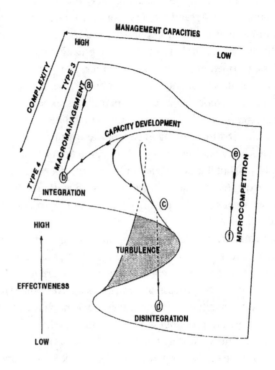

Source: Metcalfe 1998:28.

At the macro level

What is required is an effort to define a broad range of interventions designed to promote closer collaboration between Canada and Latin America and the Caribbean. In a sense, it represents a continuation (but at a renewed and more forceful level) of the effort to promote greater connectivity between the two areas. While this approach is broad-ranging by necessity, it may appear to be unfocused. However, there is much that can be done at this level to heighten Canada's capabilities.

One should not presume that there has been no effort to "organize" a concerted set of activities. A provisional framework has been on the shelves of the Department of Foreign Affairs and International Trade (DFAIT) since 1994. It is summarized in Policy Staff Paper 96/04, and proposes an action plan under three main headings: creating sustainable prosperity, promoting good governance, and building bridges (Sheck et al. 1994). They all require private/public/civic cooperation, but, as might be expected, the focus of DFAIT is mostly on the government's initiatives.

Under the first heading, creating prosperity, one finds an array of activities:

- targeting trade by sector and country in lieu of an all-encompassing strategy;
- ensuring special support for constituency building, strategic alliances, joint ventures;
- bundling of credits and business development programmes in the region;
- creating foreign investment protection agreements with targeted countries;
- significantly increasing the share of development assistance going to targeted countries in line with progress in political and economic good governance;
- creating a regular and sustained environmental policy dialogue with key regional players.

Under the second heading, good governance, one finds among others the following activities:

- advice on the process of good governance in areas such as privatization, regulatory reform, and tax collection; and
- training of Latin American military officers in the art of peacemaking.

Under the third heading, building bridges, one finds, *inter alia*, the following activities suggested:

- a Foundation of the Americas, on the model of the Asia Pacific Foundation, to develop trade links, cooperation between educational institutions, etc.;
- contacts with the Latin American groups in multilateral settings like the UN;
- build more proactively on Canada's presence in the Organization of American States (OAS) with initiatives like the one Canada promoted (Unit for the Promotion of Democracy) and funded;
- leadership with respect to internal reforms of the OAS;

- promotion and marketing of Canadian educational institutions;
- promotion of more public awareness of Latin America in Canada.

This is a list of very modest proposals. There are many others. For instance, an effort to coordinate the efforts of Canadian agencies like the Export Development Corporation, the Canadian International Development Agency, the International Development Research Council, the Department of Foreign Affairs and International Trade, many of the federal and provincial cognate agencies, as well as a host of important enterprises and concerns from the private and civic sectors, could make an extraordinary difference over a very relatively short time period.

This framework has somewhat influenced Canada's policy stand, but it remains unfinished business.

At the meso level

This second avenue is dictated by two important historical facts: the evidence of the greater effectiveness of the catalytic state at the sub-regional level, and the extraordinary success of the Canadian strategy in the Caribbean.

While, in the long run, it might be possible to imagine Canada's winning strategies of collaboration with some middle power countries of LAC (Brazil, Argentina), it must be recognized that, in the short run, each of these potential allies is also part of sub-hemispheric economic zones, and potential partners are often a hub connected with some hinterland of more or less dependent, spoke-type countries. In such a context, Canada may find it difficult to strike really useful bargains with these other middle power countries of the southern portion of the hemisphere that have their own imperial designs, unless it can bring to the table its own zone of influence.

We are thus led to re-examine Canada's very successful strategy of penetration in the Caribbean (i.e., in establishing privileged relationships within the financial and industrial sectors of smaller countries closer to Canada and to realize that it might easily be pursued throughout Central America, since most of these countries (Guatemala, El Salvador, Nicaragua, Costa Rica, Panama, but also Columbia and Venezuela) still bear the cross of the asymmetric influence of larger countries (be they Mexico, Brazil, etc.) and might welcome, as Bermuda and the Caribbeans proper did in the past, some alliance with a less imperial suitor like Canada.

This appears to be part of an explicit strategy by Quebec, which has trade offices in Buenos Aires and Mexico, and satellite offices in Costa Rica, Venezuela, and Columbia. And it may well be that Quebec's goals of trebling the number of

Quebec firms in LAC (from some 500 to 1500) by the year 2005 will materialize much more in Central America than in the larger countries of Latin America.

So the strategy of *petits pas* that has paid off in the Caribbean may hold promise if it is generalized to Central America. Canada could, in this way, build on the network of initiatives that already exists in the area, and probably also take advantage of the emerging Association of Caribbean States (ACS) as a vehicle to develop its zone of influence in Middle America. Canada is already an observer in the ACS, but will have to be creative in exerting subtle pressure in order to balance the influence of France that, through its colonies in the Caribbean, is already an associate member of the ACS.

At the micro level

It will not be possible to follow either of the strategies mentioned above without a major investment in *interpersonal resources*, because brokering a greater connectivity with LAC will rely to a greater extent on interpersonal links and trust than is generally recognized in Canada.

This is bound to entail a major effort to bring Canadians into contact with Rotary Clubs and such agencies in LAC, and to learn to make the highest and best use of Canadians who may have developed privileged relationships with groups of Central and Latin Americans. Already, some of the initiatives of Industry Canada to link up some Aboriginal groups in Canada with Aboriginal groups in Central America (where they represent a significant portion of the population in certain countries) would appear to be good demonstration projects.

These personal and cultural links have been cultivated by European countries, and the United States has made an enormous effort to create surrogates for such links by attracting a significant portion of the brightest young individuals into their educational institutions. Many of these macro and meso initiatives to build bridges between Canada and the LAC may indeed need to be bolstered by the requisite amount of investment in personal networks and flexible business networks, not only as communication tools, but also as investment in interpersonal resource capabilities (Foa 1971; Laurent and Paquet 1998: ch.1).

Conclusion

A closer examination of the data available on trade and investment in the hemisphere, and also of the new dynamics at play, as well as the recent robust efforts by the European Union to develop formal links with Mercosur, Chile, and Mexico, might provide a better sense of what might potentially be lost in the long run by not developing a meaningful Canadian hemispheric governance strategy. In the long run, the costs of inaction are immense.

But we have also put forward a few hints about a possible priority agenda for Canada in the shorter run, in the dossier of hemispheric governance. While these are not meant to be more than indicative of what might ensue if a moderate amount of commitment could be mustered, they emphasize the real potential of focusing on the whole ensemble of countries around the Caribbean Sea.

A tally of the unconnected initiatives that Canadians have nurtured and developed in the Caribbean, and more recently in Central America and the rest of Latin America, would show that they amount to an impressive capital (financial, human, trust, interpersonal, etc.) that remains largely unexploited. Much could be done with a modicum of coordination and real efforts at developing synergies.

The present lack of coordination is based largely on ignorance about the potentialities of LAC for Canada. This is the main explanation for the broad range of viewpoints in Canada about LAC. There is little knowledge, and therefore little agreement exists on what ought to be done, and hence little commitment to do anything materializes. That is why parliamentary hearings on the challenges and choices facing Canada in LAC might be most productive, cognitively, but also, as a result, economically and politically. Such hearings might resolve many of the differences of opinion within Canada, and might even be the source of a renewed and more coherent Canadian hemispheric strategy.

However, this will do little to ensure that the existing conflicting strategies, struggling for a viable compromise within the hemisphere, will be reconciled (Iglesias and Rosenthal 1995). Therefore we cannot expect that progress toward a hemispheric governance regime (however balkanized) will be anything but slow.

And again, this may not be all bad, because Canada is unprepared for any rapid evolution. It has to work obliquely and subtly at developing not only a special place in the geo-governance of the hemisphere, but also at developing the new "capabilities" necessary to acquire the different forms of leadership role that may fit Canada's role within the hemisphere. As indicated, these capacities are not only organizational and institutional, but also personal. For instance, it is clear that Canada will not be able to play a full role in LAC without our collective linguistic capabilities being improved.

There are many obstacles to a successful integration (even *par morceau*) of the Americas after 2005, and one could find many reasons (reversal of economic and political fortunes in Latin America, for instance) to ignore the challenges ahead (Wrobel 1998). In our view, the present dissipation of Canada's external efforts *à tout vent et dans toutes les directions* is unwise; Quebec's focus on LAC is by contrast both strategically and tactically effective. Some coordination and mutual learning between the different fragments of the Canadian system may be in order.

The new millennium could be a unique occasion to re-evaluate Canada's overall strategy in the Americas, and to re-assess the role Canada and its provinces wish to play, separately or together, in hemispheric governance.

Chapter 6

Techno-nationalism and Meso Innovation Systems: A Cognitive Dynamics Approach

> *"Mon crâne est tellement lourd qu'il m'est impossible de le porter.*
> *Je le roule autour de moi lentement...*
> *une fois je me suis dévoré les pattes sans m'en apercevoir."*
> Gustave Flaubert

Introduction

Currently, the most fashionable weaselword in the forum of discussions on innovation is the notion of "a national system of innovation". It refers to elusive arrays of public and private institutions and organizations, but also to public policy thrusts that are shaping stable patterns of behaviour and particular incentive reward systems. These are purported to weave different logics together in a creative way: the logic built into the technical trajectories, the logic concretely embodied in the production system, and the institutional logic defining the coherence of representations and the mechanisms of coordination of action plans by stakeholders (Niosi et al. 1992; Best 1990).

In the introductory chapter of Nelson's *National Innovation Systems*, a central hypothesis is formulated about "a new spirit of what might be called 'technonationalism'...combining a strong belief that the technological capabilities of a nation's firms are a key source of their competitive prowess, with a belief that these capabilities are in a sense national, and can be built by national action" (Nelson 1993:3). While Richard Nelson and Nathan Rosenberg are careful to explain that one of the central concerns of their multi-country study is to establish "whether, and if so in what ways, the concept of a 'national' system made any sense today", they also add that *de facto* "national governments act as if it did" (Nelson 1993:5).

The objective is to raise some questions about this hypothesis.

In the first section it is suggested that any meaningful characterization of a modern economy must start with a fair assessment of the *paradoxical meaning* of the process of globalization of economic activities, and of its impact on the national production and governance systems. This forces a confrontation both with what John Naisbitt has called the "global paradox" (Naisbitt 1994) and what I elsewhere have called the "dispersive revolution".

In the second section, I explore the dynamics of the organization and the growth of knowledge, which underpin the innovation system, and the complex way in which institutions impact on cognitive processes and learning, and, through this channel, generate the thrust that generates innovations and pressures on the existing institutional order (Johnson 1992).

In the third section, there is the suggestion that the innovation process, even when defined broadly, rarely encompasses the "national" scene, but would appear to be congruent with meso-regional/sectoral realities that are the genuine source of synergies and social learning (Friedmann and Abonyi 1976; Dahmen 1988; Acs, de la Mothe, and Paquet 1996).

In the fourth section, a critical appraisal is made of the phenomenon of the "centralized mindset" that seems to permeate the study of innovation systems. There would appear to be a strong attachment to "centralized ways of thinking, assuming that every pattern must have a single cause, an ultimate controlling factor" (Resnick 1994b). This, in turn, underpins a tendency to bet on centralized means of problem-solving that almost inevitably lead to compulsive centralization and misguided approaches of the Catoblépas-type.

Catoblépas is a legendary animal (described by Gustave Flaubert in his short-story, *La tentation de Saint Antoine*) which had become so top-heavy that it could no longer hunt for a living and, as our epigraph indicates, in order to survive, unwittingly ate its own legs. I have shown in an earlier paper how damaging such an approach may be in dealing with innovation (Paquet 1988).

In the fifth section, a very preliminary examination is undertaken of the manner in which the three countries of North America are confronting this issue, and in passing, some key research challenges facing those who are really concerned about catalyzing the innovative society are identified.

The reinvention of governance

Empirical economies are "instituted processes", i.e., they are run according to a set of rules and conventions that vests the wealth-creation process with relative unity and stability by harmonizing the geo-technical constraints, imposed by the environment, with the values and plans privileged by decision-makers (Polanyi 1968). Modern economies have substantially evolved over the last century. The wealth-creation process of the late 19th century was mainly instituted as a social armistice between somewhat rigid constraints imposed by technology, geography, and natural resources endowments, on the one hand, and the less than perfectly coordinated plans of private and public decision-makers, on the other hand.

As both constraints and preferences evolved, economies came to be instituted differently because of the degrees of freedom afforded them by the extent to which they were protected from the rest of the world by relatively high transportation costs, transaction costs, and tariff walls.

However, in the recent past, the wealth-creation process has changed dramatically: it has become dematerialized as its mainsprings ceased to be natural resources and material production, and became knowledge and information activities. Transportation costs, transaction costs, and tariff walls have tumbled. As a result of important information and communication economies, and of growing organizational flexibility, transnational firms have become capable of organizing knowledge and production globally, and have escaped to a great extent from the constraints that both geography and nation states might have wished to impose on them. Economic activity has therefore become in many instances truly de-territorialized.

This process of globalization has often been simplistically and inaccurately characterized as a process of liberalization. There has been much liberalization, but more importantly, there has been a multiplex mutation of the economic process that has transformed the fabric of socio-economies, and has left firms and nations more exposed internationally and increasingly dependent on intangibles like know-how, synergies, and untraded interdependencies which are at the core of the production of knowledge, and therefore of the new wealth-creation process. This new techno-economic world has triggered important changes in the rules of the economic game and in the governance process of socio-economies, as a result of the new challenges posed by the new economy (Paquet 1990; Courchene 1995).

In the first place, firms and governments have become rather fuzzy concepts, much akin to Klein bottles: it is often no longer possible to distinguish between the inside and the outside in the complex web of networks and alliances they are enmeshed in. Secondly, the knowledge/information fabric of the new economy has led to the development of a large number of non-market institutions, as information and knowledge proved not to be handled well by the market (Paquet 1989a). Finally, the traditional and narrow economic notion of competition has been replaced by the broader and more socio-politico-economic notion of competitiveness as a benchmark for assessing the process of wealth-creation, and as a guide in designing cooperative links among all the stakeholders.

As a result, private and public organizations have become more footloose, and therefore compatible with a variety of locations, technologies, and organizational structures (Paquet 1989b; de la Mothe and Paquet 1994b). They have also been potentially affected to a much greater extent by the synergies, interdependencies, socio-cultural bonds, or trust relationships capable of producing comparative advantages. Indeed, the central challenge of the new economy has been to find ways to create an environment in which knowledge workers do as much learning as possible—from their own experiences, as well as from each other, and from partners, clients, suppliers, etc. For learning to occur, partners must engage in *conversations* amongst themselves. But since working conversations that create new knowledge can only emerge where there is trust, trust and confidence are proven to be essential inputs (Webber 1993; Paquet and Roy 1994).

Two very significant transformations in our modern political economies in the last decades have been ascribable to a large extent to the challenges posed by the new socio-economy: a fragmentation and balkanization of existing national economies, and a concurrent massive devolution in the governance system of both private and public organizations.

(a) Balkanization

First, global competitiveness has led advanced industrial nations to specialize in the export of products in which they have "technology" or "absolute" advantages, and since those export-oriented absolute-advantage industries tend to be found in sub-national regions, this has led to the emergence of a mosaic of sub-national geographical agglomerations and regional "worlds of production", characterized by *product-based technological learning systems* resting in important ways on conventions rooted in the cultures of local economic actors (Storper 1992, 1993).

Second, the pressures of globalization have put so much strain on the nation-state that sub-national regions and communities have strongly felt a need for roots and anchors in local and regional bonds of ethnicity, language, and culture. This budding *tribalism* (to use Naisbitt's term) has in turn been reinforced by the fact that it often proved to be the source of a robust entrepreneurial culture, and of competitive advantage in the new context (Stoffaes 1987).

Third, the dysfunctionality of the nation-state has triggered the emergence of a genuine shared community of economic interests at the regional level, and the dynamics of collective action has led to the rise of the region-state, when sub-national governments or loose alliances among local authorities have become active as partners of foreign investors, and providers of the requisite infrastructure to leverage regional policies capable of making the region an active participant in the global economy (Ohmae 1993; The Economist 1994).

Fourth, as the region-state emerged, it was often in a position to provide support for the development blocs through the nurturing of complementarities, interdependencies and externalities via infrastructure, networking of economic and business competence, etc., and to dynamize the transformation process at the meso-economic level (Dahmen 1988; de la Mothe and Paquet 1994c).

(b) Devolution

The search for speed of adjustment, variety, flexibility, and innovation generated by global competitiveness has forced corporations to adapt ever faster, and this has led them to "deconstruct" themselves into networks of quasi-autonomous units capable of taking action as they see fit in the face of local circumstances. Managers ceased to be "drivers of people" and became "drivers of learning" (Wriston 1992). This required a shift from vertical hierarchical structures of governance to more horizontal networking structures conducive to innovative conversations.

The same process has been witnessed in the governance of public organizations, where the need to do more with less, and the growing pressure for more sub-national states to cooperate actively with private organizations to ensure success on the global scene, has led governments to massive privatization or devolution of power to lower order public authorities (Rivlin 1992; Osborne and Gaebler 1992; Paquet 1994).

This has led to general praise for the flexibility and genuine suppleness of the federal system as a system of governance for both private and public organizations, and to the general celebration of bottom-up management (Bennis and O'Toole 1992; Handy 1992, 1994).

In transforming the governance of economic, social, and political organizations, the growing search for flexibility has not stopped at decentralization and privatization strategies. There has been growing pressure to dissolve permanent organizations so as to allow a maximum open use of all the possibilities of networking. This has led to the proposal that virtual enterprises and governments might provide the ultimate flexibility (Davidow and Malone 1992; de la Mothe and Paquet 1994a). This form of dissolution of governance systems has not only proved to be dynamically efficient, but has also led to a reinforcement of community bonds, as private and public organizations ceased to be the main source of identification.

The organization of knowledge

Since organizations are basically information or knowledge systems, their capacity "to transform" (which is another way to say "to learn") has become crucial to their survival and their co-evolution (with the institutional environment and the other stakeholders) and has been the source of value added. While the traditional view is that learning can only take place on an individual level, more recent analyses suggest that the learning organization does not store its knowledge in separate heads, but in the relationships between and among stakeholders: it creates value through dialogue between equals (Boisot 1987, 1995; Wikström and Normann 1994).

The flexibility and adaptability of organizations have become the new gauge of effective performance in lieu of simple allocative efficiency. For in a rapidly evolving surprise-generating context, plagued with uncertainty and ignorance, the challenge is not simply to make the highest and best use of existing resources and knowledge, to exploit the available possibilities better, but also to explore new possibilities and opportunities. The strategic choice has been to strike a balance or a trade-off between exploitation and exploration. Undue emphasis on the exploitation of available knowledge may trap an organization in suboptimal situations, while undue emphasis on exploration may prevent an organization from gaining much from successful experimentation (March 1991; Marengo 1993; Dosi and Marengo 1994).

Attempting to strike this balance may be a mistaken strategy. One could probably more profitably search for the complementarities, synergies, and intercreation in work, learning, and innovation (Brown and Duguid 1991).

Our reason for adopting this strategy is that it holds the possibility of prying open the dynamics of the work/learning/innovation nexus, and this might help to discriminate among the alternative strategies that are proposed these days to catalyze the innovation process: the way in which knowledge organization underpins economic progress and the manner in which communities of practice play a central role in it. This might sharpen our understanding of the role of partnering in such a context, but also suggest a different way to deal with the central question posed by James March about the balance between coherence and experimentation, between exploitation and exploration in choosing which learning regime to promote.

In an information economy, economic progress is mainly generated through the growth of knowledge, so the way in which knowledge production is organized determines whether more or less economic progress is achieved. This is a matter that was already discussed at some length by Alfred Marshall in the early part of the 20th century, as Brian Loasby (1991) has reminded us. For Marshall, "capital consists in great part of knowledge and organization". Since not only information and knowledge are becoming the pillars of the new economy but organizations themselves are knowledge systems, knowledge has become the central engine of economic progress.

Marshall had a rather primitive but effective way of dealing with organizations as knowledge systems. It was a three-step construction. First, businessmen are expected to use their knowledge to build up the firm's *internal organization*, combining specialization and integration and making use of the diversity of knowledge, abilities, and experience of their employees. Second, when similar businesses, either collected in an industrial district or dispersed over a wide territory, recognize that they have much to learn from one another, they begin to form a sort of invisible college through which they collaborate loosely. This is a *horizontal form of organization*, external to the firm but internal to the industry. Then there are the networks linking firms to customers and suppliers in a third form of organization, for the exchange of information and ideas that Marshall called *external organization* (Loasby 1991:40–1).

These forms of organization will be the locus of on-going conversations that will produce new knowledge and value-added, through networking and partnering. This is the central message of Wikström and Normann (1994): the idea that the value-creating process is the result of co-production through interlinkages and conversations among all partners. The main challenge then is to determine what the best organization of knowledge production might be, if the objective is to generate an organization characterized by learning and innovation.

According to Marengo (1993), this will greatly depend on a balance between commonality and diversity of knowledge, between coherence and mutual learning, between exploitation and exploration. But ethnographic work on the daily life of organizations suggests that practice differs significantly from job descriptions or rules and procedures, and that the actual practices are the central feature of successful organizations. The difference then between the *de jure* and the *de facto* work procedures may indeed be of central concern, since the corporate culture embodies a communal interpretation that may have little to do with the documentation available.

Corporate culture embodies generally unwritten principles, meant to generate a relatively high level of coordination at low cost by bestowing identity and membership. This corporate culture is nested at the organization level, according to Orr (1990), through the central features of work practice: stories of flexible generality about events of practice that act as repositories of accumulated wisdom, and the evolution of these stories constituting collective learning of an evolving way to interpret conflicting and confusing data, but also an on-going social construction of a community of interpretation.

This redefinition of work as conversation, as sharing stories, as becoming members of a community of practice may appear somewhat offbeat, but it is at the core of the recent writings of Webber (1993), Peters (1994), and Handy (1995). In the same way that actual practice in the workplace has a communal base, learning also has a communal base. It is not about transmission of abstract knowledge from one person's head to another's, it is about learning to "function in a community", about the "embodied ability to behave as community members", about "becoming practitioners". Learning is *legitimate peripheral participation*, and it is fostered by membership in the comunity-of-practice of interest (Brown and Duguid 1991).

Trust is at the core of both the fabric of the communities of practice, and the fabric of shared leadership. Trust is a way of transforming "labourers into members", of converting an employment contract into a membership contract: "the concept of membership, when made real, would replace the sense of belonging to a place with a sense of belonging to a community" (Handy 1995). Belonging is one of the most powerful agents of mobilization. So what is required is an important "moral" component in the new employment contract, *a new refurbished moral contract* that is not mainly contractual but mainly moral: "a network of civic engagement...which can serve as a cultural template for future collaboration...broaden the participants' sense of self...enhancing the participants' 'taste' for collective benefits" (Putnam 1995).

However, a situation in which such a membership contract would become hegemonic would correspond to a situation in which a dominant macro-culture would prevail. If such were the case, it would in the long run become homogeneous and coherent, but would also cease to be innovative. Innovation requires a certain diversity of knowledge, and stems from the interplay of separate communities, from the interplay between the core community and emergent communities at the periphery (the suppliers and the customers of a firm, for instance), to the organization and the environment it interacts actively with.

Exploration calls for diversity; for separate stories to be in good currency. It happens at the interface between the organization and its environment, and depends on the capacity for the non-canonical to prevail over the canonical.

It is therefore in the structure of the communities of practice that one must seek the levers likely to foster both learning and innovation, by intervening with the work place. When the gap between the canonical and the actual practices widens too much, the only way to promote the growth of knowledge is to legitimize and support a number of enacting activities that may be disruptive, to foster a reconception of the organization as a community of communities, and promote the view that communities of practice must be allowed to take steps outside of received wisdom.

The very coherence that makes learning easier is likely to make innovation more difficult. The central challenge, for the promotion of the growth of knowledge, is to find the requisite degree of dissonance necessary for a system to become innovative, and to identify the most effective schemes that would decompose large organizations into quasi-isolated sub-systems likely to provoke the emergence of a workable degree of inconsistency and therefore of innovation.

The differences in the way in which the sub-organizations search for knowledge increase the scope of the search. So, as these differences are legitimized, and the different ways of searching for new knowledge have the maximum opportunity to rub against one another (as in industrial districts, or more closely interconnected communities of practice), innovation will ensue.

This is the reason why institutional learning will proceed faster when the institutional infrastructure allows a fair degree of diversity. This is a point that Granovetter (1973) emphasized when he suggested that a certain degree of heterogeneity, and therefore of social distance, might be fostering a higher potentiality of innovation due to the fact that the different parties bring a complementary body of knowledge to the conversation. This is likely to trigger more fruitful synergies.

Meso innovation systems

In an economy made dynamic by information, knowledge, and competence, and consequently balkanized and decentralized, the new relevant units of analysis have to be those that serve as the basis to understand and nurture innovation. Focusing on either the firm or on the national economy would appear to be equally misguided. Under the microscope, too much is idiosyncratic and white noise is bound to run high; under the macroscope, much of the innovation and restructuring going on is bound to be missed. One may therefore argue persuasively that the most useful perspective point is the Schumpeterian/ Dahmenian meso-perspective, focusing on development blocks, technology districts, sub-national forums, etc., where the learning is really occurring (de la Mothe and Paquet 1994b, 1996:28ff).

In an evolutionary model, the process of learning and discovery is only one blade of the pair of scissors. The other blade is the interactive mechanism with the context or environment through which selection occurs. Whether the unit of analysis is the technology or the firm, this interactive mechanism is fitness-driven, and firm search processes "both provide the source of differential fitness—firms whose R&D turn up more profitable processes of production or products will grow relative to their competitors—and also tend to bind them together as a community" (Dosi and Nelson 1994:162).

It is very important to realize that social proximity is bound to play a fundamental role on both sides of the equation. Both on the organization side and on the forum/environment side, proximity breeds interaction and socio-economic learning (Boswell 1990). Moreover, these interactive mechanisms are fuelled by dynamic increasing returns to agglomeration. In most cases, these agglomeration economies are bounded, and therefore do not give rise to monopoly by a single region or location, but they generate snowballing increasing returns (Arthur 1990).

We do not know much about the innovation process and the process of diffusion of technical and organizational innovations, but the research agenda on those issues has been much influenced by Nelson and Winter (1977). At the core of their scheme is the notion of "selection environment", which is defined as the context that "determines how relative use of different technologies changes over time" (61). This context is shaped by market and non-market components, conventions, socio-cultural factors, and by the broader institutional structure. This selection environment constitutes the relevant *milieu*, which may be broader or narrower, and may be more or less important in explaining the innovative capacity of a country and a sector/region.

The notion of *milieu* has been defined as *"un ensemble territorial formé de réseaux intégrés de ressources matérielles et immatérielles, dominé par une culture historiquement constituée, vecteur de savoirs et savoir-faire, et reposant sur un système relationnel de type coopération/concurrence des acteurs localisés"* (Lecoq 1989). Consequently, the notion of *milieu* connotes three sets of forces:

(1) the contours of a particular spatial set vested with a certain unity and tonus;
(2) the organizational logic of a network of interdependent actors engaged in cooperative innovative activity; and
(3) organizational learning, based on the dialectics between *adapting actors* and the *adopting milieu* (Maillat 1992).

Such a milieu is not a necessary condition for innovation. There are innovations and much learning even in the absence of a *dynamic milieu*, but such a milieu is likely to bring forth innovation networks; and innovation networks, in turn, are a form of organization so much better adapted to a world of technological, and appropriation uncertainty than market or hierarchy, that they are more likely to kickstart the innovation process (DeBresson and Amesse 1991).

At the core of the *dynamic milieu* and the innovation network are a number of intermingled dimensions (economic, historical, cognitive and normative), but they all depend to a certain degree on trust and confidence, and therefore on a host of cultural and social factors that have a tendency to be found mainly in localized networks, and to be more likely to emerge from a background of shared experiences, regional loyalties, etc. This is social capital in Coleman's sense, and such social and cultural capital plays a central role in both the dynamics and the capacity of meso-systems to learn and transform (Coleman 1988; Saxenian 1994).

The innovation process depends a great deal on the central features of a selection environment or milieu.

In the first place, innovation is all about continuous learning, and learning does not occur in a socio-cultural vacuum. The innovation network is more likely to blossom in a restricted localized milieu where all the socio-cultural characteristics of a dynamic milieu are likely to be found. Moreover, it is most unlikely that this sort of *milieu* will correspond to the national territory. Therefore, if one is to identify *dynamic milieux or milieux porteurs* as likely systems on which one might work to stimulate innovation, they are likely to be local or regional systems of innovation.

Second, some geo-technical forces would appear to generate meso-level units where learning proceeds faster and better. As Storper argues,

> in technologically dynamic production complexes...there is a strong reason for the existence of regional clusters or agglomerations. Agglomeration appears to be a principal geographical form in which the trade-off between lock-in technological flexibility (and the search for quasi-rents), and cost minimization can be most effectively managed, because it facilitates efficient operations of a cooperative production network. Agglomeration, in these cases, is the result not simply of standard localization economies (which are based on the notion of allocative efficiency in minimizing costs), but of Schumpeterian efficiencies (Storper 1992:84).

Third, the deconstruction of national economies, the dispersive revolution in governance, the rise of region-states and the growth of the new tribalism would tend to provide a greater potential for dynamism at the meso level. But Storper has argued that "codes, channels of interaction, and ways of organizing and coordinating behaviours" are what makes learning possible (85). He feels that the confluence of issues (learning, networks, lock-in, conventions and types of knowledge) must be rooted in politico-economic cultures, rules and institutions, and that in many countries these are highly differentiated at the regional level. Therefore, one region may trigger technological learning and innovation networks in one sub-national area much faster than in others. Canada, the USA, and Mexico are such countries, where one may reasonably detect a mosaic of politico-economic cultures, rules, and conventions with differential innovative potential (Maddox and Gee 1994). Consequently, one may say that there is a genuine "territorialization of learning" in such a Schumpeterian world.

Even a provisional attempt to map out the interface among the many dimensions explored above (the rise of the knowledge/information society, the globalization/balkanization process, the drift in the governance system, the consolidation of development blocks, the texture of the selection environment/milieu and its impact on innovation, the innovation networks, the differences in the politico-economic cultures, conventions, rules, institutions, and the new tribalism, the rise of the regional state, etc.) already suggests a few modest general propositions about the demise of the system of copyrights and patents (Barlow 1993) and about the "territorialization of learning" in a Schumpeterian world (Storper 1992).

But what might be required as a matter of priority, if the analysis is to proceed apace, is a less fuzzy vocabulary and some partial consolidation of the *terrain des opérations*. This is exactly what Storper and Harrison (1991) have attempted, with some success. What is left now is for interested parties is to continue their work.

The centralized mindset

In the face of these strong presumptions in favour of the existence of *meso innovation systems*, it is surprising to find that so little has been done to escape the mindset of "national systems of innovation". The reason for this bias is, however, not very difficult to understand. Since the cost of thinking is not zero, humans adopt paradigms and mindsets to somewhat routinize their thinking. Ideologies are simplification machines of the sort that provide mechanical responses to a battery of difficult questions by first de-complexifying and sanitizing issues.

The attraction of techno-nationalism falls into this category. Mitchel Resnick has analyzed the bizarre *travers* that explains that, in an era of decentralization in every domain, centralized thinking remains prevalent in our theories of knowledge, in our ways of analyzing problems, and in our search for policy responses." Politicians, managers and scientists are working with blinders on, focusing on centralized solutions even when decentralized approaches might be more appropriate, robust, or reliable" (Resnick 1994:36).

Indeed, despite the dramatic changes in the nature of the socio-economy, there are those in some quarters, these days, who are still calling for the Second Coming of Keynes. This mindset is a generalized blockage that has affected Canada, perhaps even more dramatically than other countries, because of our economic culture (Paquet and Roy 1992).

Over the past 125 years, circumstances have often endangered Canadian prosperity. Canada has had to learn ways and means to cope with these challenges, in a manner that reconciles the geo-technical and socio-political constraints it operates under, with the values, plans, and idiosyncrasies its diverse population choose to prioritize at the time. An *habitus* has evolved: a system of habitualized dispositions and inclinations to use certain institutional devices or stratagems that appeared to do the job of reconciling all those constraints most effectively (Bourdieu 1972).

The *economic culture* that has evolved has underpinned the governance of the Canadian economy over the last century and has been based, so Herschel Hardin would put it, on two fundamental elements: the extensive use of *public enterprise* and of *interregional redistribution* of the economic surplus (Hardin 1974). These two root-stratagies have been used repeatedly from the earliest days of the federation (Norrie and Owram 1991).

In the recent past, both these tenets of the Canadian *economic culture* have come under attack: there has been a massive disengagement by the federal government from its public enterprises, and from its massive effort at inter-regional redistribution of resources. There have been many reasons for these changes (Paquet and Roy 1992).

The results of central planning for national/regional development has resulted in a certain amount of disenchantment, and an ensuing modesty by central planners. It is now apparent that development is not technocratically ordained: it is at best nurtured and helped along by using the context and circumstances as well as one can (Franklin 1990; Côté 1991). Disenchantment with guidance from the centre has led to decentralization in its two forms: privatization and subsidiarity. Many public enterprises have been privatized or have ceased to play a central policy role, and the weakening of the central government's financial capacity has eroded its capacity for massive inter-regional transfers.

The globalization of markets and the attenuation of national economic borders, together with the greater modesty of federal policy-makers, have forced all regions and provinces to consider the desirability of developing their own development strategies. Many provinces and regions had been engaged in such activities for quite a long time, but the process has been catalyzed in the recent past. These regional/provincial initiatives have not been coordinated or integrated into an overall strategy. Indeed, they have often become part of Canada's national *adversary system*, and have contributed to the erosion of Canada's competitiveness to the extent that internal barriers and existing balkanization have been reinforced. The consequent reduction of the economic surplus has limited potential redistribution (Valaskakis 1990).

The core values of the traditional economic culture have defined economic development in a somewhat technocratic and voluntaristic way. The use of central public institutions presumed that there was a relatively clear view of what had to be accomplished, and that policy actions could be designed to effect it. At the conceptual level, economic progress came to be regarded as a mechanical process that could be engineered and dominated by a logic of production. This turned out to be the source of the failures of the traditional culture, and the root-cause of its incapacity to command or control economic growth.

A new economic culture has developed, building on a view of economic growth as emerging from below, through cities, communities, and regions which are the real loci of networks, entrepreneurship, and of un-traded interdependencies that are at the true source of economic dynamism (Jacobs 1985). Growth in that sense "cannot be commandeered; it can only be nurtured and encouraged by providing a suitable environment. Growth occurs; it is not made. Within a growth model, all that human intervention can do is to discover the best conditions for growth, and then try to meet them. In any given environment, the growing organism develops at its own rate" (Franklin 1990).

This has promoted a "gardening" view of "natural growth". In this view, the economy is a garden with trees, plants, weeds, and bushes of all shapes and sizes. The gardener may make a difference, but there is no simple rule likely to apply across the board to all plants and weeds in this ecosystem full of variety and interdependencies (Côté 1991:27). In an economy considered as a complex garden, improvement will proceed from a close collaboration between gardener and context, from creative interaction and partnership between the central and the local (public and private) to mobilize local resources (Miller/Côté 1987; Côté 1991). Natural growth is therefore not orchestrated artificially from the centre, but nurtured from its sources at the level of cities and regions. This is true as much in Western Europe (where four growth areas: Baden Wurtemburg, Catalonia, Lombardy and Rhône-Alpes—are considered as the locomotives of Western Europe) as it is in Canada. This "garden" approach imposes a completely different image of the dynamics of progress and changes the measurements of any progress regarded as meaningful.

This new economic culture calls for upside-down thinking. In the first place, there are "local circumstances". Each portion of the garden has specific needs and wants; only social interactions at the local level can play a big role in the construction of development networks, and in ensuring that the social learning they underpin is effective. Consequently, instead of broad prosperity measures translating into across-the-board development interventions, what is called for is a set of local, supportive and extremely diversified interventions because of the varied contexts, and for interventions crafted at the local level because of the better appreciation of the situation that one has from that vantage point. For that sort of action, it is not sufficient to rely on aggregate measurements or macro-indicators of progress. To monitor the "regional" progress in the garden, and to underpin effective interventions in different portions of the garden, one requires meso-indicators capturing the progress in the separate segments of the garden (Paquet and Roy 1992).

Yet although this alternative cosmology has been suggested, it has had very little impact on the Canadian gestalt in good currency. The science and technology policy or the innovation system that is currently discussed remain based on the idea of a centralized "national system of innovations" to be kick-started from the centre rather than a fragmented and localized set of *systems of innovation* that could only be nurtured from the periphery and only very lightly and subtly coordinated from the centre if need be (Paquet 1992b; de la Mothe and Paquet 1994d).

126

Indeed, one might be able to show that recent policy initiatives in Canada in areas as diverse as prosperity, social programmes, regional development, etc., have been similarly defined and processed through the same centralized mindset.

Ways of adapting

In Canada, the USA, and Mexico, the "centralized mind syndrome" looms large. In each country, however, it has taken different forms, and, in a different way, a process of questioning has begun. The existing legal framework, a common language, a shared culture—these are the facts that underpinned the presumption that national character and national boundaries not only mattered but were and are playing a determining role in shaping and catalyzing the innovation process. Indeed, Nelson and Rosenberg, in the introductory chapter of Nelson (1993) state, in connection with the post-World War II period, that "general perceptions about national societies and cultures tend to *reify* [author's emphasis] national systems", (16) echoing a strong sense that these national systems have sufficient resilience and robustness to make a significant difference, to meaningfully influence the national innovation system, in the face of the trans-national forces that tend to shape business and technology.

Little attention has, however, been paid to sub-national cultures, state or local governments, to the new powers they have acquired as international integration triggered national disintegration, and to the new rules and conventions at that level. These may not be of equal importance in every country, but there is already plenty of evidence that (1) those regional/community features compounded with (2) the joint regional/community-cum-sectoral/industrial effect built on specific synergies in the organization/location/technology nexus may indeed play quite an important role in explaining the dynamics of innovation (de la Mothe and Paquet 1994b).

These are important features of the Canadian industrial landscape where the industrial structure is sharply differentiated from region to region, where many of the ten provincial governments are powerful stakeholders and policy-makers, where certain major metropolitan private and public organizations are actively involved in providing important resources to *their* innovation system, where national and provincial institutions like research laboratories and universities and colleges have important and differential local impacts very much shaped by proximity, and where even the legal and cultural background varies widely. This explains a very diversified industrial landscape, and one that would require a thorough sub-national analysis to expose the real causes and sources of innovation and competitiveness. This also explains why, more than a decade ago, the Science

Council of Canada made metropolitan technology councils a key feature of its proposed strategy (Conseil des sciences du Canada 1984).

The same point can be made about the USA, with the extraordinary diversity of its regional/sectoral landscape, its various sub-cultures, its very different state strategies, its network of state universities, etc. And the same may also be said of Mexico, where the 32 states may not weigh equally in the innovation equation, but where a certain degree of differentiation is already obvious. A recent survey of science in Mexico has revealed to the rest of North America that there is a much greater variety on the innovation system front in Mexico than one might gather from the superficial press coverage by the rest of North America (Maddox and Gee 1994).

We know that much of the progress of the wealth-creation process in the three countries is ascribable to the innovation system, and is rooted in product-based technology-learning à la Storper, and we know that these innovation/competition capabilities are based to a great extent on what Storper has called "conventions of identity and participation" (1993:450). This remains, however, an unexplored corner in the new literature on economic development.

A shift-share analysis of the change in market share in world trade for the USA has revealed that only some 10% of the change in the market share of the USA was ascribable in the 1970–87 period to the relative changes in the relative growth of country markets or commodity markets or their joint effect. Most of the change in market share is ascribed to the residual *competitiveness effect*—a label to "cover" all the price and non-price related changes in the economy, of which the innovation system is a major portion (Guerrieri 1992). This so-called competitiveness effect reminds one of another weaselword, technical change, a label used very loosely in the old economic growth literature: the competitiveness effect can probably be regarded now much as the technical change component in the growth of GNP was in the past—as a measure of our ignorance.

These types of numbers vary considerably from country to country and from sector to sector in any given country. For instance, the competitiveness factor is much less important in traditional sectors than in science-based sectors. Of central importance is the fact that, in the Guerrieri study, for the USA, the competitiveness factor has tended to be consistently negative during the period 1970–87 across all sectors.

There is a strong presumption that the regional worlds of production may not have been sufficiently recognized as the source/cause of innovation, and that a better use of the "conventions of identity and participation" as a lever for policy-makers might pay off handsome dividends. But it is unlikely that this sort of strategy will be pursued with any robustness in Canada, the USA, or Mexico because of the "centralized mind syndrome". Even though in these three countries there are clear signs of pressures for a decentralization of public policy vis-à-vis the innovation systems, and for the pursuit of a bottom-up wealth-creation strategy, there are strong forces of "dynamic conservatism" (Schön 1971) at work.

In Mexico, the resistance is clearly built into the socio-political system: the centralized governmental institutions underpinning the innovation system are quite reluctant to build on the existing and potential regional strengths or even to allow the regional innovation systems to develop (Maddox and Gee 1994).

In the United States, although there is no sign of an integrated strategy animating a national innovation system, and there is evidence that the federal policies in the post-World War II period have "displaced the role of state governments as actors in this innovation system and contributed to some weakening in the informal ties that linked many corporate and academic research institutions" (Mowery and Rosenberg 1993:61–2), the "national" innovation system concept appears alive and well. Although, to some, it is nothing more than an *être de raison*, it has remained such an icon that even those in a position of authority, arguing for massive devolution of federal powers toward the states, have not dared to suggest that this be effected for the innovation system (Rivlin 1992).

As for Canada, the extent of the balkanization of the country and the power of the regional stakeholders who are demanding some autonomy, combined with the federal determination to maintain a centralist stand without the fiscal capacity to inject significant resources, and with a powerful set of academic forces that have been pressing for generations to neutralize the emergence of any strong "national" strategy—all these forces are bound to ensure that Canada will remain on the innovation system front a *stalled omnibus* with neither a meaningful top-down, nor a significant bottom-up strategy (Paquet 1988; de la Mothe and Paquet 1994d).

Conclusion

A presumption put forward very cautiously and tentatively by some scholars a few years ago suggested that the most effective way to analyze the innovation system and to intervene in it strategically would be to tackle the problem at the "national" level. Yet much recent work has raised serious questions about this hypothesis. Too many forces at work in the world economy would appear to suggest that, as globalization proceeds, national disintegration occurs, and sub-national components gain more importance. Consequently, focusing on sub-national units of analysis would, in all likelihood, provide better insights into the workings of the "real worlds of production", and better levers for policy intervention on the innovation front.

It might have been expected that observers, researchers, and policy-makers would have been led to focus more of their work and analyses on meso-innovation systems. However, this would be unduly discounting the power of the centralized mindset at work in so many sectors of politics, management and science. This mindset has kept the centralized model of the socio-economy in place, and the decentralized model at bay. The result is the on-going pursuit of ethereal "national systems" where there are only "regional/sectoral" systems.

The costs of such strategies are likely to be very high if, as we surmise, what is called for is a bottom-up policy. Consequently, it is perhaps time to call for a return to the drawing board before it is too late, and for a return to the cautious and tentative language used by Richard Nelson, to the realization that the hypothesis of "national systems of innovation" has not been validated yet, and a plea for a more serious and careful examination of the alternative hypothesis suggested by the new paradigms of economic geography.

Chapter 7

Smart Communities and the
Geo-Governance of Social Learning

> "We need to shift away from the notion of technology
> managing information and toward the idea
> of technology as a medium of relationships"
> Michael Schrage

Introduction

A smart community is one that learns fast and well. Learning makes the highest and best use of all the community's intelligence and resources (intellectual, social, physical, financial, personal, etc.) through the use of all available physical, social, and behavioural technologies, including the new information and communication technologies (NICT). One must guard against the temptation on the part of the technologically-inclined to ascribe the "smartness" of communities to the presence of NICTs. Given the wide range of factors contributing to the success of a smart community, it is unwise to reduce "smartness" to sheer connectedness or to a problem of wiring.

A smart community is first and foremost a community—i.e., a fuzzy geo-political entity that has assets, skills, and capabilities, but also a soul, a collective intelligence, and a capacity to transform (i.e., to learn). The fact that, in order to transform, it may use NICTs extensively, is not inconsequential, but it remains a subsidiary phenomenon. A smart community may be smart without NICTs. Indeed, NICTs are only the tip of the iceberg. The hidden and most significant portion of the iceberg is an ensemble of mechanisms, instruments, and perspectives, generally subsumed under the labels of collective intelligence and social learning. These are the basic forces that make the community ever smarter as it continues to learn.

Collective intelligence and social learning mobilize and marshal intellectual, informational, physical, and human resources in ways that produce a continuous flow of additional useable knowledge. This intelligence-cum-learning endeavour creates a geo-governance challenge: the challenge of uncovering the best way to organize geo-technical communities of practice so that they can make the highest and best use of collective intelligence, and so ensure effective social learning when resources, power, and knowledge are widely distributed.

This chapter explores why smart communities are important: how they work, and how, through a variety of means, citizens might help make their communities smarter.

Why smart communities are important and how they work

In a knowledge-based socio-economy, *extensive growth* (through additional human and physical capital) does not suffice to ensure socio-economic progress. Much depends on the capacity to ensure that the different inputs work ever better together, and therefore on the development of improved forms of collaborative organization that will fully tap into the collective intelligence, and generate effective learning. The lack of intensive growth—growth based on a capacity for continuous technical and organizational innovation—is by all accounts the source of the productivity slowdown in many socio-economies, and of the relative decline in their standard of living. Silo-type activities or conflictive turf-wars are disconcerting: they stunt the cooperation and co-evolution that are at the core of effective learning and productivity increases (Paquet 1998).

The extent of the disconcertion and dysfunction of an organization, a community, or a socio-economy has therefore much to do with the inadequacy of what Alfred Marshall called "organizational capital". Organizational capital refers to the internal organization of the units, the network of relationships (region, district, etc.) within which it is embedded, the set of capabilities they embody, the ways in which they are working in synch, and the socio-technical infrastructure required for all this to work (Loasby 1991). As Marshall put it, "capital consists in a great part of knowledge and organization; and, of this, some part is private property and the other part is not" (Marshall 1920:138). Much of it is in the form of infrastructures, rules, and social capital that are part of the commonwealth of relationships, networks, and regimes.

Collaboration and innovation demand the sort of organizational capital that is capable of generating and supporting effective concertation, but only to the point where some degree of freedom and discretion are left with all partners for discovery and learning. A lacklustre performance is therefore *prima facie* evidence that the organizational capital in place is inadequate where generating both the requisite coherence that ensures the needed collaboration, and the right looseness, imbalance, and tension likely to trigger innovation, is concerned (Granovetter 1973).

While organizational capital is not the only basic input necessary for organizational effectiveness, community success, national productivity, and socio-economic progress, it is one of the key inputs, and the most important enabling factor in these processes. It is also one of the most difficult ingredients to inject into an organization or community, because new organizational capital entails re-organization, by definition, and this breeds discontent and opposition because it modifies the sites of power, and expropriates many power-holders' existing leverage.

Still, a massive investment in new organizational capital is required to solve the sort of problems facing disconcerted socio-economies and communities. This entails a transformation of the governance and accountability structures to ensure that a more decentralized, more participative, less technocratic system is put in place, and one that draws on more effective collaboration of the private, public, and civic sectors (Hock 1995; Paquet and Roy 1998).

(a) Distributed governance and multiple accountabilities
(1) In times of rapid change, organizations and communities can only govern themselves effectively by developing, as they proceed, both the capacity to learn what their goals are and should become, and what means are to be used to reach them. This is accomplished by tapping into the knowledge that active citizens and groups already possess, and getting them to invent ways out of the predicaments they are in. This leads to more distributed forms of governance that deprive the leader of his or her monopoly on the governing of the organization: for the organization or community of practice to learn quickly, everyone must take part in the conversation, and bring forward each bit of knowledge and wisdom that he or she has that has a bearing on the issue. This calls for a dispersion of power; a more distributed governance process (Paquet 1999a).

Distributed governance does not mean only a process of dispersion of power toward localized decision-making within each sector. It also entails a dispersion of power over a wide variety of actors and groups across sectors. In the context of rapid change, the best learning experience for these variegated actors and groups can be effected through flexible multi-sectoral teams, woven by moral contracts and reciprocal obligations, negotiated in the context of evolving partnerships (Paquet and Roy 1998).

Under ideal circumstances, a multifunctional *esprit de corps* materializes and provides a most fertile ground for social learning. It is based on the development through time of a social capital of trust, reasonableness, and mutual understanding that facilitates the multilogue, and generates a sort of basic pragmatic ethic likely to promote synergies among the many potential partner organizations (Lévy 1994; Thuderoz, Mangematin and Harrisson 1999). But the circumstances are not always ideal.

This means there is a need for explicit efforts to improve the mobilization of all participants, through a wide array of mechanisms, coordination maps, and institutions. This is, however, often much more difficult to realize than is usually presumed: the workings of collective intelligence impose conditions and constraints on such efforts. Humans are not programmed units; they need to be engaged in the process of collective intelligence, the terms of this engagement are constantly re-negotiated, and much of what they know is tacit. And although social learning can be promoted, not all social learning is necessarily feed-forward social learning (i.e., promoting the advancement of social learning). Well-intentioned efforts may well be useless, turn out to be much less effective than anticipated, or even backfire and generate overall perverse collective reactions. Consequently, the designed organizational arrangements may not catalyze collective intelligence well, or may mark out only a portion of the learning terrain, or may link the different components too loosely, or may generate slow learning or even *un*learning.

(2) In a world of distributed governance, power is shared. Each person is an official, and has a burden of office. Each member of the community has ruling work to do: each participant is not simply a consumer of governance, but a producer of governance (Tussman 1989). Indeed, it is only because citizens *qua* citizens have duties and obligations that they are entitled to rights that ensure that they are fully equipped with the power to meet these obligations.

Attached to the burden of office is a commensurate accountability obligation. Accountability refers to the requirement to "answer for the discharge of a duty or for conduct". This presupposes an agreement on (i) what constitutes an acceptable performance and (ii) what constitutes an acceptable language of justification for the actors in defending their conduct (Paquet 1997f).

Officials have a complex burden of office, and are confronted with many interfaces with different stakeholders with different claims to authority (hierarchical superiors, professional colleagues, clients, etc.), many types of accounts demanded (political, managerial, legal, professional, etc.), and much complexity, heterogeneity, and uncertainty in the circumstances surrounding the activities for which one is accountable. The very complexity of the burden of office results in much fuzziness in the definition of accountability.

Defining accountability in a single direction, or with reference to only one stakeholder, or with reference to only one dimension of the burden of office, or without taking account of the context, is extremely dangerous. It amounts to assuming that only one dimension is of consequence, and presuming that all other forms of accountability can be regarded as irrelevant, or secondary in some sense. This becomes obvious in a scenario where one might define his/her burden of office entirely in terms of the diktats of the organization's financial services department. This could only lead to dangerous and truncated notions of the burden of office, accountability, and ethics.

In the face of such a nexus of accountabilities—many of them leading to contrasted and even contradictory demands—a community has no easy way out: there must be discussion, multilogue, and deliberation, leading to a fuller use of the collective intelligence and to social learning, and to an always imperfect, incomplete, and often temporary reconciliation of these different dimensions (Juillet, Paquet and Scala 2000).

This social learning can only occur if certain conditions are met: i.e., if the conversation with the situation is conducted within a context allowing for a meaningful conversation to be carried out, and if the conversation, deliberation, and accumulation of judgments are conducted with tact and civility, and a capacity to cope with multiple logics (Paquet 1999b).

The sort of learning generated by multilogue does not necessarily congeal into formalized decision-making and conclusions. To a significant degree it remains *tacit knowledge*, a capacity to deal effectively with matters of practice, and to deal with such matters in a timely manner and with a full appreciation of the local and particular context. This tacit knowing often materializes as a by-product, as a result of subsidiary or peripheral attention being given to some matters, while addressing other issues in a more focused way.

Indeed, as we shall see later, much of the effectiveness of social learning depends on a community's capacity to generate tacit knowledge, and on its capacity to accumulate it, to build on it, and to make it explicit and easily shareable (Gill 2000).

(b) Milieu and discovery

To cope with a technology-driven and dynamically evolving environment, organizations and communities must use the environment strategically, in much the same way as the surfer uses the wave: to learn faster, to adapt more quickly. This calls for non-centralization, for an expropriation of the power away from the top managers in an organization, or from any one organization in a network or a community. To be successful, decision-makers must mobilize all the favourable environmental circumstances, and the full complement of imagination and resourcefulness in the heart and mind of each team player. Consequently, they must be on the spot to take action; they must also become team leaders in task-force-type projects, quasi-entrepreneurs capable of cautious sub-optimizing in the face of a turbulent environment, and of engaging others to join in such ventures voluntarily.

This sort of strategy calls for lighter, more horizontal, and modular structures, for the creation of networks. These new modularized private, public, and civic organizations cannot impose their views on their clients or citizens. However, these structural features are not by themselves sufficient: mechanisms must be put in place to ensure the requisite degree of consultation, deliberation and negotiation everywhere.

Leaders have to become brokers, negotiators, animateurs. A consultative and participative mode must be obtained among firms, the state, and community groups; and the right balance must be found in this learning process between exploration for new knowledge and exploitation of the newly acquired knowledge (March 1991). While discovery is centrally important, it is equally important to make the highest and best use of the results of these discoveries, and to not mindlessly pursue novelty for novelty's sake.

Moreover, it must be understood that the processes and mechanisms of probing and discovery from within, so to speak, are only one blade of the scissors. The other blade is the external linking of the community with the environment through which a Darwinian selection occurs. These selection processes both "provide the source of differential fitness—firms whose R&D turn up more profitable processes of production or products will grow relative to their competitors—and also tend to bind them together as a community" (Dosi and Nelson 1994:162).

The *context* is a complex nexus of forces shaped by market and non-market components, conventions, socio-cultural factors, and by the broader institutional structure. It is this ensemble of components, conventions, rules, structures, and regimes that constitutes the relevant *milieu*.

We have shown in the last chapter how the *milieu* plays a key role in the innovation process, and how trust and a host of cultural and sociological factors that have a tendency to be found mainly in localized networks, and to be more likely to emerge in the presence of shared experiences, regional loyalties, etc., play a central role both in the process of learning and transforming (Coleman 1988; Saxenian 1994).

(c) Collective intelligence

Even though it has been established that (1) distributed governance and multiple accountabilities are the defining characteristics of the new organization or community; (2) the environment is defined by an ensemble of mechanisms, network relations, belief systems, and social capital that provide the environment with a causal texture (Emery and Trist 1965); and (3) the adaptation/adoption dynamic between the community and the environment and among the different groups inside and outside the organization or community (with their diverse frames of reference) plays itself out pragmatically much better *in situ*, i.e., in the context of practical meso-situations (Schön and Rein 1994), this does not suffice to ensure that effective coordination and learning will prevail. What is required in addition to these components to ensure that a community becomes smart is a basic coalescence of all these factors to ensure that the community has the capacity to mobilize competences effectively, and a capacity to probe and learn, to go beyond its limits (Lévy 1994).

Learning entails "the mutually consistent interpretation of information that is not fully codified, and hence not fully capable of being transmitted, understood, and utilized independently of the actual agents who are developing and using it" (Storper 1996:259). Knowledge is dispersed, and exists in a form that is not fully codified: this is a fundamental constraint imposed on the highest and best use of collective intelligence and on effective learning.

A central challenge then is to determine how such knowledge can be made explicit, and can be more effectively tapped into and shared. This is a process that has been explored most creatively by Michael Polanyi (1964, 1966). Jerry Gill (2000) has aptly synthesized Polanyi's analysis in a simple diagram that explains how cognitivity proceeds from tacit knowledge (bodily and subsidiary absorption of knowledge) as a person or community is involved in other more focused activities mobilizing their awareness, toward an explicit knowing, that can be transformed into a conceptual form likely to facilitate its dissemination.

Figure 8: Michael Polanyi's dynamics of cognitive experience

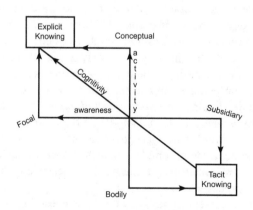

Source: Gill 2000:39.

This calls for instruments, conventions, or relational transactions to define mutually coherent expectations and common guideposts for partners who have quite different visions of the world and quite different frames of reference. The central challenge of collective intelligence often amounts to finding useful ways to effect such agreements on common guideposts in an oblique way, so as to avoid activating the powerful defence mechanisms of those parties who have different frames of reference (and often fear some power loss as a result of reframing, and are therefore likely to resist any effort to reframe the situation). These oblique strategies may be embedded in some innocuous reporting procedure that requires some dialogue, and often results in significant subsequent reframing, because of the very non-threatening nature of the process (Juillet, Paquet, and Scala 2000).

These instruments and conventions differ from sector to sector. They provide the requisite coherence for a common context of interpretation, and for some "cognitive routinization of relations" between communities and their environments (Storper 1996:259). Indeed, such coherence is a major source of nimbleness in the network socio-economy. Yet, as we mentioned earlier, a good learning network must not be too coherent: the nodes should not be too similar, nor the ties too strong or too routinized. Some heterogeneity and some social distance might foster a higher potential for innovation, because the different parties bring to the "conversation" a more complementary body of knowledge.

There is no way in which one can provide a comprehensive tabulation of all the useful mechanisms or conventions necessary to ensure the effective operation of collective intelligence. However, the ways in which mechanisms and conventions have helped to pave the way to the highest and best use of collective intelligence can be illustrated. Gill's study of Michael Polanyi's philosophy has led him to provide such illustrations in a variety of domains.

Making knowledge explicit is making communication and learning easier, but it does not ensure that a community will learn fast and become smarter. The social learning processes are based on good use of collective intelligence, but the existence of collective intelligence is only a necessary and not a sufficient condition for social learning. Therefore, both processes, though intimately related, gain from being examined separately. While collective intelligence is fundamentally raising an *epistemic challenge*, social learning raises a complementary *informational challenge*. The Boisot scheme, dealing with the latter challenge of information codification and dissemination (discussed in chapter 2), provides a useful complement to the Polanyi scheme, which focusses on the prior epistemic challenge. But, as will become obvious, these are intimately interconnected processes.

It is not unimportant to emphasize that the Boisot learning cycle of information formalization and dissemination represents only one set of key features of the learning process. It should not be seen as a reductionist ploy to occlude other mechanisms at work in parallel—like the Polanyi mechanisms that help tacit knowledge become more explicit, or the mechanisms through which the particular frames of reference of different actors or groups taking part in the learning-generating conversation are in some way transcended through the situated resolution of frame differences à la Schön/Rein (1994).

In some ways, these three families of mechanisms (at the informational, epistemic, and frame reflection levels) are integrally interconnected. And it would be unwise to argue that one is more important than any other. In a smart community, the mechanical blockages in information production and dissemination may at times appear as the least important of the blockages in the working of collective intelligence and social learning. They have been more mechanically described, and appear less opaque than the blockages in the knowledge explicitation à la Polanyi, or the frame reconciliation processes—in which a "situated resolution" of frame conflicts would appear to be possible, through actors being persuaded to engage in co-design of solutions à la Schön/Rein, for instance. But these three sets of processes interfere with one another, and, at times, any one of these sets of forces may harbour the most significant blockages.

This summary of the sort of governance challenges facing smart communities remains rather sketchy. It has not done justice to the extraordinary complexity that may ensue when the process of technological change, anchored in new communication and information technologies, plays havoc both with the ways in which the triple process of knowledge explicitation, knowledge codification and dissemination, and frame reconciliation works, and the ways in which these sub-processes interact.

These challenges can often only be analyzed and resolved *in situ*. But this summary view might guide our exploration of the existing blockages on the road to the smart community, and the various ways in which one might operate in these three dimensions to remove the blockages, and to help communities become smarter still.

Smarter communities

Citizens, action groups, and the state have to rethink their actions in the world of learning economies and smart communities.

This requires a well-aligned nexus of relations, networks, and regimes, and states can be important catalysts in the construction of the new "loose intermediation" social capital that is required: improving relationships here, fostering networks there, developing more or less encompassing formal or informal regimes at other places. This is the central role of what some have called the *catalytic state* (Lind 1992).

But it would be unwise to restrict interventions to institutional design. These sorts of frameworks have to translate into operating mechanisms and technologies, capable of carrying on the tasks envisaged by the social architects. This socio-technical engineering to enhance capacity, processes, and due diligence is a momentous task, because it must fundamentally transform *coordinating practices* (Boland et al. 1996; Kling et al. 1996). However, improving design and operational setting will not suffice, either.

To transform a community of practice in a fundamental way, one must also be able to psychoanalyze the different partners, and tinker with their frames of reference (1) through disclosing and articulating a vision of the new world of coordination and (2) by engaging them to take part in it. To do so, civic entrepreneurs must engage in *creative reframing at the level of perspectives and frame reflections* at the same time as they do a considerable amount of gap-filling at the level of mechanisms and instruments, and at times help improve the institutional designs (Henton, Melville, and Walesh 1997).

Much of this can be done as practitioners' *learning by doing*. But such work can be facilitated, and social learning accelerated, by some meta-reflections on the whole process of governance, and the crafting of more effective technologies of governance. Therefore, there is considerable merit to injecting into this world of practice a robust coefficient of *phronesis* or reflection-in-action: not only using Delta knowledge—practical knowledge—but reflecting on improving its uses (Gilles and Paquet 1989; Toulmin 1990).

This "reflection-in-action on reflection-in-action" has been somewhat ignored by the administrative sciences and by those social scientists who remain much taken by the seductions of an exclusive focus on technical rationality and deductive reasoning (Schön 1983). But the institutional design/socio-technical engineering/civic entrepreneurship nexus of activities at the core of smart communities is now challenging the academy, and forcing governance experts (1) to revisit many concepts like rationality and causality; (2) to develop a refurbished "*outillage mental*" if they wish to be helpful to practitioners in their building of smart communities; and (3) to construct better evaluative instruments to gauge the successes or failures of the new smart communities' initiatives as they emerge (Schön 1995).

The vast terrain on which civic architects, civic engineers, civic entrepreneurs, and governance experts may intervene has been poorly mapped. It ranges all the way from modest efforts (1) to ever so slightly modifying the macro-structure and dominant logic of the community; (2) to shaping its sociality (i.e., its capacity to create social glue and teams of all sorts); (3) to probing the conflicting frames of reference of the different groups (and their belief systems)

Figure 9: Anamorphosis of network governance:
a conceptual framework under construction

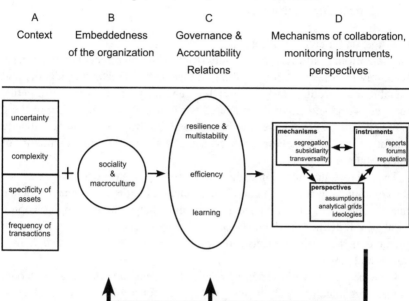

with a view to innovating by finding meta-principles likely to get enough groups to ever so slightly reframe their perspective and thus allow for some workable collaboration to materialize; (4) to transforming the whole world of institutions, rules, conventions, mechanisms, and monitoring instruments that can be more easily modified, but not always with much in the way of consequences.

Intervening in this nexus of forces is always perilous, since it is continually evolving through the feedback mechanisms that modify the system as learning proceeds.

A rough map of this broad terrain is sketched in Figure 9.

In this section, we cannot examine all aspects of this complex network governance system, but we will perform a preliminary probe of the central challenges that smart communities' governance is posing, along four axes:

What can one do to make communities smarter

(1) on the new governance/ new accountabilities front?
(2) on the social proximity/effective coordination front?
(3) on the collective intelligence/social learning front? and

(4) through a better "*outillage mental*" for reflective practitioners, and a better evaluative capability to gauge the success or failures of smart communities' initiatives?

(a) Agenda for civic architects

Organizational culture refers to unwritten principles meant to generate a relatively high level of coordination, at low cost, by bestowing identity and membership through stories of flexible generality about events of practice that act as repositories of accumulated wisdom. The transformation of these stories constitutes collective learning, an evolving way to interpret conflicting and often confusing data through the social construction of a community of interpretation.

The macroculture of a community is its worldview. It shapes the ways in which the community decodes and interprets the changes in the environment, and the manner in which it reacts to such contextual changes by developing coping strategies. It defines the dominant logic, it shapes perspectives, and it tends to promote the use of instruments and mechanisms in keeping with the dominant values and logics.

In the best of all worlds, learning relationships, networks, and regimes would emerge organically, as a response to the need for nimbleness in the face of increasing diversity, greater complexity, and the new imperative of constant learning. Moreover, organizational and community cultures would become the important bond that would make these networks and regimes operative and effective at collective learning.

Unfortunately, we do not live in the best of all worlds. The requisite relationships, networks, and regimes do not necessarily fall into place organically. Moreover, at any particular time, the organizational/community culture in place may not underpin the design of the required relationships, networks, and regimes. Therefore, there is a need to design "auxiliary conditions" to ensure that the new governance structures can be eased in, and the new accountabilities put in place. At the core of these transformations is the agency of organizational/community culture.

(b) Agenda for civic engineers

It is not sufficient to design the requisite networks and regimes likely to support collaboration: these institutions must also initiate the appropriate changes in the operations of the community. This entails a range of interrelated interventions that may be quite different, depending on the nature of the coordination game. For instance, the forces at work in choosing a legitimate new form of coordination may be quite different from those at work in shaping the technical response to particularly taxing technical or institutional demands. In the former case, much may depend on the different value systems and perspectives, and on the harmonization of belief systems (perspective making), while, in the latter case, it may depend much more on the relative effectiveness of mechanisms and instruments. These two stages are obviously not disconnected.

Often, the strength of the forces of dynamic conservatism (Schön 1971) is such that a direct effort to reform the different belief systems, or to forcefully reconcile the different logics, may prove disastrous: those whose status, privileges, or assets are challenged by these sorts of initiatives are likely to mount forceful attacks to stop them. So an oblique approach through innocuous mechanisms and instruments may prove more effective. But whatever the right strategic mix might be, these two sorts of action (on the capacity front and on the process/due diligence front) will require attention (Juillet, Paquet, and Scala 2000).

Capacity: belief systems, logics and resources
Some technologies have already been developed to allow individuals and groups to create visual depictions of their particular perspective on a situation in the form of a *cause map*, displaying their beliefs as to the major factors influencing their sphere of concern (Boland et al. 1996).

These might be used to make perspectives visible, and as an instrument to generate the basic understanding that different groups rely on different logics of coordination. Such maps provide a shared language among partners, and create opportunities for an on-going dialogue among partners capable of generating social learning and not just eliciting blame.

These diverging perspectives are not simple impediments to learning (as group-thinkers would suggest) but, through their variety, valuable resources that must be developed through time, experience, and continuous dialogue. But these resources, capabilities and "knowledges" are embedded in individuals, and they are difficult to simply pass along to new partners and colleagues. As a result, involving partners in "cause mapping" is going to be very constructive, but also very time-consuming. Moreover, this road is fraught with so many sensitivities, and may be so easily disrupted by personnel turnover (dissipating the social capital accumulated through experience by key personnel), that one will in all likelihood be often forced to opt for the roundabout way to deal with belief systems (i.e., via process and due diligence).

Process and due diligence: mechanisms and monitoring instruments
On the process/due diligence front, much depends on the focus of the system of monitoring that is put in place to continuously assess performance, and on

the generation and diffusion of mutually intelligible and trustworthy on-going information among partners and stakeholders.

Where collaborative endeavours include different levels of government, or organizations in the private or community sectors, developing a reporting framework that allows partners to meet the needs of their own internal accountability structure, while allowing for an effective form of *collective reporting*, could create significant challenges. However, it is imperative for the success of collaborative efforts to attempt to respect the perspectives and organizational realities of each partner. In particular, collaborative strategies must avoid imposing reporting requirements that could be so onerous as to result in disengagement.

Mechanisms like a shared complaint and appeal process, or citizen-centred service evaluations within a negotiated accountability framework that involves all partnering agencies, or a more formal and structured process of third-party monitoring and performance evaluation, may be difficult to maintain, as agencies are reluctant to receive criticism through mechanisms involving other agencies. Nevertheless, in a context of collaborative governance, where social learning is a requirement for effectiveness and adaptation, such mechanisms contribute to a level of transparency among partners, and to a positive form of horizontal accountability.

In all such cases, some modest tinkering with monitoring instruments may have a significant impact on the mechanisms in place (giving them more potency) and on the perspectives of the different partners (allowing them to indulge in frame analysis that may result in some reframing). Moreover, such interaction in the small may reverberate on the broader features of the community (governance relations, dominant logic, macroculture) through the feedback mechanisms.

(c) Agenda for civic entrepreneurs

Design and socio-technical engineering are not sufficient. The smart communities also require "champions"—civic Olympians—who will provide the necessary creative thrust for progress in the private, public, and civic spheres.

Spinosa, Flores, and Dreyfus (1997) have shown that the engines of entrepreneurship (private sector), democratic action (public sphere), and cultivation of solidarity (civil society) are quite similar. They are based on a particular skill that Spinosa et al. call "history-making", and that can be divided into three sub-skills: (1) acts of articulation—attempts at '*définition de situation*' or new ways to make sense of the situation, (2) acts of cross-appropriation— bringing new practices into a context that would not naturally generate them, and (3) acts of reconfiguration—reframing the whole perception of the way of life.

Such individual actions are not sufficient to generate new capabilities, nor to trigger the required *bricolage* of effective technologies of collaboration in the different worlds, but they are often important triggers. As Putnam (2000) puts it, the renewal of the stock of social capital (relationships, networks, regimes) is a task that requires the mobilization of communities. This in turn means that there must be champions capable of actions that resonate with communities of interpretation and practice.

This is at the core of the notion of institutional governance as proposed by March and Olsen. For them, the craft of governance is organized around four tasks: developing *identities*, developing *capabilities*, developing *accounts and procedures* for interpretation that improve the transmission and retention of lessons from history, and developing a *capacity to learn and transform* by experiments and by reframing and redefining the governance style (March and Olsen 1995:45–6).

Civic entrepreneurs play a significant role as "interpreters" and "promoters" on each of these fronts. They define the "style" of the community, and work at modifying the very nature of the equipment, tasks, and identities in these worlds. This transforms the organizational capital, but also transforms the rest of the assets base of the system, and stimulates a different degree of re-articulation and reconfiguration, enriching the possibilities of cross-appropriation. Civic entrepreneurs are meaning-makers. Their contributions may appear modest and symbolic, and, because of it, their efforts are often discounted as simple boosterism because they appear to deal only with peripheral realities and intangibles. But their action is fundamental.

These points have been synthesized in Figure 5 in chapter 3. It depicts the political socio-economy as an "instituted process", characterized by a particular amalgam of assets, adroitly used and enriched by political, economic, and civic entrepreneurs, through skillful articulation, cross-appropriation and reframing activities, and woven into a fabric of relations, networks, and regimes that define the distinctive habitus of a political economy as a complex adaptive system.

(d) Agenda for practice-enhancing governance
Smart communities do not only pose challenges to practitioners. They also raise questions about the contribution that governance experts can make to the understanding of these new realities. While the task of civic architects, engineers, and entrepreneurs in the governance of smart communities is relatively clear, the role of governance experts is less obvious. It might even be suggested that they have little to contribute beyond some peripheral reflections on the challenges posed to the other three groups. This is a rather simplistic view.

The governance of smart communities raises a number of conceptual issues on which governance experts have much to contribute. They can be identified under four general rubrics: (1) the challenges of collaboration: we still have a less than perfect understanding of the rationale for entering into collaborative arrangements, and of the rationale for honouring one's commitment once a "moral contract" has been entered into; (2) the challenges of coordination: what is necessary to ensure effective coordination when power, resources, and information are distributed remains unclear in many settings; (3) the challenges of social learning: the whole new epistemology of practice that appears to underpin the process of social learning (including the four complexes of mechanisms we have underlined above—the Polanyi mechanism, the Boisot learning cycle, the network governance process, and the civic entrepreneurship world) is not well understood; (4) the challenges of evaluation: the very notion of a workable template to evaluate a smart community project's success or failure remains ill-defined.

In the rest of this section, I indicate why these four conceptual challenges require a paradigm shift in administrative science research, and what the new paradigm might look like.

Why these questions cannot be analyzed usefully in a positivist mode
As indicated, the four complex mechanisms that underpin the process of social learning remain somewhat under-explored. This is largely due to that they are not easily amenable to the usual positivist methods of inquiry dealing with objective knowledge.

The matter has been insightfully examined by Donald Schön (1995). He uses the word "inquiry" in the sense of John Dewey—thinking and acting that aims at resolving a situation of uncertainty, doubt, or puzzlement—and regards inquiry as a form of *intervention experiment*. These experiments may be simply exploratory, they may also be hypothesis-testing, but they are often in organizational analysis "action undertaken in order to change a situation for the better". In such cases, success means that the intended consequences are brought about, and the unintended consequences are acceptable or even desirable.

In this sort of *intervention experiment* that lies at the centre of governance analysis, the point is not to falsify the hypothesis—a step that would be consistent with the canons of scientific experimentation—but "to create a wholly new, unprecedented situation that, in its possibility for generating new knowledge, goes substantially beyond the initial hypothesis" (Friedmann and Abonyi 1976:936). In this world, "acting and knowing are united in a single process of learning" (Friedmann 1978:86). "Through transactive planning...social practice discovers how to deal with a specific problem. Social practice may thus be understood as a process that generates not only a new tangible reality, but also the means of acquiring new knowledge about it" (Friedmann and Abonyi 1976:938).

This sort of situation does not lend itself to the usual positivist mode of analysis.

What the paradigm of social practice entails

As early as 1938, Chester Barnard introduced a distinction in the management literature between "thinking processes" and "non-logical processes", and insisted that the latter were omnipresent in effective professional practice (Barnard 1938). More recently, Henry Mintzberg has insisted that administration is an activity that is based in large part on the development of perception and strategic thinking with the right side of the brain—the locus of the implicit, of the experimental, of the synthetic. He has also often reiterated that strategies are not deduced; rather they are crafted, they "emerge" (Mintzberg 1976, 1987).

At the core of this process of *crafting* is what Schön and Rein (1994) have called *design rationality*: it connotes the capacity to reflect systematically, rigorously, and cumulatively *in action* as the inquiry proceeds. This is a process of focused rational exploration that is quite familiar in professional practice, strategy, and design. Since the problem is ill-structured to begin with, one must, of necessity, begin with the sort of exploration that Henri Lefebvre (1961:192) called "experimental utopia" (*"l'exploration du possible humain avec l'aide de l'image et de l'imaginaire, accompagnée d'une incessante critique et d'une incessante référence à la problématique donnée dans le réel"*).

This exploration is geared to the generation of a form that fits: it is a conversation with the situation, an interactive learning process. It calls for a cerebral operation that is quite different from both deduction and induction, and that Lefebvre has called *transduction*.

The process of transduction *"construit [...] un objet possible [...] à partir d'informations portant sur la réalité ainsi que d'une problématique posée par cette réalité"* (Lefebvre 1961). This process of transduction characterizes many of the cases analyzed by Schön, and fits very well with his generalized notion of design rationality (Schön and Rein 1994:167ff).

Learning in this context, is like learning to swim: it is done by eliminating misfits, by correcting errors, and by continuous re-alignment to ensure goodness-of-fit between elusive standards and circumstances. There can be no learning unless one recognizes and embraces error as a fundamental building block, as a crucial way to fuel fruitful deliberations. The new competences required in such knowledge-based learning systems develop only under certain conditions. There must be an explicit acknowledgment of the high level of uncertainty as completely irreducible; an explicit will to embrace error as the difference between what is expected and what happens; and a willingness to span boundaries across perspectives (Michael 1993).

This reflection-in-action requires a conversation with the situation. It is a social act. It is the result of "argumentation—amongst particular people, in specific situations, dealing with concrete things, with different things at stake" (Toulmin 1990). Deliberation and argumentation are possible only within the community of communication composed of the stakeholders, of those affected. Thus, *delta knowledge*, as embodied *savoir-faire,* does not materialize through an individualized process of abstraction. It materializes through a social process which resembles the one through which a child learns a complex practical system like a language.

Conclusion

Smart communities are creating new geo-governance challenges: they require a new form of governance and leadership if they are to yield their promised returns, and this will only emerge in action through the collaboration of a range of experts on *intellectual capital*, which is at the core of the smart community process.

In this exploratory paper, I have put forward a preliminary mapping of the "*terrain des opérations*", and a provisional division of labour among four groups of stakeholders.

In my view, one must recognize the central importance of the following features of smart communities, and accept that one of the key challenges will be to eliminate the blockages that appear to prevent them from playing their full roles:

- distributed governance
- multiple accountabilities
- multilogue and deliberation mechanisms
- tacit knowing
- milieu dynamics
- collective intelligence
- Polanyi's dynamics of cognitive experience
- Boisot's learning cycle
- network governance
- governance process.

These ten features may be modified in a variety of ways: through redesign of institutions or conventions, through some re-structuring, organizational carpentering or re-tooling, through reconfiguration of the game of coordination altogether, or its reframing, or through some meta-reflections likely to lead to any of the above.

A few examples have been suggested of the ways in which different actors might intervene differently in the various components of the geo-governance process, either to remove obstacles or to improve the workings of the different components of the governance process.

It must be noted that very few of these interventions are dependent on the NICTs. Most clearly call for interference in the dynamics of the community per se, through non-technical means. Indeed, the omnipresence of trust, as a facilitator of interaction, serves as a good illustration of the sort of "intangible" factor that appears to be at the core of the new governance challenges.

Whether smart communities succeed or not depends on rules of engagement and terms of agreement. Little can be resolved on this front technologically.

PART III

Ocean Governance

Chapter 8

The Governance of Sustainability: A Social Learning Approach

"But since knowing is what they do, knowledge is what they look for,
and they are likely to give the name of knowledge to anything they find"

Michael Wood

Introduction

The challenges of the governance of territorial entities, lending themselves as they do to traditional systems of appropriation, are quite daunting, and cannot always be easily and adequately met by conventional, institutional nation-state structures. There is considerable scope for opportunism and shirking, but there is also the significant possibility of external malefits and irreversible damage being inflicted on the never-fully-robust natural system on which humanity depends. It must be added that the frailty of nature has become even greater in the recent past, as globalization has triggered a dual process of fragmenting and integrating—what Rosenau (2003) has called "fragmegration"—which has considerably weakened territoriality, states, and sovereignty.

In a world of common-pool resources, or where commons abound—like oceans—the traditional appropriation systems fail, and governance challenges are even more daunting. Indeed, a whole literature has developed around the theme of "the tragedy of the commons"; it has shown that rational behaviour is likely, in unregulated circumstances, to lead to the destruction of the resource (Hardin 1968). Both markets and state coercion have revealed their limitations in coping with such threats.

This is why the governance of sustainability—concern with keeping an eye on the changing relations between people and their socio-physical environment, between the regions and the contextual ecological systems constituting their life-support systems—has become such a crucial issue. But debates about the governance of sustainability have been less fruitful than they might have been because of some *idées fixes*.

First, even though there has been no meaningful support for radical minority groups' crusades to leave the natural world unchanged, *environment fetishism* (as Sen calls it) has not been completely exorcized either. There is often confusion in the ecological literature between sustaining the lives that people can live in an environment, and with sustaining of the environment itself. There is also a failure to understand that "to live is to pollute". The "duty of sustainability" (whatever that means) is not to be confused with "leaving the world unchanged".

Second, there has been considerable fixation on property rights as a panacea. Whatever the merits of both a sound property rights system and the price mechanism, they do not constitute sufficient conditions for sustainability and a wise stewardship of nature (Perrings 1987; Laurent and Paquet 1998: ch.4).

Third, sustainability à la Brundtland-Solow (BS) has become the popular governing relation: taking all the steps necessary to allow the next generation to achieve a standard of living at least as good as our own, and to look after the subsequent generation (Solow 1992). Although the raging debates have often left unchallenged the seemingly reasonable and innocuous Brundtland-Solow standard, this uncritical attitude is not warranted. The BS standard can be contested. While the environmentalist community has embraced this so-called "reasonable" benchmark, the central questions—what we should try to sustain in safeguarding our common future, and how—are far from having been answered satisfactorily (Sen 2003).

Indeed, sustainability, as we shall see, is an essentially contested concept. It connotes a nexus of issues of such complexity that reasonable and competent persons may hold opposed and contradictory views. It raises nothing less than the problem of the conditions for the effective co-evolution of system and context, and of the requirements for the "overall diversity and overall productivity of components and relations in systems" to be maintained or enhanced (Norgaard 1988).

The problems sustainability poses are empirical (socio-economic and political), but also epistemic and moral. Sustainability refers to the empirical ways in which humankind should exploit the resources of nature (and culture) so as to ensure that subsequent generations are not left unduly impoverished. But it also refers to the knowledge system that underpins the goodness of fit between system and context, and provides the requisite guideposts for effective and sustainable co-evolution. Finally, it refers to a problem of ethics—namely, the intergenerational concerns: the need to give appropriate weight to the concerns of future generations, and the imperatives of wise stewardship in our decision-making (Euston and Gibson 1995).

For the purposes of this paper, we will define sustainability in a way that is much more encompassing than the BS standard proposes, and we will suggest that the governance challenges of sustainability in the face of fragmegration, turbulence, and a world partly made up of commons, call for nothing less than an *ecology of governance,* capable of rediscovering the paths toward positive socio-cultural and ecological co-evolution. This is a corollary of the law of requisite variety, or Ashby's law (Beer 1974): the larger the variety of actions available to control a system, the larger the variety of perturbation it is able to compensate. Consequently, the sort of governance likely to be effective in such contexts is a distributed governance that is highly disaggregated and only minimally coordinated (Paquet 2005a).

The issues are addressed in four steps.

First, I ask the basic question "what should we try to sustain", and attempt to identify some of the obstacles that prevent social scientists from answering the question satisfactorily. These obstacles are not only the complexity of the issues, but some unfortunate traits of the conventional social sciences: myopia, amnesia, imprudence, etc. Second, I sketch some of the key components of an adequate ecology of governance, based on the principle of subsidiarity and on loose partnerships, in a context at least partially consisting of commons. Third, I attempt to identify the sort of *outillage mental* capable of blending the empirical, epistemic, and moral challenges of sustainability into a workable governance regime, recognizing that governance can only provide auxiliary conditions for effective co-evolution, and that one must question the unreasonable expectations that have emerged from those quarters that have elected to transmogrify sustainability into some sort of civil theology. Fourth, I make the case for a polycentric governance as the most promising strategy, and put forward a few modest general propositions for the families of mechanisms likely to be necessary for effective governance to prevail.

This general invitation to modesty in the design of governance schemes will not prevent me from providing some hints, along the way, on the general directions this pragmatic outlook might suggest for Canada today.

Sustainability as weaselword

Despite the considerable work focusing on failure diagnosis and the design and development of institutions for governing the commons, we are still without a unified theory of sustainable environmental governance. The work on the small-scale systems (at the micro level) and on environmental regimes (at the macro level) is interesting, but it has not yet converged on a broadly similar set of questions, activities, or governance mechanisms. Indeed, the former appears to have vindicated the view that bottom-up approaches work, while the latter still depends a great deal on unduly aggregative approaches, and top-down coercive strategies.

The reason such a unified theory still eludes us is ascribable to two major obstacles, namely: the essentially contested nature of the notion of sustainability, and the fundamental limitations of traditional social sciences in dealing with such long-run issues.

These two obstacles, when compounded, have tended to derail the debate on sustainability, and to facilitate its hijacking by different tribes of ideologues: the *absolutist radicals* building on moral imperatives and ecological theology; the *politically correct* who have suppressed most of the important contentious issues and drowned sustainability discussions in banalities; and the *crafty spin doctors* who have succeeded in using the label as a way to orchestrate public relations cover-ups in the guise of green bottom lines. But some core meaning—or 'vision' in the Schumpeterian sense of the word—has evolved, around which a "*consensus mou*" is beginning to materialize.

(a) Sustainability has come to connote a whole range of meanings: from the capacity of socio-technical systems to endure and continue indefinitely at one end of the spectrum, to the maintenance of human freedoms at the other.

While environmental fetishism is unduly static, many other less extreme views are equally difficult to defend. For instance, the Brundtland-Solow focus on maintaining the standard of living and consumption that we have grown accustomed to as a norm to be sustained, and the corporate definition of sustainability as "what is corporately viable with minimal impairment to the financial bottom line", are definitions that are clearly too constrained by economic considerations.

At the opposite end of the spectrum, Amartya Sen has emphasized the centrality of "sustaining freedoms" as the key objective: maintaining and enhancing the enjoyment of undiminished freedoms (political, social, economic, security, etc.) and avoiding the burden of additional freedoms—development in this view being the removal of various types of freedoms (Sen 1999a: xii).

In between those two poles, one finds a large number of diverse definitions that have extended the notion of "sustainability" (originally related mainly to the physical environment) to deal with the much broader notion of "environment", pertaining not only to the physiographical context, but also to the whole socio-cultural domain. Indeed, it has become less and less clear in "corporate sustainability reporting", for instance, what is to be "sustained". Is it profitability? Is it the corporation? Is it development? Is it the social order? Or is it something else? (Stratos 2003) Indeed, the shorthand "sustainability reporting" is now used (in the sustainability toolkit of Industry Canada (http://www.sustainabilityreporting.ca) to refer to the broad issue of "how societal trends are affecting the company, and how the company's presence and operations are affecting society". This entails taking into account dozens of performance issues ranging all across the economic, financial, environmental, and social performance areas of the company.

Depending on the way in which sustainability is defined, there is obviously a great deal of difference in the array of means that can be suggested to achieve the stated goal. The more one leans toward the preservation of *nature qua nature*, the more coercive measures would appear to be required to modify behaviour in order to protect nature. The more one leans toward the "social and cultural" alternative of sustained freedoms, the more one is led to an anthropocentric focus, and to considering behavioural changes through dialogue, deliberation, and education.

These various definitions are in use because sustainability is an essentially contested concept, the proper use of which inevitably involves endless disputes. According to Gallie, an essentially contested concept is: (1) appraisive in the sense that it accredits some kind of valued achievement; (2) this achievement must be complex in character and its worth attributed to it as a whole; but (3) variously describable in its parts with the possibility of various components being assigned more or less importance; and (4) open in character to the extent that it admits considerable modification in the light of changing circumstances; moreover, to qualify as an essentially contested concept, (5) each party must recognize that its own use of the concept is contested by other parties, and that the concept can be used both aggressively and defensively (Gallie 1964:161).

Sustainability is an elusive notion, very much like the notion of championship performance in figure skating. Governing to steer the system in the direction of such moving, incommensurable, and differently-defined targets is therefore a task condemned to be difficult.

(b) However, this elusiveness is also ascribable to the limitations of the traditional social sciences, especially on matters pertaining to the long run.

This fundamental flaw is rooted in the unfortunate influence of positivism on the social sciences, (Paquet 1987) which has resulted in a fixation on prediction and prescription, and to a relative neglect of adequate description (Sen 1999b). Moreover, even when social scientists indulge in description, it suffers greatly from a focus on *hic et nunc* and the bizarre presumption of a world of complete continuity and divisibility.

On the one hand, this leads to the heavy discounting of anything that is not in the present, or in spatial proximity, and therefore to dwarfing the value of any benefit or malefit occurring beyond the now or the fringe. Such myopia considerably biases all calculations against taking into account the long run malefits that may be incurred in the remote environment. On the other hand, the assumption of complete divisibility and continuity occludes the possibility of irreversibility and discontinuity. These are presumed to be unlikely. *Natura not fecit saltum* is taken as an axiom, and obliterates from the usual calculation the potential for catastrophic events that may cause irreversible damage.

The conventional wisdom *problematique* emphasizes given preferences, static efficiency, and individual rational choice. Such a perspective not only heavily discounts elements that are distant in time, and not proximate in space, but pays little heed to learning and dynamic efficiency, or matters of interaction or coordination. Moreover, it relies unduly on a notion of mechanical reversible time that builds in myopia, amnesia, and imprudence in the conventional practice of these social sciences, and leads them to pay little attention to discontinuities (Clark and Munn 1986; Redclift 1987; Braybrooke and Paquet 1987; Laurent and Paquet 1998: ch.4; Boudon 2003).

These five blind spots have led traditional social sciences to privilege a sort of cartography of reality lacking in both comprehensiveness and *prudentia*. It has trapped social scientists into restricting themselves to being type I cartographers. As Schumacher has explained (1977) there are two types of cartographers. Type I live by the rule "if in doubt, leave it out", while type II live by the rule "if in doubt, show it prominently". Traditional social sciences have celebrated Cartesian type I cartographers even though, in our turbulent and totally connected world, we may actually need more type II cartographers.

(c)   The combination of an essentially contested concept and the handicaps of conventional social sciences has led to the promotion of the most whimsical notions of sustainability. Sustainability has become synonymous with sustaining whatever anyone wished to sustain, for whatever reason. But despite these difficulties, a "vision" of sustainability has begun to emerge, built around a number of core beliefs that have begun to generate a minimal consensus: limits, irreversibility, scale, co-evolution, sustaining our inheritance and our degrees of freedom, the precautionary principle, etc. (Norgaard 1999).

This "vision" (in the sense of Schumpeter) is still only a loose and provisional arrangement of the key elements of the issue domain. It does not provide a conceptual framework capable of generating theoretical propositions (Schumpeter 1949; Perroux 1960). This "vision" accommodates approaches that are pluralistic, i.e., that use a multiplicity of frameworks.

What it demands is "appreciation" à la Vickers (1965), i.e., making judgments of facts and value about the state of the system both internally and in its external relations. These entail the readiness to see and value the situation from a plurality of viewpoints. Indeed, the dream or fantasy of "unity" and "coherence" is a major source of the problem (Norgaard 1999:12). This form of loose appreciative framework (to the extent that it embeds mutual inconsistencies) generates considerable frustration with those who wish to predict and prescribe. This explains the popularity of the simplistic "escapist" images in good currency: in the face of a complex issue domain, marred by essentially contested concepts and crippled social sciences, ideology as a form of false consciousness thrives, and everyone feels empowered to impose his/her own notion of sustainability as dictated by his/her own interests.

The "market", "business" and "deep ecology" approaches are examples of selective attention being given to one dimension of the problem. In their search for comfort, they privilege either an act of faith in property rights-cum-market mechanisms as panaceas, or a broadening of perspective (to include such an array of social and environmental dimensions that one can easily fuzzify the whole picture), or a fixation on geo-centric, bio-centric or theo-centric oracles (Perrings 1987; Stratos 2003; Lovelock 1979; Devall and Session 1985; Daly and Cobb 1989).

The same may be said about the environmental rights-based approach: there is a sharpness to rights (easily transformed into entitlements, powers, or immunities) that does not match the fuzziness and complexities of the environmental world. Insisting on legislating what one might best see as ethical claims can only lead to using instruments that will prove unduly intrusive and very ineffective.

The freedom-based pluralistic approach suggested by Sen focuses on the truly important dimensions of sustainability, i.e., the degrees of freedom to be preserved for the next generation (economic and financial, but also political and social) and concerns for transparency, security, legitimacy, and participation. But it remains rather vague and relatively anthropocentric. Since humans are explicitly placed in a context that requires attention to the natural world, Sen's approach need not deny some taking into account of environmental dimensions (McDonald 2004), but it does not answer the key questions: what should we try to sustain to ensure sustaining freedoms, and how this be done?

Governance

Government cannot just respond to the sustainability challenge by fiat or decrees. What needs to be sustained does not necessarily fall under the control of governments, who are not in possession of all the required information, power, or resources to get other agents to modify their behaviour in any particular direction. So a workable strategy must mobilize the public, private, and civic sectors, and build on their collaboration. Governments must change their role:

they must cease to be controllers, and become catalysts and animateurs. This is a drift from government to governance that has endured extensive analysis (Paquet 1999a,1999b).

(a) There has been a significant growth of mixed organizations to deal with the challenges at hand, because they combine the features of the three basic mechanisms at work in the three sectors (coercion, quid pro quo exchange, and reciprocity): the long-term horizon and fair stewardship of the public sector, the creativity and dynamism of the private sector, and the compassion, commitment, and trust in the not-for-profit sector.

These "partnerships" have proved effective. What may at first have been mainly opportunistic efforts to take advantage of certain specific skills of sub-contractors (with the need to constrain them with strong legal contracts and numerous specific requirements and penalty clauses) has often evolved into true joint venturing, based on a flexible continuing relationship, rooted in loose arrangements that respond to the expectations and needs of the other parties, and in soft horizontal accountabilities. The parties must be mutually accountable. Such accountabilities must provide the sorts of incentives needed for the parties both to wish to join the game in the first place, and to ensure that they will meet their commitments even if and when it might not be to their short-term advantage to do so. As the strength of the partnerships grow, the underlying conventions require less and less formality. This does, however, generate an immense problem regarding the definition of performance, or the fair sharing of the surplus.

These challenges may initially make these partnerships appear unmanageable.

In fact, in a concrete setting, committed partners find ways to co-design viable arrangements, even when each of them has a different frame of reference. Indeed, it is as a result of this very process of co-design that the intentions and meanings of each partner are revealed, and that negotiation in a situated context can be conducted. Such a process of co-design helps to identify (1) the sorts of interfaces likely to exist and on which partnerships might be built; (2) where compromises might be sought; and (3) ways in which the "proceeds" may be shared (Vaillancourt Rosenau 2000). Since the partners may not all be after the same sort of loot, sharing the "proceeds" in specific circumstances may not be as intractable a problem as one might anticipate.

This is not the place for an inventory of all the possible rationales partners may harbour as they first enter a collaborative arrangement. It is, however, important to underline a few that have been widely mentioned in the specialized literature. Partnership may simply be a device used to trigger management reform by destabilizing the system. The partner, in this case, is an *agent of subversion*. The objective may also be to effect a problem conversion—a way to redefine one's business through some reframing. Here, the partner acts the part of an *agent of seduction* that helps elicit a different way of tackling a task: for example, by brokering a typically public interest issue such as environment protection into one that is of interest to entrepreneurs. Partnership may also be sought for the purpose of moral regeneration—to inject a concern for the long run in myopic quarterly-earnings-fixated organizations. The partner's role in this case is one of an *agent of moral refurbishment.* Partnership is also an instrument of risk shifting; it is a way of unloading a portion of the responsibility for some commitment. The partner thus becomes an *agent of risk sharing.* Finally, partnership may simply be a mode of power-sharing, as a result of the recognition that no one party has the resources, information, and power to govern appropriately. The partner would under these circumstances wear the hat of an *agent of cooperation* (Vaillancourt Rosenau 2000).

Most partnerships are based on a mix of these rationales: they are multi-purposed instruments used for various reasons. Indeed, most of the time, partnerships are not defined clearly *ab ovo.* They emerge from cautious and limited arrangements into deeper and more robust partnerships through unpredictable meanderings. This has been the experience both in the Gulf of Maine, as well as with the World Weather Watch, where limited information-sharing has led to robust forms of collaborative governance (Schroeder et al. 2001; Cleveland 2002).

If partnerships fail, it is usually because, along the way, one or more of the partners refuse to accept the basic conditions of power sharing. One partner or another may simply want to use the partnership as a tool to reform, convert, rekindle, or shift risk, without relinquishing some power, accepting the need to negotiate fair terms of agreement, developing relational capital and trust, etc. The result is a phony partnership, bound to fail. Fortunately, partners who know that they are in the game for the long run appear to be willing to pay the price.

(b) The core contribution of these partnerships is the construction of collective intelligence and the fostering of social learning.

Social learning is the interactive process by which individuals and organizations learn from each other, adapt, innovate, and consequently develop new arrangements and conventions among themselves, in turn leading to new rules of behaviour. It is through social learning and its resultant increase in collective intelligence that a community may harness its intellectual, informational, physical, and human resources to produce a continuous flow of innovative and usable knowledge. Collective intelligence refers to the creative and discriminative capacities of a community, and effective social learning increases collective intelligence over time.

Collective learning requires a context that allows for meaningful conversations to be conducted, and these conversations, deliberations, and accumulations of judgments require a capacity to support and integrate the multiple logics of community members, in an atmosphere of tact and civility. This sort of learning does not necessarily result in formalized decision-making and conclusions. It often remains as tacit knowledge—a fuzzy implicit recognition of the local and particular context. This is where communities of practice have the most impact.

This sort of collaborative dynamic requires technologies and mechanisms of collaboration. Such technologies and mechanisms must, however, fit the context. One of the most important challenges is to design governance mechanisms in keeping with the complexity and deep interdependence of the environmental context. Dale (2001), Howlett (2001) and others have all emphasized the complexity of the environment as open-system, and the non-linear impacts of any policy intervention. This has led Audrey Doerr (2003) to suggest that a Vickersian approach would appear very well suited to the challenges at hand.

In Vickers's world, governing is not built on goals and objectives, or even on setting permanent governing relations or norms. It is an on-going process that involves the evolution and modification of the standards and norms within a context where interdependencies impose constraints and limits on what the very possibilities of an organization are (Vickers 1968; 1983). Governing requires setting up the largest number of quick feedback learning loops. It seeks behaviour modification through persuasion, participation, and perseverance. These mechanisms may take many forms: round tables, forums, networks, coordination agreements, etc. They must focus on communications as a way to improve the broader arrangement of governing relationships, and the adoption and adaptation of new values and norms. Such mechanisms have to get away from the seduction of ethereal long-term trends and focus on generating multilogues that are inclusive, integrated, and relevant for the ordinary citizen. This is the only way to generate a change in the appreciative system, and therefore to modify behaviour. Is there a need to remind anyone of the great accomplishments of GATT?

But such mechanisms do not automatically produce a coherent and comprehensive scheme, generating maximal synergies among the different actors and organizations. Maximal collective intelligence and social learning may in other words not ensue, and intervention may prove necessary.

One of the most important and most difficult lessons is the realization that the law of requisite variety calls for an ecology of governance to regulate the world of sustainability, and that an ecology of governance is anything but integrated and neat.

(c) W. T. Anderson (2001) has made both these points on an ecology of governance vividly.

> Complex systems cannot be governed effectively from a single center...What we have and are likely to have for some time is what I call an ecology of governance: many different systems and different kinds of systems interacting with one another, like the multiple organisms in an ecosystem. This won't be necessarily be neat, peaceful, stable or efficient; despite what some nature lovers may believe, ecosystems are not necessarily neat, peaceful, stable or efficient either ...it will be in a continual process of learning and changing and responding to feedback" (251–2).

An ecology of governance entails a variety of things: (1) a "thick" understanding of environmental decision-making; (2) a new way of thinking about social-ecological resilience; (3) a mix of co-evolving institutions, processes, and ideas from the private, public, and civic sectors, leading to a form of regulated self-regulation; and (4) effective transition management.

Only a "thick description"—identifying the basic connections and general patterns that are characteristic of a certain context—is likely to lead to decisions that are legitimate and context-sensitive (efficient, effective, and equitable) (Adger et al. 2002). This in turn calls for more emphasis on the institutional framing and embeddedness of decisions: decisions are taken in various arenas of action influencing the behaviour of actors, but the contexts are all continually evolving and generate institutional creations that follow different rules of decision-making, and interact in complex and changing ways. Without a thick description, decisions are likely to be made on the basis of false or incomplete information, and therefore mistaken.

Intervention must be seen as an effort to "sustain and enhance the capacity of social-ecological systems to cope with, adapt to, and shape change" (Folke 2003). This puts the notion of resilience (and its flip side, vulnerability) front and centre (Paquet 1999c). The central question is to identify behavioural responses that sustain social-ecological systems—and therefore sustain freedoms—in a world that is constantly changing. Folke has identified four critical factors: learning to live with change and uncertainty, nurturing diversity for renewal, combining different types of knowledge for learning, and creating opportunity for self-organization.

These factors entail nothing less than a new way of thinking about resilience. It is not only a capacity to spring back undiminished after shocks; it is the capacity for self-renewal, self-re-creation, that allows an organization to learn its way out of evolving predicaments by making the highest and best use of all the knowledge (whatever its form) available to it. Consequently, the governance of sustainability goes well beyond traditional state-centric, top-down policy-making. It is a mix of ideas (awareness, knowledge, approaches, rules), processes (mechanisms and linkages) and institutions (roundtables, research units) rooted in all sectors, and it needs to be somewhat coordinated.

Bregha (2002) has argued that the decentralized Canadian model of governance of sustainability has significant limitations because of its fragmentation, and has called for a fuller and more coercive role for central agencies. This is ill-inspired. While the decentralized model is imperfect, it is the most promising strategy. "Governance clearly takes place in multiple arenas, partly within and partly outside the scope of the state. It involves polycentric steering institutions, with a strong emphasis on subsidiarity which has become prominent as a guiding principle" (Bleischwitz and Langrock 2003; Héritier 2002; Young 1999). This co-evolutionary, polycentric governance approach calls for a mix of institutions, puts emphasis on knowledge generation, and uses targets not as absolute objectives, but as a set of incentives to readjust expectations, change habits, and search for a new direction of innovation.

Transition management is necessary because of two important sets of obstacles or barriers to the emergence of a coherent ecology of governance: (1) the fact that the governance schemes are often locked into short-term benefits trajectories; and (2) the fact that there is much fragmentation in the issue domain leaving the various policy fields somewhat disconnected at times.

Taking that into account it is apparent that transition management is an exercise in soft planning and vision-led incrementalism: it feeds adaptive, interactive, and multilevel governance, and improves them by taking long-term sustainability visions into account (Kemp and Loorback 2003). Transitions are no blueprints: they are long-term-oriented evolutionary processes that do no more than create possible development pathways, arenas capable of generating evolving agendas and experiments. This may be done either directly, or through the development of monitoring and evaluation mechanisms underpinning short learning loops (Loorbach 2002).

Blending, complex adaptive systems, and bricolage

The governance of sustainability consists in maintaining a complex pattern of relationships through time, within limits that have somehow come to be set as governing relations (Vickers 1965:27). Such "governing relations" can be seen as an evolving corridor, aiming at making possible a regime more acceptable to all concerned than what the logic of the situation would otherwise provide. This runs contrary to the conventional taste for comprehensive and centralized planning—considered as the only way to avoid chaos (Resnick 1994; Rheingold 2002).

Such governing relations are built on a blending of many perspectives, an appreciation of the dynamics of complex adaptive systems, and recognition that thoughtful interventions often cannot be more than bricolage.

(a)   Blending is a generative cognitive operation (on a par with analogy, mental modeling, framing) that produces a conceptual structure not provided by the perspectives that serve as inputs. It generates new viewpoints partly on the basis of old (Turner 2001).

It serves a variety of cognitive purposes: ideas, arguments, and inferences developed in the blend have effects on cognition. Blending also contributes to consensus building.

There are three operations in the construction of the blend: composition, completion, and elaboration. These three operations lead to the emergent perspective or "mental space" of the blend. Composition provides the new frame and relations that did not exist in the input spaces; completion draws from the background knowledge to complete the pattern; elaboration develops the blend through imaginative mental exploration (Fauconnier and Turner 1998/2001).

In the case of sustainability, there may be a wide variety of blends that could be instrumental in forging new consensus in a variety of contexts. For the purpose of general illustration, one may use the blend of the three perspectives referred to earlier: sustainability as an empirical/institutional challenge, as an epistemic challenge, and as an ethical challenge. If successful, such blending provides an "emergent" meaning that underpins governing relations.

The first perspective is focused on institutional design and the self-reinforcing mechanisms that generate behavioural learning, i.e., learning that builds on past experience to respond to new situations. But existing institutions and their collective memory suffer from *structural amnesia* (Clark and Munn 1986: 433). The institutions doing the recognizing and the classifying of the risks worth taking into account may systematically disregard problems that would threaten values and deconstruct institutions. Even when the basic facts are confirmed, there is no assurance that they will become socially defined as problems worth worrying about (Braybrooke and Paquet 1987; Hilgartner and Bosk 1988).

The second perspective is focused on *usable ignorance*, i.e., on an awareness of our own ignorance and on learning designed with the ignorance factor in mind. Such learning occurs through environmental representations that are reframed, and strategies consequently being modified. This evolution is always unfinished: a culture is always imperfectly adjusted, because actors have imperfect and incomplete information and limited rationality, and because adjustments take time (Ravetz in Clark and Munn 1986).

The third perspective is based on *trans-science*, i.e., on questions that cannot be answered by science: that "transcend" science. Sustainability is a subject matter too complex and too variable for only scientific canons to apply; moral judgments are involved (Weinberg 1972).

Blending composes the elements (institutional, epistemic, moral) of the input spaces into a new space that recognizes the multidimensionality of sustainability, and attempts to merge them into a pattern of learning: learning from the past, learning from usable ignorance, and learning from appreciation and judgment, rather than only from facts. Such blends are at the core of social learning. They play the same role as prototypes in learning in general. A child learns the notion of a bird through a prototype—a sparrow—and the rest of his life will simply be the story of how he/she adds some flats and sharps to this prototype to encompass penguins and ostriches (Johnson 1993).

The most interesting aspect of blending is obviously elaboration—the imaginative extension of whatever space has ensued to generate a dynamic blend with a life of its own, capable of carrying the argument further.

The blend that maps the *problematique* of governance of sustainability (a composite vision or provisional arrangement of the objects of the inquiry into a pattern) remains quite blurred. But its construction is a major challenge facing environmentalists. Without it, one does not have the required complex image of the system to be governed, or the basic pluralistic *outillage mental* needed not only to grapple with this complex system but also to elaborate an evolving guiding vision and elicit a workable regime.

(b) A provisional blend that can guide the learning process through the complexities of sustainability, is the notion of a complex adaptive system. It is a notion that encompasses the institutional, the epistemic, and the moral dimensions that are of interest.

A complex adaptive system (CAS) is first and foremost a system, i.e., it is composed of a structure (a set of roles and relationships among actors), a technology (the tools and techniques that extend the human capability of its members), and a theory (views held within the system about its purposes, its operations, and its future). These dimensions are interdependent, so that any change in one produces change in the others (Schön 1971:33–6).

This interacting and evolving set of individuals and groups bound together by structures, technologies, and theory has certain features: (1) it is open, and receives resources from the external environment; (2) it must adapt to its environment through modifications of its social and technical texture; (3) it entails a process of differentiation to respond to the different challenges posed by the environment; (4) it generates a system of interactions so complex that agents

166

cannot analyse them *ex ante*; they must simply adapt and discover new rules and new behaviours that generate the requisite coordination and integration for the system's high performance to ensue.

Any CAS (like our central nervous system, our immune system, our ecosystem) is made up of parts that are well interconnected, where complexity and organization arise in a non-linear fashion from interaction. The system is self-organizing, and is guided by vague schemata or templates that evolve through Darwinian selection and guide the system to dis-attend to aspects of experience. Such a CAS develops a variety of schemata, often highly local and provisional, as recognition devices, and their evolution is path-dependent, contingent, and based on developed entrenched patterns.

While such a blend is intellectually satisfying, it resembles early maps—elegant but not necessarily very helpful to navigation. Much refinement is therefore required if one is to offer a pragmatic diagnosis of the sort of governance relations required, design them accordingly, and allow them to develop creatively (Metcalfe 1993). However, work in progress is already showing the way (Holland 1995, 1998). Indeed, for the last ten years, James Kay has, together with his colleagues and graduate students, been using an ecosystem approach to sustainability, and has gained much recognition for the sort of governance arrangements that were suggested for complex settings (Kay and Schneider 1994; Kay et al. 1999).

It suggests that the best we can hope for is to create conditions that may lead to the requisite cooperation for effective governance to take place. New rules and new behaviours simply have to be discovered along the way. This, of course, provides a sharply deflated vision of what can be accomplished through governing.

Taking advantage of these organic and emergent forces means living with complexity and harnessing it. This perspective is predicated on an acknowledgement of our ignorance. It is the reason massive mechanical interventions often prove futile, while relatively small interventions, making the highest and best use of the inner dynamics of the system, may be surprisingly effective. These paradoxical results are ascribable to the lesser or better way of taking into account the reactions of mutually adaptive players to interventions that promote (or not) effective adaptation, fruitful interactions, and powerful social learning. Since one does not know enough to "control" the system, one can at best "provoke experimentally" some variation, interaction and selection processes by thoughtful interventions (Axelrod and Cohen 1999:xv; Paquet 2005b).

(c) These small thoughtful interventions may attempt to modify the actors' time horizon, to accelerate the process of social learning, to tinker with interaction patterns by modifying proximity and space, or to exercise leadership by creating shared space or forums, by sharpening performance measurements and by helping to catalyze a better selection of agents and strategies. But in all these interventions, it must be understood that what can be expected at best is to stimulate and "excite" the complex adaptive system without any guarantee that the desired outcome will be reached.

Reform must accompany the system and not try to remake it: muddling through and *bricolage* are thus more valuable than disruptive and so-called transformative restructuring.

In ascertaining the sort of intervention that might be most helpful in the case of the environment, one may derive some guidance from an examination of interventions in the health care system, as an example of a complex adaptive system in need of repairs.

What has been proposed in the case of the health care system is less a complete revamping of the system than (1) a multiplication of access and information points; (2) more transparency regarding waiting time; (3) multiple service lines within emergency rooms; (4) increased support for carers and self-carers, etc. (Glouberman and Zimmerman 2002:24). On the supply side, this has translated into rewards for differentiated knowledge, respect for complementary professional perspectives, lack of disruption of the workable division of labour, etc.

The challenge is to identify particularly effective tipping points, capable of triggering the equivalence of epidemics, and making full use of the power of context (Gladwell 2000).

The difficulty with *bricolage* in a complex adaptive system that might drift into irreversible discontinuities is that it calls for type II cartographers, armed with a strong version of the precautionary principle. And yet there are dangers in making such a principle part of the judiciary or in otherwise casting it in strong legal forms when faced with a diffuse and fractured field, where interactions defy the possibility of prediction. It may lead to many sorts of *débordements*, such as: (1) the danger of requiring nothing less than an impossible clairvoyance from agents, and of indulging in misplaced hard accountability (Paquet 2004a: ch. III); and (2) the danger of slumping into the position of situationologists, relying exclusively on moral reasoning when policy-making calls for a mix of moral and prudential reasoning (Paquet 1999b:ch.2).

These two dangers are quite significant. The first one may completely pervert the notion of accountability, and taint it with a great deal of arbitrariness as the courts attempt to punish sins of omission and lack of clairvoyance. The second one may uproot the policy process and sterilize it, by promoting moral reasoning and "sermons from the Mount" to a dominant role: in the real world, prudential reasoning (acting in a way that is efficient in achieving one's goals) prevails, and prudential maxims therefore apply only to segments of societies, i.e. to those seeking these specific goals. Consequently, pluralism is what is needed.

This is where transition management may turn out to be helpful. It represents a way of providing some broad directions for the less than perfectly concerted *bricolage* that one is condemned to practice. But it must be understood that only soft, oblique, and thoughtful interventions are likely to work: interventions making use of context, and aiming at "integral governance" (not "integrated governance") through convening, intelligence and thoughtful leadership (Integral Governance Initiative 2002; Badaracco 2002). This in turn can only be effected through polycentric governance.

A plea for polycentric governance

In the face of such a messy situation (sustainability being defined along the lines of sustained freedoms; the high level of turbulence and uncertainty; such an ill-defined and ill-structured problem; the likelihood of irreversible discontinuities; the wide distribution of resources, power and information; the lack of a unified view of environmental governance and the need for ecologies of governance; the complex adaptive system and the need to be satisfied with *bricolage*) it is crucial to draw some conclusions about the sort of governance of sustainability likely to be workable.

One of the important results of the work of the last quarter of a century on the governance of common-pool resources has been that polycentricity works best. Only this type of governance appears to be able to nurture the communities' self-governing capabilities (McGinnis 1999a, 1999b, 2000).

Polycentricity is a *manière de voir* that is built on two presumptions: (1) that there is no single source of authority vested with all the power, resources, information, and legitimacy, and which has exclusive responsibility for determining public policy; and (2) that the diversity of circumstances calls for a diversity of arrangements that may appear overwhelming and even ungovernable at first, and most certainly not very neat, until one realizes that such is the case only from the viewpoint of the centralizing mindset, that it need not be so once the perspective point is modified, and the powers of self-governance are allowed to unfold.

Self-governance need not generate chaos. Indeed, self-governance flows naturally from the principle of subsidiarity that suggests that decision-making should be located at the most local level where it can be efficiently and effectively executed, and that collaborative or higher level decision-making should prevail only when individual, local, and lower-level instances have demonstrated that they cannot do it well or at all.

So, self-governance does not entail a chaotic or disorderly division of labour among sectors and levels of organizations, but an "ecology" of loosely coupled arrangements, likely to be most effective in ensuring that adjustment tasks are delegated to the sub-systems that can handle them best. It is a commitment to as much decentralization as possible, but as much centralization as necessary. As a result, there is a full spectrum of "scales", "levels", and "sites" of governance—from nano-governance schemes to global regimes, from operational-level rules-in-use to collective choice of rules to change the rules-in-use, etc.

This is not the place for proposing a periodic table of sorts of all possible governance arrangements, or a grammar of such institutional schemes. Indeed, such general frameworks (at least satisfactory ones) are not yet available in the governance literature. This is all the more true in the world of environmental governance, where even a unified and integrated problematique remains unavailable.

Yet as we have mentioned above, a provisional "vision" is in the making, and one may put forward a number of modest general propositions that would appear to have validity. They should serve until an alternative and more robust *problematique* has been developed.

These modest general propositions could be subsumed under two general rubrics: loosely coupled arenas, and learning through multilogue.

(a) Loosely coupled arenas
Open systems evolution is dictated to a large extent by external pressures. Yet the vulnerability of open systems to external shocks can be mitigated somewhat, and some stability ensured, through a partitioning of the system into loosely coupled segments. This allows the segments best able to do so to react to certain external shocks and to provide the adjustments required. Multistability is thereby acquired.

This governance for multistability entails a fragmentation into sub-systems, and a degree of decentralization of decision-making toward arenas where the challenges can best be handled (Paquet 1978). These segments are built around arenas where communities of practice, networks of persons, and groups with some stake in the issues, etc., congregate to shape the modus vivendi, or at least to defend their interests.

While broad political arenas generate certain political structures, such structures can only handle issues of the broadest generality. Most of the time, governing requires a focus on what Les Metcalfe (1993) would call the three Ds: diagnosis, design, and development. Issues areas therefore generate arenas where they can be debated, and where governance responses can be designed.

Most of the time, the starting point is some governing failure. The response to the failure is the consolidation of a sub-system capable of tackling the issue through the use of certain instruments, or the development of certain coalitions.

As society becomes more diverse and volatile, the likelihood of governing failures through disconcertation increases, and it becomes clear that such a dynamic, complex, and diverse world can only be governed in a complex, dynamic, and diverse way, through modes of governance that will vary according to time, place, and circumstances.

While there is an assumption implicit in much of conventional thinking that governments and states may ordain such responses, this is not necessarily true. Citizens and groups increasingly refuse to be governed top-down without their consent, or an appropriate degree of consultation. Moreover, the degree of complexity, diversity, and dynamism in open systems is such that they have become *de facto* ungovernable from the centre.

The conditions have been explored for the "effective structuration" of the system, so as to make it as resilient and innovative as possible, and they call for the system to be decomposed into separable but interdependent arenas (Bessières 1969). Consequently, one must face the dual challenge of living by the principle of subsidiarity, and working at defining the optimal structuration, i.e., the optimal partitioning and division of labour among sectors and between levels. This calls for a much higher degree of decentralization than conventional wisdom would appear to favour.

From this perspective one may derive a few modest general propositions.

(1) Governance of sustainability goes much beyond traditional, state-centric policy-making and must coordinate and constrain the stewardship contributions of the meaningful stakeholders.

Agents from all levels of the state, as well as the corporate and the not-for-profit sectors have to be mobilized. This is clear as one observes both market and government failures. What is less clear is the full range of stakeholders that need to be involved if effective governance is to ensue, and the very different composition of the communities and groups to be accommodated within the different arenas (Bleischwitz et al. 2003).

This does not mean that the state stands without a role. It must accept the challenge of providing the framework for self-regulation, and this in turn requires a fundamental reframing of many conventional views. For instance, the metaphor of "corporations as persons" has subtly, yet craftily, invaded the forum. This view underpins the credo of those who feel that corporations deserve the same freedoms and rights that real persons must have, and that laissez-faire therefore is the cherished ideal. It has led the state to lose sight of the basic fact that "corporations" are a creature of the state, a product of public policy, and therefore exist "at the pleasure of the people and under their sovereignty" (Bakan

2004:157). Corporations must therefore serve the public interest, and it is the role of state to ensure that they do. Laws are meant to constrain corporations, not to meet their needs.

(2) Governance of sustainability aims at behaviour modification, is anchored and develops in multiple arenas, and must be deeply rooted at the local level.

This range of stakeholders is quite different from place to place and time to time. Workable arrangements will not take the same form in all arenas, and policy instrument choice is likely to differ according to circumstances. The principle of subsidiarity is likely to be the dominant force. This is an imperative that contradicts the states' propensity to centralize and tax their immodesty, but one that experts in the field have long recognized. Ann Dale's framework for governance (1998) insists on the need for a redesigned institutional order and loosely coupled domains of governance that would be quite different one from the other.

This need not imply incoherence, only questions the usefulness of homogeneity and standardization in a diverse world. Behaviour modification entails learning, and learning is maximized when the agent closest to the context, and confronted with it, is faced with making the adaptation. Indeed, in situ, that which might have appeared to be intractable "in theory" gets resolved (Schön and Rein 1994). As a result, organizations and agents evolve; they become different from what they used to be. This is the essence of learning. And it takes place with more ease locally.

(3) Governance of sustainability relies on "regulated" self-regulation.

Governance in this new context is seen as "regulated self-regulation". It recognizes the multiplicity of loci where decisions are taken, and the need for polycentric steering institutions with as much self-regulation as possible, even though it also provides for as much imposed regulation as necessary (Bleischwitz et al. 2003). Such "regulation" may take different forms (property rights regime, stabilization, insurance, regulation, conflict management, etc.) but it must most importantly provide fail-safe mechanisms when self-regulation would appear to fail.

This obviously means that the regulatory system has to be strengthened to deter corporations from acting against the public interest (significant liability for directors and managers, graduated fines for offences, exclusion from public markets in the case of repeated offences, "suspending the charters of corporations that flagrantly and persistently violate the public interest" (Bakan 2004:161), or even seeking a court order to dissolve a corporation, take its assets, and sell it at public auction to those who will operate it in the public interest).

While there have been hesitations (and rightly so) pertaining to the use of the precautionary principle to legally prescribe that "corporations be prohibited from acting in ways that are reasonably likely to cause harm, even if definitive proof that such harm will occur does not exist" (Bakan 2004:162) (because of the possible abuses it might lead to), one must find ways to bring forth the spirit of the precautionary principle into the regulatory regime, even if it is not in the law.

(b) Learning through multilogue

The core of the arena is communication. As Yankelovich (1999:15) puts it: "dialogue is a process of successful relationship building".

Vickers has identified five levels of communication: communication by (1) threat, (2) bargaining, (3) request, (4) persuasion, and (5) dialogue (Vickers 1987:ch.8). This emphasizes the growth in the minimal trust and understanding necessary for communication to proceed: each level demanding from each party to the communication a more complex and reliable model of the other, or more trust in the other, or both. As Vickers suggests, negotiation may be no more than level 1 or 2, but may also rise to level 5.

The extraordinary experience of GATT—what economists have come to call the General Agreement on Talking and Talking—in generating a negotiated agreement to reducing international tariffs from some 45% in 1945 to an insignificant level in the year 2000, has been built on a multilogue marred by very little executive power. While it may not have been designed as such, and may even be the successful result of an institution that many dominant countries wanted to see remain a toothless tiger, GATT has proved to be a most impressive success.

One of the extraordinary weaknesses in our modern governance institutions is the lack of sites or loci for multilogue. This is true at the local, national, and international level. Steven Rosell and Daniel Yankelovich (www. viewpointlearning.com) have shown that unless such forums exist where citizens can not only become conscious of the issues, but can reflect, confront their perspectives, values and opinions, and deliberate, little social learning will ensue.

Such forums must be inclusive and permeate the whole of society if they are to be effective. Closed forums of experts (often with closed minds) are not very effective: they preach to the converted, and generate debates that produce more heat than light since experts often claim to know it all (or almost) to begin with. This is why roundtable exercises (of a closed and experts-only variety), hoped to be useful in allowing the new forms of governance of sustainability to emerge, have often floundered. They have neither been successful in reaching out to the citizenry nor in driving out "corrupt" communication. For there is in communication the equivalent of Gresham's Law in economics: bad communication drives out good communication (Vickers 1987:125).

From this perspective also, one may derive a few modest general propositions.

(4) Effective governance of sustainability is unlikely to emerge unless one can elicit a plurality of inclusive deliberative forums.

In the beginning is the issue, and there is a need for those in the issue domain to meet and deliberate. What has been missing in the sustainability debate, and (until recently) in the debates over ethics, are public spaces where deliberation can occur. And when such forums have emerged, they have been largely closed to the citizens, policed by experts, and without meaningful local roots.

It is only through the multiplication of local forums, involving cross-sections of the citizenry and debating, in situ, issues of relevance to their communities, that any behavioural change may be expected. This is most certainly the lesson that one may derive from the policy controversies of the last decades on such things as tobacco use. Science is important, but cannot suffice.

(5) Governance of sustainability demands short feedback learning loops.

Communication and deliberation are meant to generate better understanding and greater trust. But another function of communication is watching for signs of misunderstanding and errors, in order to correct them. So it is not sufficient to have public spaces for deliberation. Deliberations have to be able to generate learning. As it stands now, much of the discussion in open forums is marred by a high degree of cognitive dissonance and political correctness. This means that multiple monologues ensue: an undue amount of tact and civility often results in little learning.

One of the most important indirect and subtle techniques to foster social learning has been the development of voluntary reporting procedures. These are often innocuous processes that appear at first to be both unhelpful and likely to generate much disinformation. For instance, there was a great deal of skepticism when corporations were urged to report on their sustainability strategies.

While, in many cases, this has led to tepid exercises in public relations, based on very little accomplishment, it has also generated a momentum for better reporting tools, more imaginative ways of gauging the impact of activities purportedly geared to improving sustainability, and an educational thrust that has led to the production of various sustainability indexes. These instruments remain rudimentary, but have begun to have an impact on the climate of opinion (Stratos 2003).

(6) Governance of sustainability requires experimental prototypes to play with.

In environmental governance, as in other domains, the best is enemy of the good. Being overly ambitious often leads to a quest for comprehensive approaches. Such approaches often stall all potential corrective activities until a comprehensive plan is available (which is often socially costly), or even make the situation worse when the plan is insensitively implemented top-down.

One of the important impediments to learning is the belief that one can optimize. In fact, in the face of complex issues, one must be ready to experiment with quick-and-dirty prototypes that can serve as a medium for fruitful conversations and a basis for co-development. Otherwise, very little can be accomplished.

As Schrage (2000:15) puts it, "creating a dialogue between people and prototypes is more important than creating a dialogue between people alone". Prototypes are, as we have argued earlier, at the core of learning. There must be a prototype to begin with, if flats and sharps are going to play their role.

One must therefore develop a spirit of experimentation if one is to foster social learning, and such experimentation requires a great dose of imagination and gumption. Those virtues are not, for the time being, in good currency, any more than the other politically incorrect virtues—compromise and patience—and yet they are essential in wise policy-making (Rocard 1996).

Conclusion

To borrow a phrase from one of Geoffrey Vickers's books (Vickers 1983: xxvii), this argument "is concerned not with solving problems but with understanding situations". According to Vickers, problem-solving is never more than 15% of governance: the rest requires a deeper understanding of less fully describable and less well-structured realities.

To deepen our understanding of the governance of sustainability, we have argued that we need a new, open, and creative approach; a new language; imaginative organizational design; and shared beliefs and frames with the communities one wishes to influence. We have also argued that only polycentric governance (i.e., pluralistic regulated self-governance) can deliver this outcome.

This argument is unlikely to be well received: self-governance has its enemies. An important bias of the traditional social sciences is the belief that social order will not emerge organically, that some coercion or top-down governing is required.

Yet there is enough evidence that it really works to "force" the discussion about self-governance into the open. Both in the world of commons proper (Ostrom

1990) and in the world of business (Hock 1999) it has been demonstrated that self-governing structures can be effective governance structures.

The next phase in the discussion has nothing to do with "existence theorems" —debates about whether there are self-governing structures that work—but about the technologies of governance, the definition of effective ways to get the job done. This is the work of social architects.

Such work is not entirely without difficulties. It is not only a matter of generating the most useful prototypes, or ensuring that social learning progresses. One must also deal with demolition jobs. It may well be that the source of many difficulties, and much disconcertation, has to do with the dysfunctionality of existing structures, with pathologies of governance that need to be rooted out (Paquet 2004).

One such source that might require attention as a matter of priority is the whole legal framework surrounding "private corporations". Much has been written since Berle and Means or Galbraith on the pathology of this techno-structure. Maybe it is time to take it in for repairs.

Another more profound obstacle to change may be more difficult to root out. It is a cultural trait of Canadians—a natural tolerance and torpor—that would appear to make them less sensitive than other communities to the malefits inflicted by structures. What is needed is nothing less than a revolution in the Canadian psyche.

Shaking off our natural torpor and the shackles of the unfettered corporation is the order of the day on the way to the effective governance of sustainability.

But given the constraints we are operating under, this creates a puzzling paradox: how can one effect such a revolution in our structures and in our psyche in a non-revolutionary way, since this seems to be the only way Canadians find palatable. This will call for much ingenuity, and a *bon usage* of our typically Canadian capacity to scheme virtuously in an oblique and unassuming way.

Chapter 9

Features of a Governance Regime for Oceans*

"Social dilemmas are situations in which individual
rationality leads to collective irrationality"
Peter Kollock

Introduction

With the second largest offshore territory in the world and the world's longest coastline, Canada has a vast oceanic world to survey and govern. However, the governance challenges are daunting for reasons that extend well beyond the sheer physical dimensions of the domain in question. Canada's marine dominion underpins numerous industries including commercial fishing, aquaculture, transport, shipbuilding, tourism, mining, and oil and gas extraction. Access to the oceans is also required for purposes of scientific investigation, defence, and recreation. The activities of these stakeholders are not necessarily very well coordinated, and may interact negatively not only within the Canadian sphere of influence, but also with other oceanic socio-technical systems under foreign or international jurisdiction.

For instance, on Canada's Atlantic coast, conflicts have arisen because of the restriction of access to oil and gas lease areas for other activities, the impacts of fishing gear on telecommunication cables, the impact of scientific investigations on fishing activities, and future conflicts are anticipated if the shelf is mined for minerals (McCay and Jentoft 1998). Recent disputes over fishing rights on Canada's eastern and western coasts underscore the importance of developing

---

* In collaboration with Kevin Wilkins.

modes of operation and patterns of stakeholder interaction that will minimize the incidence of conflict. Indeed, as marine activity intensifies, concern over resource depletion increases, and the citizenry demands a greater participation in the decision-making process. This underlines the need for a coordinating framework for marine activity.

The economic importance of such a coordinating framework for Canada is clear: the direct and indirect impact of the numerous activities within the "oceans sector" contributes an estimated $150 billion annually to the Canadian economy. It is also essential to the economic and cultural survival of innumerable coastal communities (Felt and Locke 1995; Thompson 2000). The collapse of commercial fisheries in the Atlantic led to the loss of thousands of jobs, the demise of local communities, and to significant increases in social welfare expenditures (Harris 1998). This provides but one example of the cost of ineffective stewardship of ocean resources and maritime activities.

The ecological imperatives of improved stewardship of marine-based resources are also evident: a rapidly increasing world population and the industrialization of harvesting have placed new stresses on marine species. An estimated 35% of the world's 200 major fish stocks (representing 75% of global landings) are estimated to be overfished (Constanza 1998). Moreover, as the sources and amount of marine pollution intensify and marine industries grow, the health of those species that remain is increasingly threatened. Biologists are beginning to cite pollution and habitat destruction as a contributor to the decline of fish populations and marine mammals (Elliott et al. 1998).

The ocean world

(a) The natural/technical ecosystem
Oceans are complex entities characterized by considerable natural variability and significant uncertainty regarding resource conditions. Much of the uncertainty surrounding the status of fish stocks stems from a lack of knowledge regarding the impact that physical changes in the environment have on species populations. The controversy surrounding the role of changes in water temperature, water salinity, and habitat damage as contributors to the collapse of the Northern Cod fishery attests to this fact (Atkinson and Bennett 1994; De Young and Rose 1993).

In particular, the uncertainty introduced by species interactions presents a formidable challenge to natural resource management agencies. There is much ignorance, even about interspecies dynamics: for instance, the uncertainty regarding the role that seal predation had on the cod population is still a matter on which there is much debate but little agreement. In Canada, it was only after 1985 that interspecies relationships began to be considered in the determination of catch quotas for most fisheries, despite a large body of evidence that pointed to the importance of the dynamics of interacting species. As a result, fisheries management was mainly predicated on most unreliable stock assessments, that employ "models that treat one species at a time, as though they were rows of garden vegetables which do not interact with each other" (Larkin 1997).

While current estimates of the total allowable catch (TAC) are formulated using complex models of interspecies relationships, that body of knowledge is relatively new, and therefore considerable knowledge gaps remain. Moreover, the migratory nature of species, and other difficulties involved in the measurement and characterization of marine resources, create a situation where the margins of error in estimating fish populations are likely to be 30 to 50% of actual population size (Wilson et al. 1994).

Finally, there is also much uncertainty regarding the impact of land-based activities on marine ecosystems, and the interdependence of terrestrial and marine environments. For example, it has only recently been recognised that agricultural, forestry, and urban activities have likely impacted Atlantic salmon stocks (Elliott et al. 1998). As the type, intensity, and pattern of human activity on- and offshore changes, the possibility that marine ecosystems will be impacted in unforeseen ways increases.

(b) The socio-cultural-economic-legal-bureaucratic context
While ocean science is essential for improved management of ocean resources, it is not sufficient (Lane and Stephenson 2000). Socio-political forces also have a significant impact on the resources, ultimately lending support to the view that environmental managers do not manage natural systems, but rather human interactions. Indeed, there is much to be said in support of the view that the socio-political context is increasingly becoming the dominant force in the dynamics of ocean life: the multiplicity of international and national rules imposed on oceans, the immensely important and growing impact of population growth and marine-based industries, and the varied ways in which the socio-cultural context constrains the uses of ocean resources, are as important as the dynamics of the natural system in the governance of oceans.

Indeed, not taking some of these socio-political dimensions into account may explain the extraordinary crises experienced recently in ocean resources governance.

Given the uncertainty regarding the impact of any level of fishing effort, politicians are confronted with the possibility of making two types of mistakes in managing ocean resources: a type I error (restricting fishing effort when an increased harvest is sustainable) and a type II error (supporting a level of effort that is unsustainable). The natural tendency of politicians in the face of scientific uncertainty and the pressure of social demands is to embrace type II error, because it is politically convenient to hope for the best and to appease voting communities dependent on the fisheries for their livelihood. As a result, it is not surprising to find that prior to the moratorium, the Total Allowable Catch (TAC) set by the Canadian Department of Fisheries and Oceans was often in excess of what scientific estimates suggested as wise (Hutchins 1996).

Resource managers are also bound to honour a growing body of transnational and international agreements. The legal framework is as daunting as the incertitude regarding jurisdiction over resources is important. In a coastal area, for example, rights over the seabed, mineral resources and development activities, fisheries, navigation, recreation and riparian rights, to name but a few, may exist simultaneously and be dispersed among numerous actors. Delimiting jurisdictional or administrative boundaries is often technically difficult (Nichols et al. 2002) and the nature of ecosystem processes is such that those boundaries rarely coincide with natural features or culturally based communities of practice.

(c) A propensity to centralize decision-making
Despite the inherent difficulties in managing ocean resources, the natural tendency of the official state agencies mandated to ordain sound management of ocean resources has been to presume that they have all the relevant information, power, and resources to do the job themselves (Wondolleck and Yaffee 2000).

Concomitant with the centralization of decision-making authority regarding ocean resource use has been the emergence of a paternalistic approach to stakeholders in many jurisdictions (Lane and Stephenson 2000). An unfortunate by-product of such centralized and hierarchal structures of governance is often a suppression of the diversity of perspectives and values that multiple stakeholders can bring to the management process. This "we know best" view among resource management institutions has not only hindered genuine citizen engagement, but has also resulted in considerable discounting of the rich contextual knowledge of the individuals and communities that interact daily with the resources.

This sort of "disengagement" of stakeholders from the operational and strategic decision-making processes of resource management has contributed significantly to the "structural amnesia" of natural resource management institutions (Clark and Munn 1986:433) and to their propensity to disregard problems that threaten their own values or priorities (Braybooke and Paquet 1987).

As a result, one might characterize current ocean governance practices as (1) a complex series of interactions between a social context that is largely rigid and centralized and a technical context that is significantly turbulent and chaotic, (2) a poor alignment between the social and technical contexts; and (3) an overall lack of resilience in the system as a whole.

Socio-technical systems and resilience

The fact that oceans are complex adaptive socio-technical systems imposes constraints on their effective governance. Governing such intricate physical, material, and socio-political processes bound together by a large number of relationships and rules, is made all the more daunting a task since (1) the oceans' natural/technical ecosystems are still poorly understood; (2) the socio-political fabric is also still not fully mapped out; and (3) the interaction between these two universes leads to evolutionary transformations in the structure and functioning of both that are often unpredictable.

Figure 10: The interdependence of the social and technical contexts

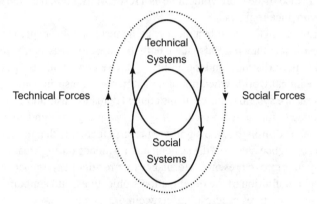

Adapted from Ziman 1991.

(a) Resilience as the key imperative

Resilience, in the face of turbulence and shocks of all sorts, is the capacity to return to a sustainable state without permanent damage.

Traditional notions of resilience in dealing with natural systems emphasize the ability of a system to return to a particular steady state following a perturbation or level of harvesting. This is equilibrium resilience [R1] and it connotes a capacity to successfully face a mild range of fluctuations around a homeostatic norm. Estimates of sustainable harvests are invariably built around the concept of a "normal" equilibrium for renewable marine resources.

Ecosystems also exhibit a second form of resilience. Instead of having a single steady state, they often have many. When perturbed beyond a certain range, altered structures and processes may lead the system to adopt "another regime of behaviour—to [find] another stability domain" (Holling 1973; Holling and

Meffe 1996). Marine ecosystems have the capacity to adopt multiple stability domains. This is ecosystem resilience [R2].

There is a strong likelihood that oceans may face sudden and significant change; in fact, for centuries the term "sea change" has been employed as an analogy to describe dramatic and significant transitions of all sorts, and the scientific community is beginning to accept the hypothesis that shifting regimes may be normal for oceans.

Holling has suggested that command-and-control governance, geared to increase harvests may have produced natural systems that are less resilient to perturbation, and also less capable of finding a stable equilibrium after a shock: "when the range of natural variation in a system is reduced, the system loses resilience" (Holling and Meffe 1996). The social systems dependent upon those resources are also made more vulnerable as a result of traditional command-and-control governance regimes.

The institutions in the socio-technical system must not only adapt to these dual forms of resilience; they must also have both the capacity to assemble resources to respond to perturbations, and the ability to devise new relationships between the socio-technical worlds when minor adjustments are insufficient.

The governance system required in this context demands institutional resilience [R3]: the capacity for the socio-technical system to spring back undamaged from pressure or shock through some significant re-arrangements that do not modify the overall coherence nature of the system; and resilience through learning [R4]: the capacity to improve present performance as a result of experience through a fundamental redefinition of the organization's objectives, and a modification of behaviour and structures as a result of new circumstances.

When the natural or technical system reveals vulnerability to type 1 and type 2 resilience failures, "social resilience" kicks in, i.e., the ability to learn, to operate in an iterative environment and adjust outcomes and objectives as one proceeds. However, these governing relations are in creative tension: institutional or type 3 resilience calls for preservation, while resilience through learning, or type 4 resilience, means change. They must be balanced. The governance challenge revolves around the creation of an institutional order with the capacity to integrate these four types of resilience as circumstances change.

(b) Continuous learning as the road to higher-level resilience
A resilient socio-technical system has the capacity to employ both single-loop (or adaptive) learning and double-loop (generative) learning as required.

On the one hand, organisations capable of single-loop learning are able to find new ways to solve problems (Argyris and Schön 1974). They are able to cope with varying circumstances by bringing together numerous and diverse sources of information relevant to the problem. As such, building knowledge networks is important for the agglomeration of the numerous and diverse sources of information about the environment (Wondolleck and Yaffee 2000:25). The result is a more comprehensive view of problems and opportunities that grows from a transdisciplinary perspective that integrates the natural sciences, the social sciences, and the policy process.

On the other hand, double-loop learning "occurs when error is detected and corrected in ways that involve the modification of an organization's underlying norms, policies and objectives" (Argyris and Schön 1974). This form of organizational learning allows stakeholders to build new mental maps of their organization and the problem domain, to reassess purposes and change processes, and to create and adjust goals, norms, and assumptions in the face of major perturbations.

Multi-looped learning leads to higher-level resilience through a process of interaction, enabling individuals and organizations to learn from each other and consequently adapt, innovate, develop new arrangements, conventions, and rules (Paquet 1999b). Learning is rooted in a social or collective mobilization of knowledge: harnessing the collective intelligence of the team as a source of continuous improvement (Florida and Kenney 1993). It is predicated on the existence of a social capital of trust, reasonableness, and mutual understanding that facilitates debates, and generates synergies among the many potential partners from the civic, public, and private sectors. This entails a mobilization of all participants through a wide array of coordination maps and institutions.

Such a coherence within a social learning system is a major source of its nimbleness. Yet a good learning network must not be too coherent: the nodes should not be too similar, nor the ties too strong or too crippled by routine. This is the sense in which one may speak of "the strength of weak ties" (Granovetter 1973). A certain degree of heterogeneity, and therefore social distance, might foster a higher potentiality for innovation because the different parties bring a more complementary body of knowledge to the conversation. More fruitful synergies may ensue.

An effective governing system for oceans must therefore be capable of modifying its technologies, its processes, and its structures in an effort to respond strategically and effectively to the diverse social and technical forces that impact the system. It must be able to learn—to recognize and absorb social and technical fluctuations and transform as required. In fact, a governance system for the oceans must employ multi-looped learning: it must be as varied, diverse, and complex as the environment and the interactions it contends with. It is the law of requisite variety.

To be effective then, a governing system for oceans must be able to evolve, as required, into more complex forms of differentiation and integration, to be able to deal with the variety of challenges and opportunities in novel ways, and to maintain its coherence through time, while retaining or shedding some characteristics that are sources of good fits or misfits if higher-level resilience is to be achieved.

Figure 11: Forms of resilience in socio-technical systems

The Natural System

R1	R2
Equilibrium Resilience:	**Ecosystem Resilience:**
The capacity for a natural or technical system to absorb perturbations within certain limits and return to steady-state conditions or a general and relative condition.	The capacity for a natural or technical system to operate at multiple steady-states and adopt a new regime of behaviour with noticeably different relationships between the different elements.

The Social System

R3	R4
Institutional Resilience:	**Learning:**
The capacity for the economy-polity-society-bureaucracy nexus to spring back undamaged from pressure or shock through some slight re-arrangements that do not modify the nature of the overall system.	The capacity to improve present performance as a result of experience through a redefinition of the organization's objectives, and a modification of behaviour and structures as a result of new circumstances.

Distributed governance, co-evolution, and networks

In a turbulent environment, organizations can only govern themselves by becoming capable of learning both what their goals are, and the means to reach them, as they proceed. The central question is how to organize for faster learning. This is done by tapping into the knowledge and information that the various stakeholders possess, and getting them to invent ways out of the predicaments they are in. Systems based on centralized control and the concentration of power respond poorly to complex environments. Hierarchies designed for stable environments lack the nimbleness to react to the torrent of inputs that this complex multi-stakeholder environment provides. As Osborne and Gaebler (1992) note: "today information is virtually limitless, communication between remote locations is instantaneous, ... employees are well educated, and conditions change with blinding speed. There is no time for information to go up the chain of command and decision to come down." Hierarchal regulation and management systems work poorly when the scale and scope is as large as the marine environment (Brundtland Commission 1987).

Distributed governance is a *sine qua non*. More innovation results when local agents are empowered to take decisions on the spot (Naisbitt 1994). Most problems are unsolvable by one person, but require insights from a variety of perspectives (Cicourel 1990) as this generates more learning, and it is through learning that complexity is managed (Argyris 1996). The objective is to integrate multiple and differentiated forms of expertise (Tenkasi and Boland 1996). For institutions to learn quickly, everyone must take part in the conversation, and bring forward each bit of knowledge and wisdom that he or she has that has a bearing on the issue (Paquet 1992b;1996–7).

(a) Co-evolution

Distributed governance is embedded in a broad set of organizations and institutions built on market forces, the state, and civil society. But it is most importantly nested in the transversal links relating these three families of institutions and organizations, and allowing them to be integrated into a sort of neural net. These transversal links neither echo the traditional, functional top-down organization, nor the matrix form of organizations, where vertical-functional and horizontal-process rapports are supposedly keeping one another in check. Rather, in a transversal world, processes are dominant, and the reaction to external challenges is for the different stakeholders to coalesce laterally to create informal links and multifunctional teams, capable of promoting faster and more effective learning (Tarondeau and Wright 1995).

The ecological concept of co-evolution provides an apt way to synthesize these transversal links among the three universes of state, society, and economy. Co-evolution in biology refers to an evolutionary process based on reciprocal responses of closely interacting species. Reference has been made to the co-evolution of the beaks of hummingbirds and the shape of the flowers they feed on. The concept can be generalized to encompass feedback processes among interacting systems (social, economic, political) going through a reciprocal process of change. The process of co-evolution becomes a form of organizational learning: that is, of joint learning and inter-adjustment of economy, society, and state (Norgaard and Dixon 1984).

What evolves from these linkages and mixed institutions are new modes of cross-functional coordination that are largely supported by moral contracts. Actors within each sector learn about the knowledge and competencies of the other through dialogue. The sort of learning that emerges from these interactions does not always lead to formal conclusions and codified knowledge (Paquet 1999b). To a large extent it remains tacit knowledge that allows actors to deal effectively with practical matters within particular contexts. Linkages within institutions that span the three sectors build this implicit type of understanding that allows institutions to evolve concomitantly as they shift between different families of integrative methods (exchange and negotiation in the economic sector, coercion and redistribution in the state sector, and reciprocity and solidarity in the civic sector) in response to particular problems.

The versatility embodied within a co-evolutionary system allows it to shift into different stability domains, and imparts greater resilience to the system. As suggested by Wondolleck and Yaffee (2000:9, 42): "reliance on one sector of society is unlikely to produce satisfactory outcomes"; instead, resource management agencies must "build bridges with the world outside the agency walls" to enhance organizational and individual learning.

(b) Networks

The capacity to reach higher-level resilience is in large part dependent upon an organization's ability to collect, assimilate, and react to information. As previously mentioned, vertical organizations lack the required flexibility to react quickly to this rapidly changing environment; however, horizontal organizations do not always have the necessary accountability structures or cohesion to mobilize teams towards the accomplishment of complex tasks. To achieve the required rigidity and flexibility, we must rely on networks that are capable of building relationships and of nurturing collaboration (Paquet 1999b).

Networks therefore have a distinct advantage over vertical and horizontal organizations. Actors within a network are often better able to modify their processes and activities as circumstances change, as they have a greater capacity to respond autonomously to changes. Moreover, within a network, often what cannot be accomplished by the individual may be realized by the aggregate.

Within a network that spans hierarchies and vertical lines of power there will be overlapping memberships, personal ties, temporary coalitions, and special task organizations; the organizational structure is therefore created by the most powerful as well as the least powerful within such a paradigm (Hine 1977). In some cases, networks can give rise to the mixed institutions that provide the basis for cooperation, harmonization, concertation, and even co-decision-making involving agents in the public, private, and civic sectors (Laurent and Paquet 1998). The mix of political, social, and economic mechanisms that results provides the capacity for a system to strategically shift among these integrative mechanisms according to the circumstances. Networks are thus an essential facilitator of co-evolutionary processes.

A social learning governance system must balance the need for interdependent actors to have the requisite coherence to collaborate as well as the requisite distinctiveness to foster innovation. In fact, in a situation of environmental turbulence, adversarial methods produce outcomes of limited value, so that collaboration emerges as the dominant strategy. In such contexts, organizations and individuals become highly interdependent, their fates become correlated, and collaboration is thus seen as a necessary and logical response to environmental turbulence (Trist 1977). Turbulent conditions trigger collaboration because of the stabilizing effect that coordinated activity can have on the sociotechnical system. Uncoordinated actions on the other hand can accentuate destabilization (Gray 1985). Collaboration also generates the synergies and tensions necessary to foster the multi-looped learning that, as we have seen, is the cornerstone of resilient institutions. In fact, the resiliency of the governing regime depends on forms of learning that are steeped in collaboration. Engendering trust and bestowing identity and membership will be key requirements in the development of the patterns of interaction between stakeholders that create conditions that foster forms of collaboration.

Several features of the ocean world pose extraordinary governance challenges. One, in particular, is worth describing here—oceans as common property resources and the inherent difficulties in generating adequate appropriation systems for diffuse marine resources.

Common property resources and appropriation systems

The common property nature of the fisheries and ocean resources creates a major impediment to collaboration. Scott Gordon has shown how a system of universal access leads to overexploitation. Given a situation of diminishing yields at a given level of effort, the rational actor is led to increase the fishing effort rather than yield resources to other users (Gordon 1954). Everybody's property is nobody's property. Therefore, it appears rational to appropriate as much as possible, as soon as possible, for there is no assurance that any will be left tomorrow. Defection/non-collaboration is the dominant strategy, and stock depletion is therefore to be predicted despite the fact that cooperative solutions would leave everyone collectively better off.

(a) Common property resources
Common property resources create a social dilemma where individual rationality leads to collective irrationality (Kollock 1998). Traditional solutions to this

dilemma are either government control or privatization of the resource. But a growing body of research into commons dilemmas has indicated that solutions other than privatization and state control exist, and that both government ownership and privatization are themselves subject to important coordination failures (Ostrom et al. 1999).

Private property regimes, while often successful at increasing the rents generated by resource users (if properly designed and administered), can be unworkable for a host of reasons. Difficulties arise due to the necessity to make decisions regarding who is to be excluded from the resource, a dilemma that often generates conflicts and a deterioration of the social order. As summarized by Bromley (1991), privatization can cause "tragedies of enclosure". The exclusivity of property rights can also lead to sub-optimal use of resources, or an "anti-commons dilemma", where "multiple rights to exclude" prevent plural uses, or lead to underusage of commons property (Buchanan and Yoon 2000). In an environment as highly diversified as the oceans, the probability is high that rights-based regimes will lead to increased conflict and less than optimal use or access to ocean resources. Moreover, numerous factors influence the choices that users make regarding the amount of resources they extract, and individual time lines are not always congruent with public time lines.

State ownership is also subject to failure under certain circumstances. Mancur Olson (1982) outlines how public institutions can be captured by specific interest groups, and thus make decisions contrary to the interest of the majority of citizens. The failure of the former Soviet Union to effectively conserve resources, and prevent large-scale pollution, provides an example of the mismanagement of resources under state control.

In the last quarter century, the possibility of successful management of common-pool resources (CPRs) has been documented in a variety of settings (Baland and Platteau 1996; Berkes 1989; Bromley 1992; McCay and Acheson 1987; Ostrom 1990; Ostrom et al. 1994; Pinkerton 1989). It has been shown that resource users define value and risk in a more complex fashion than the traditional model predicts.

As a result, the assumption that resource users will adopt defection strategies has come to be challenged by the acknowledgement that "users can communicate and cooperate when it is in their interest to do so and when the resources at their disposal and the socio-political context permits it" (Ostrom 1998). This does not suggest that the rational actor's model is inaccurate or without utility: incentives have an integral role in appropriation systems; however, incentives alone provide an incomplete basis for the development of management strategies.

In the rational actor's model there is no consideration of resource appropriators as moral agents who are also members of communities. As noted by Clark

(1981), "[t]o assume that fishermen 'always have an incentive to cheat', that they constitute a kind of 'homo economicus' that is completely immune from most social pressures, is an absurd hypothesis upon which to base an analysis of fisheries". Sociocultural conditions and the structures that influence the mix of collaboration and competition have a significant impact on the efficacy of public, private, or community-based regimes.

(b) Appropriation systems, governing institutions, and social learning
Because the rules that govern resource access strike a balance between social and technical circumstances that are context-specific, a standard set of rules for all marine communities cannot be devised. However, case studies of self-governed CPR resource appropriation systems (Ostrom 1990) indicate that there are some features common to many successful appropriation systems: defined boundaries; rules of access and withdrawal that are accepted by the appropriators, rules which are tailored to resource and managing institutions; dispute resolution mechanisms; user participation in rule changes; monitoring and enforcement of rules with graduated sanctions against offenders, recognition of the collective rights of the group by outside authorities. A system need not employ each of these characteristics to be successful; however, as noted by Ostrom (1990), the chances of failure are greater the more of these features are missing.

Other investigations of commons dilemmas and experiments involving simulated commons dilemmas support Ostrom. They indicate that resource users choose to restrict their consumption when the resource is important to the survival of the community (Wade 1987); when they receive timely feedback

Figure 12: Potential success factors for common-pool resource appropriation systems

Exclusion of non-members through territorial or technological rules
Rules of access and withdrawal tailored to environmental and social conditions
Monitoring, enforcement, graduated sanctions, detection of defectors, visible behaviours
Dependency on the resource
Feedback on the impact of extractions
Dispute resolution systems, users can communicate
User participation in rule changes
Small community, mutual ties among members, shared identity
Recognition of authority by external agencies

on the impact of their extractions, when their behaviours are visible to others; when they can communicate with resource users; and when users share a group identity (Kollock 1998).

These inquiries indicate that the outcomes sought by appropriators are both economic and socio-political. The rational choices of stakeholders depend also on relationships, trust, political influence, and values. Collective action can take precedence over defection when the socio-cultural and institutional arrangements provide incentives that allow the appropriate mix of appropriation rules and norms.

The importance of institutions cannot be overlooked. Institutions are the organizational constraints that structure incentives and shape human interactions (North 1990). The rules, norms, and conventions they encapsulate define what is allowed and what is not. As such, they serve as orientation maps concerning future actions: they enable a large number of actors to co-ordinate their actions by means of orientation to a common signpost. They are the vehicle for sustainable governance as they guide the development of appropriation systems that are appropriate to the social and technical context, as well as influencing the social context.

Sustainable governance refers to creating an institutional order that fosters the development of appropriation systems and governance institutions that balance the creative tension between the need for resilience and learning. External shocks emerging from the environment, and strains and stresses generated by the network of interactions among agents and groups, continually shape the institutional order. Institutions evolve through minor technological modification to existing rules, or through major transformations of roles, rules, and structures within the game, or through a reframing of the whole game. The relationship between governance institutions and appropriation systems is depicted in Figure 13.

For an ecology of governance

Oceans are a common property resource that is not under the full control of any single national jurisdiction, but they are also fundamentally, from a governance point of view, collectives of stakeholders of the most varied sort who are pursuing conflicting objectives, and they are an assemblage of extraordinarily complex adaptive socio-technical systems that require very sophisticated governance regimes if they are to remain in a healthy state. Such regimes are a constellation of mechanisms capable both of mobilizing the appropriate degree of cooperation and of ensuring the degree of engagement necessary for stakeholders to honour their commitments.

In ocean governance, the nature of the environment demands a particularly nimble institutional order, able to include the views, knowledge, and contribution

Figure 13: Governance institutions and appropriation systems

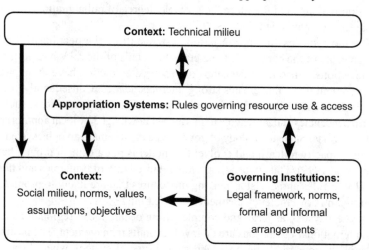

of numerous stakeholders on the one hand, and able to create the necessary cohesion group dynamics to mobilize actors to contribute to a collective good. Oceans represent a global commons that cannot be governed by a single actor. It is a game without a master, and it calls for a "nobody-in-charge" ecology of governance.

As a result, the mechanistic models that have guided policy-makers and resource users have failed to provide solutions to dilemmas. This is because these models neither take account of the complexity of the socio-technical system, nor provide frameworks for accommodating either the diversity of perspectives or changes within that system. They are inadequate navigational tools for at least three reasons: (1) they rely on a definition of problems, structures, and context that remains static, rather than acknowledging that they are in a process of continuous evolution and co-evolution; (2) the continual learning of stakeholders and the resulting redefinition of their competencies are overlooked; and (3) choices are assumed to be only individual, rather than also social (Schön and Rein 1994).

Sustainable governance depends on an approach that recognizes the inherent uncertainty of the environment, the role of tacit knowledge in the policy and planning process, and the need for learning and innovation to adapt to change. Because of the common-property nature of the resource, as the appropriation systems explored by Ostrom and others illustrate, a second imperative of the sustainable governance of ocean resources is the fostering of a socio-political environment that facilitates the alignment of individual choices with collective benefits. Creating those conditions involves the modification of an ensemble of factors, such as norms, values, laws, and rules that influence behaviours and decision-making, and therefore the possible degree of collaboration and of the integration of syncretic mindsets.

The most successful appropriation systems allow the peculiarities of the resource and of the community to dictate the details of the rules and norms that guide actions. Since local decisions on resource extraction have an impact on other communities, this creates strong interdependence. Consequently, there is the need for a layering of decision-making, or nesting of institutions, such that interdependencies and larger constraints are acknowledged by local appropriators, and vice versa. Such an ecology of governance must remain an open system that has the capacity to learn and evolve: the model is not a cathedral but a bazaar (Raymond 1999). This in turn shapes the required mix of principles and norms, but also of rules and decision-making procedures that are likely to promote the preferred mix of efficiency, resilience, and learning.

In an ecosystem as large and complex as an ocean, local, regional, national, and international institutions are all involved in its management. The nesting of these institutions refers not to a hierarchical type of system, where local rules and norms are subjugated by regional rules or laws, which in turn are trumped by national laws. There are so many exceptions to this cascading sphere of influence, and such intermingling of the different levels of coordination in different circumstances and in different contexts, that one may best describe the organization chart as a knotted fishnet.

For example, a highly local scientific endeavour may, because of its contribution to the efforts of a global institution, be more concerned with international standards than with local norms. A local industrial activity, for example, because it may principally impact an ecosystem or a species that straddles or migrates across a border, may be influenced by national or provincial agreements more than by local rules. By the same token, the necessity to respect local value systems may prevent international organizations from proposing stringent guidelines, which might reduce the options of the localities in question. What emerges then is a complex web of formal and informal patterns of coordination.

Basic principles

Although any ecology of governance connotes a complex system of interaction among a variety of sub-systems, this variety does not mean that there is no common philosophy underpinning this arrangement. It has already become clear that chaordic systems (i.e., self-organizing, adaptive, complex systems, exhibiting characteristics of both chaos and order, competition and cooperation) need not be without core determining principles.

Much has been learned from the VISA experience, and Dee Hock has suggested a few basic principles that outline why VISA has a viable governance structure.

These principles have been used extensively in the attempts to generalize this learning to other domains. They are discussed in detail on the Chaordic Commons website (www.chaordic.org).

These principles necessarily remain very generic, in order to have wide applicability. Our interest here is to develop a workable set of such principles that would appear to be applicable to the ocean governance domain.

From our examination of the ocean domain, we have come to the conclusion that its inherent environmental uncertainty, turbulence, social complexity, and cacophony calls for a governance system that would have to meet at least certain minimal norms if sustainability is to be achieved.

As a result, a workable ocean governance system would have to be open and participative, subsidiarity-geared, and multistable. The following principles (principles 1, 2 and 3) define these embryonic norms. An integral ocean governance system would also need to be apt at creating the conditions under which, when situations evolve such that the socio-technical system is thrown outside the boundaries of normal circumstances, certain temporary rules would kick in to deal with these abnormal circumstances, but with clear limitations being imposed on such suspension of the normal rules of the regime. This puts a premium on monitoring organizational learning and relational leadership. So the fourth principle below offers the necessary stewardship that this demands. It is here, incidentally, that we can see most clearly the new role that needs to be played by government.

Principle 1: participation
In the world of oceans, as in many other domains, broad public involvement in decision-making is being increasingly embraced in response to important management failures and growing public distrust of resource managers and scientists (Kennedy and Quigley 1993; Endter-Wada et al. 1998; Daniels et al. 1994; Endter-Wada and Lilieholm 1995). More public involvement increases the amount of relevant information available, helps resolve conflicts, and makes difficult political decisions more acceptable (Sinclair and Diduck 1995). Stakeholders are often led to support decisions that are contrary to their interests if their voices are heard and taken into account.

In a society that is now increasingly based on participation, negotiation, and bargaining, rather than on universal rights, decision-making should be shared with the resource users in order for them to become responsible participants in a sustainable management system (Jentoft and Kristoffersen 1989). Various private–public arrangements worldwide, where resource users enter into partnerships with governing authorities, have demonstrated that real participation increases awareness and appreciation of the issues, and contributes to improved stewardship and management of the resource (McColl and Stephens 1997; El-Sabh et al. 1998; Jentoft 2000; Holland 1996).

Stakeholder participation is essential for ocean governance because a participatory system allows the users' intimate knowledge to shape the rule system according to the unique features of local circumstances. Ostrom (1990) observes that successful resource appropriation systems rely on local rules that are not only specific to local circumstances, but modifiable by local actors. In successful self-governance systems, users "convene regularly in a deliberative body to make decisions about opening and closing the commons", set harvest dates, decide "rules governing the commons", and also "adjudicate conflicts" among themselves (McKean 1992).

As it can lead to highly contextual rules, participation can also increase compliance with rules (Kuperan et al. 1998). Greater legitimacy is achieved when the rules established suit the circumstances well, a situation observed in enduring self-governed resource appropriation systems (Peternoster et al. 1997; Ostrom 1990). Perceptions of legitimacy come from fairness within the procedures used to develop laws and regulations (Tyler et al. 1989). Wondolleck and Yaffee (2000:31) have studied numerous successful collaborative resource management regimes, and found that despite the fact that the decisions that come out of participatory systems may not differ from a regulatory regime, participation in the decision-making process leads to ownership of outcomes, a sense of legitimacy, and better compliance.

Participation builds commitment: "the reliable and loyal actions of the users [are] a product of involvement and commitment, as opposed to being the offspring of calculations of self interest" (McCay 1995) and "public involvement is a 'technology of legitimization' which can be seen as a means by which managerial legitimacy is maintained in the context of an increasingly pluralistic policy arena" (Jentoft 1989). Building such commitment and fostering involvement is important, because it enhances the probability that resource users can successfully engage in collective action towards shared goals, and also because it reduces the costs associated with regulatory compliance.

Public participation in resource management dilemmas not only provides socio-political empowerment (Rocha 1997), but it has been shown to create a sort of "social rationality", and to increase social cohesion (Pateman 1972). In many successful collaborative processes, the public is involved from the very earliest stages of the process, and in a substantive fashion (Wondolleck and Yaffee 2000:103).

Through sincere involvement of the stakeholders in planning and problem-solving, all parties "learned together, understood constraints, and developed creative ideas, trust and relationships." (Wondolleck and Yaffee 2000:105) By its nature, participation provides an education that can shift users away from 'possessive individualism' to social rationality that transcends the myopic objectives of individuals and interest groups (Friedmann 1987). Participation achieves this by altering each individual's frame of reference (Diduck and Sinclair 1999), and thus engenders social learning.

Principle 2: subsidiarity
The subsidiarity principle states that "power should devolve on the lowest, most local level at which decisions can reasonably be made, with the function of the larger unit being to support and assist the lower body in carrying out its tasks" (Bellah et al 1991). The contextual richness of subsidiarity-based regimes allows for the development of appropriation systems tailored to local circumstances. Noncentralization is required to use the environment strategically in this manner, as more innovation occurs when local realities are empowered to make decisions on the spot (Naisbitt 1994). As noted by *the Economist* (1995), "central authorities often lack the information they need to design a regime for the coast and fisheries, let alone enforce it." A distributed governance regime with local or regional foci is often more effective than a centralized one, because regional systems can more effectively solve complex problems and facilitate citizen involvement.

The subsidiarity principle is obviously an extraordinary support to the participation principle: by shifting decision-making to the lowest possible level that can effectively despatch a function, it augments citizen engagement.

A governance system for the oceans must have the adaptability to take on as many equilibrium structures as the oceans themselves. Subsidiarity provides the flexibility required in a system as inherently unpredictable and complex as oceans. Without this flexibility to change rules locally, there is a high cost to rule change because any desired local modification to the rules requires that an exception be made, or the rules governing everybody be changed (Ostrom 1990).

In addition to rules and patterns of interaction appropriate to the local context, subsidiarity can, through multistakeholder participation, thus lead to socio-cultural benefits. The necessity of user participation demands human interactions, and therefore also provides a valued good since "human beings are social creatures, and creatures with values. Among the things that we value are our relations with each other" (Scheffler 1997). Through repeated interaction, such involvement can enhance social capital.

Learning is also facilitated by the combined effect of the flexibility and authority to change rules according to the context and the social benefits of subsidiarity. When the components of the institution that are confronted with different local realities are empowered to make decisions on the spot, learning is accelerated (Naisbitt 1994). It is in this way that the citizen becomes a co-producer of governance in a subsidiarity-based system (Paquet 1999b).

Principle 3: multistability

The diversity of the actors involved in ocean governance generates tensions and conflicts. It is therefore necessary for the system to have the necessary resilience to withstand perturbations, as well as the flexibility to make changes as necessary. It is for this reason that a governing system that can adapt to strategies that are paradoxical and contradictory is required: it must concomitantly be organized and structured while being disorganized and unconcerted; becoming more and more minute (as organizations fracture) and larger (as networks grow) and having more autonomy and latitude, and more partners (Peters 1992).

Because of the importance that interpersonal relations will have in facilitating cooperation by building trust, there are practical limits on the size of the groups that can participate in a subsidiarity-based institution. There are inherent problems of organizing, agreeing on rules, and enforcing rules within large groups. It becomes necessary to break the system down into manageable units that can define modes of engagement that are appropriate to their circumstances. This demands modular structures that allow each unit to define its mission and clientele more precisely, shaping the members while the members shape it (Paquet 1999b).

Many have been critical of such fragmentation and have deplored the sluggishness that one might anticipate in the consequent reactions of the socio-technical systems to external shocks. This preference for centralization is a mistaken view. In the same way that double-looped learning enables a system to react by minor adjustments in the system's operations when faced with small changes in the environment, and by major changes in the institutional parameters and directions when the external turbulence has generated a change in essential variables, the adjustment process may benefit immensely from a fragmented system.

Ashby and others have shown that such a partitioned and balkanized system is multistable: it is less vulnerable and fragile because the adjustment to modifications in essential variables might be facilitated by delegating it, so to speak, to a partial system better able to cope with it. This enables the overall process to adjust more effectively, and more quickly, than if the overall process had had to be modified (Ashby 1960; Paquet 1978).

Since scale mismatches between ecosystems and human governance institutions underpin many ocean management problems, it becomes important that compartmentalized and interconnected systems also exist at multiple levels. The nesting of rules into multiple layers facilitates innovation, because it allows the participation of those affected by operational rules in the modification of those rules (Ostrom 1990), without adjustment of the whole system.

The multiplicity of subdivisions also permits multiple memberships and multiple associations that create overlapping and redundant connections. This redundancy in connections also affords the system resilience (Paquet 1999b) by allowing, to a certain extent, the coexistence of different principles. The intermingling of opposing views minimizes the destabilizing impact of changes from within the internal environment, or from the exterior, while the feedback loops and interdependencies of these relationships impart a certain resilience to the system (the capacity to react to pressures and shocks through minor rearrangements, without modifications to the complete system) and capacity for learning (the ability to respond to new circumstances by changing the organizational structure and redefining objectives) (Paquet 1999b).

Principle 4: stewardship of organizational learning and relational leadership
As we have seen, a sustainable and effective governance regime for oceans needs to be resilient and continuously learning, and therefore needs to be built around distributed governance, co-evolution, and networks. This means that it will always be evolving and changing. But not all the adjustments are the result of the workings of some invisible hand. And it is going to need stewardship of organizational learning and relational leadership.

This is a role that can usefully be played by government. The state has an important role in maintaining healthy communication in the forum, and workable competition in the market. It also has an important intelligence function if it is to act as catalyst in an innovative learning process (Wilensky 1967; Lundvall 1992).

Within a subsidiarity-based and participatory regime, government must abandon some degree of control to become a supporting and subsidiary actor. Such a system deprives the minister of a monopoly on leadership of the organization. In many successful participatory regimes, the government has been able to transform its role from that of the ultimate authority, a role which "limits information exchange, hampers creative thinking, and undermines the ownership of decisions by regulated parties" to assume "a broader set of roles, including those of expert, stakeholder, partner, facilitator, and leader" (Wondolleck and Yaffee 2000:130).

Governments have an important role coordinating the assembly of resource users, providing information that helps identify the problem and possible solutions, and legitimizing and aiding the enforcement of agreements reached by local users. Thus, they are the stewards of organizational learning. They not only seek to learn how to ensure better functioning, but also, and more importantly, they are charged with finding the right goals, and learning whether the objectives pursued are the right ones (Argyris and Schön 1974).

The state as animateur then becomes a partner who shares decision-making powers and risks and responsibilities with other stakeholders, but establishes the broader set of objectives, promotes local management, and verifies successes (NRTEE 1999). As defined by the Government of Canada:

> A partnership is an undertaking to do something together. It is a relationship that consists of shared and/or compatible objectives and an acknowledged distribution of specific roles and responsibilities among the participants which can be formal, contractual, or voluntary, or between two or more parties. The implication is that there is a co-operative investment of resources (time, funding, material) and therefore joint risk-taking, sharing of authority, and benefits for all partners (Heritage Canada 1995).

The role thus proposed for the federal government is more than simply a technical or coordinating role. The state must develop a new interactive regime with the citizenry to promote the emergence of a participation society where the citizen has both a recognized voice and an obligation to participate (Paquet 1999). As noted by Yankelovich (1999), decentralized regimes require relational leaders whose defining tasks are to develop "webs of relationships with others rather than handing down visions, strategies, and plans as if they were commandments from the mountaintop". A leader in this context must be able to ensure that the institutional setting is capable of promoting and ensuring a requisite amount of social learning. In many ways, central governments are the designers and builders of subsidiarity-based regimes.

The key role of governments (either as separate entities or as the basis of federations) is to guard against the possibilities that the system of systems might, through cumulative movements, be led to go beyond the boundaries of the "viable corridor". In such circumstances, a discontinuity occurs, as the normal re-equilibrating mechanisms would appear to no longer be able to ensure the resilience of the systems. This is a moment when rules must be altered, if only temporarily, to avoid the complete collapse of the systems in place.

The conditions must be clearly specified under which different government-driven regimes kick in, in abnormal times, to replace the one in use in normal times, and the process through which the normal-times regime will be re-instated must also be specified clearly. It must be clear that this switch to the abnormal-times regime is a fail-safe system to be used when the self-organized regime is in danger of collapsing. In such circumstances, the power of coercion of the state or states becomes hegemonic. Power rules, and survival is the objective.

Such interventions would be required in situations akin to epidemics, when the impact of a few may make a difference in tipping the process in certain directions (Gladwell 2000). One cannot presume that epidemics-type phenomena cannot occur, and there must therefore be a way to invoke a regime-switch when it becomes obvious that the cumulative causation of micro-decisions is becoming the source of a dangerous irreversibility (Kahn 1966).

These principles are not sufficient to freeze rules and procedures, but they will tend to move them in certain directions. As a result, the "practice" will be modified. For example:

Participation entails:
  Openness
  Taking diversity seriously
  Information exchange
  Catering to interdependencies

Mechanisms for consultation, negotiation, and conflict resolution subsidiarity entails:
  Decentralization
  Empowerment
  Much attention to context
  Attention to boundaries
  Multi-layered governance

Multistability entails:
  Long-term focus
  Primacy of the whole
  Division of labour
  Graduated sanctions

Organizational learning inside/outside of the corridor entails:
  Attention to fragility of the system
  Benchmarks for what is normal
  Monitoring
  Attention to larger systems

These principles emphasize the need (1) to be inclusive in order to mobilize the dispersed information and to gain legitimacy; (2) to delegate decision-making as locally as possible in order to obtain maximum efficiency and learning; (3) to subdivide and deliberately fracture the governance system, so as to make it more robust and less likely to crash *in toto*; and (4) to ensure that a meta-governance process is in place to guide the learning process and the adjustment of the regimes in case of crisis.

Cases

It is useful to apply these principles on existing realities in the ocean world to see if they make sense. We have chosen three examples: the Waterfront Restoration Trust[1], the Gulf of Maine, and Australia. They illustrate how regimes can tap into a greater portion of the codified and tacit knowledge of a wider array of stakeholders, and mobilize them to contribute to problem solving. In many cases, this does not require the dismantling of current institutions. New forms of coordination, specifically at the micro- and mesolevels (between micro and global or macro) are often sufficient to create functioning regimes that can spontaneously distribute knowledge, power, and resources in a fashion appropriate to the circumstances.

(a)   The Waterfront Regeneration Trust: a microscopic perspective
In most industrialized nations, the predominant governing regimes for oceans concentrate power, resources, and scientific knowledge at the national or sub-national (state, provincial) level. This is often a useful arrangement, as certain activities, such as scientific research or international negotiation, require a larger resource or population base to be effective. In fact, the subsidiarity principle demands that certain activities occur mainly at the national or international level for that very reason. Nonetheless, the concentration of power, resources, knowledge, and capacities at the level of provinces and nations can be problematic when it comes to solving dilemmas that are increasingly complex. In many cases, the relevant unit of analysis is to be found at the local level.

The complexity of multiple demands on scarce resources is perhaps most evident at the level of communities. Moreover, the uncertainty and turbulence that characterizes the oceans often has its most dramatic impact on those that live in coastal communities. Quite often the problems that are present at the level of the community or region cannot be effectively dealt with within the framework of national strategies. Moreover, the "authority" that exists at the national or sub-national level is often highly fragmented, creating roadblocks for community-based action.

---

[1]   While stricto sensu the Waterfront Restoration Trust does not deal with an "ocean" but only a "great lake", the coordination challenges are not dissimilar to those raised by larger maritime common property resources. Moreover, the fact that the Trust as leader had no legal authority replicates in the small the situation that exists in the large with oceans: nobody is in charge (Cleveland 2002).

The *problematique* of regimes of concentrated power at the national and sub-national level surfaced along the North Shore of Lake Ontario in the late 1980s. Within this string of communities there was much agreement among stakeholders that action was required to improve the waterfront from an environmental standpoint, notably, by reducing the levels of pollutants flowing into the lake, and creating more green space along the shoreline. There was nonetheless considerable difficulty coordinating that action among the interested parties.

This case with respect to the Western Lake Ontario waterfront has been well documented by the Canadian Centre for Management Development (CCMD). The reader is encouraged to consult the original CCMD documents and the publications of the Royal Commission and the Toronto Waterfront Regeneration Trust. This section provides an overview of the case, and the importance of the challenges that were overcome from the perspective of the distribution of knowledge, resources and power in regimes.

The Western shore of Lake Ontario spans from Oshawa to Niagara Falls, and is characterized by heavy industrialization and a high population density. It is also characterized by overlapping jurisdictions, with numerous municipalities abutting one another, and with the province and the federal government having distinct and shared responsibility for numerous dossiers that impact development and conservation within the area. Environment, for example, is a shared jurisdiction of the federal and provincial levels, but with much involvement of multi-municipality conservation authorities. With the inclusion of non-governmental organizations, over 100 organizations have some involvement in the management of this waterfront area that spans approximately 300 km.

While the distribution of responsibility among different organizations can provide an efficient means of developing expertise and stewarding resources, at the local level, due to the lack of effective coordination, it can lead to an incapacity to develop and implement initiatives. The problems created by this web of responsibility were termed "jurisdictional gridlock" by the Royal Commission, sponsored by the federal and provincial governments to explore potential solutions to the dual desire for development and conservation in this rapidly growing lakefront region.

The committee's former executive director, David Crombie, describes "jurisdictional gridlock" as a situation where "horizontal problems are being dealt with by vertical organisations" (Canadian Centre for Management Development 1996). The consequences of the difficulties involved in coordinating activities horizontally among a fragmented group of authorities, many of them hierarchical, is illustrated by the case of the ferry from Prince Edward Island. In 1986 the ferry was set to sail to the Caribbean with a cargo of two transformers filled with PCBs. When the deal faltered, the ferry was locked in Whitby harbour as government agencies argued about its fate. Because harbours are federal domain, the town of Whitby and the government of Ontario could not act. However, because of the potential toxicity of the cargo, Environment Canada would not let it sail. Nonetheless, Transport Canada continued to collect docking fees. In 1990, the ferry broke loose from its moorings and sank to the bottom of the harbour.

The need to overcome dilemmas that span the numerous jurisdictions was therefore evident. To achieve this, the Royal Commission instituted the Waterfront Regeneration Trust. While the Trust introduced a new agency to a landscape cluttered with them, the Trust was not regulatory and without statutory authority. Instead, it opted to work horizontally among the existing stakeholder and regulatory groups. The Trust attempted to identify where competing jurisdiction was countered by overlapping interests, leveraged the reconciliation of interests and proposed solutions to yield influence.

The Trust advanced the ecosystem approach advocated by the Royal Commission, favouring solutions that were inclusive of the natural system, extending beyond artificial barriers that emphasized more meaningful units, such as watersheds. To engage in decision-making frameworks that also encompass the communities' economic, social, and cultural environments, the Trust moved towards the development of a regime that valued widespread participation. As an advisory committee, the Trust brought persons together to meet, discuss, and facilitate discussion aimed at turning gridlock into action. Turning discussion into action required collaboration among the multiple interest groups and agencies implicated in the region.

The success of the Trust was ascribable to its lack of legal authority. It acted as a facilitator, arranging and mediating dialogues as required, connecting stakeholders and advising, ultimately helping them sort through their responsibilities and interests. The temporary and flexible nature of the Trust was also integral to its success. As the former executive director, Ron Doering, remarked about the 'messy' organization that lacked formal responsibilities, authority, and accountabilities: "Complexity cannot be managed, intellectually or practically, through increased control or top-down management. There is nothing linear about the environment. We need to be flexible and adaptive."

The messiness of the environment was matched by a messy institutional arrangement. Coastal problems are complex; competing interests and objectives must be balanced.

As noted by David Crombie, the Chair and Chief Executive Officer of the Trust, this can only be achieved by the extensive "talking and listening" that enables decision-makers to know the intricacies of the terrain, and allows stakeholders to "exchange information and experiences, discuss priorities, monitor progress, address common issues, and continue the momentum". The Trust was integral in the organization of the numerous minor steering committees that handled fragments of the overall problems facing the waterfront. It has also linked research and information networks, and used them to develop programmes. Often this resulted in subwatershed plans that fit within the framework of the larger lakeshore level plan and stakeholder involvement in the monitoring of progress and outcomes.

The Trust was successful in rallying stakeholders around plans, not only because it fostered participation, but because it also promoted greater awareness, understanding, access and recreational use of the waterfront and encouraged a sense of community pride. This link to community-level engagement was essential in encouraging the involvement of local service clubs (Waterfront Regeneration Trust 1995).

The local emphasis was also key to raising funds. In several circumstances, the proposals of the Trust found support by linking environmental objectives to existing government funding programmes for community-based projects of all sorts, rather than allowing them to collapse for lack of a single significant source of funds (Waterfront Regeneration Trust 1995).

Where there were numerous overlapping jurisdictions and diverse stakeholders, an approach was required that recognized the "chaos" that the diffusion of responsibility created, but was able to give it "order" through the mobilization of stakeholders around limited agreed objectives; to tackle the complexity of the situation. It was the coherence (consistency or cohesion are too rigid) that was created through informal influence that was the key to success, ultimately expropriating power from above in a temporary fashion. As the Lake Ontario Greenway Strategy outlines, they "coordinate the actions of existing agencies rather than impose solutions from above".

(b) The Gulf of Maine Environmental Information Exchange: a mesoscopic perspective

The Gulf of Maine Environmental Information Exchange (GOMINFOEX) exemplifies the importance of the four guiding principles—participation, subsidiarity, multistability, and the stewardship of organizational learning and relational leadership—in the development of a functional chaord.

GOMINFOEX is a regional knowledge-sharing network of governmental agencies, local non-profit organizations, and educational and research institutions, dispersed throughout the American states and Canadian provinces that border the Gulf of Maine. As described by Schroeder et al. (2001), the network is locally based, widely distributed, and non-hierarchical. While Schroeder et al. adequately describe the network and its origins, and the reader is encouraged to consult this document and the GOMINFOEX website, a brief outline is provided here to underscore the exemplary qualities.

The network grew out of the Gulf of Maine Council for the Marine Environment, a conglomeration of provincial, state, federal, and private sector partners that actively promoted public participation in environmental decision-making. The network arose as an effort to create a large-scale central data-sharing arrangement among the participating scientists, for use by resource managers. The diversity of information and uses for it, as well as a lack of resources to gather and maintain information, and the importance of encouraging participation and a sense of regional solidarity, led to a system with central access and dispersed responsibility for information collection, presentation, and storage, that extended beyond scientists to all interested parties.

The vision statement of GOMINFOEX stresses the sharing of information to maximize the benefits to coastal communities. The principal outcome sought through these exchanges is "to foster wider awareness of the range of interests and efforts that are alive in the region, so that participants can take the needs and goals of others into consideration as they attempt better to achieve their own" (Schroeder et al. 2001). Moreover, through increased awareness of the related projects of other GOMINFOEX members, interested stakeholders have forged partnerships and alliances, contributing to each other's success, and identifying additional projects that would be desirable. The result is a proliferation of partnerships where geographic proximities overlap with interests. Having fostered these processes, the network contributes to the main objective of the Gulf of Maine Council, i.e. to enhance participation in environmental initiatives throughout the region.

Secondary objectives of the network include enhancing the capacities of member agencies, and fostering a sense of regional citizenship. A people-centred approach has emerged, rather than a data-driven approach, and a distributed rather than a centralized system has been adopted. For example, on-line sharing is enriched by the sharing of other documents, and leads to holding face-to-face meetings. Other elements of the exchange focus on the ecosystem and the constitutive communities, to underscore and increase the sense of community in this region that transgresses provincial and national boundaries. This reframing of the traditional identities that are primarily attached to a nation, Canada or the U.S., or a state or province, is achieved by representing the region using maps that emphasize ecosystem characteristics or community elements. One such map omitted the political boundaries, and thus had a large impact on raising awareness of the natural characteristics that bind these communities (Kelly 1999).

The integration into the e-Atlas of technical reports, project information, and stories on the Gulf of Maine, enhances the range of interpretations not otherwise possible. The layering and real-time information collection and communication capacities of GIS systems, and GIS systems built from the ground up, based on public participation, are recognized to have an important role in the basic information-sharing component of the network.

Figure 14: Gulf of Maine Watershed

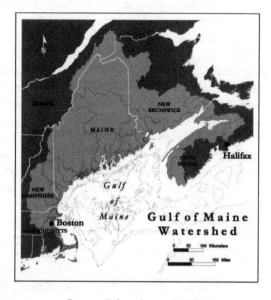

Source: Schroeder et al. 2001

The fostering of a regional identity, and the establishment and strengthening of relationships, may continue to build the coherence necessary to form flexible arrangements based on moral contracts, and to mobilize the necessary forces to reap the rewards of limited resources. In fact, in the area of fisheries, the recognition of local interdependence on the resource has led communities to collaborate and devise initiatives from the ground up, in response to the failures of their national resource management authorities. This may be just the type of arrangement required to balance the need for institutional resilience and learning.

The network has also generated peripheral benefits that demonstrate not only improved coordination, but that the groundwork for a social learning system can be installed through bottom-up processes. It has been acknowledged that information sharing benefits both decision-makers from government resource agencies, and those involved in community-based initiatives, by contributing to the tacit knowledge base that inevitably influences planning and policy-making. Moreover, sharing and dialogue has led participants to discover the range of interests in the region, instead of just the issues and efforts underway to address them. Members attempt to share their different worldviews, and have expressed a commitment to acknowledging the differences and striving to accommodate them. In addition, the partners have begun to perform exercises that differentiate between fact and value-based conflicts. It is this form of reframing that can lead to double-looped learning.

As described by Schroeder et al. (2001), this form of double-loop learning has been most prominent in community-based efforts to manage fisheries. Planning at this level must be highly inclusive, and decisions must be widely communicated, in order for governance structures to maintain their legitimacy. This bottom-up approach demands much public participation and is upheld by extensive systems for information exchange. The connections that develop between individuals, and the capacity building that this facilitates are the source of mutual learning and collaboration. However, not all collaboration and action is based on widespread consensus. In many instances, stakeholders have concentrated their efforts in different areas, focusing on different elements of the community plan, from promoting improved marine education to pursuing economic development (Schroeder et al. 2001).

This is an emerging information system that is currently in its infancy. One can see, however, that it is likely to remain evolutionary, and thus possibly avert the impediments that prevent most institutions from responding rapidly to change. In fact, no institution or member has a formal leadership role, and the development of central bureaucracies is forbidden. Rather, the notion that purposes, principles, and organizational structures must evolve together has been embraced. Thus, what began as an effort to exchange electronic data has matured into an endeavour to encourage participation, the distribution of resources, and a sense of identity and citizenship. In fact, it is now acknowledged that the development of this general sociality is a prerequisite for the full development of the network.

That government can catalyze this ground-up activity is demonstrated by the role of the Gulf of Maine Council on the Marine Environment's importance in developing the GOMINFOEX network. The Council assembles the federal and sub-national governments of the Gulf with industry, and exists to promote participation. The Council got the ball rolling, and from there this institution without a master has taken over.

(c) Australia: a macroscopic perspective
In the latter half of the twentieth century, Australia, like Canada, experienced developments in the oceans sector that resulted in overfishing and overcapacity

in the fishing industry; a lack of trust between industry, resource managers and scientists; a lack of input of user-groups in management plans; a perception that resource management services were not cost-effective; and increasing conflict (McColl and Stevens 1997). These socio-economic-political consequences, coupled with augmenting concern over the conservation of marine resources, provided the impetus for both countries to develop a comprehensive "ocean policy".

The policy that each country has presented over the last five years is reasonably similar, promoting an integrated management of ocean resources, such that planning and decision-making incorporates the economic, environmental, social, and cultural concerns of stakeholders, promoting multiple uses of marine spaces, while attempting to sustain the resource. Despite the fact that the Canadian Oceans Act and the Australian Oceans Policy employ similar terminologies and accentuate similar principles, there are differences in the institutional frameworks that have emerged from these policy overhauls that have substantially impacted the forms of governance that are emerging.

Both policies acknowledge the need for governments and industry to cooperate in order to reduce conflict and improve the effectiveness of resource management. However, in the case of Canada, there is an implicit unwillingness to relinquish the centralized control that has existed since the establishment of Fisheries and Oceans Canada. Australia, on the other hand, has adopted political mechanisms that distribute power over a greater number of actors, specifically enhancing the involvement of state and territorial governments and offering significant opportunity for industrial and civic organizations to participate in the decision-making process.

The first major divergence between the Canadian and Australian models may be noted at the federal level. The Australian regime vests the final responsibility for decisions on marine resources with their National Oceans Ministerial Board. The board is composed of the federal ministers from the departments that are implicated in decisions most likely to impact the oceans: industry, resources, fisheries, science, tourism, and shipping. Other ministers, such as the ministers for defence and foreign affairs for example, are incorporated when conditions warrant. There is in such a structure an implicit recognition that a negotiated approach is required to coordinate the multiple uses of ocean resources.

Through the establishment of a National Oceans Advisory Group, the Ministerial Board is provided the input of experts from industry, science, and conservation. In Canada, a similar advisory board exists, and advises the minister of fisheries and oceans; however, its role is immensely less important.

In addition to integrating the considerations of experts through the Advisory Board, and the integration of the ministries, the consultations that occur between the state and federal governments are coordinated through the ANZCC (Australian and New Zealand Environment and Conservation Council), a body designed specifically to coordinate the accommodation of cross-jurisdictional consultations. This is necessary as the state government has jurisdiction over fisheries out to three nautical miles, and the federal government has jurisdiction out to the limit of the exclusive economic zone (EEZ).

The second important difference between the Australian and Canadian regimes is the regional participatory approach endorsed in Australia. In fact, the primary function of the National Oceans Ministerial Board is to approve the plans of Regional Marine Steering Committees. Regional Committees are formed of government and non-government stakeholders. The government members represent federal and state agencies. The Regional Committees are responsible for developing regional plans that integrate the demands on ocean resources from multiple industrial sectors.

This delegated and integrated approach to the complex issues of marine resources is an extension of the regional and species approach to fisheries management that has existed since the 1992 establishment of the Australia Fisheries Management Authority (AFMA). The AFMA was instituted to transfer the administration of fisheries resources from a government department to a statutory authority. The authority has a corporate structure and a board of directors that are selected by the minister, but are nominated by government and industry officials, according to their expertise within the fields related to fisheries management, such as ecology, science, management, and processing and fishing.

The AFMA develops and submits plans for the fishing industry that must be approved by parliament. The minister responsible for the authority can only provide directions to the AFMA if they are consistent with the authority's objectives, and they too must be tabled through parliament (McColl and Stevens 1997). The citizen's voice is heard in parliament, but also directly, as local and fishery specific plans are publicly available and cannot be approved without consideration of those voices.

Under this regime, power is shared between industry and government. The AFMA has delegated the role of developing management plans to Management Advisory Committees (MACs). MACs have been established for the major fisheries, by geography and species. The MACs are primarily a joint government-industry body that consults and develops management arrangements. While the AFMA acknowledges that a consultative approach can be time-consuming and expensive, they believe "it is the key to gaining broader industry acceptance and ownership of management decision" (McColl and Stephens 1997).

Observers from within AFMA have noted that this consultative approach has resulted in "more informed discussion of management arrangements, research priorities and stock assessment" (McColl and Stephens 1997). Moreover, "instances of industry advocates or self-interest groups lobbying the Minister have almost ceased since the establishment of the AFMA" (McColl and Stephens 1997). This is significantly different from the Canadian regime, where partnerships are limited by the fact that the Minister maintains the "ultimate authority" over the resource, rather than delegating to a regional board (Lane and Stephenson 2000). Lobbying the minister, therefore, remains a daily reality at Fisheries and Oceans Canada.

The MACs have five industry representatives, a state or territorial government representative, a scientific member, an AFMA member and an independent chairperson. In addition, many now include an environmental and recreational fishing representative. This regime does not only promote a sharing of power, however, but a reallocation of resources as well. Fishery management plans often depend upon the sharing of information between industry, government, and scientists, regarding catch and effort data. The involvement that stakeholders have in the management process, and the fact that the AFMA recovers 100% of management costs related to the fisheries from industry, provides the impetus to co-operate actively. It is thus that they take a stake in the management and policy process, and the setting of research objectives.

The efforts of Australia, in the areas of fisheries and oceans, attest to a sincere commitment to distributed governance and a stronger regional autonomy. The greater range of voices consequently incorporated into decision-making frameworks allows a more comprehensive view of the implications of different policy options and, perhaps most importantly, places strategic and operational decisions in the hands of those that interact with the resource regularly, potentially enhancing the resilience of the overall system.

As is clear from these three examples, the four principles seem to make sense. But it is important to understand that these principles were not explicitly used to shape things in any of these cases. Both in the Waterfront and in the Gulf of Maine examples, what began as modest attempts at generating coherence have taken on a life of their own. While the overall results were not unwelcome, they were not initially planned. In the Australian case, the matter is still evolving, but the consequences of some of the original choices of collaborative technologies in changing mindsets and embracing distributed governance are undeniable.

Conclusion

The ocean world is a complex adaptive socio-technical system. It is clearly a world without a master. The ecological and economic importance of oceans, and the disastrous implications of a lack of effective coordination in the ocean world, have forced the discussion of its resilience onto the policy agenda of most nations. While the difficulties of governing a global commons are undeniable, the impossibility of doing so top-down is equally obvious.

The features of the emergent governance regime are difficult to define. Yet it has become obvious that the most likely contours of such a regime—for reasons of efficiency and resilience—are those of a distributed governance network.

Such a network is only emerging *par morceau* and *par étapes,* but it would appear to be inspired by some basic principles—participation, subsidiarity, multistability, and a regime-switch mechanism in case of crises.

It has been shown that distributed governance—even though it challenges the traditional state-centric centralized mindset—is workable at the micro, meso, and macro levels. But this is not, in and of itself, sufficient when it comes to persuading the skeptics and hypercentralists. Consequently, it is necessary to probe further into the ways in which a regime of distributed governance of oceans is likely to translate into mechanisms of polycentric governance, and technologies of collaboration. This is explored in the next chapter.

Chapter 10

Polycentric Governance and
Technologies of Collaboration*

> "We must learn that in complex systems
> we cannot do only one thing"
> Dietrich Dörner

Introduction

While important, the principles cited in the last chapter may appear to be insufficient for effective ocean stewardship. This is ascribable to a general distrust of self-governance, and to the dual challenge of (1) the ocean governance design not being approximated by a single game framework, and (2) it not being presumed that all the information available to the stakeholders can be synthesized in game-type matrices.

As a result of the first challenge, ocean governance must be conceived of as a set of multi-level games, in which the stakeholders must operate simultaneously and concurrently at several levels. As we shall see, this means that the game is polycentric and must be resolved by a set of integrated social contracts.. For the purposes of our preliminary exploration, it may be sufficient to consider only three levels: the global level, the specific ocean level, and the intra-ocean level.

As a result of the second challenge, ocean governance cannot be modelled as a game with complete information. It must be recognized that, in such a world, each stakeholder is a Bayesian rational actor who continually updates his/her beliefs on the basis of whatever information they find useful from whatever source,

---

* In collaboration with Kevin Wilkins.

including the behaviour of other actors. This is important because Bayesian rational actors, in a non-cooperative game with incomplete information, must find some way to implicitly correlate their behaviour.

To effect such coordination, the different actors must make use not only of their rationality and preferences but also of the rich repertoire of their historical experiences. Such a repertoire serves them well as basic references and focal points when all else fails. For instance, when participants in experimental games are asked to suggest, where in New York, acquaintances (who have agreed to meet on a certain day, at a certain time, but with the location for some reason having remained unclear) will tend to converge on Grand Central Station. In Paris, it might be the Eiffel Tower; in other capital cities, the characters' embassy. Such dimensions are impossible to model, and yet they provide "effective responses" to seemingly unsolvable conundrums. Such decisions are echoes of conventions or conventional wisdom that remain contingent on personal history.

To understand how best to meet these challenges, it is useful to examine polycentric games, design principles, and evolving priority rules (Schelling 1960; Ostrom 1990; McGinnis 2000). We deal with these issues in the first section of this chapter. In the second section, we examine some of the key levers, or families of mechanisms that might be used to ensure the requisite degree of collaboration.

Polycentric games, institutional design, and priority rules

(a) Polycentric games
A polycentric system is a label used to refer to "a political order in which multiple authorities serve overlapping jurisdictions". It is made up of a wide array of concurrent games, linked into complex networks of interactions. In such a system, it is presumed that "actors in any single game can draw on a vast array of informational cues and strategic interactions to help them understand the behaviour of other participants in that particular game. To do so, they can draw on commonly understood norms or rules, and they can use institutional procedures to organize their interactions" (McGinnis 2000:2).

Polycentric games connote an image of a network of overlapping and interlinked arenas of choice: operational choice (the world of action where individuals take action or adopt a strategy), collective choice (the world of collective decisions taken by officials, and enforceable against non-conforming individuals), and constitutional choice (the world of decisions about decision rules).

Obviously the arenas of choice are nested in broader games and constrained by them: constitutional choices defining broad orientations constrain collective choices by social groups, and collective choices constrain operational choices at the community level. But there is also a powerful learning feedback: as a result of operational level initiatives to meet local challenges, pressure is brought bottom-up on collective choice, and even on the constitutional framework, and forces them to evolve. Indeed, this is the sort of two-way learning loop that shapes all three arenas of choices over time.

In chapters 3 and 7, different images have been provided of this process of social learning that underpins such an evolution. A third version, presented here, is better equipped to throw some light on the choice dimensions in ocean governance. This one makes use of the three cascading worlds (global/constitutional, meso collective choices, and operational action in more local sites).

It is our view that oceans can be stylised as multi-level games pertaining to three layers of choices (global, single ocean, sub-oceanic site) and that corresponding to each of these three layers, there are rules that become progressively less constitutional and more operational as one proceeds from the global scene to sub-oceanic areas. The whole governance apparatus pertaining to oceans may well be inspired by the principles mentioned in the last chapter, but this will translate into quite different moral contracts among stakeholders because of the different nature of the tasks at hand. The law of the sea has a constitutional texture; the trust relationships at the local level make sense only in situ and regarding practical matters.

Polycentric games are often solved by conventions rooted in history and values. We have chosen the language of moral contracts to express these conventions.

Donaldson and Dunfee's integrative social contracts theory (1994) defines different layers of moral contracts that are developed from shared goals, beliefs, and attitudes, of groups of people or communities. These social contracts serve as a tool to measure the moral performance of organizations.

These moral contracts are at three levels: hypernorms (core human rights, obligation to respect the dignity of each person, etc.—at the core of constitutional arrangements) that would apply generally to all concerns; macro social contracts, providing conditions under which the different communities can develop their micro social contracts—contracts that best serve the different communities and correspond to the earlier level of collective choice; and micro social contracts that guide action at the operational level. Fritzsche (1997) has sketched the different layers of moral contracts pertaining to different relationships, and illustrates somewhat the sort of guiding norms, values, and rules pertaining to it.

Integrative moral contracts
Hypernorms
Primum non nocere (first do no harm)

Personal freedom
Physical security and well-being
Informed consent
Political participation

Macro social contract
Moral free space
Free consent and right to exit
Compatible with hypernorms
Respect of international agreements
Priority rules

Micro social contracts
Don't lie in negotiations
Honour all contracts
Give hiring preferences to native born
Give contract preference to local suppliers
Provide a safe workplace

Source: Fritzsche 1997:44

In the ocean world, such social contracts would appear to be quite sensible. One can easily imagine a cascade of social contracts that are designed to fit particular circumstances, while maintaining the overall integrity of the ocean governance.

One may readily suggest that hypernorms are likely to be negotiated at the global level, i.e., as an evolving form of law of the sea. The stakeholders are likely to be nation states, together with their strategic advisory groups, and the norms evolving from such negotiations are likely to remain rather vague.

One may expect to go further in macro social contracts, negotiated by a smaller number of stakeholders around particular oceans.

One may surmise that the array of forms, and the multiplicity of bilateral arrangements will create a very dense network of relationships of the sort we have noticed in the Gulf of Maine. Another example might be the Association of Caribbean States.

But discussions at these three levels cannot be conducted in isolation. We are faced with tri-level games in which negotiations are carried out by somewhat different stakeholders at each level, in ways that have to ensure not only a basic coherence of the overall game, but also compatibility between the different levels, and an adherence by lower-order arrangements to the norms of the higher-order conventions.

d.   Institutional design and evolving priority rules

Until such time as the conventions at the global level, the rules at the ocean-specific level, and the norms at the intra-ocean level have been negotiated and made coherent, the mishmash of existing practices will prevail. And yet that mishmash is not necessarily ineffective. The powers of self-organization are greatly underestimated, and there is no reason to expect disaster, even if there is agreement on only a few guiding principles. The chaordic VISA is a case in point.

But one needs to keep in mind the fundamental stewardship function that is bound to require that certain design principles in institutional architecture and certain priorities in decision-making be respected.

On the design front, Ostrom (1990: 90) has identified a few of the elements that would appear to account for the success of some governance arrangements. However, it is not impossible to provide some guidance about the sort of mechanisms likely to be effective:

- clearly defined boundaries
- congruence between rules and local conditions
- wide participation of those affected by operational rules
- monitoring
- graduated sanctions when rules are violated
- rapid and low cost conflict resolution mechanisms
- right of appropriators to devise their own institutions.

On the priorities in decision-making, Donaldson and Dunfee (1985) have proposed a set of priority rules within the context of their integrated social contracts framework:

- transactions within a community when there are no adverse external effects should be governed by the community norms;
- community norms should be applied as long as they have no external adverse effects on other humans and communities;
- the more extensive the community which is the source of the norm, the greater the priority that should be given to the norm;
- norms essential to the maintenance of the socio-economic environment should be given priority over those potentially damaging to that environment;
- when multiple conflicting norms exist, patterns of consistency among the alternative norms provide a basis for prioritization.

These design principles and priority rules are provided only as an example of the general sort of guideposts that might be required to ensure the appropriate stewardship of an otherwise self-governed ocean world, steered by the principles of participation, subsidiarity, multistability and the safeguard of a stewardship of organizational learning through relational leadership.

The central question has to do with the ways in which one might be able to engineer such a governance-cum-stewardship.

Key lever points

Such a regime can neither be imposed top-down, nor be expected to emerge in one swoop bottom-up. It requires the auxiliary support of technologies of collaboration that take advantage of key lever points.

The notion of technologies of collaboration may for some readers wrongly connote the application of information and communication technologies as devices allowing a central agent or pace-setter to control and manipulate complex systems, through the generation of appropriate quasi-mechanical incentive reward systems. Such an interpretation fits quite well some efforts by central agencies to impose their dominion. However, this does not fit the notion of ocean governance that we are trying to define.

Complex systems like oceans are not truly controllable by any single pace-setter. They are always in a process of self-organization, emergence, and adaptation. Complex adaptive systems do not draw their guidance from a single "executive branch", but from a bottom-up aggregation of simple mechanisms of adjustment, or rules, into complex assemblages of interactive agents capable of rather sophisticated adaptations of their own. Intervention from above may be necessary at times, but it has to be in a form that takes maximum advantage of the self-governance forces.

Over the recent past, there has been much exploration of these complex adaptive systems, but it is only in the last decade that there have been significant advances in the design of ways to exploit self-organization and its laws to subtly modify complex systems (Johnson 2001).

In order to be able to intervene in effective ways, one must be able to map the lever points in a complex adaptive system. A vaccine, for instance, is a lever point capable of getting the immune system to "learn" about a disease, and to produce enough antibodies to make the system immune, and to avoid having the system learn about the disease "on line" (Holland 1995).

Oceans as complex adaptive systems have such lever points (and even tipping points) wherein small amounts of input produce large directed change. The central challenge in the design of an effective regime is to gauge the properties and mechanisms underpinning the process of emergence, to identify these lever points, and to make the highest and best use of them.

For oceans, this search reveals three intervention domains.

First, the "right kind" of interventions—i.e., the use of effective technologies of collaboration; second, the appropriate use of monitoring, accountability, and learning schemes; third, a paradigm shift in mindset on the part of all those involved in oceans to recognize the new drivers that are likely to be useable as lever points.

(a)   The right kind of direct interventions

To be the architects and stewards of collaborative regimes, state agencies must be able to employ processes that move stakeholders past defensive and adversarial strategies and nurture collaboration. Common obstacles to collaboration are the historical and ideological barriers of stakeholders: power disparities, cultural norms, different perceptions of risk, the technical complexity of issues, institutional incentives, etc. (Gray 1989).

Technologies of collaboration are the ground-level processes and incentive reward structures that overcome these barriers and nurture social learning. The word "technology" in this sense refers to techniques and social processes that help increase knowledge exchange, generate trust and commitment, and ensure a more effective coordination.

They provide guideposts that shape the expectations, incentives, and reward systems that induce cooperation, as well as the conventions, moral contracts, and regimes of accountability that are necessary for cooperation to prevail and survive. I believe that the most useful technologies of collaboration will include: forums and public spaces, loci for dialogue and multilogue, capacity and competency building, and exchange of information schemes.

These are all instruments capable of generating "reframing", and frame reconciliation is the key to social learning. The points of view of the different stakeholders are informed by what Schön and Rein (1994) call "frames" (i.e., underlying structures of beliefs, perceptions and appreciations) which are different from group to group. These frames are usually tacit and exempt from attention and immune from appeals to facts and reasoned arguments. Without frame reconciliation, little progress can be anticipated in the collaborative debates.

Forums and public agoras

As Lenihan reminds us, the historical notion of the "commons" refers to a public space that is a "locus of information and learning, support and solidarity, friendship, commerce, entertainment and connectedness" (Lenihan 2002). The governance dilemma created by the complexity of the oceans is increasingly portrayed as a problem of cooperation and learning. So it is a commons dilemma of another sort.

217

Observations from simulations of commons dilemmas demonstrate how the alteration of individual frames of reference can facilitate cooperation. Subjects have been shown to enter the dilemmas with "egocentric interpretations of fairness"—the common assumption by appropriators that the rule that benefits them is the fairest (Wade-Benzoni 1996). In other cases, stakeholders assume their way of looking at the problem is best, and all the different perspectives are regarded as inadequate (Gray 1989:12). However, "as resource appropriators learn more about other users' perceptions of fairness—and the reasons for those perceptions—the user's own view of the fairest result grows less biased", and increases the possibility of coming to mutually acceptable agreements (Baron and Jurney 1993).

Within a governance regime that emphasizes social learning, the processes that influence stakeholder interaction are critical, because of their important role in the exchange of codified and tacit forms of knowledge. The requirement to build the necessary trust and communicative capabilities will be critical to the ability of the governing institution to establish and maintain a social learning system for the oceans.

For agreements to spontaneously evolve there must be a modicum of freedom of association and the flexibility to create arrangements that match the requirements of specific circumstances. In such an environment, "traditional mechanisms for ensuring accountability that constrain flexibility and creativity need to be changed" (Wondolleck and Yaffee 2000:232). This demands that moral contracts form the foundation of the regime, for "[t]he formal law, [...] is less likely to provide a successful default regime of direct regulation that is sufficiently contextual and dynamic" (Dagan and Heller 2001).

Formal law "is often not powerful enough, by itself, to establish directly the trust, cooperation, and mutual reliance that any successful commons requires for the day-to-day routines of self-governance" (Dagan and Heller 2001). Therefore, trust becomes an important outcome: trust enhances probability of success, and success reinforces trust, creating a cycle where trust "builds on trust" and may "grow with use" (Pettit 1995).

But this essential part of effective ocean stewardship requires the existence of a place for public discussions and debate, and in modern times such places have either disappeared or have been marginalized. As a result, providing forums and creating such public spaces (that are necessary in an informational commons) is an important aspect of collaboration.

Fostering dialogue and multilogue
Public spaces are necessary but not sufficient. They merely provide the boards needed to foster dialogue and multilogue. Without deliberation, one cannot hope

to generate and re-inforce moral contracts, and thereby contribute to building and sustaining the informational commons.

As Wondolleck and Yaffee (2000:52) suggest, the hierarchical and paternalistic process of natural resource management agencies has led them to make decisions on the basis of "their sense of science and public interest". This arrangement "pushes groups to accentuate their differences rather than searching for common ground" and "judicial processes are explicitly adversarial; groups are cast as opponents who need to make the strongest case for their own interests, and only one will win. It is in no one's interest to think of outcomes that split the difference, or produce creative, win-win decisions" (Wondolleck and Yaffee 2000:51).

Comparisons of successful and unsuccessful endeavours to resolve resource management disputes (Wondolleck and Yaffee 2000) indicate that the "attitude" that stakeholders bring to the table greatly influences the possibility of collaboration. Preconceptions (even presumptions that the parties are not even aware they are harbouring) are powerful impediments to double-looped learning. The heavy emphasis on adversarial approaches and a corporatist perspective can impede reframing.

When stakeholders are steered into deliberative processes that focus their attention on carefully defining the problem, they are often guided away from the biases they bring to the process, and they can move away from their preconceived notion of the solution and into explorations with the group. This requires that the solution-finding process be led by groups that can move people away from the conflicting positions of stakeholders and towards their common interests.

But epistemic and cognitive communities need to be persuaded right from the start that there is something to be gained/learned from information-sharing and collaboration, so the first step involves teaching stakeholders that collaborative solutions may exist. A lack of precedent needs to be countered by knowledge of exemplary arrangements that have succeeded. Images and ideas of success can be more influential than equations or prescriptions (Wondolleck and Yaffee 2000:18). Moreover, images of success can also be accomplished by working on more modest objectives in the early phases, to build support for collaborative processes (Wondolleck and Yaffee 2000:187).

A vision that collaboration is possible often comes from entrepreneurial individuals who yield influence on a local level. "Many collaborative partnerships have gotten underway and succeeded due to the efforts of dedicated, energetic individuals who worked at being proactive and entrepreneurial." (Wondolleck and Yaffee 2000:177) Oftentimes the entrepreneurs achieve this by exploiting existing social networks to "create effective communication links, mobilize support, and achieve a legitimacy that they could never achieve on their own" (Wondolleck and

Yaffee 2000:185). Often the individual can mobilize support and break people out of purely competitive notions by framing the issue as "us as innovators against the possibility of failure" (Wondolleck and Yaffee 2000:190).

This step towards collaborative governance depends upon leaders who can act in the capacity of an *animateur* and a *rassembleur,* overcome the current difficulties and blockages facing stakeholders in ocean governance. A leader of this sort often has an informal authority, such as position and influence in a network, expertise and knowledge, or credibility to stakeholders. The credibility of such a third party can provide assurances that concerns are addressed and positive outcomes are possible (Gray 1989:61).

When collaborative processes do take hold, they are often stymied by interpersonal dynamics that are left unmediated. To keep dialogue from becoming debate, it is necessary to have a facilitator who can keep the flow of dialogue going so that mistrust can be minimized (Yankelovich 1999). Indeed, Wondolleck and Yaffee (2000:33), in their extensive observations of successful collaborative processes, find that third-party engagement is often required to prevent disputes from hindering the whole process.

A facilitator can establish a sense of fairness in the process, which is critical (Gray 1989:93), and can help overcome psychological barriers to allow concessions to be made (Gray 1989:164). In most successful processes, stakeholders (through the action of this third party) have adopted ground-rules that shift the focus away from blaming others, and redirect the attention of the group to the problem at hand in a constructive manner (Wondolleck and Yaffee 200:145). Successful facilitators often establish rules of process on how to deal with other parties in a tactful manner and establish a climate of trust (Gray 1989:15).

The biases that hinder mutual respect are often ideological. As described by Clark and Reading (1994): "Effective information transfer is further hampered by the different ways in which professionals from different fields communicate (via jargon) and learn. [...] The highly specialized training of experts can thus prevent them from understanding other perspectives." Such barriers are accentuated when the experts "defend their disciplines and discount the opinions of 'outsiders'" (Clark and Reading 1994). Another role of the facilitator is to prevent these professional frameworks from hindering collaboration through the creation of a group culture that exposes biases and favours the reframing of perspectives.

The facilitator must also use conflict as a positive force that advances issues through the identification of inadequate or misleading information (Mitchell 1995), or any form of impaired probing (Lindblom 1990). The most important purpose of a facilitator is engaging stakeholders in dialogue that breaks them out of common assumptions that "their interests directly conflict with the other party's interests" (Bazerman 1986), and allows them to reconcile seemingly divergent frameworks.

Capacity and competency building
The third technology of collaboration is capacity building. It is often required so that stakeholder representatives have the communicative competence to articulate their views. This not only has the impact of reducing the tendency for the best communicators to influence the process, but it also enhances the ability for each stakeholder to engage in dialogue that can build the necessary trust to sustain the governing network.

The education of stakeholders can enhance appreciation of the complexity of choices facing resource managers, and allow them to better comprehend the biases in their frame of reference. Moreover, a technical understanding of the numerous factors influencing resource conditions and decisions taken regarding resources prevents stakeholders from identifying a "scapegoat". That is, it prevents them from developing the perception that others are responsible for declining resource availability, and demanding that sacrifices are borne only by others (Wade-Benzoni 1996). It will also enhance the ability of decision-makers to reframe scientific advice presented using a probabilistic approach that outlines the likelihood of certain outcomes under alternative management decisions, and thus improves the decisions of resource managers (Shepherd and McGlade 1992).

The required competencies can be grouped into four categories: contextual competencies; interpersonal skills; creating an effective organizational climate; and value systems (Michael 1980, 1988a, 1988b; Morgan 1988).

In the first category (contextual competencies) we can identify a number of important skills and tools that are unlikely to be developed by traditional management techniques: acknowledging uncertainty, recognizing the full implications of the fact that there is no reliable theory of social change; developing a capacity to entertain multiple logics simultaneously; accepting and embracing errors; and reframing problems to explore new solutions.

The second category (interpersonal skills) includes a whole range of communication skills and tools that are going to be required in a variety of contexts: consultation, negotiation, deliberations, conflict resolution, facilitation, action as a broker, a preceptor, an educator, an *animateur*. There is also a need for the capacity to adopt new roles and attitudes, according to the specific characteristics of a particular issue or process.

In the third competency grouping (creating an effective institutional environment), one might retain the central importance of facilitating a shift toward perceiving the organization as a learning system; a capacity to truly empower individuals, and a culture of productivity, of responsiveness, of creativity. These are the core elements of a learning culture. Actors should then learn "process" skills aimed at improving their ability to structure and facilitate efforts towards problem-solving (Wondolleck and Yaffee 2000:218).

In the fourth category (value systems), there is a new ethic driven by the emerging realities of interdependence. In our economic and political cultures, our values often still emphasize individual rights and autonomy, whereas the circumstances of life make imperative the acceptance of obligations and interdependence (Michael 1988a). This ethic forces a redefinition of leadership: away from leaders as authoritative generals to leaders as catalysts of change and creativity—removing obstacles that prevent followers from making creative and effective decisions by themselves (O'Toole and Bennis 1992). These obstacles are at the heart of the move away from rigid bureaucracies and hierarchies.

Information exchange schemes
The final dimension of collaboration relates to processes. Observers of successful collaborative processes note that, through dialogue, opposing groups develop relationships that allow them to respect differences and "agree to disagree without attacking each other" (Wondolleck and Yaffee 2000:101). This process of successful relationship building comes forth through dialogue in which individuals generate the cohesiveness to overcome different values, interests, status, political orientations, and professional backgrounds (Hackett et al. 1994).

As observed by Ostrom (1990), a forum for stakeholder interaction and conflict resolution is common among enduring common property resource arrangements. Similarly, Hackett (1994) found that face-to-face communication contributed to efficient rule formation. This occurs when actors are steered away from initial positions, and focus on a reframed definition of the problem that emphasizes common interests rather than their proposed solution (Wondolleck and Yaffee 2000:128).

In order to search for answers to difficult quandaries, it is often necessary to explore many potentially useful but seemingly impossible directions. More often than not, this process is hindered by important assumptions that one is not even aware that one is making. Revealing these underlying presumptions and informing actors of the presumptions of others prove crucial in any collaborative process: "Collaboration operates on the premise that the assumptions that disputants have about the other side and about the nature of the issues themselves are worth testing. The premise is that testing these assumptions and allowing a constructive confrontation of differences may unlock heretofore disguised creative potential." (Gray 1989: 13)

Thus it becomes necessary for stakeholders to engage in discussions that reveal their priorities, assumptions, and values. In many cases, this allows them to collaborate to develop a shared vision of the future (Constanza et al. 1999). Effective stakeholder forums that facilitate exchange are an important step in the creation of a collaborative governance regime.

These four collaboration techniques can breathe life into the abstract governance regime pertaining to oceans.

(b) Accountability structures

While the moral contracts that are founded in trust and norms of reciprocity form the foundation for collaborative processes and negotiated arrangements, accountability structures are required to ensure the continuity of such arrangements. Collaboration holds great promise, but must be bounded by mechanisms to ensure accountability. Cheating, shirking, and abuse of power can never be completely eliminated; as long as the possibility of free riding exists, the continued cooperation of stakeholders requires processes that minimize such behaviours and provide those who do cooperate with the assurance that their efforts towards collective objectives are warranted. In addition, many agreements falter when implementation is ignored, so accountability structures are imperative to ensuring the continuing commitment of stakeholders.

Monitoring and enforcement

Monitoring and enforcing marine regulations is both difficult and expensive. Enforcement is commonly the largest cost of regulatory programmes (Wade 1987). However, various researchers have observed that compliance with fishery regulations is typically in the 50–90% range, despite a less than 1% probability of getting caught (Kuperan and Sutinen 1998; Sutinen and Gauvin 1989; Furlong 1991). This suggests that compliance is largely a normative decision based on a sense of moral obligation, or social influences such as a desire for peer approval (Bean 1990), rather than self-interested decisions by actors who weigh potential gain against the severity of sanctions, as deterrence models assume.

Normative models of compliance assume that compliance decisions on internal norms of what is just, moral, and appropriate, may have utility for the management of ocean resources. Compliance occurs because participants perceive a collective objective to be obtained, and perceive that others are complying with the rules (Ostrom 1990; Klandermans 1992). As indicated by Ostrom (1990), "commitment is obtained by providing rules, monitoring compliance and enforcing them". In the most effective resource management systems, the users act as monitors and are accountable to the group: the monitoring rules bring potential defectors and victims together. They provide limits on defection strategies.

It is thus not surprising to observe that "where resource users defer to a regulatory authority, they prefer authorities who they trust and know, with whom they share common attributes, and who treat them with dignity and respect" (Van Vugt and de Cremer 1999). Central governments are less effective at rule enforcement because their relationship with resource users is rarely founded on trust.

Nevertheless, the necessity for coercive measures is evident. Even those that argue against government control agree that reputation and shared norms are insufficient in developing commitment. Some coercion is required for compliance, as the temptation to adopt defection strategies will otherwise arise (Ostrom 1990; Feeny et al. 1996).

In a collaborative system, it is the regulators who should also be involved in monitoring and enforcement. The law then serves as a backdrop to the user-based monitoring and enforcement regime. As described by Dagan and Heller: the commitment that most appropriators have to the group is an essential component of the success of the appropriation regimes described by Ostrom. When the probability of future interactions is reduced, the incentive to engage in cooperative behaviour is reduced as retaliation becomes unlikely. While moral codes are likely to prevent cheating in most circumstances, law can play a supportive role and can "supply the anti-opportunistic devices that reassure prospective commoners that they will not be abused for cooperating" (Dagan and Heller 2001:578).

Collective reporting and feedback loops
In a study of twenty collaborative efforts in the area of forest management, Wondolleck and Yaffee (2000: 149) found that commitment was "the single most significant difference between successful and unsuccessful negotiations". Commitment to a collaborative approach, and to the realisation of objectives arrived at through negotiation, resulted in a greater likelihood of success and enhanced stakeholder satisfaction (Wondolleck and Yaffee 2000: 149). Collective reporting can be an important method of maintaining commitment, because it provides a reminder of the collective objectives, and reinforces the fact that consultation has resulted in genuine efforts to achieve those goals.

Observations from business and natural resource management indicate that first-step ventures or partnerships with specific joint activities build relationships and help the partners learn to work together (Kanter 1994). Researching facts together allows parties to forge interpersonal bonds rather than seeing other stakeholders as adversaries (Gray 1989). Moreover, a mutual examination of relevant data provides a common framework for discussion regarding differing interests (Gray 1989).

Collective reports may centre on resource conditions or management outcomes. In either case, they reinforce commitment. Social ties provide valuable feedback.

This feedback regarding resource conditions and the effectiveness of management processes is also likely to improve the functioning of a social learning system (Lane and Stephenson 1997; Stephenson et al. 1999).

360-degree and softer accountabilities
Defining accountability in a single direction, or with reference to only one stakeholder, or without taking account of the context, is extremely dangerous. It would amount to assuming that only one dimension is of consequence, and presuming that all other forms of accountability can be regarded as irrelevant or secondary in some sense. Yet the notion of accountability is still not widely regarded as a 360-degree process, i.e., as pertaining to all the stakeholders surrounding any one official.

The framework proposed by Robert Nozick (1981) with ethics as its foundation is most useful in analyzing accountability, for accountability is in a way the flip side of ethics. Nozick presents ethics as a tension between the moral forces that push persons because of their inner values to act in certain ways (the supply side, as an economist would put it) and the moral forces that pull persons to act in certain ways as a result of expectations by others (the demand side, as an economist would put it). Ethical action, he suggests, is the result when the moral push is equal or greater than the moral pull, and there is an ethical gap when the push is less than the pull.

The reason why this loose framework is very useful is that it applies easily to a vast network of relationships among very many different stakeholders, who may have various levels (legal, organizational, professional, political, etc.) among them.

Dubnik (1996) uses the Nozick push-and-pull framework, and applies it to four types of institutional forms in order to illustrate eight species of accountability.

Table 2: Species of accountability

Settings	Moral forces	
	Conduct of accountability External moral pull	Accountability of conduct Internal moral push
Legal	Liabilities	Obligations
Organizational	Answerability	Obedience
Professional	Responsibility	Fidelity
Political	Responsiveness	Amenability

Source: Dubnik 1996.

On the pull or demand side, one finds an array of institutional factors that frame the challenges faced by any official in the face of diverse, multiple, and conflicting expectations—ways to ensure the fulfilment of the legal, organizational, professional, and political expectations. But there is a flip side to that coin: on the push or supply side, the dominant factors are more personal and may be regarded as some sort of internalized drive to act ethically that materializes in some traits: the internalized sense of obligation, obedience, fidelity or loyalty, and amenability (i.e., a desire to actively pursue the public interest).

This ethical approach to accountability has the merit of embodying a variety of tensions between supply and demand, and to allow different degrees of internalization or embodiment of a moral push along different spectra. One may readily imagine a graduated progression between the external pull and the internal push at various degrees of moral development in the sense of Kohlberg (1981), and there may be some co-relation between the degree of moral development at those different levels. But it would be unwise to assume that in a network-type net of relationships, every stakeholder will have the same ethical valence. Indeed, this may well be an important source of flexibility in the adjustment mechanism: the same fit does not need to be there at all levels, and there may be quite wide variations in the nature of the norms internalized. They may be universal hypernorms, or globally-based or community-based norms.

(c) Four drivers

While raw power struggles, and complex game-like interdependencies are having an impact on ocean governance, our sense is that, in the longer run, cognitive or epistemic communities are likely to dominate the scene. They are the communities of practice that are the major producers and users of information and knowledge about oceans, and the most fundamental stakeholders. Their participation and information inputs are essential. While these epistemic communities may not appear to have the upper hand on official terrain, they hold the most strategically important positions and resources.

The mobilization of communities of practice, with the help of the developments triggered by new technologies, will effect a dramatic shift in mindset.

These developments are: the rise of e-governance; the growing sophistication of new technologies like geographic information systems (GIS); the emergence of informational ecologies and commons—the domain of publicly-accessible information; and the development of new forms of organization like chaords (a crasis of chaos and order) designed explicitly to bring some basic coherence and survivability to organizations in a complex adaptive world.

These four broad sweeping forces are not in any way restricted to any particular policy field. They have dramatically transformed governance in all sectors and areas. But while they have been a source of concern in stable traditional sectors, and the source of much unwanted turbulence, they may have a most beneficial impact in sectors already living with this sort of turbulence.

None of these four areas of effervescence have been properly mapped and subdivided yet. They remain terrain still being cleared. They themselves are perspectives *en émergence*.

E-governance

The notion of e-governance is a somewhat diffracted one. It has been used to connote a variety of realities. In our context, the notion is used to refer to the new family of governance regimes that has evolved as a result of the commutative revolution (Guillaume 1999). This revolution has triggered the erosion of traditional communities, and the emergence of a new sociality (i.e., a new form of social cement) based on much weaker ties. These weaker ties are rooted in the fact that individuals have become more spectral (i.e., diffracted into a multiplicity of roles in which they invest only a portion of their emotional commitment and resources). This has led to a certain anonymity, and to new forms of partial and temporary identities developed by persons who have a multiplicity of attachments, none of which exercise dominion over their whole behaviour. In this world created by the commutative revolution, any person can choose to connect or disconnect at will, and can modulate his attachments to any other portion of the system at any moment. This enables any agent to avoid being pinned down to one location, identity, etc. and forces the development of relationships based on weaker ties, from which the agent can at any time disengage.

There have always been networks of that sort, based on more or less robust ties. However, as commutation has become much easier (i.e., as agents have become able to engage or disengage more easily, rather than being trapped in particular settings) networks have become more fluid, less constraining, and better able to serve social learning, since such flexibility allows for a much smoother possibility of adapting to the evolving context.

This greater looseness of networks, and the continuous process of dis-integration and re-integration that accompanies social learning, puts a much greater emphasis on the ways in which connectedness will materialize. The commutative revolution has entailed a sort of "dematerialization" and "virtualization" of those linkages. What was in the past based on blood ties, or formal contracts, tends today to be built on more ephemeral, fluid, and informal relations.

Communication technologies have made possible the operationalization of these "fragile communities" and their development as cyberhoods. The Internet is already serving as the basic tool to build a peculiarly varied array of such fluid communities.

The emergence of these more fluid and informal rapports has had an impact on traditional organizational forms. They have all become more fragile and temporary. This has in turn transformed the governance process, and made it easier (since the organizational system to be governed is immensely more malleable) on the one hand, yet more difficult on the other (since the temporary and evanescent nature of all rapports makes the governing task much more daunting).

The ocean world remains obviously anchored in a solid material and natural system. However, the new communication technologies have already transformed much of the production process built on it. Every stakeholder is now involved in a multiplicity of networks, yet is related to others in a more tenuous way. This means that governance as effective coordination is faced with new challenges. One needs to establish a coordination of stakeholders that have significantly less in common and less of a sense of identity and commitment. The links among them have also become increasingly virtual, in the sense that the governing institutions have become less representative and more deliberative and participative.

The high-speed, high-risk socio-technical systems emerging in the post-commutative revolution have had to become more entrepreneurial and more cooperative. But to achieve such a degree of co-opetition (word coined by Brandenburger and Nalebuff 1996), one must meet three basic conditions: first, one must develop a minimum of trust among these weakly-connected agents; second, one must find an answer to the dual problem of information dispersion and agent motivation; third, one must find ways to neutralize the impact of the negative unintended consequences of the governing structure in place.

This has generated a demand for a new sort of state, capable of ensuring that the higher risks would be shared somewhat fairly, and of nurturing the requisite degree of trust necessary for collaborative governance to thrive. The sort of state likely to do the job has to find the right balance between the need to protect the persons negatively impacted by change, and the need to help those who require the assistance of the state to ensure the requisite amount of social learning and transformation.

In the face of this important governance challenge, two reactions appear to be in good currency.

First, there is the "governmentality approach", that is based on the presumption that nothing has fundamentally changed, and builds on efforts by the state to use a panoply of instruments to manipulate representations in order to keep hierarchical control on this turbulent world. This is a strategy based on a perceptive awareness of the fears and anguish of the population, on an apt use of this knowledge to persuade the citizenry that the state has their interests at heart, and on a clever use of instruments to lead them to voluntarily submit to the canonical position of the state, and to rationalize their voluntary submission in the name of self-realization.

Second, there is the "social learning approach", that is based on an effort to transform dynamically through better use of collective intelligence via distributed governance and a transformed state—the Commutator State. This approach is based on a redefinition of the underpinning logic of the state: from a logic rooted in a propensity to centralize in order to be able to redistribute, to a logic of learning based on the role of the state as facilitator and *animateur*. It squarely faces the challenges of e-governance through three complementary strategies: a strategy of connexity (to guard against exclusion), a strategy of catalysis to boost collective intelligence and accelerate social learning), and a strategy of completude (to engineer additional new possible technologies of collaboration in the face of governance failures) (Paquet 2000d).

The first approach is tempting for those state officials who are in denial vis-à-vis the new realities, and are crippled by a centralized mindset. It serves mainly to sustain "la raison d'État" —a state geared entirely to its own sustenance and using society as an instrument. The second approach entails the deployment of a distributed governance which challenges the centralized mindset in good currency, builds on the highest and best use of collective intelligence, and on experimentation. While the second approach is the only viable one, one should not underestimate the dynamic conservatism at play, and the vulnerability of the citizenry to the manipulation of state officials bent on defending their power.

In a collaborative e-governance regime, the key element to success is the ability of the institutional order to facilitate innovation through multi-looped learning. Building such a regime rests upon four basic objectives: 1) improved knowledge of the natural, social, and institutional environments; 2) improved knowledge use; 3) the integration of syncretic mindsets; and 4) sufficient social capital to engage in collaborative endeavours. The governance regime we have outlined stresses the development of a negotiated order that contributes to the realization of each of these objectives.

Communication and information technologies have contributed greatly to the evolution of the more distributed form of governance that is emerging on the global scene. At the same time that they contribute to the dismantling of centralized and hierarchical structures they also provide important means for enhanced learning, and for the creation of the transversal linkages important to supporting the networks that are emerging within the knowledge economy.

New technologies
The techniques of collaboration outlined earlier can be filled in by information and communication technology. Because communication and information technologies have the potential to improve the quantity and quality of data

available to decision-makers, and because they can improve the linkages between stakeholders, they can make a positive contribution to the good governance of ocean resources. The linkages are important because within a social learning regime this can lead to greater employment of resources to increase collective intelligence, and potentially lead to improved knowledge use and more double-looped learning. Technology in this case is an enabler.

There is no doubt that the extent of learning and the processes that generate learning can be greatly enhanced through the use of information and communication technologies. In the context of oceans, geomatic technologies show particular promise. Geomatics is an evolving discipline that is concerned with the acquisition, transformation, management, and distribution of spatially referenced data. In particular, geographic information systems (GIS) and web-based extension of this technology can play an integral role. Their contribution to both single and double-looped learning enables the substitution of hierarchical and centralized regimes with ones that are distributed and fortified by e-governance.

While traditionally seen as a decision-support system, a mere tool that improves the assembly of information available to decision-makers, it is increasingly being recognized that GIS can influence the process and extent of learning within a system (Hendriks 2000). GIS technologies have the capacity to enable restructuring and reframing (i.e. changing the vision that underpins an organization, a rethinking of its role, purpose, priorities, and objectives).

From the perspective of restructuring, the main contribution of GIS to the learning process is assistance in scanning the environment, the creation of links between people that would not otherwise be connected, and enhanced organizational memory through the building of databases (Hendriks 2000). GIS technologies, and web-based ones in particular, assist the integration of information across organizations (Campbell and Masser 1991). The combination and layering of information, not to mention the social processes required to coordinate sharing, can stimulate inter-organizational alliances (Kumar and van Dissel 1996).

The highly visual elements of GIS technologies can also lead to transformations of perspectives. As stakeholders share perspectives and contrast values there can be enhanced understanding and reconsideration of what the organization is in relation to its environment. Mental models of the organization and/or of the environment can be integrated, transformed, generated or destroyed. Processes, rather than outputs, then become dominant. As described by Talen (2000), "the goal of bottom-up GIS is not to capture all meaning, but rather to strengthen the quality and depth of communication about residents' issues and preferences".

The reframing process can be stimulated in a GIS environment because visualization and data models produce and communicate interpretations. Individuals working on separate projects on a common map or database learn more about each other's work and perspectives, and better identify conflicting interpretations (Hendriks 2000).

The potential for GIS technologies to accelerate restructuring and reframing within group processes has been demonstrated by the Gulf of Maine Environmental Information Exchange (GOMINFOEX). As described earlier, the varied representations of the environment have accelerated processes that develop a modified perception of the interdependencies between stakeholders (Schroeder et al. 2001). This reframing reinforces the collaborative dynamics that develop when stakeholders commit to work towards collective goals. Moreover, it has shown that such transformations can be effected among a diverse group of stakeholders over large distances.

The layering and real-time information collection and communication capacities of GIS systems have enhanced the access to information among stakeholders. In addition, GIS systems, built from the ground up and based on public participation, are acknowledged to have an important role in the basic information-sharing component of the network. This extension of the information available in the common space enhances the potential for capacity-building exercises to lead to more informed and constructive dialogue about the problems stakeholders must address.

The visual impact of maps that illustrate non-traditional features, such as ecosystem components instead of political boundaries, has raised awareness of interdependencies and enhanced the regional identity of participants. In addition to maps, the integration of the maps with the technical reports, project information, and stories on the Gulf of Maine e-Atlas enhanced the range of interpretations not otherwise possible (Schroeder et al. 2001). These types of overlay allow the inclusion of qualitative and quantitative information, essentially assisting story-telling and enhancing the communication of perspectives (Harris et al. 1995).

Information ecologies
One of the most important contributions of the GIS technologies might be the creation of information ecologies and the necessary informational commons.

Informational commons have extended the idea of the public domain. The domain is more than just a physical space; it also consists of the information that is publicly available to citizens (Roberts 2000). The efficacy of regimes that adopt models of e-governance to enhance public consultation, and employ new technologies to enhance the breadth and scope of public participation, depends on the continued expansion of the information commons. As demonstrated in the Gulf of Maine Environmental Information Exchange, inter-sectoral partnerships, based or instigated through information sharing, are essential components of distributed governance. Publicly accessible information and a willingness to share information among participants is an integral component of distributed and participative governance.

The information commons is the foundation of an information ecology. As defined by Nardi and O'Day (1999) an information ecology is "a system of people, practices, values, and technologies in a particular local environment". It is important to note that Nardi and O'Day emphasize that in information ecologies, the emphasis is not on technology, but on human activities that are served by technology. It is a complex system of relationships. The ecological metaphor is crucial because diversity is as important to sustaining an information ecology as keystone species are in nature.

A library and a hospital emergency unit are information ecologies. They are complex systems of parts and relationships involving tools, people, and practices, with a special emphasis on locality. The different parts of information ecologies, like those of their biological counterparts, co-evolve.

At the core of the information ecologies, one finds an information commons—shared by all at the site. But in the same way that the physical commons may be affected by the activities of the stakeholders (either being maintained and nurtured, or by being destroyed), the structures that shape the interactions of actors in the system, and the behaviours of those actors, have overwhelming influence on the information commons.

New information and communication technologies have increased the ease through which citizens and actors in all domains can obtain documentation on governments, private institutions, and civic sector organizations. The view that holds that a "Global Information Society" has spontaneously emerged, and will continue to develop with the continued penetration and advancement of information and communication technologies, is, however, not universally accepted. Persuasive arguments can be made to demonstrate that recent technological change has nonetheless resulted in a diminished transparency of public institutions, and may therefore reduce the amount of publicly accessible information (Roberts 2000). Therefore, information can be accessed more easily, but there may not necessarily be more available.

Alasdair Roberts argues that cultural, economic, and political forces are combining to limit the types and amount of information that is publicly available.

> The informational commons is contested terrain. Governments and corporations—and citizens themselves—have all taken steps to preserve secrecy, often spurred to do so by the power of new modes of surveillance, or by the

desire to gain economic advantage by asserting their property rights over the central commodity of the new information economy (Roberts 2000:176).

The new restraints are, in addition to being the product of the advancing capabilities of the technology, in some cases a consequence of the diffusion of power over a wide variety of actors and the diminished influence of governmental agencies.

In other cases, governments' reduced financial means have prompted direct reductions in the resources devoted to, or peripherally related to, access to information. Moreover, the indirect consequence of the shift towards the increasing privatization of government agencies, outsourcing of standard government tasks, and private–public partnerships has been new restrictions on accessibility.

Roberts's warnings underscore relevant concerns that could impede the establishment of an information commons adequate to the task of transforming the way in which we govern the oceans. In much the same way that geomatic technologies can influence social processes for the better, changes that are instigated by technological advancement can be harmful to the advancement of governing relations. Warnings have already been issued regarding the impact of GIS on social relations. The capacity of governments to employ GIS for surveillance activity exists, a development that can lead to more resistance to accept their use (Sheppard et al. 1999). Moreover, without an equitable distribution of access to technology, those disadvantaged by their exclusion may not be able to contribute to the policy or decision process (Harris et al. 1995). The technologies of collaboration, and the mechanisms involved in creating the networks, chaords, and dialogues of a sustainable governance regime, must preserve and enhance the breadth and scope of information that nourishes those systems.

Yet the information commons are not the whole of information ecologies. One may regard information ecologies as the flipside of socio-technical systems: the information flows are the infrastructure of socio-technical systems. Every transaction or transformation corresponds to an information signal. Information flows are also the foundation on which the governance system is built, so effective governance entails an effective merging of information flows—it being understood that perfect information is as elusive as perfect competition.

An effective governance system needs to build on common knowledge and information, but also to integrate or articulate in a workable way the array of informational resources at hand (much of it tacit, proprietary, or even unmapped). Information ecologies are the main terrain where levers to trigger incentive reward systems, dialogue, and deliberation, are to be found.

The information ecologies that underpin ocean governance are segmented sectorally, nationally, and professionally. Coordination cannot simply build on the information commons being expanded: it is part of the solution, but only part of it. Much needs to be done to elicit more modest and more partial forms of information exchange, sharing, and compounding, if one is to ensure that the diverse information available is tapped into as fully as possible, and the information proprietors enticed as much as possible to share it.

The compounding of e-governance schemes, of new information and communication technologies, and the consolidation of diverse information ecologies (public, private, social, and mixed) are at the core of effective coordination in the ocean world. These broad forces not only integrate the different stakeholders somewhat differently, but they are reshaping the nexus of the relationships, conventions, and contracts that define the governance regime.

Chaord as the new organization form

Complexity, turbulence, etc. have not only led to a transformation of governance regimes, but they have also trans-substantiated the organization of our socio-technical systems. It was not accomplished top-down through grand designs, but bottom-up, through experiences and experiments.

One might define the new emerging generic organizational form as the Chaord—to use the word coined by Dee Hock, the founder and CEO Emeritus of VISA.

The success of the organizational form is such that if VISA were converted into a stock company it would be worth $150 billion. Yet it cannot be bought or sold, traded or raided, since ownership is held "in the form of perpetual, non-transferable membership rights" (Hock 1995:14).

If such an organizational form can coordinate the work of 23,000 financial institutions operating in over 200 countries, and serve 335 million users, and if it can do it effectively, it may well serve as a template in our search for a model of ocean governance.

Conclusion

Oceans form a complex, adaptive socio-technical system requiring a certain kind of sustainable governance regime for its effective stewardship. The "right kind" of regime will be one that ensures resiliency and continuous learning, with state agencies playing a stewardship role.

Such a regime can be built on four principles:

- participation;

- subsidiarity;
- multistability; and
- stewardship of organizational learning and relational leadership.

It will translate into an integrative scheme of multi-layered social contracts.

Such a regime cannot be imposed top-down; it must be allowed to simply emerge. And it will require a change in the way that people think about oceans. I think this paradigm shift could be triggered by an awareness of the current existence of the "chaord" as an organizational form, and by the general emergence of collaborative e-governance in the country. But the route to the "right kind" of regime will probably prove circuitous and take some time.

For the "right kind" of regime to emerge, furthermore, the "right kind" of intervention will be required at key lever points, as well as an acknowledgment of the long-term importance of the community of practice that comprises the major producers and users of knowledge and information about oceans, because they will come to dominate the scene.

The "right kind" of intervention, furthermore, will be one that enables, builds, and nurtures the necessary collaboration (thereby also fostering the necessary social capital and trust) and that does not lend itself to rigid rules—thereby requiring new forms of softer accountabilities.

Effective technologies of collaboration can foster the new GIS technologies and create:

- forums and public spaces;
- loci for dialogue and multilogue;
- capacity and competency building; and
- exchange of information schemes.

At the same time, it will be important as well to build/ensure:

- appropriate monitoring;
- hard, soft and 360-degree accountability arrangements; and
- learning and feedback loops.

These are the central features for effective stewardship of oceans. They offer a general direction for further exploration, and if adopted, they would show that bottom-up governance works, and that there can be a paradigm shift in how people view this resource.

PART IV

The New Stewardship

Chapter 11

Toward a Baroque Governance
in 21st Century Canada

> "Our natural mode is therefore not compromise
> but irony, the inescapable response to the presence
> and pressures of opposites in tension.
> Irony is the key to our identity."
> Malcolm Ross (1954)

Introduction

Canada will have to meet the three fundamental challenges of 21st century society: complexity, new forms of collaboration, and citizen engagement. The new information and communication technologies, and the greater connectedness they have generated, are only one of the families of forces, albeit an important one, that have increased the level of relevant complexity, uncertainty and turbulence in the Canadian system. Over the last thirty years, Canada has also become (partly by design and partly due to circumstances) dramatically more demographically variegated, culturally diverse, socially diversified, and politically complicated. Finally, it has also evolved into a country in which citizens have become not only better informed and better able to express their dissent, but also better equipped to assert their multiple identities and to demand participation in the governing of their affairs. As a result, the coordination problems that Canada has been confronted with and has had to resolve have become increasingly daunting.

This quantum of additional variety and complexity has been denied or significantly downplayed by ideologues from the left and the right—*ces terribles simplificateurs* whose purpose is to propose a flat-earth view of reality in order to rationalize the choice of "the solution" (more state intervention, lower taxes, etc.) they are propounding. These solutionists' calls for univocal responses—whether the "solution" is meant to rely on the powers of the invisible hand of the market or of the hidden (hiding?) hand of government—have compounded the difficulties.

Fortunately, ordinary Canadians have been more pragmatic: they have acknowledged the greater variety in the environment as *incontournable*, and have built on this premise a more pluralistic set of reactions better able to deal with it: they have embraced the old Ashby law of requisite variety (Ashby 1970). Such an approach has required more of a bottom-up, muddling-through, distributed and collaborative governance, based on the more or less successful efforts at coordination of a large number of actors and participants—in lieu of the simple top-down hierarchical process of governing that was in good currency in earlier and less complex times.

This fourth and final part of the book proceeds in four stages. First, it defines Canadian distinctiveness as an *habitus* characterized by irony and bricolage. Second, it explains why Canada has been rather slow in adapting its governance to cope with the challenges of its disconcerted learning socio-economy. Third, it suggests that repairs for the many different forms of disconcertation that have been noted require a more vibrant *bricolage communautaire*—dealing with disconcertment in a low key, differently from place to place, with the use of different assets, skills, and capabilities. Fourth, it illustrates, through vignettes of what is happening on three construction sites, how the Canadian governance system of the 21st century is evolving.

From bonding to loose intermediation

While much has been written about the decline of social cohesion and the transformation of Canadian sociality over the last few decades (Helliwell 1996; Paquet 1996b, 1997a, 1999a), most of it has been couched in terms of erosion of the old bonding social capital that was so good at undergirding reciprocity and mobilizing solidarity (Coleman 1988; Putnam 2000). The erosion of the superglue of family, church, community, hierarchies, etc., was an erosion ascribable to the fact that these institutions were not nimble enough to fit the requirements of the new knowledge-based learning economy. Much less work has been done on what would appear to be required to construct a new sociality, one based on much weaker ties and more loosely coupled networks (Granovetter 1973; Paquet 1999a).

In Canada, the transition from bonding to loose coupling has been less smooth and rapid than it should have been because of significant resistance to this sort of *virage* by a portion of the federal elites. This has led to a vigorous counter-argument being mounted in favour of "bridging social capital"—the need for a fairly high degree of centralization to be maintained in order to bolster redistribution, and therefore to save the country from falling apart. This has been presented as "the Canadian way" (Paquet 1995a; Chrétien 2000).

This rearguard action has been fueled by a degree of diffraction in Canadian society, generated by greater complexity and heterogeneity and a demand for greater citizen participation. It was wrongly presumed by Pierre Elliott Trudeau (among other Canadian leaders) that a response to these challenges was to be found in overarching principles, abstract norms, or grand designs and narratives. One of the most prominent of these intellectual devices was the focus on human rights and the increasingly judiciary nature of governance via charters, courts, commissions, etc., and it acted as an extraordinary support for a more centralized and hierarchical system. Such schemes are most often intellectually disingenuous, practically unhelpful, and perhaps even dangerous for democracy (Gauchet 2000).

More recently, there have been efforts in the country to hide such centralizing schemes behind efforts at "branding" Canada—a language falling halfway between business and rodeo lingoes—or efforts at creating new devices aimed at "bridging" divisions. These have been novel ways of redistributing income and wealth across regions, social groups, and organizations in order to equalize their circumstances, and thereby reduce social tensions and envy. Many people in public discourse have even come to declare these redistributive schemes to be the social cement that binds Canadians together, and constitutes their "distinctiveness".

But "distinctiveness" is neither a matter of "branding" nor one of "bridging". It connotes a dynamic *"habitus"* or *"manière d'être"*, while branding refers to static markers and identifiers. As for the seemingly innocuous language of "bridging" "[...]what are potentially big fractures in a society between rich and poor, between language groups,[...]"—the language used by the Canadian Senate Committee on Social Affairs (1999)—it is misleading and trivializes a *manière d'être* by reducing it to fiscal plumbing.

Bonding, with its exclusiveness, is an echo of traditional society, and does not fit the realities of modern Canada; neither does bridging, with its emphasis on mechanical redistributive schemes. Circumstances would appear to call for a looser and more temporary coupling—*cohabitation avec commutation* (i.e., a system in which anyone can claim or deny attachment), but these weak ties can nevertheless provide much strength (Granovetter 1973; Guillaume 1999; Putnam 2000). This is the paradoxical result of a number of reflections on the Canadian perplexities, generated by Canada's experience in creating a new "multiculture" (Paquet 1999b:ch.7; Iyer 2000:part IV).

Fortunately, these subtleties have not been lost on Canadian citizens. Their response *qua* citizens (to both the new circumstances and to the "magnificent" efforts to deal grandiosely with them) has been much irony vis-à-vis grand schemes, and a plea for *bricolage* first and foremost to effect the needed repair to the institutional order.

The drift from bonding to loose intermediation has, however, been slowed down by efforts to impose either–or choices on Canadians (when the new realities confronting Canadians called for choices of the more-or-less variety—less centralization, more subsidiarity in the name of efficiency, etc.) or redistributive bridging schemes (when what was required to facilitate risk-taking and to ease transition in a high-risk society were better insurance schemes). As a result, Canadians have over the last decades defined their "distinctiveness" almost in spite of their leaders, and they have been quite good at it. And this distinctiveness as *habitus* has been characterized by expressions such as "a passion for bronze" (Valaskakis) or "slow adrenaline" (Iyer).

The rejection of grand schemes by the majority of Canadians has at times been deplored as *occasions manquées*. But Canadians, with their hefty dose of tolerance and apathy, are ironists, "never quite able to take themselves seriously because always aware that the terms in which they describe themselves are subject to change", and they spend much time worrying about the possibility of having been initiated into the wrong tribe, and taught to play the wrong language game (Rorty 1989:73–5). Thus they prefer (1) understatement, irony, and self-mockery in their rhetoric, and they most certainly resist being "branded" like cattle, or "bridged" in a crippling way in the face of liquid modernity (Bauman 2000); and (2) they prefer a sort of pragmatism and *ad hoc bricolage* in their practice, and a gamble on a combination of plural, partial, and limited identities, even though that often actually increases the distances between groups of Canadians. This is Canadian distinctiveness.

Malcolm Ross put it very aptly almost fifty years ago when he said: "we are inescapably, and almost from the first,...the people of the second thought. To remain a people at all, we have had to think before we speak, even to think before we think. Our characteristic prudence is...this necessity for taking second thought... (Ross 1954:ix). In 2000, an outside observer like Pico Iyer (2000) came to almost the same conclusion using almost the same words.

This pragmatic liberalism, couched in a prudent pluralistic and ironic language, has often led to discourses that are difficult for outsiders to decode and understand. Canadians will often pretend ignorance and willingness to learn from others for the sake of making the other person's errors conspicuous by means of their adroit questioning. They will even slide into "a manner of discourse in which what is literally said is meant to express its opposite".

Canada as a disconcerted learning socio-economy

The transition, over the last few decades, from an industrial age to a knowledge-based economy has revealed a separation between the world of physical objects and the world of ideas. These two worlds exist by quite different rules. On the one hand, the world of physical objects is characterized by scarcity and diminishing returns, and focused mainly on allocative efficiency in a static world. On the other hand, the world of ideas is essentially scarcity-free, inhabited by increasing returns, and focused on Schumpeterian efficiency (i.e., on the discontinuities in the knowledge base over time, and in the dynamic learning ability of the new evolving arrangements these entail) (Boisot 1995). Canada is still deeply rooted in the old economy, but it is shifting more and more toward a world dominated by the logic of the new learning economy.

(a) The learning socio-economy

In the new economy, the success of individuals, firms, regions, and national economies has come to depend upon their capacity to learn, to a much greater extent than was the case before. In such a context, responsive or passive flexibility will not suffice. What is required is *innovative flexibility*: learning, and not simply adapting (Killick 1995).

The emergence of the learning economy has transformed the division of labour in Canada, and the Canadian social fabric. While a technical division of labour based on hyper-specialization was efficient during the industrial era, such *travail en miettes* does not promote learning. In order for learning to proceed, one must build on conversations, on communities of interpretation and communities of practice, and specialization must proceed to a greater extent on the basis of *craft*, i.e., of competencies. This requires a cognitive division of labour (Moati and Mouhoud 1994): a division of labour based on learning blocks (innovation systems, skill-based production fragments, etc.) that entails a very different mode of coordination.

In the old system, coordination meant standardization, and economic integration was a way to effect standardization. As a result, hierarchical coordination prospered. But in the new system, wherein the challenge is to harmonize the *capacity to learn and progress together*, the organization (private, public, or civic) must focus on its core competencies, but also consciously recognize that it operates in an ecosystem and must mobilize its community of allies (Moore 1996).

The challenge to foster collective learning calls for the development of much more horizontal coordination of a looser sort among all the stakeholders. And since the relationships with the stakeholders (suppliers, customers, partners, etc.) cannot be built on simple market relations (because these may not promote efficient co-learning), *networks of relational exchange* have emerged. In such arrangements, long-term relations based on trust are negotiated. Forms of cooperation that would never otherwise materialize evolve as a result of the emergence of important positive feedback and self-reinforcing mechanisms that are generated by external economies or neighbourhood effects, and learning curves yielding increasing returns (Goldberg 1989).

These dynamic processes, involving the interrelationships of groups of actors, generate a variety of *conventions of identity and participation* among these different agents, and proximity (in the different senses of that word: spatial, technological, social, etc.) plays a not insignificant role in the learning process. Co-learning entails co-evolution in an ecosystem that evolves by finding ways to "charter" cross-functional teams from which no important power players are left out and, if feasible, in which "all major players have some stake in the success of the strategy" (Moore 1998:177; Arthur 1994; Krugman 1996; Durlauf 1998).

Such are the trends as Canada drifts into the 21st century.

(b)   Canada's slouching toward the learning economy
These challenges facing Canada are well known. Yet little in the present structure and functioning of the Canadian economy, in the private, public, or civic sectors, appears to indicate that Canada is progressing as well as it might through this transition.

As a matter of consequence, while Canada scores well in terms of certain indicators in international comparisons, when other indicators are used (gross domestic product per capita, Tobin's measure of economic welfare, the so-called Genuine Progress Indicator, or Fordham's index of social health), they appear to suggest that Canada's relative performance has been deteriorating (Paquet 1998). This is also reflected in the relative measures of productivity growth, in the coefficient of attraction of foreign capital to Canada, etc.

One broad hypothesis has been offered to explain why the Canadian political socio-economy is losing ground: it is a general failure of the Canadian system to adjust its governance to the new requirements of the learning economy, and to abandon its antiquated hierarchical and confrontational governance structures. According to this diagnosis, the Canadian socio-economy is suffering from *disconcertment*: i.e., there is a disconnection between its governance and its circumstances (Baumard 1996) that has not been noticed, and therefore has not been repaired. Indeed, as R. D. Laing would have put it, Canadians have failed to notice that they have failed to notice this discrepancy.

It has been noted by many observers that the Canadian socio-economy remains marred by important cleavages and torn by adversarial systems (federal–provincial, public–private, labour–management, small firms against one another, etc.) that have prevented it from developing into an effective learning economy (Valaskakis 1990). Indeed, the major conclusion of a recent study by the Public Policy Forum is that the most important reason behind Canada's relatively lacklustre performance on the productivity front is the lack of a culture of cooperation, especially between government and business (Public Policy Forum1993). André Burelle (1995) has shown extremely well that the federal–provincial quagmire is not far behind as a major source of friction that has prevented the development of an effective coordination/governance system.

(c)   States as catalysts

Some have argued, quite rightly, that tension and disconcertion may not be all bad. They are a fount of novelty and a source of enhanced learning: heterogeneity and somewhat weaker interpersonal ties (less groupthink) may in fact yield more innovation than a very homogeneous order. But excessively confrontational patterns of interaction slow down learning. The central challenge is to ensure the requisite flexibility of the institutional system so as to bring "the skills, experience and knowledge of different people, organizations and government agencies together, and get them to interact in new ways" (Johnson 1992:43). But this requires an important social capital of trust, and, in Canada, the social capital needed for such cooperation is eroding.

The World Values Surveys provide a very rough gauge of the evolution of the degree of interpersonal trust and associative behaviour in the country over the past few decades. Despite the jelly-like character of the available data, some important trends have emerged: 1) the degree of confidence and trust in one's neighbours has remained higher in Canada than in the United States; 2) there has been a significant erosion of social capital in the United States; 3) the gap between the two countries has declined, meaning a more rapid decline in Canada than in the United States; and 4) the decline of trust and associative behaviour has been even more rapid in French Canada than in the rest of Canada over this period of the post-Quiet Revolution (Paquet 1996b, 1997a; Helliwell 1996). Given this significant relative erosion of the social capital of trust in Canada (and even more so in Quebec), one should not be surprised by the failure of various initiatives à la Gérald Tremblay to stimulate networks or industrial clusters in Quebec. The requisite social glue was not there, and there is little evidence that public policies have been at work to develop the requisite new type of social capital that would allow learning networks to thrive (Paquet 1999a).

The state has to rethink its action in the learning economy. As Dalum et al. suggest (1992), this means intervening to improve the means to learn (education and training system), the incentive to learn (government programmes supporting networks and projects of cooperation), the capability to learn (promoting organizations supporting interactive learning: i.e., more decentralized organizations), the access to relevant knowledge (through relationships between agents and sources of knowledge, both through infrastructure and mediating structures), but also fostering the requisite amount of remembering and forgetting (acting to preserve competencies and capabilities, but also helping groups to move ahead and to let go of older ways). This in turn requires a well-aligned nexus of relations, networks, and regimes.

States can be important catalysts in the construction of the new "loose intermediation" social capital: improving relationships here, fostering networks there, developing more or less encompassing formal or informal regimes in other places. This is the central role of what some have called the *catalytic state* or the *resurgent state* (Lind 1992; Drezner 1998).

Currently, this catalytic action is not too vibrant. Canadian governments appear to be characterized by a certain centralizing mindset, and by a chronic neglect of governance issues (Paquet 1995a; Canada 2000). It does not mean that the Canadian governance system is not evolving, or that it does not invent innovative ways to meet the present challenges (Paquet 1999b). But fiscal imperatives in the last decade would appear to have mesmerized our governments to such an extent that those in a position to act as catalysts have missed key opportunities (Program Review, for instance) to effect the sort of repairs to the governance system that might have gone a long way toward providing the Canadian political socio-economy with the non-centralized guidance regime it requires (Paquet and Roy 1995; Paquet and Shepherd 1996).

So if one had to characterize Canada, retroactively so to speak, one might stylize Canada as follows: (1) a disconcerted socio-economy caught in a tectonic transition between an old, somewhat centralized political economy and a new, somewhat more decentralized and subsidiarity-driven one, and (2) experiencing a sort of relative lull in its socio-economic performance and a mild form of midlife identity crisis. Moreover, in the face of these circumstances, Canadians are perplexed, but also persuaded both that (1) there is no simple fix to their predicament and (2) their "passion for bronze" (Valaskakis)—in other words their belief that "le mieux est l'ennemi du bien"—may not be such a bad thing after all.

New capabilities and bricolage communautaire

There are times when the evolution of the institutional order is such that one can really speak of a change of kind, and not simply a change of degree. Such a tectonic but silent change has been underway in Canada in the last few decades

(Paquet 1999c).To cope with an ever more turbulent global environment, Canadian organizations have had to evolve and to learn to use their environment more and more strategically, in much the same way that the surfer uses the wave.

Managers in the private, public, and civic sectors have had to exploit not only favourable environmental circumstances, but also the full complement of imagination and resourcefulness in the heart and mind of each team player. They had to become team leaders in task-force type projects, quasi-entrepreneurs capable of cautious sub-optimizing in the face of a turbulent environment. This dual sort of challenge has pressed public, private, and civic organizations to design lighter, more horizontal and modular structures, to create networks and informal clan-like rapports, and to develop new rules for the game. In general, this has generated some pressure for *non-centralization*, for an expropriation of the power to steer that was once held by the top managers.

(a) Distributed governance

As globalization proceeds, international economic integration increases. As the component parts of the system become more numerous, the central driving force is the pressure to organize for faster learning and more innovation, and this occurs when the actors, confronted with different local realities, are empowered to take decisions on the spot. In this way, international integration has led to some erosion of the relevance of the nation-state—globalization has led to the localization of decision-making, to the dispersion of power, and to a more distributed governance process.

These new modularized organizations cannot impose their views on their clients or members. Indeed, there has been a significant decline in deference to authority in all sectors. To compete effectively, firms, in much the same way as state or civic organizations, must consult: they are moving toward a greater use of the distributed intelligence and ingenuity of their members. A good example is Linux. The strategic organization is becoming a broker, an animateur, and, in this network, a consultative and participative mode obtains among firms, states, and communities. The reason for this is that the best learning experience appears to be effected through flexible intersectoral teams, woven by moral contracts and reciprocal obligations, negotiated in the context of evolving partnerships.

In our new high-risk and turbulent environment, strategic hierarchical management is no longer sufficient. What is required is the development of capacities for collaborative action in managing large-scale re-organizations and structural changes at the macro level: the ground is in motion, acting independently not only may not ensure effectiveness, but it may even make things worse and amplify disintegrative tendencies.

What is required is collective action by "dissimilar organizations whose fates are, basically, positively correlated". This requires trust-enhancing mechanisms like stronger relationships, networks, and regimes.

(b) Deficits on the capabilities front

It is easy to document a decline of trust and an erosion of social capital in Canada, a weakening of the pattern of networks defining the old Canada, and governance structures that have consequently been less helpful than they might have been. This situation has not been improved by the Canadian habit of self-doubt that is extremely difficult to shake off.

And yet, while, as Jan Morris (quoted in Iyer 2000:122) would put it, Toronto is "a capital of the unabsolute", it is also an extraordinarily successful experiment in multiculturalism, and one of the most peaceful cities of such size in North America. Organically, Canada would appear to be able to distill a way of life capable of accommodating this growing diversity, and to do it somewhat unconsciously.

This does not necessarily provide the basis for a satisfactory strategy for improvement in other realms. It only indicates a general direction for action.

The only thing that would appear to be certain is that Canadians feel that there might be ways to catalyze those local processes, to improve the situation on all three of these fronts (trust relations, networks, regimes).

On the civil society front, the repairs have to help regenerate some new forms of loose solidarity at the very time that diversity is growing exponentially, and shared values appear to have diminished. Boutique multiculturalism and the reliance on symbolic recognition devices would not appear to be satisfactory strategies (Fish 1999). And yet, given the fact that Canadians are hypersensitive to any form of intolerance, such new weak ties cannot be constructed on a retribalization that would carry with it any sort of exclusion.

On the political front, we in Canada now live in a world of plural, limited, and partial identities in which multiple citizenships are common currency. A rethinking of the notion of citizenship is necessary to accommodate these new realities (Paquet 1989; 1994b), but one has also to reconsider the existing political structures, and to modify them (in the sense of a greater decentralization) in order to provide maximum leverage to the strategic/catalytic state (Lind 1992; Paquet 1996–7).

On the economic front, the development of a stronger basis for stakeholder capitalism, and the transformation of the property-rights regime, are equally necessary: a shift from the absolute property rights doctrine in good currency in the English-speaking legal tradition (shareholders own absolutely all the enterprise), and the formality of market contracting, toward a pluralistic and more encompassing view of property rights, and a greater reliance on relational, trust-based and moral contracts.

(c) The elusive Canadian style

It is quite tempting to highlight one dimension or one aspect of this nexus of forces, and to suggest that it has a defining impact on the whole structure. Many have elevated certain patterns of rights to this role; others have suggested that the whole system revolves around certain identities. In fact, this misses the central point: that this broad-ranging canvas has an overall dynamic, the sort of dynamic that underpins all social systems. In the words of Donald Schön, a social system "contains structure, technology and theory. The structure is the set of roles and relations among individual members. The theory consists of the views held within the social system about its purposes, its operations, its environment, and its future. Both reflect, and in turn influence, the prevailing technology of the system. These dimensions all hang together, so that any change in one produces change in the others." (Schön 1971:33).

What defines the "Canadian way" is the transversal manner in which these assets, skills, and capabilities are integrated into a social technology, how they constitute an interpretative scheme, a system of beliefs, and a stylization of the world, and how they translate into coordinating governance structures and schemes of intervention. Such schemes are inspired by a root framework, but take different forms *hic et nunc,* because the circumstances call for *ad hoc* action. Indeed, as was mentioned earlier, this is the very nature of the Canadian style.

One may observe the "Canadian way" at work in various spheres—key cauldrons where Canadian distinctiveness is being shaped (schools, workplaces, cities, arts and culture, politics and government, etc.). Each of these loci is a laboratory in which Canada has tackled, with greater or lesser success, the challenges of complexity, collaboration, and citizen engagement in designing an ensemble of assets, skills, and capabilities that has given its shape to the Canadian *habitus.*

While no such local vignettes can pretend to exhaust the Canadian distinctiveness, they may act as powerful *révélateurs* of the nature of this distinctly Canadian *manière de voir et de faire,* but also of some features of this distinctiveness that may be *en émergence.* Such illustrations are useful to understand the ways in which the Canadian style may serve the country less effectively than it should, and to disclose where catalytic action might be required as a matter of priority.

But what may be most fundamental in the characterization of the Canadian style is that Canada is the "capital of the unabsolute", that Canadians are uncomfortable with any form of distinctiveness that excludes. This, in turn, generates a phenomenal degree of tolerance for diversity, and a robust rejection of any form of *embrigadement* that binds.

In certain circumstances, aloofness may become complacency, irony may lead to denial, tolerance to diffraction, openness to the erosion of the differences between the outside and the inside, and political correctness to greater social distance between groups. So this particular *manière de voir et d'être* is not without a dark side, that has sometimes been exploited by shrewd manipulators to manufacture denial and complacency.

Three problematic cauldrons

We have chosen three loci to illustrate this Canadian distinctiveness *en acte*: workplace and enterprise[1], education and health, and the national multilogue about patriotism and social cohesion.

(a) Workplace and enterprise

Canada's productivity growth has been relatively lacklustre over the last while. This is linked to coordination failures in the workplace and enterprise, and to the lack of effective coordination among the different sectors (private, public, and civic). And yet there is a systematic denial of the seriousness of this situation, and feats of analytics to demonstrate that, despite the stagnation of Canadians' material standard of living, everything is all right with our total well-being.

Canadians have an uncanny capacity to occlude their macro-organizational problems. John Porter had considerable difficulty in persuading the equality-conscious Canadian population of the 1960s that Canada was a vertical mosaic of classes and elites (Porter 1965). In the same manner, Canadians are in denial in the face of ample evidence that the Canadian governance apparatus is marred by hierarchy and confrontations, and that this situation has translated into a relative lag in adopting new technologies, an immense lag in the productivity of our service sector, and a certain slowness in its capacity to transform.

Many of these difficulties are a result of a misalignment of Canada's structural capital: *systems* (processes and outputs), *structure* (the arrangement of responsibilities and accountabilities among the stakeholders), *strategy* (the goals of organizations and the ways sought to achieve them), and *culture* (the sum of individual opinions, shared mindsets, values and norms within the

---

[1] Workplace refers to the physical locus of activities, while enterprise refers to the broader set of relations weaving together the stakeholders; the first refers to a smaller and more physical milieu, while the second refers to a broader and more legal context.

organizations) (Saint-Onge 1996:13). The major barrier to good performance is misalignment among these four elements, and, in particular, the disconnections between strategy and culture.

In Canada, the "culture" in which both enterprise and workplace are embedded, and which also shapes them, is problematic: (1) the framework of corporate law is dominated by the shadow of the shareholders, and does not provide much place for stakeholders; and (2) the culture of the workplace (which is a significant source of social capital) is not one of learning and innovation, and is not geared to taking full advantage of alliances, partnerships, and network externalities.

While in dozens of US states, corporate law allows boards of directors to allocate portions of the net operating surplus to stakeholders other than the shareholders (through amenities, better working conditions, lower prices to consumers, etc.), in Canada, any shareholder has the power to sue the board, if it were to adopt such a policy. This considerably cramps the board's style in generating the requisite commitment from these other stakeholders.

The same sort of dysfunction can be seen in the workplace, where a discourse of confrontation is still prevalent, along with the centrality of job action as a method of conflict resolution. As a result, the sort of collaborative governance that might ensure better dynamic (Schumpeterian) performance fails to materialize. This has resulted in Canada's relatively poor showing in the OECD league in a number of areas.

And yet, the rhetoric of competition and confrontation continues to prevail at the front of the stage, while new forms of cooperation, partnering and joint venturing materialize every day *en catimini* in all sorts of quarters throughout the land. So it is not that there is no progress, but the progress is local and informal (as it should be) but without the benefit of a supporting infrastructure.

(b) Education and health

Canada spends immense resources on both education and health care, and both the Canadian education and health care systems are national icons and a source of national pride. This explains our sense of accomplishment over Canada's gold medal in the United Nations international ranking of nations in terms of 'human development'.

Canadians boast about their superior systems, and are concerned about the quality of education and health care, but they turn a blind eye to the important signs of dysfunction that experts (in Canada and elsewhere) point to, in both our educational and health care systems. Gross lapses in efficiency and effectiveness, counterproductive silo-type organizations, and confrontational policy developments, entailing critical blindspots, lack of voice or role for the users, etc.—all factors that experts acknowledge (Keating 1995; Angus and Begin

2000) but that are deliberately suppressed in public debates in Canada. There is an amazing chasm, for instance, between the grim reality that Canada spends 50% more than the UK on health care per capita, with results that are inferior to theirs, and the public display of sacramental denial that there might be any need for repairs in the governance of our "superior" health care system.

Our education system also shows symptoms of ill-health: for instance, young Canadians spend significantly fewer days in class each year than students in other advanced countries; a recent report has suggested that up to 40% of high school students in Ottawa are dysfunctional as learners (Keating 1995:82); our commitment to lifelong learning is minimal, and the resources dedicated to formal manpower training remain a fraction of the sums spent by our industrialized competitors in Europe and Asia (one third of what is committed by Germany, ten percent of what is committed by Japan). And the same critical diagnosis might be made about our health care system: a very chaotic system that generates indices of morbidity and mortality well above what one might expect, and yet at quite a high cost (Angus and Bégin 2000).

Canadians enjoy damning the two-tiered American systems in both education and health. And yet all this occurs with many winks and nods showing some appreciation of the degree of disarray of both Canadian systems. What is resented, though, is any radical in-your-face criticism of the Canadian systems. These are regarded as most unhelpful (if not unpatriotic) and as such likely to discourage action à petits pas meant to repair those systems.

Obviously, in the face of suppressed criticism, a major overhaul of both systems is most unlikely. What is likely is a magnificent and uncompromising rhetorical defense of the status quo, while, through a piecemeal and quasi-underground approach, establishments will select particular reforms, and somewhat covertly implement them. Any radical challenge will continue to be denounced as a betrayal of our "perfect" institutions. This is the way in which 'universality' was assassinated in Canada: piecemeal, covertly, without a national debate, while on the hustings the political classes pretended that they were staunchly defending it.

This might explain what Harold Innis meant when he said "a social scientist in Canada can only survive by virtue of a sense of humour" (quoted in Neill 1972:93).

(c) National multilogue about patriotism and social cohesion
As global integration proceeds ever more deeply, the nation-state has been transformed. Its territoriality has become problematic to the extent that borders have become porous, its sovereignty has begun to come unbundled, and this

has led the citizen to a re-assessment of *what belonging means*. The problem of belonging echoes the new situation where Canadians are themselves increasingly of mixed origins, and authority has become dispersed in a multiplicity of sites. A multiplicity of allegiances have ensued. While citizens have traditionally associated their main loyalty with the nation-state, the state has lost its privileged position as the main anchor of belonging, as non-territorial modes of organization have become increasingly important (Elkins 1995:74–5).

New principles of social cohesion are *en émergence,* and we know that they are likely to evolve at the local level, and to echo a non-centralizing philosophy, but the timing of the tipping moment bringing a new sociality remains largely unpredictable at this time.

Not all observers agree on the reality of this tectonic change. Many continue to hold the view that "bridging capital" has been the basis of the Canadian "social glue" that has bound us together in the past, and believe it should remain the main adhesive in the years to come.

That is the position of the Standing Committee on Social Affairs, Science and Technology of the Senate of Canada (Canada 1999), which has suggested that the three pillars on which Canadians' sense of social cohesion rested in the post-World War II era were the federal programmes of redistribution of income; the shared-costs programmes through which the federal government provided federal grants to support health care, post-secondary education and social assistance; and a system of grants to equalize the average quality of public services throughout the country. Thus, the Committee suggests, nothing short of a new wave of federal institutions can provide, through redistribution, the requisite degree of security to Canadians.

This is the central theme used by those who argue that medicare is what makes Canada hang together, and that anything that threatens the present inter-regional process of money laundering is bound to put the Canadian edifice in peril.

This "bridging social capital" interpretation may not be anything more than a slogan in aid of rationalizing compulsive centralism (because it is necessary for redistribution). However, it has been put forward by certain groups in English Canada, as a founding national myth. The same individuals who defend the view that income and wealth redistribution supplies the essential Canadian social glue have also found evidence of a latent demand for such glue, and evidence of latent patriotism in the Molson beer commercial "My name is Joe and I am Canadian".

In such a bizarre rendition, Canadians, a people that defiantly harbours limited and multiple identities, are characterized, almost in the same breath, as both crassly opportunistic in defining themselves through some federal-provincial fiscal plumbing arrangement and, at the same time, as naïvely sentimental.

Another interpretation is rooted in our national irony and our taste for *bricolage*.

Medicare is a prime example of a popular federal redistributive scheme. It is a collectively expensive scheme, in which health care is presented to the population as a free good, through the hiding hand of the state. It is hardly surprising that the population is favourably disposed toward such a scheme. The fact that the elected officials have wished to be seen as providers of a valuable free good is also hardly surprising. This manufactured win–win situation (in which the population pretends that it receives free and universal health care, and the politicians pretend that they provide it free) is at best a sleight of hand. But only in government-sponsored polls or political harangues does this ever get confused with national identity and citizenship.

In the real world of Canadian health care, the principle is simply that it is unhelpful to rock the boat. *Bricolage* has already begun to effect some of the required repairs to the system through appropriation of whatever techniques would appear to be most effective, including those emerging from the United States. This movement of silent reform will slowly replace the existing emphasis on redistribution (which is costly and ineffective) with more effective and cheaper insurance schemes (Mandel 1996). The same may be said about education: the staunch defence of our public education system has never been stronger than at the very moment when Canada is *sotto voce* creating both private schools and universities galore.

Canadian distinctiveness does not, therefore, lie with the safety net. And this may be good news, since the safety net is under strain. Rather, it lies with the Canadian mastery of weak ties, with Canada's capacity to build on loose casual social connections, with its capacity to elaborate a *modus vivendi* of heterogeneous and diverse groups. The *leitmotif* is therefore likely to be the appropriate insurance for our high-risk society, rather than income and wealth redistribution.

This emphasis on weak ties in the new social arrangements reminds one of Schopenhauer's parable about porcupines: in the cold of winter, these creatures have found ways to be close enough to bring each other some warmth, but not too close to hurt each other. This new form of civic engagement should not be confused with the sort of social cohesion and passivist attitude that is supposed to ensue from the massive redistribution of income and wealth (Paquet 2000).

As for the success of recent commercials about "Canadianness", it is an interesting illustration of Canadians' general taste for self-deprecation and irony. The success of the Molson commercial is less evidence of suppressed patriotism than evidence of our immense taste for an ironic view of ourselves, for self-mockery. The popularity of "*La petite vie*" or "This Hour Has 22 Minutes" can be explained in the same way.

Conclusion

To clearly restate the main point: Canadian distinctiveness is not a set of static and arrested traits, but a certain *habitus*—i.e., a certain set of propensities or proclivities which become the dominant logic in the face of challenges and pressures. This dynamic *réactique* defines the characteristics of the socio-economic system in its dual process of *adapting* to its environment and *adopting* (i.e., bestowing a greater probability of success on) certain types of behaviour by actors or organizations in the system. This is what we mean when we refer to the "Canadian world", a distinctive world rooted in special equipment (physical, organizational, legal, etc.), tasks and identities—all integrated into a certain style. This dynamic is in turn anchored in an integrated ensemble of assets, beliefs, skills, and capabilities which are also evolving, as a result of pressures both from the external environment and from the evolving internal "Canadian world" itself.

It is not possible to define this dynamic "Canadian distinctiveness" in all its complexity in a few paragraphs, but one may identify the main features of the worldview that underpins it, and the ways in which this distinctiveness has crystallized in reaction to anomalies and pressures in different sites.

Our hypothesis is that this *habitus* has been characterized by irony + *bricolage*, i.e., a certain denial and disingenuousness at the rhetorical level, and a certain ad hocery at the practical level. This approach, by avoiding grand narratives and grand designs, generates an aloofness *de bon aloi* at the level of discourse, and the sort of practicality in action that is capable of generating piecemeal reform in a country that is relatively averse to change.

One major benefit of this approach (devoid of ideology, except perhaps for some latent soft egalitarianism) is that it de-dramatizes even the most ambitious endeavours, and makes adjustment appear less painful than it really is. Some side malefits of this vision-less approach are that it enables Canadians to avoid fully taking part in a number of major modern debates (the appropriate mix of liberalism, democracy, and republicanism, centralization vs decentralization, egalitarianism vs subsidiarity, redistribution vs insurance, etc.) and to surf over change during major periods of transformation without a full awareness of the depth of the reforms underway, or even an adequate appreciation of the auxiliary precautions that might be required.

The other papers in this book illustrate very well the canonical Canadian capacity for ironic denial and ad hocery. Yet it should not be presumed that

Canadian distinctiveness is somewhat "arrested". Ours is "dynamic irony" (Ross 1954:xii), for the institutional order is an emergent phenomenon: it is adaptable, evolvable, resilient, boundless and it breeds novelty, but it is also nonoptimal, noncontrollable, nonpredictable and fundamentally nonunderstandable (Kelly 1994:22–3). This explains why the discourses about social transformation of the institutional order are so vague and non-committal (Drucker 1994). We have to be ironic, since we have to be satisfied with observing the "emergent properties" of the new order as they materialize.

In the transition period to the new millenium, one may expect the strong affirmation of "limited identities", considerable disconnection, and challenges to most of the rigid and centralized institutions. There will also be a growing tendency for the emergent order to become anchored in communities of practice at the meso-level, and to be couched in informal rules of the game agreed to by persons who share a "web of trust". One may even expect that, at some point, key signposts or standards will mutate—the minting and issuing of currency, for instance. The main challenge will not be mastering the switch from one dominant logic to another, but learning to cope with multiple dominant logics, and therefore with concurrent distributed institutional orders (Paquet 1995b; 1997d).

The new "coordination" *en chantier* will loosely intermediate the spectral and distributed network world generated by the information age. In the network age, fluidity is the foundation of dynamism and survival, and institutional stability imposes constraints to relational fluidity. Many predict the emergence of an "imperial age" reminiscent of the Roman empire under Hadrian, where the "institutional order" will aspire to being no more than a loose web of agreements to ensure compatibility among open networks (Guéhenno 1993; Paquet 1994b). A baroque governance!

Obviously, this is not an ideal situation, but an ideal situation may not provide the optimal result after all. There is much to be deplored about the Canadian way of degenerating into denial and complacency, and revealing a tendency towards lethargy. Such a way of governing Canada will be costly in the long run. But there is also much to be said for a country that has decided not to take itself too seriously, and to take the economic counsel of John Maynard Keynes to heart: avoid dealing with big problems, emulate the dentists and deal with the small holes (Gordon 1975).

For those who would welcome more passion, an afternoon at a soccer game in Rome might be the requisite cure. There, they would experience passion about trivia: armed guards body-searching those coming into the stadium; vigilantly guarding the safety of the visiting team's band, and ready for gratuitous violence at any time.

Back in our aloof country, one finds on the editorial page of the national newspaper—The Globe & Mail on June 15, 2000—an editorial article not calling the population to arms, but one entitled "a call to irony".

Qui dit mieux!
In 1999 (Paquet 1999a), I suggested that, in the construction of the requisite new sociality in keeping with the Canadian/Quebec "spirit" (and Quebec's spirit is much more akin to the Canadian spirit than Quebecers like to admit), it might not be unreasonable to start with tact and civility. Many ridiculed such a modest start as too much like a celebration of Band-Aid—"solving a problem with a minimum amount of effort and time and cost" (Gladwell 2000:256).

This sort of approach always generates disdain in Canada—at least at the rhetorical level—for it conveys a sense of dogged and indiscriminate effort. This is missing the point. Rather, it is meant to convey that the most effective way to respond to the central challenge is to find ways to partition big intractable problems into small tractable ones. This is why the Canadian way is *une foule de petites choses*.

Chapter 12

Governance and Emergent Transversal Citizenship: Toward a New Nexus of Moral Contracts

"Liberalism is a doctrine about the external organization
of society. It is silent on the more important question:
How shall we live? "
Michael Lind

Introduction

Pluralism is a world view that defines societies as fragmented and discontinuous, as composed of incommensurable complementary/conflictive parts or spheres, and therefore cannot be reduced to a single logic. In plural societies, there is a constant and active process of reconciliation, harmonization, and effective coordination of the logics in these different spheres to ensure a minimal degree of coherence, resilience, and effective learning.

Citizenship is a covenant based on the values, principles, and reciprocal privileges and responsibilities that define our ways of living together. Therefore, in a plural society, citizenship cannot be anything but *plurielle*—i.e., limited and multiple—since the citizen in such a world has multiple and limited relationships, and multiple, limited, and overlapping identities (Cairns 1999).

Many political scientists and jurists are critical of this notion of limited/ multiple citizenships. To bring commensurability to the incommensurable, they routinely reduce this rich and variegated nexus of values, principles, privileges and responsibilities that connote citizenship to a common denominator, for the purposes of governance, by granting politics a transcendent role. Through a sleight of hand, they invent a projection of this n-dimensional socio-economic reality (that citizenship synthesizes) onto a single transcendent plane where all agents are defined as equivalent and equipotent, and make it the sole locus of citizenship. The citizen becomes an *être de raison* operating in the transcendent plane of politics, a sort of lowest common denominator *soul* in all agents.

In such an ethereal world, there is a denial of diversity, no possibility of considering any differences within the n-dimensional world, and a refusal to establish lucid and responsible rankings among dimensions. This reductionism is even presented as the essence of democracy: inferring that without the transcendence of politics, democracy would not prevail (Gauchet 1998).

Plural societies need a much richer notion of citizenship. The argument is developed in four stages. First, the strategy of a sanitized locus for agent–state intercourse is described in a cursory way, and the limitations of this strategy on which politics has built its purported dominion are exposed. Second, an analytical framework is proposed to explore various crucial dimensions of citizenship. Third, we develop a broader notion of citizenship, one rooted in civil society and in the notion of moral contracts, showing how it is likely to be better adapted to pluralist contexts. Four, there is a brief sketch of the different ways in which Canada and Australia are drifting toward this position.

Pluralism and the perils of transcendent politics

The notion of an open society (Bergson 1934; Popper 1942) suggests societies that have escaped the dominance of holistic values, and have managed to put the individual at the centre of the stage. In the traditional stylizations of this open society, one finds a private sphere for the individual, where his negative freedom (freedom from constraints) is guaranteed through arrangements like private property, and a public sphere where an *état de droit* regulates the relationships between individuals and between the individuals and the state (Reszler 1990). The restricted power of the state is meant to ensure that the society will never be closed.

A pluralist society is a much richer concept than an open society. It goes beyond this notion of negative freedom and calls for *"un ensemble composé (à compartiments) librement aggloméré"* where the constituent parts maintain a good portion of their original autonomy. These sectors are regarded as *"autant de domaines irréductibles, en interaction permanente...chaque sphère particulière trouve son expression dans un pouvoir à part...à la division des pouvoirs correspond...une véritable démultiplication des allégeances"* (Reszler 1990).

Plural societies are societies that explicitly recognize that individuals and groups are motivated by different values, and that they can legitimately have different value systems. To pursue their different objectives, they require positive freedom: capacity and opportunity to actively and effectively pursue these values, and the elimination of the constraints or freedoms that prevent them from doing so. Moreover, plural societies deny that there is any constantly overriding value (Kekes 1993:19). This entails the inevitability of conflicts, and the need to develop reasonable conflict-resolution mechanisms based on some core credo (however minimal) that the disputants may share. While the plurality of conceptions of a good life increases the range of valued possibilities, not all possibilities are reasonable. So there is also a need for limits, and for the justification for such limits as excluding unreasonable possibilities, or unreasonable ways of pursuing them, or ways that might simply maximize conflicts.

The central strategy of many political scientists and jurists in the face of "plural" societies has been to focus on finding complexity-reducing devices for the purpose of governance.

One favourite stratagem has been the reductive assumption that there are only two spheres: the private and the public. According to this device, there is a private sphere relying on a right to privacy, and a public sphere where individuals interact under the aegis of the state. It is in this public space that citizenship is nested, and in which the citizen participates in a restricted way (through representation in Parliament) giving a voice to "*la volonté générale*".

For those who defend such a dichotomy, the two spheres represent the private and public faces of the lifeworld of individuals. Groups and communities are simply considered as insignificant symbolic markers, citizenship pertains to the public sphere, and is dominated by state–agent relations. This occluding of communities, and the emphasis on the private–public dichotomy and the vertical notion of citizenship associated with it, are both altogether too Manichean and reductive.

The real plural world is much more complex and characterized by deep diversity: it is filled with communities (real and imagined), there are many more spheres, and they all overlap to such an extent that it is of little use to build any analysis on an assumption of tightly compartmentalized spheres (Janoski 1998; Paquet 2000c, 2001d). Consequently, citizenship cannot be restricted to the public sphere. State, market, private, and public spheres, and there may be others in the material and symbolic orders, overlap to such a significant degree that it is unreasonable to limit the ambit of citizenship to the state sphere. Indeed, as T. H. Marshall (1964) would put it, the development of the nexus of privileges and obligations defining citizenship has evolved sufficiently that it has invaded all spheres (market, state, private, public, etc.).

Moreover, citizenship cannot be reduced to state–agent relations. At a certain level of generality, political scientists and jurists recognize that citizenship is fundamentally a dual relationship that is both *vertical*—between the members of the political community and the political authority and the state—and *horizontal*—among members of the community. But they overemphasize the former relation to such an extent that the notion of citizenship becomes totally absorbed therein (Cairns 1999; Jenson and Papillon 2000).

The bias toward the vertical is based on the special importance of the public sphere, and of politics and state within it, through the process of political representation. Politics and state are purported to play transcendent roles as the agents of transfiguration of society—*"une élévation tranfiguratrice de la société"* (Gauchet 1998:112). And there is a quasi-doctrinary belief that it is a *necessary* elevation, since only politics, through the process of conflicts among parties and collective adversaries, can lead to a meaningful taking-into-account of the common good (Mouffe 1993). For those holding that view, the state is the centre of the public sphere and the privileged locus of conflicts between power groups. Consequently, any relativization of the role of the state can only be regarded as a deplorable erosion of the political, even though the state is said, by the same persons, to have generated a *"primat de la représentation des acteurs sur la résolution des problèmes qu'ils posent"* (Gauchet 1998:123).

It is my view that in a modern, pluralist, knowledge-based socio-economy, there is no privileged or transcendent locus of conflict, and, therefore, that the valence of politics and state is considerably overstated. In a more realistic approximation of the socio-economy, the horizontal (community) relationships are as important (or perhaps even more important) as the vertical ones. The reduction in the relative importance of the stato-political, any disenchantment of the political, or any drift toward a reduction of the intermediation role of the political (Touraine 1999), or toward its implosion or its reconfiguration in new sites, means a shift from government to governance (Paquet 1999b).

Governance may be defined as effective coordination when resources, information, and power are distributed. Citizenship—in a context of governance—means the ensemble of values, principles, reciprocal privileges and responsibilities that define the nexus of moral contracts. These contracts constitute the necessary social technologies of coordination, capable of bringing forth good life in all its various senses for the different agents. The perils of maintaining a fixation on the stato-political are clear. Since citizenship is a nexus of relationships dominated not by the state but by a much richer array of relations throughout the socio-economy, the fixation on the political can only rob the notion of citizenship of much of its meaning.

An analytical framework

Refusing to reduce citizenship to the realm of the political does not suffice, however. One must suggest an alternative and broader framework within which citizenship might be usefully analyzed. While there are many monist schemes playing up one dimension of citizenship or another, none of the efforts at producing an acceptable synthetic scheme has been totally successful. This is ascribable to the very nature of the societies that have become plural through historical times: no single template would appear to be applicable to all.

At this stage of the debates, one can only hope to identify an "analytical framework"—"a set of relationships that do not lead to specific conclusions about the world of events...[but] may be looked upon as the mold out of which the specific types of theories are made" (Leibenstein 1976:17–18).

I have identified three major dimensions to be taken into account in a classificatory scheme presented in Figure 16 (Paquet 1992a, 2001a).

(1) The first dimension pertains to the dichotomy between material and symbolic orders. This notion has emerged clearly from the works of Raymond Breton, among others, and has contributed to broadening the debate on culture in Canada (Breton 1984). The insistence on the importance of the symbolic order has allowed the discussion to escape from the traps of traditional analyses of interest groups' demand for material or financial gratifications. The broader analysis has focused on problems of collective identity (traditions, customs, norms, *genre de vie*, etc.) that are embedded in the forms and styles of private and public institutions. It has re-affirmed something that is often forgotten, i.e., that the symbolic order underpins the workings of the material order, and is also a prime target of government interventions (Tussman 1977).

For Breton and others, the construction of the symbolic order is as important as the construction of the material socio-economy. Citizens traditionally have sought a certain concordance between their private way of life (their "culture") and the style of their public environment (their "national identity"). Their demand for status (that is, for recognition) will often be as vociferous as their demand for access to economic and political resources (Tully 2000). Indeed, recognition and redistribution are often alternative ways of transferring different sorts of capital. Governments of plural democracies must be increasingly involved in monitoring and understanding the symbolic order, and in intervening in it, both in response to demands by diverse groups, and in order to temper the behaviour of groups by reframing their representations and perceptions (Tussman 1989).

This more inclusive framework helps to provide the basis for interpretations encompassing "material" and "symbolic" dimensions, and in probing the growing centrality of "recognition capital". Membership and identity are simply less structured forms of social and symbolic life, but they naturally either progress through the development of culture and institutions, or fade away.

(2) The second broad axis of the analytical block defines an increasing degree of formality in social arrangements: from membership, which may be regarded as a minimal set of conditions to belong to a club (the difference between members

and strangers); to identification/identity, which is the subjective recognition of some salient features as the basis for self-categorization; to culture, which represents a somewhat formalized set of rules, laws, customs, and rituals; to governance, which amounts to the development of a stable pattern of social interaction and institutions (Walzer 1983; Edwards and Doucette 1987; Roberts and Clifton 1990).

The notions of membership, identity, and culture are extremely difficult to define precisely. Essentialist definitions of belonging are anchored in certain traits. Others have insisted on some primordial features as determinant. A third group has fundamentally defined these notions in a relational way: shared differences that are the result of negotiated arrangements (Drummond 1981–2). In the first two instances, a number of ethnographic features are said to provide the basic or dominant characteristics necessary to qualify for membership (Nash 1989). In the last case, membership, identity and culture are in the nature of a *persona*, which is the result of a creative and interactive process through which relationships are constructed and evolve in a manner that makes them a matter of conventions and agreements with outsiders (Goldberg 1980).

Figure 15: A citizenship problematique

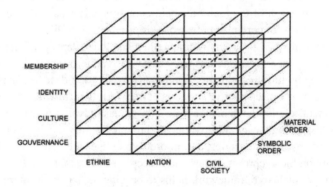

In that sense, membership, identity, and culture may be regarded as increasingly more complex forms of "social glue" or social capital (Coleman 1988). This sort of capital simultaneously provides the basis for differentiation, structuration, and integration: i.e., it serves to provide a basic partitioning based on negotiated differences, but also as a basis for assembling those disparate elements into a coherent whole (Porter 1979; Lussato 1989).

Since heterogeneity may *de facto* generate a segmentation of the social space into disconnected groups, and since such segmentation may well degenerate, through multiplex relationships, into cumulative processes accentuating and crystallizing such a segmentation, an increasing degree of balkanization and anomie of the segments may ensue (Gluckman 1967; Laurent and Paquet 1991). Consequently, it is crucial that we spell out these conventions, along with the pattern of rights and obligations of each party, if active and vibrant citizenship is to ensue, rather than a mosaic of disparate groups in conflict on all fronts.

Membership will be easier to negotiate than identity, and identity easier than culture, but corresponding to these different degrees of cohesion, there are different types of "moral contracts" (Paquet 1991–2).

(3) The third broad axis of the block identifies three complementary and yet intricately interwoven terrains of social integration: ethnos, nation, and civil society. These are the different grounds on which these moral contracts, however loosely negotiated or otherwise arrived at, are embedded. They are alternate/joint foundations for moral contracts.

The case of ethnos used to be regarded as quite distinct because of the fact that membership was perceived as rooted primarily in physical characteristics and the material order. But even ethnicity has tended to become more and more symbolic, so that growing importance has been given to symbolic recognition in defining ethnic boundaries (Gans 1979).

Ethnos, nation, and civil society are different ways of anchoring membership and identity, and may be regarded as tending to become substitutes (or at least the basis for a complex compound) rather than being the basis of absolutely non-intersecting realities. Ethnos, nation, and civil society are valid bases for discussing membership, identity, culture, and governance, but depending on which one is the hegemonic terrain, the "moral contracts" will contain a different set of collective rights and obligations. Determining the valence of each terrain has therefore become crucial.

Such determination is difficult, and fraught with Manichean dogmas and nasty discussions that reveal the full powers of naïvety and political correctness. Ethnos has become the target of many attacks as it serves as a source of exclusion. Indeed, the dichotomy between "bad" nationalism (based on ethnicity) and "good" nationalism (based on territory and constitution) has become a mantra. Connection between government and an ethnocultural nation upon which the nation-state is based has become regarded as "xenophobic, nativist and even fascist" (Lind 2000:44).

In its place, the politically correct conventional wisdom has proposed a sort of "civic" nationalism as "progressive because it is committed to a political ideal". This represents a subtle but futile stratagem to capture the "psychological economies of scale" of the nation-state, without having to pay the price of ethno-cultural commonality broadly defined. For, unfortunately, it would seem that "the ethnic nation is the largest community with which ordinary beings can have an emotional attachment" and that civic patriotism is simply an *être de raison* (Lind 2000:46).

So far, these attempts to completely exorcize ethno-cultural dimensions having failed the test of reality—ethno-cultural nations and nationalisms are thriving. There has been a recent attempt to salvage the civic nationalism paradigm by insisting that ethno-cultural dimensions may be factored in, but only as subsidiary/secondary features. These features are regarded as important only at the symbolic level, as a support system for the "liberal-civic-nationalist" citizen whose "liberalism" remains the only fundamental value. Michael Ignatieff underwent such a minor conversion between 1993 and 2000 (Ignatieff 1993, 2000).

This has led to the emergence of a form of "boutique multiculturalism"—i.e., a multiculturalism one can invoke only in matters inconsequential, because as soon as there is an effort to leverage or parley these ethno-cultural values into anything significant, the dominant liberal view of the individual-without-ethnocultural-qualities is used to forcefully trivialize the ethnocultural dimensions (Fish 1999).

This analytical block leaves a great deal of room for a wide variety of complex notions of citizenship, anchored in quite different terrain. This captures the central fact that citizenship as a set of ligatures (values, principles, reciprocal privileges, and responsibilities) is an essentially contested concept—i.e., one about which reasonable persons may never agree (Gallie 1964) because it is a multidimensional concept, and different individuals may legitimately put more emphasis on one aspect or another within the citizenship analytical block. What crystallizes as the relevant notion of citizenship is a set of ligatures or moral contracts defining a transversal syncretic entity within the citizenship analytical block: a mixture of values, principles, and reciprocal privileges and responsibilities that provides citizenship with its broad diffuse base and its syncretic unity.

Terms of integration and emergent transversal citizenship

In the process of defining citizenship as ligatures of all sorts, it is easy to understand how different groups may focus on different cells of the block. Ethnic membership may be regarded as the essential feature by some, while others may elect to emphasize symbolic identity in civil society exclusively. But in a world characterized by much spectrality—multiple memberships, limited identities, a mélange of ethnic/national/civil society identification and cultures, layered governance structures, and a most fluid boundary between the symbolic and the material world, citizenship is unlikely to be captured in one cell or dimension of the block. Indeed, and this is our main argument, citizenship is a transversal concept: it is nested in a diagonal cluster within the analytical block (Paquet 1989a, 1994c, 1994f).

This means that citizenship might be regarded as a nexus of ligatures defining a covenant or pact cutting across the block, across the many boundaries, and attempting to reconcile in an evolutionary way the many different perspectives that coexist, within a given society or at the intersection of many societies, through a nexus of fluid "moral contracts" (Paquet 1991–92). Moral contracts are more or less informal arrangements and conventions that embody values and norms on which people agree. They define mutual expectations, legitimate entitlements and obligations, and the corridor or boundary limits within which people have agreed to live.

Only such a transversal notion of citizenship, based on moral contracts, can capture the array of ligatures capable of meeting individuals' complex needs for autonomy and belonging, the needs for responsibilities, and opportunities for participation in an active democracy, and the challenges of a spectral society with its new type of sociality based on weak ties. This notion of citizenship need not be univocal, since there are multiple citizenships anchored in different terrains, and there may be differentiated citizenships—in degree and in kind.

For instance, one can easily imagine a basic set of minimal norms corresponding to basic citizenship, but also differential levels of rights-cum-obligations that individuals and groups might choose in order to equilibrate their entitlements with the sort of responsibilities they are willing to accept (Paquet 1989). In the same manner, in a world of limited identities and multiple citizenships, one can imagine layers of citizenship corresponding to different pacts entered into by individuals or organizations. These may echo either different degrees of rootedness, or complementary ensembles of commitments, or, in some cynical scenarios, flags of convenience that can be used alternatively or strategically by individuals or organizations, depending on circumstances.

In this context, the multiplication of citizenships has called for some ordering (strong or weak) if the notion is not to be trivialized. The notion of primary and subsidiary citizenships connotes a sense of priority among the different limited affiliations. This ordering cannot be embodied in a formal legal arrangement. At best, it would correspond to an always emergent and never fully crystallized meta-moral contract defining the relative valence of the different ligatures that make up individuals' and organizations' citizenships of all sorts (Paquet 1998).

(a) Coordinates

To facilitate the discussion, one might identify some important dimensions of citizenship: citizenship as legal status, as participation in governance, and as belonging. These are illustrations of the range of meanings that might be attached to a transversal concept within the block, and of the wide array of flavours that can emerge as layers are multiplied, and one dimension or another is emphasized. This is presented in Figure 17.

At one apex of this citizenship triangle is the liberal notion of citizenship, fundamentally rooted in the notion of legal status—a notion that is in good currency in the Anglo-Saxon world. Here, citizenship inheres in individuals, who are seen as the bearers of rights, and it is couched in a language of rights and entitlements. Citizens do not have to do anything, or at least not much, to become or remain citizens. It minimizes participation requirements and expects little sense of identification. This notion emphasizes the centrality of negative freedom (i.e., protection against interference with individual choices).

At a second apex is the civic republican view of citizenship. It is largely couched in terms of duties, and defines citizenship as a notion with a high valence to practice and participation: the citizen is a producer of governance. It calls on individuals to become members of the community, to participate in the culture and governance of the community. This concept emphasizes positive freedom (i.e., a person's being able to do this or that, and the duty to help others in that respect).

A third apex emphasizes neither status nor participation, but the process of belonging. In this zone of the triangle, what is of central importance is the "recognition", respect, esteem, given to the individual and his circumstances. There are two important variants of this polar case: one in which recognition is simply a *"mise en visibilité"* of some basic characteristics that are already there; and the second which focuses rather on the "construction" of status and differences by activism designed to transform the symbolic order (Tully 2000; Markell 2000).

These three ideal-type conceptions are only meant to illustrate the broad range of different notions of citizenship in good currency. One may find countries having anchored their notion of citizenship all over the terrain of the citizenship triangle, corresponding to different mixes of status, participation, and belonging. In any concrete real-world situation, citizenship in a plural society is a transversal mix of these three components. Indeed, a given notion of citizenship condenses some of these dimensions, and represents a nexus of moral contracts that deals with these different dimensions in a particular way. Consequently, citizenship may cover a whole range of possible meanings, with all sorts of intermediate cases giving different weights to each of these dimensions.

Moreover, one may easily imagine, as was suggested earlier, different layers of citizenship within which the individual may be embedded through his/her membership in different organizations, and a variety of families of citizenship within which individuals and organizations are nested as they take part in the different arrangements pertaining to different countries.

Figure 16: The citizenship triangle

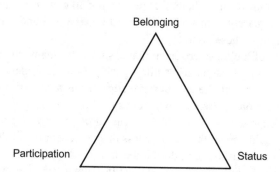

(b) Guideposts

Over the last few decades, the dynamics of the debates about citizenship have led to an evolution of the concept. From the original formulation of T. H. Marshall (1964) emphasizing the development of citizenship entirely in terms of rights (civil rights in the 18th century, political rights in the 19th century, and social rights in the 20th century), one has seen it evolve toward an ever greater importance being given to the participation aspects of citizenship, but also in ways that give more import to the whole dimension of belonging and symbolic recognition.

Moreover, there has been a tendency for the notion of citizenship not only to change the valence of these three components, but also to react to the ever greater "liquidity" and complexity of modern societies (Bauman 2000) by an increase in the degree of "informality" in the normativities embedded in the moral contracts, and by a multiplication of the contracts dealing with these more complex relationships (Paquet 2001a).

Instead of being absorbed into a simple, formal, and legal linkage between the citizen and the state, the citizenship relationship has evolved into a looser but more encompassing covenant, covering a web of relationships among members of the community, but also between them and the state.

Finally, the proliferation of multiple citizenships has heightened the complexity of these arrangements, and has generated a whole new set of problems for persons or organizations purporting to hold membership in many clubs at the same time. This has led both to ugly abuses of power (when a group of citizens are branded by a paranoid state as likely to collaborate with the enemy, as happened to

Japanese Canadians during World War II), and to individuals and organizations using their "citizenship of convenience" to take opportunistic advantage of all possible entitlements while shirking the responsibilities of citizenship.

This should have led to debates about meaningful arbitrages among competing allegiances, or at least to the emergence of a dominant logic acting as lodestar to guide collectivities in such choices. However, not all countries have had the fortitude to deal squarely with such problems. Many have found it politically incorrect to even raise these issues.

The emergence of the loose covenant that ensues faces many challenges. In two recent documents, Jenson and Papillon (1999, 2000) have identified some of them. A few of these challenges deserve attention as a way of probing the process of construction of citizenship underway in all countries.

The first challenge has to do with the increasing *diversity and spectrality* of populations. It would appear that nothing less than a recognition of differential and asymmetric citizenships can do the job in a world where diversity and spectrality entail a multiplicity of limited identities that may be complementary or competing. (Van Gusteren 1998; Paquet 2000d). Unless one can define some rank ordering among these attachments, citizenship becomes meaningless.

The second one has to do with the multiplication of the *sites of citizenship*. While the power and legitimacy of the nation-state would appear to be lessened, there are reasons to believe that this proliferation of sites of power is even more important when the ethno-cultural basis of society is more diverse.

When new entities at the supra-national and infra-national levels become meaningful actors, and alliances and joint ventures blur the old distinction between the state sphere and the rest of society, one must either firmly re-establish the state sphere to salvage the old notion of citizenship, or transform the notion of citizenship to deal with the new realities (Paquet 2000d). This latter route calls for citizenship to be broadened, and for new social ligatures and arrangements to be negotiated. While different groups may wish to obtain symbolic recognition, others may want some political autonomy, or a portion of the economic surplus. This is true for groups at the local and regional levels, but particularly for ethnocultural groups.

The third challenge has to do with the evolving nature of *solidarity*. The old notion of citizenship associated with rights has simply been driven to extend rights to cover all sorts of social entitlements on the ground that social and political equality are linked. This has often been discussed without any consideration of a citizen's responsibilities, and often rooted in the basic assumption that only the state could be trusted to take action with a view to the common good.

This has led to a strong emphasis on redistribution as a way to ensure that the so-called collective rights of communities would be honoured, and on a reiteration of the importance of a strong central government as a source of redistribution—for only a centralized state can bring the requisite resources to the centre, and redistribute them to lessen inequality. However, it is far from clear that redistribution (be it of material or symbolic resources) is the only or even the right way.

A return to the principles of insurance might be a more appropriate response in a world of weaker ties and greater turbulence, where what one wants to encourage is a more efficient allocation of risk-taking through a wider use of risk-sharing (Paquet 2001c). And this refocusing may be all the more important if one accepts (only in part) the argument of René Girard, who contends that reducing inequality by redistribution may increase the risk of envy and violence (Laurent and Paquet 1991).

A final challenge has to do with *participation*: i.e., with the taking part in the governance process. Again, this may take two forms: either opening the political process through strategies of inclusion, or accepting that citizenship does not necessarily have to be restricted to the political. This latter approach would require a broadening of the notion of citizenship to encompass more than individuals and communities, and the design of appropriate mechanisms to define and enforce the rights and responsibilities of these other "organizational entities" (Paquet 1998).

There are daunting challenges in eliciting the requisite participation and engagement for a society to thrive and prosper when faced with a more and more variegated population in a more and more turbulent world.

The mix of negative and positive freedoms likely to provide the optimal integration (i.e., one capable of providing ample possibilities for differentiated citizenship, while ensuring the minimal rules of engagement for the society to succeed) need not necessarily have evolved organically. One must therefore identify the ways in which the state wittingly or unwittingly is influencing the "terms of integration".

Australian and Canadian musings

It is only since 1947 (Canada) and 1948 (Australia) that the members of these societies can claim Canadian or Australian citizenship. Before that time, these persons were either British subjects, or without citizenship. One may reasonably ask whether this discontinuity per se has made any difference. The answer is not clear. It has obviously entailed the creation of some symbolic capital around the new label, but it is fair to say that, in and of itself, this re-labelling has done little to effect the instant crystallization of a new identity. It has only triggered the process of learning about what it means to be a citizen, for citizenship always remains *en émergence*.

This process of social learning has been experienced quite differently in Australia and in Canada. Australia has tackled the issue more openly, frontally, and transparently. In Canada, the birth of citizenship came just a few years after a very divisive fracture in Canadian society created by the Conscription Crisis (Laurendeau 1962). This crisis split Canada along ethnic lines right in the middle of World War II, when the federal government tried to escape from a promise (that it would not invoke conscription) made to secure Quebec's agreement to support Canada entering actively into the war effort. This particular experience was so traumatic (Quebec leaders being jailed) that it had quite a chilling effect on the post-war debates in Canada.

So the two countries entered these citizenship debates under quite different circumstances. In Australia, debates and documents registered progress in the emergence of a syncretic notion of citizenship. In Canada, the debates were muffled, the arguments less vibrant, and the documents not very clear as markers.

A preliminary examination of the two experiences suggests that the Australian approach has led to faster progress toward a clear definition of the meaning of citizenship. Most certainly, this issue has received more attention, has generated more debates, and has led to a much sharper sense of what constitutes the nexus of the moral contracts of citizenship in Australia than it has in Canada.

Yet one should not conclude too hurriedly that the Canadian way has proved dysfunctional. A closer examination reveals that a slower process of social learning in Canada was not only well suited to the Canadian circumstances and ethos, but also a strategy not necessarily unhelpful in dealing with ever more complex citizenship issues in a country that does not have the robust debating culture of Australia. It has been a strategy of small steps and ad hocery.

In this next section, some hypotheses are put forward about the different routes that these two countries would appear to have followed over the last 50 years, about the different nexuses of moral contracts that have emerged as a consequence, and about the paradoxical efficiency of the Canadian approach.

(a) A few contrasts
One might suggest the following differences between Australia and Canada as deserving some probing:

- the importance of "citizen commitment" in Australia, and its relative unimportance in Canada; the centrality of discussions about the moral contract embodying this commitment in Australia, and the diffidence vis-à-vis any such discussions in Canada; and the consequent sense of the limits to tolerance that ensue in Australia as a result of the debates about the emergent moral contracts, while almost unlimited tolerance prevails in Canada, because no norms have been agreed upon, and a no-norm convention has emerged by default;

- a carefully constructed bottom-up social cohesion built on commitment in Australia, and a top-down mechanical social glue, supposedly generated through the redistribution of resources in Canada;
- a capacity and taste for robust national debates in Australia, while in Canada there is a "sociality of consensus" and a taste for obfuscation, irony, and *bricolage* in the public sphere; and a certain differential in the degree of political correctness (higher in Canada than in Australia) which seriously stunts social debates in Canada and is a source of differential social learning between the two countries.

i. From the "white Australia" policy of yesteryear to the "commitment to Australia" expected from citizens today, there has been significant clarity in Australia's position. In Canada, on the contrary, much has been done to equivocate. Canada's immigration policy was almost as quasi-racist as Australia's 50 years ago, but without being stated as bluntly as in the Australian case. There is still great difficulty in Canada even today in accepting that this ever was the case. This hypocritical policy of obfuscation, about an era when soft but effective discrimination was in force, is easy to understand, and is ascribable to the "Quebec factor": it is not possible to openly debate the rights, responsibilities, values, participation, *appartenance*, etc. that underly the moral contracts of citizenship, when a significant segment of the Canadian population of ethno-cultural extraction has not been persuaded that such moral contracts are internally acceptable, and provide for the identity and lifeworld of communities.

Indeed, as a result of the Quebec factor, the conditions for becoming a Canadian citizen have had to remain strategically ill-defined: at first, admission was based on opportunistically defined norms rooted in no clear principles. It then evolved toward the present situation where any person putting one foot on the tarmac at any Canadian airport is automatically granted almost all the same rights as long-term Canadians, with the exception of the right to vote.

The Canadian Parliament's recent granting of a "Canadian citizenship" to Nelson Mandela has gone further, and expanded the definition of citizen to include someone who meets none of the standard criteria for citizenship. Whatever the merit of this particular individual, the Canadian Parliament admitted into "our community of fate" someone who has only the most tenuous possible reciprocal relationship of obligation with other members of our community, and through this gesture, it has all but declared that there are no firm conditions for becoming a Canadian citizen, and it did much to establish that Canadian citizenship is simply an honorific title.

ii. Canadians as individuals are inclined to be much more demanding in their definition of citizenship than are Canadian officials. They define it not only in terms of a bundle of rights and liberties, but also in terms of responsibilities, attitudes, and identities. Pragmatism is a core determinant of public officials' behaviour: in a survey, public officials claim to have no concern about defining any such set of expectations about the terms of integration for newcomers, on the ground that one cannot ask anything from newcomers that one does not explicitly require from the native born (Gow 1994; Dwivedi and Gow 1999:21).

Making any additional demands from newcomers is automatically branded as intolerance, chauvinism, or racism. As a matter of consequence, officials are not much concerned either about ensuring that newcomers are provided with the requisite help to make them capable of participating fully in the host society, and feel that they have no legitimate basis to refuse to modify the Canadian ways in response to requests by newcomers claiming that such ways constitute a discriminatory stance against them.

The result is not only a lack of debate in Canada about the limits to tolerance and diversity, but a natural drift, as the jurisprudence cranks out case after case, toward a refusal to recognize that there are any limits. This is no longer pluralism, but a flimsy hope that if some form of limits prove necessary, they will emerge organically. It is quite a gamble since the required terms of integration are in fact likely to emerge only from a continuous renegotiation as the expectations and environments change, and to coalesce into an explicitation of rights and responsibilities, but also of the host society's limits to tolerance, and of the obligations this entails for the newcomers to adapt. This challenge Canadian leaders refuse to confront.

To clarify these expectations, Australia has spelled out the content of the "Australian Compact"—seven basic principles based on "commitment" that Australian citizens must accept (Australian Citizenship Council 2000:82)

- to respect and care for the land we share;
- to maintain the rule of law and the ideal of equality under the law;
- to strengthen Australia as a representative liberal democracy;
- to uphold the ideal of Australia as a tolerant and fair society;
- to recognize and celebrate Australia as an inclusive multicultural society;
- to continue to develop Australia as a society devoted to the well-being of its people;
- to value the unique status of the Aboriginal and Torres Strait Islander peoples.

Moreover, the community consultations conducted by the Australian Citizenship Council revealed that it was perceived by a majority of respondents that "Australian citizenship should be valued emotionally rather than purely as a way of gaining certain legal rights and responsibilities…should also signify a commitment to Australia and to shared civic values" (Australian Citizenship Council 2000:92–3).

iii. The present Canadian refusal to engage in an exercise of definition of terms of integration is understandable but not inconsequential. The lack of a clear notion of the responsibilities of citizenship can only lead to a great fuzziness in the definition of the limits of tolerance. More than any other factor, the very reluctance of the Canadian government to foster debates leading to a clear articulation of what the guideposts are in this land is probably the main source of concern for those who would like tighter controls on immigration to Canada.

Australia has chosen to establish these limits clearly. They are defined in terms of acceptance of the basic structures and principles of Australian society (the Constitution, the rule of law, parliamentary democracy, English as a national language, equality of the sexes, etc.), of the responsibility to accept the right of others to express their views and values, and of an overriding and unifying commitment to Australia, to its interests and future first and foremost.

While Canada is reluctant to develop any such "moral contract" defining the responsibilities of citizens, this is a matter that has been explicitly raised and discussed by the Quebec Government in the Gagnon-Tremblay report on immigration (December 1990). Quebec has stated clearly the basis of the "moral contract" it would wish newcomers to accept: recognition of French as the language of public life, respect of liberal-democratic values, respect for pluralism, etc. This was not well received by the federal government, and Quebec has fought for these principles without much success. Of late, the creation of a separate Quebec citizenship has been proposed as a way to clarify these citizenship requirements. There is obviously some inherent danger in trying to overformalize such contracts and covenants, but there is also much merit in providing a statement of some substantial principles on which to build these arrangements.

The unfortunate effect of Canada's unwillingness to establish clear conditions of admission and terms of integration is that it has allowed some extreme forms of erosion of trust as significant groups have found it opportune to take advantage of Canadian benefits without accepting any of the obligations that constitute the flip side of this "moral contract" of citizenship. This can only lead in the longer run to greater exclusion than would otherwise be desirable, and both old and new Canadians are consequently bound to be worse off.

iv. The last two hypotheses mentioned at the beginning of this section are less closely related to citizenship per se. They pertain to the ethos of Canada and Australia respectively and underline the fact that, on two important fronts, the different perspectives of the two communities have resulted in the social learning process evolving differently.

First, the sort of social glue that is regarded as binding the citizenry together is quite different in Canada and in Australia. While Australia builds on commitment of the members bottom–up, to construct the identity and the commonalities, Canada has proved unable to follow this route, and bets on inter-regional and inter-group redistribution schemes as the foundation of citizenry. This is done on the basis of the assumption that egalitarian rights yield belonging (Vipond 1986).

This has maybe unwittingly generated an instrumental view of citizenship— citizenship being viewed as a way to get access to the privileges of being a member. Some observers (Banting 1999) pretend that Canada's perspective is not strictly instrumental, but this is a most unpersuasive argument. They also suggest that the only way to generate solidarity is through inter-regional and inter-group laundering of money, but this is also questionable, even though, if all else fails, it may understandably be regarded as a defendable stratagem to generate social cohesion.

Secondly, Canada has developed a sociality of consensus that has made public debate and harshly critical appraisal of opposing views most unwelcome because they are likely to be both painful and divisive. This most un-Australian modus operandi has led to undue restraint in public debates, and greater timidity in tackling difficult policy issues (Caldwell 2001). This modestly satisfying approach and the omnipresent search for appropriate compromises have had important positive impacts on the socio-economic performance of the country. Some, like Joseph Heath, would even say that it is a particularly apt approach, that has generated a very successful society (Heath 2001).

This oblique and timid approach to crucial policy issues has been considerably strengthened by the extraordinarily high degree of political correctness that continues to marr public debates in Canada. A few years ago, Judge John Sopinka, of the Supreme Court of Canada, even suggested that political correctness in Canada had become the greatest enemy of free speech. It is most certainly a powerful enemy of vibrant debates on issues like citizenship.

Canadian timidity has stalled the process of social learning by suppressing or stunting national debates. For instance, one is not allowed to discuss the required transformation of the costly and inefficient health care system in Canada—that is a taboo topic because medicare is purported to be part of the social glue that forges Canadian citizenship. One must pay homage to the Canada Health Act as an untouchable icon, despite its inadequacies (Paquet 2002a).

The fact that public debates are more robust, and political correctness less crippling in Australia, has accelerated social learning, and made it possible to generate national debates on many fundamental aspects of Australian society— even the possibility of becoming a republic. In Canada, such debates have not often been possible, and the painful experience with the Meech and Charlottetown accords has made such initiatives unlikely in the future.

Finally, much has been done explicitly in Australia (as in Switzerland) to root citizenship in sites at the local and state levels. This was part of a process that was rooted in a wish to ensure membership being felt bottom–up. Citizenship has been an active and emotional commitment, built in consort with local authorities. In Canada, the federal government has hijacked the citizenship file. It has forcefully defined it as a status bestowed passively by the federal government as the monopoly agent entitled to do so. Citizenship has therefore degenerated into a federal gratification.

Moreover, to the extent that citizenship has come to be used as a federal instrument of Canadian unity, and used as an instrument of propaganda by the federal government to promote its view of the good life in the federation, this was bound to generate reactions on the part of fragments of the population that had a different point of view on what the good life is. And indeed, this is now happening. Quebec, being unable to find a place to locate its identity, its participation or its sense of belonging within the federal discourse, is searching for a new site where it might be easier to do so. This has led to the recent proposal for the construction of a Quebec citizenship that would attempt to articulate separate rules of the game for Quebec. Australia, on the contrary, has used citizenship as an integrative feature involving state and local authorities, and has chosen to explicitly promote the involvement of local and state authorities in the liturgy of national celebration, especially at the time of public ceremonies to confer citizenship.

(b) Different emergent transversal ligatures

In both Australia and Canada, the notion of citizenship has not fully crystallized yet—it is still *en émergence*, but the nature of the moral contracts also appears to evolve quite distinctly in each case.

i. Canadian citizenship is fundamentally anchored in the notion of legal status, and gives scant attention to participation. Australia, by contrast, emphasizes the participation dimension. Both countries pay attention to belonging, but in a starkly different manner. In Australia, belonging is an emotional force to be emphasized as the foundation for commitment and participation; in Canada, belonging is looked upon with suspicion, for it has an echo of sub-national communities (national, ethnic, or other) that evokes emotional forces likely to undermine the integrity of the "national" political collectivity. Belonging is not abstract but visceral, and in Canada belonging is feared because it is seen as pertaining primarily to sub-Canadian communities. Yet outbursts of emotion on the occasion of Canada Day reveal the depth of this untapped "national" resource.

ii. Another important difference in Canada and Australia is the relative importance given to the vertical and horizontal relationships (between state and citizen, and among citizens) in the definition of citizenship. In Canada, the emphasis is clearly on the vertical dimension, and citizenship is rooted fundamentally in the entitlements of the citizen from the state. The social glue integrating groups is supposed to emerge from the inter-regional, inter-group, and inter-personal redistribution of resources, effected top–down by a centralized state. This has bolstered the instrumental notion of citizenship as a one-way contract to gain access to certain rights. In Australia, citizenship more truly emphasizes the relationships among Australians, and the commitment to other members of the community by citizens themselves. There is some hostility to the instrumental notion of citizenship, and a strong emphasis on an emotional commitment, on the recognition of obligations, and on an agreement to actively participate as a condition of entry.

iii. Australia and Canada have explicitly recognized the constraint of diversity in some formal way. However, in the case of Canada, there has been a greater reluctance to accept primary communities like Quebec (or aboriginal groups) because of the very size of the Quebec fragment (and because of the multitude of smaller aboriginal groups), as it might result in a significant balkanization of the country. In Australia, the existence of aboriginal communities has been acknowledged, and there has been a genuine attempt to reconcile unity and diversity through a composite citizenship. Canada has been nervous about following the same strategy, so, in general, has done so somewhat timidly, with the noteable exception of the Nunavut case (Paquet 1999c).

iv. In Australia, the debate about the nature of the "civic" deficit has been robust since 1995. It is still inert in Canada. Instead of dealing forcefully and explicitly with this need to square the circle and ensure national unity while fully legitimizing the diversity of civil society and fostering community participation, as was done in Australia, the debate on citizenship has remained moot and inexplicit in Canada.

v. Despite the differences in approach, both countries are still grappling with some important challenges that are likely to materialize in each country in the form of moral contracts that define:

- the way in which one can recognize a multiplicity of citizenships and some order among these different allegiances;
- the way in which citizenship can accommodate some priority among the multiplicity of allegiances to different ethno-cultural or sub-national communities within a nation-state;
- the way in which to congruently define the degree of ease of entry and the power of deportation—it being understood that the easier the entry is, the more powerful the instruments of expulsion might have to be;
- the way in which communities can be provided with a democratic voice in the governance of the country, either through some form of self-government, or some sort of effective community representation;
- the way of ensuring the requisite mix of status/participation/belonging in a world of multiple and limited identities, through an explicit recognition that "ethnos" may well be forging the largest possible site of belonging (Lind 2000). The narrow interpretation of ethnicity as a static entity instead of as a form of cultural practice has led to a very narrow definition of community and to a demonization of ethnicity. What is required is a capacity to recognize the social need for difference, and a democracy of communities deriving from it, while not mandating that this should be the case for all communities, and therefore running the risk of balkanizing the country (Howard-Hassmann 1999);
- the way in which one might be able to use differentiated citizenship as a way to reconcile the multiplicity of allegiances and the different levels of commitments;
- the focus on "recognition" and the redistribution of symbolic resources, and the extent to which it can be a substitute for the sharing of real resources, or the protection against real contingencies.

(c) The paradoxes of the Canadian way

The Canadian ethos would appear to make it more difficult than in Australia to face squarely the need to explicitly negotiate the terms of integration for citizens and newcomers, and to determine what these terms might be in the new world of citizenship. Yet the task is clear: what is needed is a nexus of moral contracts (1) that ensures the requisite degree of rights, obligations, participation, *appartenance* and identity necessary for the country to prosper; (2) that ensures that all the stakeholders retain their basic freedoms (political, economic, social) in order to increase their capabilities; and (3) that the appropriate trade-offs are defined between these two sets of priorities.

The more timid and *étapiste* Canadian way is not necessarily an inferior strategy, since it fits the Canadian ethos. However, it entails a complex and somewhat erratic process of social learning, where progress comes most of the time in fits and starts, locally, by trial and error rather than as a result of broadly debated revolutionary transformation. This often means that social learning is fractured and slow. This fundamental Canadian conservatism may prove extremely costly in an evolutionary learning sense.

However, this way of gauging the opportunity cost of the Canadian way may be somewhat unreasonable, for it presumes that Canada has the choice of doing it otherwise. While theoretically that is true, de facto, it is not. Compulsory debates imposed on a Canadian citizenry that has neither a taste for them, nor a capacity to sustain them, does not represent a meaningful alternative.

Canada can no more adopt the Australian way than the Swiss or Japanese way in defining its moral contracts of citizenship. Even though Canada has to face many of the same challenges as these other countries (globalization, growing polyethnicity, and multiculturalism, etc.), it is forced to confront these challenges with a different habitus (Bourdieu 1972). This habitus constitutes Canada's idiosyncratic propensity to deal with issues in a particular way that has been inherited from its history and experience.

Canada's habitus is its organized reaction capability, its *manière de voir*, a sum of its dispositions, and it has to be taken as a given at least in the intermediate run. Changing it amounts to changing Canada's culture. The peculiar Canadian habitus is undoubtedly a source of slower learning, and of a lesser ability to confront these challenges head on, but it is not without some advantages.

However frustrating and ineffective the Canadian way may appear by radical standards, it is not only efficient à la Heath, but it may even constitute a truly attractive strategy for polyethnic, multicultural, and plural societies in general, when they do not have the capacity to orchestrate the sort of open and vibrant debates that Australia has seemingly managed to conduct in a legitimate and peaceful way. It may well be that Australia is rather unique, i.e., not representative of the social capabilities of most societies, and that Canada with its crab-like, oblique mode of operations, is a more realistic approximation of what is observed generally: a fractured and somewhat disconcerted socio-economy incapable of anything but ad hocery. As a result, the slow, scattered, unfocused and small-stepped approach that Canada has been known for might not be an unreasonable strategy for most countries.

De facto, Canada is slowly moving toward a supra-national and community-based federalism, while fruitless "official" debates continue unabated in a manner that appears very unpromising (Paquet 1999c). This de facto modest and oblique way of getting there is obviously a roundabout way of tackling the unity–diversity problem, but, in many cases, it may be the only practical way to proceed. Unwittingly, then, Canada may have invented an approach useable by many small nations to engineer the right strategy to preserve their cultural identity in a globalized world, while allowing their component communities to maintain both their integrity and their capacity to be heard. This Canadian approach is characterized by a two-tracked strategy—a cacophonous public forum where the powers of disconcertion are modulated by a systematic avoidance of general, ambitious, and all-encompassing debates, while, in parallel, difficulties are resolved ad hoc and *in situ* most imaginatively.

This social technology to square the unity–diversity circle is exportable, and citizens of most small and medium-sized countries may well come to the conclusion upon reflection that, in this sense, "*ils sont tous Canadiens*" (Paquet 2002c).

Conclusion

Australian and Canadian citizenships are emergent idiosyncratic realities. These complex institutions are the result of the on-going interaction between values and environment. The sort of social armistices and moral contracts embodying the workable notion of citizenship at any moment, and the sort of adaptive learning process defining the dynamics of the terms of integration over time, are different from one society to another.

First, this paper has suggested that the syncretic notion of citizenship may be usefully analyzed through a prism that reveals its complexity, its fundamental transversality, and its essentially emergent nature. A two-stage process has been sketched to identify the basic dimensions of interest, and to suggest the mix of ligatures that would appear to be useful to compare different types of citizenship.

Second, these templates have been used to contrast the Australian and the Canadian way of evolving their notion of citizenship. In the Australian case, the nexus of moral contracts defining citizenship would appear to have been arrived at through more vibrant national debates, and to have elicited a more explicit and proactive set of moral contracts.

In Canada, a more ad hoc and pragmatic process avoiding national debates has generated a more tacit, passive, and vague set of arrangements.

While the former experience appears to be more satisfying from an intellectual point of view, it depends a great deal on the existence of a national ethos and habitus that carry the capacity to underpin such national debates. Canada's ethos would appear to be unable to promote and support such robust debates without generating much divisiveness.

It is not unreasonable to suggest, however, that Canada may be more typical of most pluralist societies, and that, in such societies, the low road of ad hocery appears to be the only way to avoid divisive, destructive and perilous national debates.

This chapter is therefore led to conclude that the slow and erratic road to citizenship adopted by Canada might be a useable model in our post-modern world. While one might deplore Canadians' incapacity to conduct a high road debate on such issues, and bemoan the ad hocery of citizenship construction in Canada, the extraordinary excesses and violence that would appear to ensue when such broad national debates are engineered, or simply experienced in contexts that are not suited to them, would appear to favour the more modest Canadian way.

This conclusion should not be interpreted, however, as condoning the centralized mindset that underpins the current federal "liberal constitutional project" (Carter 1998) in vogue in Canada nor its top–down, heavy-handed, arrogant efforts to "devoice" communities, and to use citizenship as a way to smother deep diversity.

Canada may be right in general, but wrong in the particulars on this front. We have made the case for it being right in general. As to the ways in which one might be able to use the citizenship debates to correct some of the most destructive particulars, it is a topic for another discussion.

Chapter 13

The Limits of Territorial/National Federalism as a Social Technology of Governance

> "For every complex problem there is an answer
> that is clear, simple and wrong"
> H. L. Mencken

Introduction

One of the central features of modernity is the existence of a plurality of conversations that practical persons hope to be able to reconcile and to articulate in some loose and comprehensive manner through some common "mode of conversation" (Tully 1994).

In this quest, federalism has come to be regarded as a social technology that has the capacity to build such means of articulation. Indeed, the very variegated fabric of Canada explains why federalism was seized upon early in Canadian history as a workable social technology, and why much of Canadian political philosophy is dedicated to debating these issues.

In the recent past, there has been an extraordinary growth in diversity of all sorts in our modern societies, and the plurality of conversations has made most societies truly polyphonic. Moreover, the coefficient of diversity has deepened significantly. This has considerably heightened the degree of difficulty of the reconciliation task, and eliminated the possibility of simply "papering over the differences" (Kymlicka 1998).

In the face of such deep diversity, traditional federalism does not appear to be as powerful an instrument as many had hoped. It has mainly developed along territorial lines and become fundamentally associated with a form of geographical essentialism that is "politically naïve, constitutionally undesirable and theoretically irrelevant" (Carter 1998:55). Even when federalism has attempted to inject a "national" flavour into such geographical essentialism, or when it has tried to transform itself into a "multination federalism", the results have been less than successful because diversity has by now acquired such polymorphous dimensions that these simple categorizations—territory or nation—have failed to grapple with deep diversity in any significant way.

This chapter proceeds in four phases. It examines (1) the new challenges faced by pluralist societies facing deep diversity; (2) the process through which deep diversity generates a process of diffraction that challenges the viability of unitary forms of governance; (3) the limits of conventional (territorial/national) federalism in enabling societies to deal with the many types of conflict generated by deep diversity; and (4) the directions in which federalism as social technology may have to develop in order to adjust to these new realities.

Pluralism and deep diversity

It has become quite evident over the past few decades that most modern societies have become much more diverse. Globalization has triggered a significant increase in mobility, which has transformed most societies into communities that are diffracted in a multiplicity of ways. Growing polyethnicity and multiculturality, and the emergence of various "identity groups" (Piore 1995) have, in particular, raised significant questions about the capacity of the "practices of modern representative government" (Tully 2001:49) to ensure the emergence and sustenance of a legitimate order.

In some sense, so-called "territorial" and "national" societies have become more akin to "global and transversal arenas" where only loose, fluid and partial regimes may hope to prevail.

This deeper diversity—in which the plurality of ways of belonging is acknowledged and accepted (Taylor 1993:183)—has led to a new *manière de voir* that has accompanied (more or less fitfully) the development of the deep diversity in modern societies. Pluralism is the name of the *new manière de voir*: it is an attitude, a philosophy. Deep diversity connotes the stark new reality of diffraction. Deep diversity calls for a pluralistic governance approach, and a pluralistic outlook welcomes deep diversity. Yet there is no necessary fit between these two "realities". Pluralism may be more or less extreme, and diversity may be more or less deep.

(a) Pluralism
There is no corpus stating clearly what a pluralist society is, and what its institutions and laws should be.

The notion of open society has been developed and expounded by Bergson and Popper (Bergson 1934; Popper 1942). It connotes societies that have escaped the dominance of "wholistic" values and have managed to put the individual at the centre of the stage. This has translated into the following traits for open societies: a private sphere for the individual, freedom within that sphere, the principle of private property, *un état de droit* to regulate the relationships between individuals and states, and a restricted power for the State, so that it never allows the society to be closed (Reszler 1990).

In such a context, the challenge is to find ways to eliminate the "unfreedoms" (Sen 1999) likely to emerge when any group becomes hegemonic, or is allowed by the institutions to become so. It entails the assurance of some positive freedom—possibilities of development—for groups that might be marginalized or side-lined by the society-building efforts of an abusive ruling majority (Kymlicka 2001, 2002).

One may imagine a gradation of intensities of pluralism. At one extreme, one may posit complete relativism and the cult of diversity qua diversity: this entails a *"démultiplication des allégeances"* and a gamble on solidarity, emerging as a result of a multiplicy of competitive foci in the different cultural groups. At the other extreme, one may posit the unitary and closed society.

(b) Diversity
In the past, diversity was a matter of accident. Globalization has accentuated the intermingling of populations, and most societies have become more or less polyethnic, multilingual, etc. Some societies feel disconcerted by such trends, while others embrace it as a desirable goal. But it is not clear what optimal diversity is, and what diversity really means. Is it diversity of agents, of traits, of values, of interests?

Variety, like any "social chemical", cannot be examined in isolation, for it interacts with other social chemicals. For instance, there has been an extraordinary growth of symbolic group recognition as a result of the Charter of Rights and other such developments in Canada. This sort of phenomenon has quickly translated symbolic recognition into entitlements, and that has meant that symbolic recognition has not been a substitute for material gratification but a complement of it. This has had revolutionary effects, since diversity has become a lever underpinning and legitimizing seemingly unbounded social demands from the state (Tully 2000).

For many observers, such variety would appear to be undermining other social characteristics such as belonging, identification, commitment, etc. Indeed, it is widely presumed that there is a trade-off between these desirable social features and variety-cum-diversity. This entails that there is often a celebration of diversity, but only as long as there is no sense of threat to these values. As soon as diversity would appear unbounded—i.e., without limits, and of necessity threatening those other values—there is a slip in support even though it does not always dare show its face.

One should not, however, reduce the trade-off to one between diversity and social cohesion. Social cohesion is a most extraordinarily tainted word. There should be no confusion between social capital (i.e. the tonus underpinning the capacity to work together) and social cohesion (i.e., a state of homogeneity and stale uniformity). Social cohesion is a proxy for "social peace" and uniformity, and egalitarian actions have therefore been propounded as the core source of social cohesion/uniformity. In fact, the creation of social capital as a basis for civic solidarity, organized reciprocity and social networks based on trust may be facilitated by a certain degree of commonality and security, but it also emerges from conflict, since social learning is enhanced by diversity and contrasted perspectives (Paquet 2005b:ch. 2).

Consequently, diversity is a source of social energy, but also a source of dissipation of social energy. The interaction with evolving contextual factors has made diversity more than a matter of nominal recognition, respect, and tolerance of otherness. It has translated into a legitimate tool to generate group rights, balkanization, and entitlements. As a result, diversity has become associated with the erosion of certain basic values. But these trade-offs that diversity imposes on a society are not easily discussed. They have become truly taboo topics. Indeed, the very notion of the governance of diversity (i.e., of the intentional use of instruments to ascertain how much is too much, and to ensure that such a threshold is respected) is challenged as politically incorrect.

This is a remarkably naïve position, yet one that is in good currency. Diversity in this perspective would not be a matter of choice, but a matter of fate. Refusing to govern the diversity interface would appear to be blessed with the name of virtue, while any effort at attempting to manage the diversity of a society is immediately perceived as an effort to limit it, and is therefore chastised as a sign of latent fascism. It is our view that the governance of "deep diversity" is a central challenge facing pluralistic societies, and that no responsible society needs to agree to be shaped by faceless external forces. The question is: how is this job to be done?

Deep diversity and the diffraction of society

Shallow diversity leads to arrangements that one might lightly characterize as "boutique pluralism"—to adapt an expression used by Stanley Fish (1999: ch.4).

Boutique pluralism recognizes the legitimacy of diversity as long as it does not lead to any significant adjustment to the prevailing order.

The political process engineered by democracy is such a strategy, which strips individuals of any characteristic except their citizenship, in an effort to find a legitimate way to aggregate preferences. It has created the citizen as "*être de raison*": erasing all differences in order to impose the "*citoyen sans qualités*" (CSQ) as the arbiter of all decisions. This is cognitive dissonance at its best. Deep diversity is not so easily erased. In a world of deep diversity, the CSQ cannot claim to be the sole source of power, or even a legitimate source of power.

If the social fabric cannot be reduced to the cohabitation of CSQs, differentiation is not circumstantial, but essential. This in turn calls for an explicit recognition that the governance of the socio-technical system must take these differences seriously.

The diffraction of society, generated by deep diversity, has two major impacts.

First, it poses numerous intractable challenges to unitary governing bodies. Even with the best of intentions, it is quite difficult to ensure that all the varied points of view will be fully acknowledged and appropriately weighted in collective decision-making. Aggregating such intractable challenges in macro-baskets, allowing for some horse-trading, is clever but not helpful. It may lead to certain expedient and opportunistic balancing acts at the higher level, but such aggregation of social choices does not necessarily lead to the best choices either or to consistent and fair choices, or even to choices that take diversity seriously.

Second, it generates different sorts of conflict between or among factions. And all these conflicts are not necessarily of the same nature and resolvable in the same ways. For instance, one must distinguish between routine distributional issues that can be resolved by discussion and negotiation, and categorical conflicts that cannot be resolved by debates and negotiations, because things such as identities "cannot be changed by rational arguments" (Fleiner 2001).

These impacts impose certain constraints on the design of a workable governance system.

They raise serious questions about the possibility of any unitary government being able to provide reasonable guidance on the sole basis of the rule of law. Therefore, it has led to much interest in federal systems that would appear to be capable of resolving problems at a less aggregated level, by maintaining a diversity of rules of the game.

It suggests that some issues are not at all resolvable except at the "community of meaning" level. Indeed, deep diversity generates numerous "categorical" conflicts: identities are based on a mix of objective and subjective realities that cannot be transformed by discussion. One does not become a Croat in the same manner as one changes one's view about income redistribution.

Deep diversity also calls for a modification in the modes of reconciliation of the various discourses. While there has been much use made of rights and "*le droit*" in the past, this is an orthopedic tool that has the knack of ossifying power relations in absolute ways. This may not be as effective a method of reconciliation in the dynamic context of present-day diversity. Softer and subtler institutional forms of power-sharing governance have the merit of allowing for some balanced representation of a variety of groups in specific terrains (Cassiers 1999; Paquet 2001d).

The required governance principles and tools are not easily designed, for they call for a partitioning of both the "governance terrain" and the "issues terrain" to provide acceptable arrangements of different sorts according to the nature of the issues, and of the stakeholders. Yet these principles and tools can be designed.

Conventional federalism as a flawed social technology of governance

Two modes of federalism have been proposed to deal with the challenges of diffracted societies: territorial federalism and multination federalism (Resnick 1994). Both of them are flawed because of the limited number of dimensions that they can accommodate. The first one emphasizes only the link between federalism and self-government for territorial entities, while the second one emphasizes only the link between federalism and self-government for national minorities.

The most obvious example of territorial federalism is provided by the United States. It was adopted not in response to ethno-cultural or other diversities, but simply as an expedient administrative device to reduce the danger of tyranny, and to make more room for a broader base for experimentation (Kymlicka 1998: 137–8). Defenders of communities of meaning have shown that such an approach has done little to help them take part in the conversation (Carter 1998).

Multination federalism adds nationality-based units (NBUs) to the region-based units (RBUs). This enriches the original model, and is more promising in certain circumstances, but it is not truly a general solution. The main reasons are: (1) that it does not go far enough in taking diversity into account (diversity is more than simply national); and (2) that it proposes an uneasy cohabitation of these two principles of partitioning especially in the face of what remains a profound and ill-founded commitment to a centralized governance structure. Such arrangements—as has been demonstrated in Canada—usually drift into acrimonious debates between the contradictory imperatives of the two principles of partitioning: one calling for territorial equality while the other calls for special treatment for national entities. One becomes buried in debates about asymmetry, special status, and the like that quickly run into stalemates as a result of the inequality of rights that they demand.

These two forms of federalism have failed because of their built-in pressures for centralization as an unstated assumption, and by the zero-sum game setting they thrive on. They have also been erected on the presumption that this is a game with a master—the central government. In that sense, the founding value at the origin of American federalism—that power at the centre must be dramatically limited—has been lost track of. What has ensued is a perception of federalism as a negotiated form of organization under the dominion of a dominant logic of centralization. Consequently, negotiations slipped into futile efforts to design all-purpose-organizational forms that came to satisfy neither the need for centralization required for effective redistribution, nor the need for decentralization necessary for the full autonomous development of the regional or national fragment. This has given both processes a bad name.

This centralization mindset injected into the core of the notion of federalism has led to a perverse dynamic.

Instead of being built on a commitment to decentralization (as much decentralization as possible, and only as much centralization as necessary)—as deep diversity would command—the system of governance has been allowed to be torn between the centrifugal forces pulling the multiple groups into strengthening their limited identities, and consolidating their status and share of power (and being branded as illegitimate in doing so); and the centripetal forces imposed by the administrative rationality of a central authority pretending to regulate and maintain the system in this turbulent environment (and claiming to be the sole legitimate level of government) (Carter 1998).

The result has been a conflictive equilibrium among the different levels of government, each with a legitimate portion of the sovereignty, but quite aware that it cannot rid the system of the other, and that a compromise is necessary if one is to reach one's own objectives (Crozier 1970). Yet informal bargains require a modicum of mutual understanding and trust between the parties. In Canada, and elsewhere, the game has been plagued by mutual threats: arrogant use of executive federalism galore, with the use of unilateral action by the feds, and threat of exit or disengagement or sabotage by the regional/national groups (Paquet 1977).

The federal government's mix of cognitive despotism (most of the time) and the sabotage by fractious regional/national groups (sometimes) has shown the limitations of the conventional apparatus. This has led to deteriorating organizational effectiveness, and to ineffective policy-making. Both federal and national/territorial groups have lost much legitimacy in this process. Territorial/national federalism has not succeeded in partitioning sovereignty in a useful way or in creating an effective social oligopoly.

Toward a reframed federalism

Reframing federalism requires two sets of operations. First, it calls for nothing less than the questioning of unstated assumptions that many students of federalism are not even aware they are making. These unstated assumptions have significantly deflected the governance design process. Second, it calls for the construction of an alternative approach to federalism, based not only on territory and nations, but also, and more fundamentally, on regimes.

Clearing the ground
There are three sets of assumptions that must be challenged:

a.   the assumptions underpinning the "liberal constitutional project" (Carter) that there is a need for central control
b.   the assumptions that a bottom-up federalism is unworkable, and that it is impossible to design a legitimate and effective chaordic (i.e., mixed centralized/decentralized) system
c.   the assumption that one cannot accommodate a variety of "whatever" or singular communities in the body politic, and therefore that the CSQ is a necessary detour.

These assumptions have been challenged before, but they have proved quite resilient.

Stephen Carter (1998) has made the point that the "liberal constitutional project" (built on the presumption that central government is "more likely than anybody else to find the answers that are right") is in a powerful sense anti-democratic, and anti-communitarian (Carter 1998:20). It is based on the foundation that the views of the people are irrelevant except when they happen to be in support of the liberal constitutional project, in which case they are crucial (Carter 1998:21).

The assumption that no system can function without some central control is widely held and is best expounded by Dror (1997, 2001) and Jaques (2002) as a binding rule of living organizations. It posits the need for some constraints to be defined in order for a freedom-based organization to avoid floundering and collapsing. This body of doctrine has a profound following among people who prefer centralized explanations (Resnick 1994).

The second set of assumptions flows directly from the first, but it complements it in a fundamental way and may be regarded, in part, as an enriched corollary. It suggests that no fully decentralized solution is viable, but it also adds that one cannot mix centralization and decentralization. The first portion of these assertions raises questions about the process of emergence, and has been countered effectively in recent work by Holland (1998). The second portion of these assertions—the impossibility of effectively mixing elements of centralization and decentralization—has been regarded as a categorical imperative by Jacobs (1992). She has argued that mixing systems that are defined by different syndromes (centralized, decentralized) could only generate monstrous hybrids. This argument is entirely spurious as we have shown elsewhere (Hubbard and Paquet 2002). Bottom-up chaordic organizations (mixing chaos and order) have proved that they are workable, viable, and effective (Hock 1999).

The third set of assumptions is more difficult to unplug. But it is also a derivative of the first two sets of assumptions in the sense that the need for centralization and the impossibility of mixed institutions, can only entail an incapacity to take into account the variety of singular communities generated by a deep diversity context. This difficulty is ascribable both to the large number of such communities, and to the coefficient of rigidity of many "identity groups", and is used as the basis for relying on the CSQ as the only fall-back option. Yet one cannot see how a pluralist political system could ignore such diversity and not take seriously these singular communities (Agamben 1993, 2000).

These three sets of assumptions pollute most debates about federalism.

They presume a "natural" dominance of centralization and a need for control, the impossibility of building bottom-up structures or mitigating the malefits of centralized organizations by mixed forms of organizations, and the need to ignore singular communities simply because they cannot be effectively represented by a simple and rigid system.

A reframing of federalism must be based on the converse of these assumptions: the primacy of decentralization as a design principle, the possibility of constructing hybrid organizations to ensure that effective coordination ensues, and the requirement that singular communities be afforded a requisite voice through flexible instruments like regimes.

A regime-based federalism
This cannot be done without breaking down the traditional structures of territorial/ national federalism.

(a) Meeting the challenges
Plural societies have an explicit recognition that individuals and groups are motivated by different values, and that they can legitimately have different value systems. To pursue their different objectives and goals, they require positive freedom: capacity and opportunity to actively and effectively pursue these values, and the elimination of the constraints or unfreedoms that prevent them from doing so. Such communities and groups cannot be ignored.

The governance of diversity entails the harnessing of the forces at work in defining the desirable degree of decentralization, balkanization, and *métissage* in the governance system. For true variety does not simply consist of additive layers or groups of individuals living in totally separate worlds as in a quilt. Such a patchwork generates apartheid societies that are neither plural nor diverse in a true sense. They are simply parallel worlds; worlds of separate facilities.

If the degree of interaction between groups cannot be zero, it may vary greatly according to the different regimes in place pertaining to various issues. Indeed, not all groups have an equal interest in all issues. So it becomes more expedient to attempt to govern by segments.

Internationally, since there is no world government, the only alternative is to govern the world by segments. In each case, one can map out the terrain, identify the stakeholders, and design the relevant coordination mechanisms more or less separately from what is done in other terrains. This is the case with oceans, for instance (Paquet and Wilkins 2002). Consequently, a bottom-up approach to governance emerges piecemeal, segment by segment, with the reconciliation task being somewhat simplified by the fact that a dominant logic of "*une décentralisation incontournable*" has to imbibe the whole order, and so increases the probability that congruent regimes will in all likelihood emerge (Lachmann 1971).

The diffraction of socio-technical systems has shaken the foundations of the territorial/national state. Insisting that a dominant "territorial" or "national" logic should prevail is sufficient to derail federalism into a conflictive game. A decentralized subsidiarity-cum-multistability approach suggests that the best way to ensure that a system will be resilient is to devolve its governance downward, as much as possible, in a system deliberately fragmented or balkanized to ensure both that it is immunized against total crashes by enabling portions of the system to tackle external shocks independently, and that it can better deal with singular communities (Paquet 2005b).

A refurbished notion of federalism, built on principles of decentralization, subsidiarity and multistability, would appear to be promising. But it must be erected on a sort of partitioning of the system into segments that is likely to lend itself to the emergence of both sustainable regimes and a legitimate, if loosely-integrated order.

(b) Regimes

Stephen Krasner has defined regimes in international context as "sets of implicit and explicit principles, norms, rules and decision-making procedures around which actors' expectations converge in a given area of international relations" (Krasner 1983:2). This definition has been refined and expanded by Hasenclever et al., who have made more explicit the different conceptual elements of the definition: "Principles are beliefs of fact, causation and rectitude. Norms are standards of behavior defined in terms of rights and obligation. Rules are specific prescriptions or proscriptions for action. Decision-making procedures are prevailing practices for making and implementing collective choice" (Hasenclever et al. 1997:9).

Regimes are arrangements designed to ensure effective and robust coordination when power, information, and resources are widely distributed. Different regime theories have emphasized one aspect or another of this challenge. For instance, some have insisted mainly on the power variable, and made the other dimensions more or less dependent on the outcome of the power struggle. Others have emphasized the resources base of the interest groups in competition, and used the language of interdependency of game theorists to emphasize the dominant role of patterns of resources and situational variables in shaping the outcome. Another group has focused on information and knowledge as the key dimensions, and posited learning as the core force at work in epistemic communities.

There is no reason to believe that these simplifying views are mutually exclusive.

All these forces are at work in shaping the sort of regime likely to be effective, robust and capable of generating social learning. Consequently, regimes are likely to be hybrid forms of organization that will accommodate these three sources of tensions.

The component elements of a regime have been described in various ways. They are of necessity only loosely definable, since they have to adjust to the particular circumstances of each issue-area, and to the configuration of interests and communities at play.

One might suggest, however, a useful aggregation of the sources of order generated by regimes into two broad components that are in continuous interaction: (1) the principles defining the general normative framework, and (2) the rules and decision-making procedures defining the instrumental framework into which these norms will be echoed (Wolfe 2001).

These two sets of forces are in a constant process of inter-creation: principles and norms shaping rules and procedures, but rules and procedures also having an impact on the evolution of principles and norms as social learning proceeds.

The terrain on which regimes grow can be simply mapped in a three-dimensional box, spelling out the major families of *forces at work* (power, interdependency, cognition), the two *sources of order* (principles and norms, and rules and decision-making procedures), and the three main *objectives pursued* (efficiency, robustness, and resilience/learning).

Regimes are arrangements around which actor expectations converge. They are neither orderly nor systematic, but reveal some internal consistency and technical proficiency. They are identified in terms of problem areas, and define the framework prevailing in the coordination function in this area or domain. For instance, while a country may espouse the globalization syndrome in matters of trade, it may remain mercantilist when it comes to human capital, and outright exclusionist when it comes to immigration and social integration.

To the extent that the *terrain des operations* is quite diverse, and the array of interested stakeholders also quite varied, it might be that the best way to accommodate such terrains and such stakeholders is by dealing with them "relatively separately". In the same way that internationally we try to define regimes pertaining to special terrains, we would suggest that the same imperative applies on the national scene, in the face of turbulent times.

By partitioning the terrain into issues and "communities of meaning", it is possible to identify a vast number of sub-games that require specific treatment. This partitioning does not exclude some attention being given to territory and nation, but it does not provide these dimensions with the dominant role. Each issue-domain is multifaceted, and dealt with on an ad hoc basis.

(c) Chaords and forms of organizational *métissage*

The expression "ecology of governance" has been proposed by Walt Anderson to identify this new fluid form of governance: "many different systems and different kinds of systems interacting with one another, like the multiple organisms in an ecosystem" (Anderson 2001:252). Such arrangements are not necessarily "neat, peaceful, stable or efficient...but in a continual process of learning and changing and responding to feedback". This represents a transversal nexus of arrangements within the regime space.

An ecology of governance amounts to a group of loosely integrated "uncentralized networks", designed around issue-domains. A regime-based federalism would be one designed to facilitate social learning by ensuring that such networks correspond roughly to both issue-domains and "communities of meaning", while taking into account territorial and national dimensions.

Such an ecology of governance must remain an open system that has the capacity to learn and to evolve: the model is not a cathedral but a bazaar (Raymond 1999). This open system in turn shapes the required mix of principles and norms, but also of rules and decision-making procedures likely to promote the preferred mix of efficiency, resilience, and learning.

Issue-domains would not be simply allotted to "territories" or "nations" but would be the locus of an arena where the different interested communities

Figure 17: The regime space

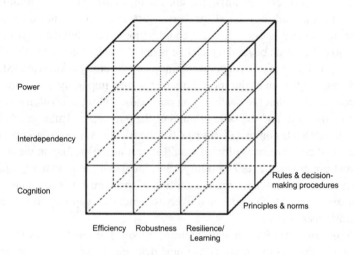

Power

Interdependency

Cognition

Rules & decision-making procedures

Principles & norms

Efficiency   Robustness   Resilience/Learning

would partake in the design of a participative organizational form allowing the appropriate mix of collaboration and competition. One would, for instance, deal with the issue of health with an appropriate forum, in the same way that forums are created internationally to handle critical issues, and accords or agreements of all sorts are arrived at in such forums.

Such efforts to fit the forum to the issue may appear unwieldy if pushed beyond certain limits, but if it is traded off against the convenience of pure territorial or national partitioning as a third meaningful dimension, it opens organizational forms to all sorts of new mixes that are bound to accommodate the variegated nature of the fabric of socio-technical systems in a much better way. In some cases, devolution should delegate to local communities that are both geographically homogeneous and socially connected, the decision-making process most likely to fit both territorial and community imperatives. In other cases, however, one may have to sacrifice some territorial expediency to satisfy the demands of variegated communities. It is questionable whether a meaningful debate about cultural policy could be conducted in local forums.

The template likely to be of use in a regime-based federalism may not be available yet, but it has been established by experiments in the private sector that uncentralized networks are workable arrangements, even in complex transnational arrangements. The most interesting example is the "chaord " (Hock 1995).

(d) Federalism as a mix of principles, regimes, chaords, and mechanisms

Moral contracts, conventions, etc. are the mechanisms and technologies of collaboration, and they lie at the very heart of regimes—not only do they outline the processes through which coordination occurs, but the ways in which, implicitly, the limits beyond which one is not allowed to proceed are defined.

De facto, the set of rules in good currency, and generally acknowledged, define the limits, very much as the speed limit on the road implicitly spells out what is regarded as the tolerable death toll on our roads. But there is often a large gap between the rules and the state of mind of the population. Rules are defined in the light of sanctimonious discourses that do not always take into account the unintended consequences of what would appear as reasonable on the surface.

Good governance entails a transparent, inclusive, participative, and fairly effective form of guidance via the crafting of mechanisms in keeping with the dominant logic of the regime, and likely to generate a capacity to transform as circumstances change.

Up to now there has been an attempt to collapse most issues into arenas and agoras defined by territorial/national debating areas. This is unreasonably reductive. In a diverse world, where no such reduction is possible, the only way to construct an order has been to build piecemeal on arrangements pertaining to particular issue areas.

This would entail a form of functional/personal federalism built on issues/ segments that lend themselves to some coordination scheme.

Instead of trying to allocate all the issues of interest to rigidly defined "layers" of decision-making, we need to design collective decision-making arrangements around issues. This would have the advantage of providing a basis of operation on an issue-by-issue basis, and allowing for a design process that suits the circle of stakeholders who have a true interest in the issue.

Instead of territory becoming the "essence", it remains a convenient conduit on occasion. Nationality can also be a useful conduit. But there may also be other conduits depending on the nature of the issue. For instance, in the case of health, it may turn out that the catchment area is the only relevant variable. This would mean that planning health governance on other bases is most inefficient.

For instance, it may well be that Eastern Ontario is a relevant unit in health care. This would entail a form of organization that would overview the catchment area. One could then propose an organizational form that is in keeping with this reality: a regional health authority. In other cases, personal federalism may be the obviously superior solution: dividing the state into associations, each of which comprises only individuals of the same nationality. In other cases, one might want to use the *"communauté nationale"* as the "best" basis of operation, in the sense proposed by André Laurendeau (Paquet 2000a).

There is a need for a set of basic principles that could apply to all these arrangements, much like those defined by the VISA company. Such principles may not generate instant unanimity, but they would probably be based on maximum participation of all interested stakeholders (to ensure legitimacy), on competition (i.e., overlapping jusrisdictions), on subsidiarity (i.e., a gamble on devolution) and on multistability (i.e., segmentation as a strategy to immunize against total crashes).

This would allow a new reconfiguration of federalism taking "communities of meaning" seriously, and allowing their presence to weigh heavily in the definition of federalism as social technology. Territory and nation would continue to have their importance, but they would see their import mitigated by the new imperatives of diversity.

Such an approach would not only force the re-examination of certain dossiers, and suggest very different arrangements, but would underline the importance of regarding any such arrangement as temporary—since the ground is in motion, and diversity is likely to acquire new faces. Consequently, a regime-based federalism would not only rely on a much more flexible toolbox, but would probably require that any formal or binding arrangement be revisited every ten years in the same way as is done with the Bank Act or company law.

Conclusion

Would a federalism based on territory, nation, and regime be more cumbersome than the existing schemes? Obviously. Would it be more effective? Probably. Would it solve all the problems generated by deep diversity? No.

It would, however, open the door to the design of more complex and innovative arrangements likely to deal less ineffectively with deep diversity. For the time being, most federalist schemes are in denial in the face of deep diversity. As a result, friendly dictatorship (Simpson 2001), territorial acrimony, and integrist nationalism have been allowed to shape the social technology, but little effort has been made to accommodate the new challenges of deep diversity. Factoring it in, even in a modest way, might revolutionize and modernize federalism.

Conclusion

Governance as Subversive Bricolage in the 21st Century: The Missing Links

"How might a new literacy of cooperation look?"
Howard Rheingold

Introduction

The shift from a geo-government based on the old trinity of state–nation–territory to a new and more fluid, mobile, slippery, shifty, evasive geo-governance has created new challenges. In this new game where geographical space plays a lesser and different role, where the state has lost its full grip on governing, and the nation and various other territories of the mind have woven a multiplicity of powerful reciprocal extraterritorialities of determining consequence, the game is without a master, and collaboration is the new imperative.

This is eminently subversive since it amounts to nothing less than an expropriation of the power base of most traditional and well-established potentates. Whatever the pretenses of state (national or territorial) leaders might be, they are faced with a turbulent environment marred by much disconcertation and conflicting equilibria, where each group recognizes that it cannot rid the systems of either its partners or opponents, but has to live and compromise with them to survive.

While this state of affairs may be perceived as a challenging novelty in certain countries, it has been a leitmotif in the history of Canada. Canada's identity has been shaped by a sequence of failed top–down planning efforts by French and British colonists (Paquet and Wallot 1987). Such failures yielded a fragmented world of groups with limited identities and very incomplete interaction, and generated "the many-coloured but miraculously coherent, if restless, pattern of the authentically Canadian nationhood" (Ross 1954:x–xi). Underpinning this baffling Canadianism is a creative and dynamic irony "opening outwards against—and through—a world of shut-ins. A hope confronting both the anarchic and the totalitarian" (Ross 1954:xii).

However, the powers of dynamic irony and self-organization do not guarantee good governance. In a book on *Governance Through Social Learning* a few years ago (Paquet 1999b), I explored the immense difficulties in achieving good governance in a turbulent world. A little later, I tried to respond to friends and foes in a debate about the strengths and weaknesses of the governance problématique developed by *l'Ecole d'Ottawa* (Cardinal and Andrew 2001).

It is only in the more recent past that I have become convinced that the amount of subversion required to effect a suitable transition to 21st century governance (and the amount of institutional carpentering needed to operationalize it) might be much greater than had been anticipated. The powers of creative irony are corrosive, but also at times too feeble to overcome the high degree of inertia and dynamic conservatism embodied in existing structures (Schön 1971). These forces may prevent the organic emergence of the new order.

Although the new evolving order may not emerge organically as easily as it should, it cannot be scripted *ab ovo* and installed ready-made by a *coup d'état* either (except temporarily). Modern socio-economies are complex adaptive systems that are always in a process of emergence. Consequently, much of their evolution cannot be deterministically designed: they co-evolve with their environment. The evolutionary process may proceed smoothly, but it may also get stalled and freeze the socio-economy in a dysfunctional state. When that is the case, the governing apparatus of the socio-technical systems in place must be significantly destabilized in order to ensure that the emergence process is not brought to a halt.

Much has been written about these traps, blockages, and pathologies, and about the ways to shake social systems free of them. We have explored these themes from different perspectives in three documents that have helped shape the nature of this chapter (Paquet 2004a,b, 2005b).

In the first section, the two basic conclusions one may draw from this extensive set of analyses are sketched: a *pessimisme mesuré* about what can be accomplished by social scientists at this time, and the presumption that one might benefit from using a mediological approach in tackling the challenges ahead—i.e., an approach attempting to understand, and to intervene, mainly through an appreciation of the mechanisms and shared spaces underpinning the key social ligatures and the ways in which ideas get translated into action (Debray 1991, 1994, 1997). In the next section, this provisional diagnosis is buttressed by an analytical framework emphasizing mechanisms as *primus inter pares* among the tools one might use to modestly guide the redesign of the governance apparatus such a transition requires. In the following section, the contours of some key terrains where investment in missing mechanisms may have the highest returns are briefly etched. The final section illustrates how such mechanisms might be used in the construction of technologies of collaboration.

Pessimisme mesuré and missing social learning loops

From our various forays into the always subversive and often pathological world of governance, two robust propositions would appear to emerge.

First, there is no satisfactory theory of governance providing a guide to good governance. Governance and geo-governance remain a series of challenges that have elicited only imperfect responses. One cannot even gauge the full extent of the repairs to the existing order needed to reach better governance. Indeed, we do not even know how to ascertain what the optimal amount of subversion required may be, or what terrain one might have to prospect to gain a good basic understanding of the underlying forces defining the necessary and sufficient conditions for social learning to proceed quickly and effectively. For now, complex adaptive systems are simply beyond the grasp of our understanding and our social engineering.

Some have suggested that these difficulties are temporary; that it is only a matter of time before we can come up with rules of good governance for our social systems, since we already have been able to suggest simple rules to govern complex systems in the animal world (Reynolds 1987; Resnick 1994). Others are more pessimistic and suggest that, in the case of truly complex adaptive systems like human societies, emergence is a constitutive dimension of reality, and one cannot hope to do more than to intervene lightly in the spirit of experimentation: governance through social learning, coping with the obstacles to good geo-governance through *bricolage* and tinkering with existing processes, structures, mechanisms, and rules. I tend to side with the pessimistic lot on this issue.

Second, in this sort of *bricolage* that we seem condemned to practice, central attention should be given to the installation of missing mechanisms likely (1) to limit the negative impact of the inertia associated with dynamic conservatism, and to neutralize the sources of these undesirable results, or (2) to broaden the basis of experimentation, and to catalyze the innovative forces at the root of the evolution of the institutional order.

The focus on mechanisms and "social technologies" (i.e., forms of coordination arrangements rooted in some particular physical support but shaping social relations) may at first appear to be less effective than focusing on principles, rules, or structures. Mediology has underlined the importance of paying attention to technical support, but only as a means to probe and understand forms of social coordination and mediation, and their evolution. What is interesting is not so much the details of the postal network, but the ways in which such a network has shaped the nation.

Principles are powerful instruments, but their generality is measured by what they ignore. They are often nothing but a mask for reductive ideology, and their reductionism is a major impediment to social learning (Fish 1999). Structures are also somewhat utopian devices: an approach built on structures presumes it to be sufficient to modify structures to transform behaviour. It is a bit of a gamble to so presume. The focus on processes has, on the other hand, proved too myopic as the process re-engineering literature has amply demonstrated.

Finally, it would appear premature to attempt to develop rules at this time, since we do not yet have a good theory of emergence. As for culture, it is such a diffuse phenomenon that it cannot provide a useful grip for transformative action. Cultural change is more likely to be an outcome or a cooperation-amplifying outgrowth than a direct lever for action.

Mechanisms offer a much less precise instrument, but an operational one. They lend themselves to improvisation and experimentation. Consequently, it is not that we feel particularly well served by mechanisms, but they are one of the few workable levers we have. Indeed, when one reflects on some of the broad features of the new ligatures that have been found particularly useful in seeking to construct good governance arrangements in practice, mechanisms would appear to be the operational unit most likely to be of use in our social architecture endeavour.

As Schön (1971) suggests, structure, theory, and technology are closely intertwined: any change in one of these three components of existing social systems triggers modifications in the others. New mechanisms usually transform the array of possible choices by extending the zone of possibilities. This in turn shapes choices differently, and generates new patterns of habituation and values. So new technological supports impact on organizational forms.

Individual priorities being transformed by changes in the array of possibilities represents only one sort of learning loop, however. There are also ways in which new technologies modify the structures and views of the world, and, through double-looped learning, redefine both means and ends as experience brings forth new information, and transform the ways in which both individuals and organizations learn (Kim 1993).

An analytical framework emphasizing mechanisms

Canada has chosen to face the challenge of intervening in this complex maze of relationships in a rather idiosyncratic way, inspired by much disappointment with grand theorizing. Canadian history has been plagued with magnificent failures of grandiose attempts at socio-political architecture (from the Colbert plan of a prefabricated society in New France, to the Meech and Charlottetown non-accords).

This Canadian emergent strategy has taken the form of a semi-passive, semi-active stand, allowing the resolution of social problems to emerge largely as the result of self-organization, with interventions being planned mainly as ways to eliminate blockages, to catalyze processes that would appear to be unduly slow, or to add missing links likely to straighten the sometimes crooked incentive reward system.

As a result, the modifications of the governance practices have proceeded *à petits pas, par morceau et par étapes*, often in informal ways. This eclectic approach has obliquely catalyzed a certain range of compatible but different principles, structures, processes, mechanisms, cultures, and rules throughout the land, that have ensured a sort of coordination that may appear at first rather inefficient (in a static sense), but has proved dynamically efficient, i.e., capable of ensuring much resilience and innovation.

Governance through social learning has therefore generated an assemblage of arrangements that lacks the coherence and integrity of an integrated top-down governing initiative, since it is the result of the emergence of meso-level solutions to "regional"/"sectoral" problems. In the face of such mobius-web governance, one must be satisfied with effecting modest improvements to the governance of the socio-economy as a learning system. This entails less focus on "big ideas", and more attention to mechanisms likely to provide an acceleration of the process of social learning. Much of this sort of intervention has been built on very simple lessons that would appear to have been learned unwittingly: incentives matter, markets fail, etc. (Heath 2003).

An analytical framework represents, at best, a toolbox from which one may draw the instruments to design the specific contours of the governance scheme likely to be effective in a particular setting.

The sort of analytical framework we have used to deal with geo-governance is an amalgam of some guiding metrics like opportunity costs; a few complementary basic principles (importance of true price–cost relations, subsidiarity, competition, maximum participation, multistability, etc.); enabling structures (markets, hierarchies, and networks); efficient processes—without minimizing the role of culture—and of a few mechanisms to ensure appropriate dialogue, inclusion, deliberation to help work things through, moral contracts, and applicable social conventions or norms.

This baroque apparatus has been used to analyze the governance of various transnational, national, and intra-national socio-technical systems. It has been used to construct the sort of social architecture and the panoply of ligatures, principles, structures, processes, mechanisms, and rules likely to weld together assets, skills, and capabilities into complex temporary communities of practice (Wenger et al. 2002), capable of generating both the requisite coherence and as many degrees of freedom as possible. Such experimentation often entails the construction of missing mechanisms, linking otherwise less well connected nodes, or providing for richer interaction.

This cautious approach—it is worth repeating—should not be interpreted as an abandonment of the quest for principles or rules that might hold the key to human complex adaptive systems (Gell-Mann 1994). But we still lack a full-blown theory of emergence, and a second-best strategy would appear to start with mechanisms (Holland 1998).

Yet mechanisms are most unreliable links: they may as easily work in one direction as another. This elusiveness is best captured by Jon Elster's formulation—"if p, then sometimes q" (Elster 1998:52). Much depends on circumstances and situational features. For instance, an increase in opportunities may either increase a group's level of satisfaction, or (if aspiration levels increase faster than the opportunities) generate discontent. This explains why economic progress sometimes causes contentment and sometimes ignites a revolution.

The choice of a mediological (mechanism-based) approach is, however, not easy for those social scientists still haunted by the dream of grand theories and 'magnificent macroscopic dynamics' applicable to all circumstances. This still eludes us most of the time in the social sciences. During the 19th and the first half of the 20th century, the social sciences were obsessed by the challenge of building some fort of "social physics". It is only of late that this sort of ambitious programme has been revised to fit better with the sort of practices in good currency, and with the sort of results they can reasonably be expected to produce: probing the mechanisms at work that underpin middle-range phenomena and mechanisms of communication, and mediation as building blocks (Hedström and Swedberg 1998).

For example, we have explored the dynamics of inter-cultural relations through the lens of three interacting mechanisms: cumulative causation à la Myrdal, the link between egalitarianism and envy à la Tocqueville, and the mechanism of mimesis and violence à la Girard (Laurent and Paquet 1991). This represents an experiment in the small that has revealed how interacting mechanisms may hold the key to a better understanding of the emergence of complex phenomena like intercultural relations.

The objective here is to suggest that this strategy could be somewhat generalized to a large number of sub-assemblies of mechanisms capable of (1) inducing dialogue, (2) amplifying cooperation, and (3) fostering emergence.

Some sub-assemblies of mechanisms

A useful way to probe mobius-web governance patterns might be to map out in two dimensions both the broad families of ligatures making up governance arrangements (horizontally)—partnering (P), accountabilities and ethics (AE), leadership and trust (LT), and enaction, control and stewardship (ECC)—and (vertically) the variety of instrumentalities used to embody and operationalize these different families of ligatures—principles, structures, processes, mechanisms, cultures, and rules.

The families of ligatures needed for effective governance are not exhausted by PAELTECS, and neither are the instrumentalities exhausted by our list of bonds. However, we feel that the interfaces revealed by this provisional framework are the loci of the major sources of blockages and pathologies.

Table 3: An analytical framework for subversive intervention

	Partnering	Accountabilities & ethics	Leadership & trust	Enaction, control & stewardship
Principles				
Structures				
Processes				
Mechanisms				
Culture				
Rules				

As discussed in the last section of this chapter, the particular focus of our inquiry is on the array of mechanisms that would appear to be missing under each of the broad families of ligatures. These missing mechanisms are preventing the emergence of an effective geo-governance, and putting them in place would appear to be the most promising levers to catalyze the emergence of improved geo-governance arrangements.

In the case of each of the broad families of ligatures, an effort has been made to identify the reasons why they are particularly important for good governance, what functions the missing mechanisms may play, and how one might make good use of them to provide the requisite subversion.

(a) In the new geo-governance, the first and foremost need is for *partnerships*, for there can be no effective coordination if the different stakeholders do not find ways to work together. This in turn calls for two different sets of specific mechanisms that we have labeled P-mechanisms: the Yankelovich mechanism, and the Sacconi mechanism.

The first P-mechanism pertains to dialogue, i.e., the forum or agora for deliberation. In order for a partnership to be formed, there must first be a place where the stakeholders can struggle to reconcile their viewpoints, and can work through their relations to others, and frame reconciliation via dialogue (Yankelovich 1999; Rosell 2000).

The second P-mechanism pertains to the basic conditions necessary for a partnership to work. While the specific conditions may vary widely from situation to situation, two fundamental requirements stand out in a workable "social contract": ensuring that all parties gain from the arrangement, and that each party is provided with the incentives to honour its obligations even when they do not constitute the preferred option (Sacconi 2000).

The P-mechanisms required (to ensure the existence of a place for deliberation and the appropriate social contracts to ensure interest and compliance in the accord) are often missing. So it will be necessary to design some version of them in line with the feelings, values, and moral convictions of all parties, as illustrated in the discussion on ocean governance (Paquet and Wilkins 2002).

This entails creating the requisite agoras (information sharing places, shared spaces, consultation/negotiation tables, and the like) for clusters of stakeholders in different sectors or regions. These agoras often suffice to trigger the conventions modulating the interactions among the partners. Such innocuous "territories of the mind" acquire their own dynamics, and often generate an expanding set of richer and deeper interactions. What was at first a simple information exchange mechanism, at the origin of the world weather network, has become the basis of extensive and deep partnerships and binding agreements (Cleveland 2002). Yankelovich-Rosell-type mechanisms would appear to generate the conditions for the emergence of Sacconi-type mechanisms.

The information commons that is usually the launching pad for such arrangements explains why the integration is done bottom–up, piecemeal and stepwise. It builds on a perceived limited zone of common interests that may take time to develop and to take hold, and may not be amenable, anywhere but locally, to the sort of loose monitoring that generates the incentive not to shirk.

Quite clearly, the creation of loci for multilogue and deliberation is not an instrument that will necessarily ensure that particular objectives will be met. These mechanisms only provide for better communication and interaction, and therefore for potential accelerated social learning. They are likely to produce an array of new and resilient forms of collaboration but without ensuring that this collaboration will take the form or lead to the results that some of the opinion-molders would favour. Social learning will thereby be improved, and consequently collective intelligence, but not necessarily the pursuit of objectives favoured by officials.

In the summer of 2003, Premier Jean Charest of the Council of the Federation introduced a mechanism, hitherto missing, that would provide a permanent forum for Canadian Premiers to meet and sort out their zones of agreement and differences. No one can really ascertain what might emerge from such a new mechanism of coordination, but it would most certainly constitute much more than simply another layer of bureaucracy—a mistaken evaluation that unreflective journalists were quick to propose (Cohen 2003).

(b) One must also ensure that the appropriate mechanisms of vertical, horizontal, and transversal *accountability* and *ethics* are in place, so that the requisite feedback and social learning operate well, that the system stays within the bounds of acceptable behaviour, and good governance ensues. This calls for a multitude of AE-mechanisms, ranging from routine feedbacks and rendering of accounts to ethics-based mechanisms.

Such mechanisms of accountability cannot solely be based on financial accountability to superiors. Accountability is a much more complex concept than is usually presumed. And one has to recognize that only "softer forms" of accountability are plausible when most agents are faced with 360-degree accountabilities and a rendering of accounts in many dimensions (financial, administrative, operational, etc.).

The development of an effective pattern of accountabilities is the most important challenge of the new geo-governance. In a game without a master, the very multitude of accountabilities has led some cynics to suggest that anything goes. Such is not the case. But the new constellation of accountabilities calls for a multitude of mechanisms that deliver feedback and provide the basis for a constant process of construction of trade-offs among these various dimensions (Juillet et al. 2001).

Such accountabilities are embodied in moral contracts that can only be couched in the most general terms. Covenants of that sort, though vague, are binding. However, they are binding only to the extent that a battery of moral and social control mechanisms give credence to them. Accountability without feedback and discipline does not mean much.

It is the very multitude of reference or focal points generated by the 360-degree accountabilities that makes the collective decision-making process so complex: the guideposts for effective feedback and social learning are numerous and pull in different directions, yet their conjunction stewards the socio-technical system.

There is much resistance to the very notion of soft accountability, and to the deployment of 360-degree accountabilities (and therefore to the abolition of one over-riding accountability) as a foundational feature of the new geo-governance. As a result, very little effort has been invested in developing a clearer notion of what they are, and of the ways in which they might be operationalized. It is even more difficult when one attempts to gauge the workability of "moral contracts" according to their ethical content. Depending on the reference points used in defining the "ethical mechanisms" (fear of punishment, satisfaction of personal needs, need approval, respect for law and authority, contractual moral obligations, broad principles of justice and universal rights) there can be a significant difference in the nature of the corridor of acceptable behaviour (Kohlberg 1981).

The "moral contract mechanisms" therefore perform a dual task: they provide a working definition of expectations for the different actors vis-à-vis the different stakeholders, and a rough definition of the boundaries of the corridor of acceptable behaviour. Again, these constraints do not ordain specific results, but somewhat limit or shape the acceptable outcomes. They also provide levers for intervention that may be determinant since they construct the foundation for new accountabilities or redefine the feasibility boundaries of the bargaining zone.

It is easy to imagine how new consultation and bargaining mechanisms underlining different accountabilities or ethical focal points within the federation, or within continental groups, might completely transform the game.

However weak the mechanisms at work in buttressing the Kyoto Protocol are, or however feeble the moral power of a Fair Trade Organization (à la Monbiot 2003) charged with debating the ways in which gains from trade are shared, they would generate an incentive to take into account the full impact of the present sharing of gains from trade, and would inevitably lead to some accommodation. They might have the same impact on amplifying the negotiation space that ensues when accounting procedures do not simply measure returns on the shareholders' investments, but establish clearly—as *la méthode des surplus* does (Perrin 1976)—how the surplus generated by the operations have been shared among the stakeholders.

(c) One must ensure that the geo-governance scheme provides the required *leadership and trust* to shepherd the socio-technical system in a manner that will ensure a sustainable and workable state of affairs likely to satisfy all parties. We have labeled these LT-mechanisms and they are of two types: those eliminating or attenuating rivalry and envy à la Myrdal-Tocqueville-Girard (MTG), and those building social capital and trust à la O'Toole.

These mechanisms are geared (1) to eliminating the blockages that prevent the appropriate degree of listening and open-mindedness to other parties in the forum (likely to lead not only to deliberation but to the overcoming of rivalry) and (2) to generating the requisite degree of trust for solidarity and followership to blossom.

The first family of LT-mechanisms pertains to overcoming the rivalry and envy that always threaten the possibility of cooperation. We have explored elsewhere the ways in which intercultural relations are corrupted by the MTG-mechanism: (1) according to Gunnar Myrdal, cultural differences create transaction costs among groups, and this leads to intra-group networking and social capital accumulation that accentuate intercultural differences through a cumulative causation process, and create blockages to cooperation; (2) such differences can only be further exacerbated by the "decreed equality" that has become the staple of democratic societies (as Tocqueville suggests, the passion for equality in a world of increasing inequalities can only generate envy); (3) such envy in turn, as René Girard has suggested, can only lead to competition and violence (Laurent and Paquet 1991).

Many strategies and mechanisms of concealment or sharing have been used to tame these destructive forces, but the only workable schemes would appear to be based either on a certain degree of segmentation and social distance or on the development of a certain civil theology that would allow, through new solidarities and citizenship, the requisite degree of trust to emerge, minimizing envy and therefore the probability of non-cooperation and violence.

Neutralizing MTG-type mechanisms at work in geo-governance will require tinkering with existing structures, which are fundamentally undemocratic. As long as the United Nations general assembly is dominated by the Security Council's permanent members and their veto, as long as major decisions at the International Monetary Fund and the World Bank require an 85% majority and the U.S. holds 17% of the votes, a few can veto any resolution they dislike (Monbiot 2003). One must therefore create mechanisms capable of circumventing these formal structures, or ensure that they operate in ways more fair: the institution of the Summit of Spouses of leaders of the countries in the Americas, and pressures to democratize the UN general assembly are examples of such strategies.

The second family of LT-mechanisms pertains to the degree of effective orientation one may impart to collective action through mechanisms of respect. Tact, civility, and rituals are the foundation on which respect often rests. There can be no agreed acceptance of leadership (and therefore consensual following) unless the roots of envy and violence have been eliminated, and respect reigns.

These trust-building mechanisms are the foundation of robust leadership, and underpin the whole institutional order (Fukuyama 1995; Thuderoz et al. 1999; Braithwaite and Levi 1998; Solomon and Flores 2001). They also underpin a variety of strategies used to build system trust—i.e., trust not only in individuals, but also in socio-technical systems like ISO 9000.

James O'Toole (1995) has shown that all true leadership is based on a good measure of listening, and that respect is the foundation on which trust is built. Leadership mechanisms are indeed based on a foundation of trust and respect; however, building trust requires the development of routines and practices that allow confrontations and engagements, commitments and promises, offers and requests in an atmosphere of "civility". Civility is the word Vaclav Havel has used to connote the respectful attention paid by leaders who want to earn the trust of their followers. The mechanisms of civility are often underestimated, in spite of being most powerful.

An example of the most effective use of such a lever is the experiment with the enforcement of the use of "vous" instead of "tu" in some French-speaking Quebec schoolyards. Schoolyard violence was reduced dramatically as a result.

(d) As a matching set of mechanisms congruent with the constellation of accountabilities/ethics mentioned above, one must have in place a constellation of feedback mechanisms to ensure social learning. We have labeled these mechanisms (they are the flip side of the accountability/ethics mechanisms) *enaction, control, and stewardship* mechanisms, or ECS-mechanisms. They are self-regulation mechanisms that provide the requisite feedback at the source of collective intelligence and social learning, and contribute to their evolution.

These mechanisms can be categorized into four types.

The traditional Wiener-type mechanisms (Wiener 1948) are strictly self-correcting and stabilizing feedback mechanisms that are meant to ensure some degree of self-conservation. A good example might be the usual automatic stabilizers like transfer payments, used in economic policy.

A second group of Arthur-type mechanisms (Arthur 1994) are "feed forward" or amplifying mechanisms that generate cumulative causation. This family of mechanisms brings the system beyond certain thresholds and may generate discontinuities. The mechanisms are not necessarily disruptive, for they may also be amplifiers of cooperation, and therefore a source of stimulation to social learning.

Often the mechanisms in place operate well within the corridor of normal times, but fail when cumulative causation feeds abnormal circumstances. What is required then is the installation of mechanisms that operate only in abnormal times, and are triggered by the system's being dragged beyond certain thresholds. A good example is the switch in codes of conduct in wartime.

A third group of Varela-type mechanisms (Varela 1989) are geared to guide the evolution of the socio-technical system through a process of enaction or creative "*faire-émerger*" that springs from the cognitive process itself.

It contributes to the creation of "new worlds" through articulating and integrating the interactions between the context and the cognitive capabilities as they have emerged from history. These schemes change the "visions of the world" of actors and groups and the frames or reference through which they view the world.

Failure to put such mechanisms in place would slow down the work of the social learning cycle considerably and therefore also the transformation of the socio-technical system. Such reframing capabilities may come from neutralizing the deafening impact of ideology, or from mind-expanding experimentation, or from the design of new ethical guidelines. Often, such transformations of the cognitive process are generated by the emergence of guidelines like ones suggested by the federal government on July 14, 2003 (at the summit on progressive governance). These outlined a code of responsibility regarding intervention in cases where the intervention violates national sovereignty arrangements, but human rights violations would appear to warrant such *ingérence*.

A fourth group—Wright-mechanisms—transforms the very nature of the game: these mechanisms inject new dynamics into socio-technical systems, act as cooperation amplifiers, and point to the progressively greater use of more and more complex meta-technologies (like money, charters, etc.) to enable humans to transform zero-sum games into more and more complex non-zero-sum games (Wright 2000). The new mobile communication technology and pervasive computation facilitate the further emergence and use of meta-technologies capable of elevating the degree of non-zero-sum game playing, and thereby contributing to better geo-governance (Rheingold 2002).

These four sub-assemblies of ECS-mechanisms are at the core of the governing of socio-technical systems. They underpin the resilience of the system, i.e., its capacity to spring back vibrant and more or less transformed after shock. Each of these sub-assemblies of mechanisms is a different regime of self-organization: from simple self-correction, to self-stabilization and regulation, to self-reorganization, to self-re-creation.

The temptation to intervene in only one of the four pillars (P, AE, LT, ECS) or to do so only at the most general level (sermons on principles or culture) is very high. Focusing in this way on only one domain, and only on evasive thinking about it, avoids the tedium of designing the assemblage of mechanisms, structures, processes, and rules that might incentivize high standards of governance.

Mechanisms are of great importance, but one ought not restrict one's attention exclusively to mechanisms: while they are the most important lever, they cannot be insulated from the principles that underpin their use, or from the processes, structures, and rules they are meant to subvert. Consequently, the sort of "hybrid governance" likely to ensue from tinkering with mechanisms often refuses to lend itself to neat and tidy descriptions. What we are faced with is often an "ecology of governance"—"many different systems and different kinds of systems interacting with one another, like the multiple organisms of an eco-system" (Anderson 2001: 252). And the result is a sort of institutional *metissage* that may not be peaceful, stable, and efficient (in a static sense) but rather a baroque assemblage in a continual process of learning and changing and responding to feedback (Jacquet et al. 2002; Hubbard and Paquet 2002; Paquet 2003b).

An ecology of governance and cooperation-amplifying mechanisms

Although there are some examples of particularly creative and fruitful confluences of mechanisms that have triggered important surges of cooperation, one of the great tragedies of the governance world is the fact that such confluences are relatively rare. It is more often the case that the required mechanisms are either missing, fail to live up to expectations, or neutralize one another. There is either (1) no place for dialogue and deliberation, or for collaborative arrangements to be negotiated; or (2) no way to neutralize and overcome rivalry and envy; and little possibility of building much partnering and leadership on inexistent trust; (3) or little in the way of intelligent mutual accountability mechanisms; or (4) not much of the requisite enaction, control, and stewardship mechanisms for effective social learning. As a result, geo-governance flounders.

Reflecting on the best way to intervene in this nexus of forces, it becomes clear that the only successful way to catalyze the social learning process somewhat is to build on the dynamics at work within the ecology of forces presented earlier.

(a) a sort of cascading effect in the innovation commons
One of the most important aspects of this dynamic is a sort of cascading effect among these mechanisms: when a place for dialogue and deliberation emerges, collaborative arrangements blossom, trust is built, intelligent accountabilities materialize, and enaction, control, and stewardship mechanisms that allow the socio-technical system to evolve meaningfully materialize. There is also a "thickening", so to speak, of this string of mechanisms: they expand to incorporate structural and cultural changes, and coalesce into new principles and rules. Well-designed interventions therefore have an impact (not always conscious or deliberate) that promotes an amplification and a deepening of cooperation, both horizontally and vertically.

While we do not fully comprehend the dynamics of this *innovation commons*, it is clearly at work. We have observed it in the Gulf of Maine, and in smart communities; Harland Cleveland has noted it in the world weather system; Howard Rheingold tracked it down in a variety of areas. New mechanisms lead to a reverberation throughout the organizational space of forces (shown in figure 1) that underpin collective intelligence and social learning.

Some have suggested a focus on mechanisms grafted onto the state.

The state has a useful role to play, but it may be counterproductive to ascribe to states the whole responsibility for such anchoring. In modern democracies, the sort of citizen participation entailed by the mechanisms sketched above is a challenge to the usual method of representation: it short-circuits the usual process through which the collective will is supposedly expressing itself in the polity—the ballot box (Cardinal and Andrew 2001). The mechanisms that promote dialogue, partnering, leadership and the like are the very fabric of governance, but have a subversive impact on the state.

The Economic Council of Canada and the Science Council of Canada—instruments of direct group intervention via advisory bodies—were soon seen as challenging the views of elected governments, whatever the merits of the messages they voiced. These interesting mechanisms of communication between Canadian interest groups and governments were abolished because they were opening channels of unwelcome communication.

That proliferation of roundtables on all sorts of issues have fizzled out after a few seasons should serve as a cautionary tale. The same may be said about carefully designed task forces that have simply been ways for the government to forcefully express its views through third parties. Neither approach is promising.

But other forces are at work. Some say that the new "social imaginaries"—"the ways people imagine their social existence, how they fit together with others, how things go on between them and their fellows, the expectations that are normally met, and the deeper normative notions and images that underlie these expectations" (Taylor 2004:23)—have now generated new ideas of collective agency, new senses of belonging, and new ways to come to a common mind without the mediation of the political sphere (91). The rise of a public sphere that is not state-centred may well be a harbinger of the end for the state-centric "jacobine illusion" that all must be handled through the political sphere and through enforced uniformity (Balladur 2005). Much will depend on the capacity of civil society to play its subversive role.

(b) Civil society as the main source of contestation and subversion

Both the private and the public sectors are somewhat limited by the prevalence of their dominant logics: the logic of profit, and the logic of power respectively. Civil society is more unpredictable. It may generate the most varied initiatives, rooted in a wide array of constellations of interests, and based on quite diverse logics. This very unpredictability prevents or slows down the development of counter-powers, and this may at times prove an important asset (Angus 2001).

Greenpeace is an interesting constellation of members with quite different concerns, which has been able to articulate radical positions and engineer daring methods of intervention. It has probably had a potent impact on environmental policy in most industrialized countries. Countries that were trying to counter Greenpeace—France, e.g.—had to engineer covert operations leading to explicit violence. Yet these efforts proved futile.

Civil society partnerships elicit bottom–up leadership based on trust, and are able to fend counter-attacks largely thanks to their very fuzziness and diffuseness. States are often forced—*en dernière instance*—to fight them through various forms of restriction on their financing. For instance, the legal requirements for charity status from national revenue agencies—and the consequent right to collect tax deductible financial support—put very stringent limitations on the advocacy role of such groups. Similar constraints are constantly generated to paralyze the citizenry, and to prevent civil society from reclaiming its primacy (Gairdner 1996).

One of the main ideological sacred cows used to prevent civil society from having its way is the phony presumption that key social concerns like education and health if not handled by the state, (1) will either not be handled at all or (2) will be done inequitably.

The first contention is disproved daily by the ingenious ways in which citizens deal pragmatically with a variety of coordination problems through mutual agreements and contracts. Ostrom (1990) and McGinnis (2000) have provided numerous examples of such effective coordination in polycentric games.

As for the inequity argument, it is an ideological one used to prevent the citizen from taking control of his/her own affairs by promulgating as a foundational tenet the bizarre principle that "unless everyone can have some thing, nobody should be allowed to have it". By turning egalitarianism into such an icon, and by denying that mutuality could lead somewhere, the state edicts that only coercion works, and that loyalty to the state should prevail over accountability to one's neighbour. Yet, this statist argument fails to persuade.

And although the idea of a global society appears somewhat utopian, there is no reason to believe that a global civil society is not in the making. It may emerge *par morceau* and informally in the guise of a "covenant", but this is the very best way for it to immunize itself from the centralized mindset and control of global state institutions.

(c) Centralized mindset versus prototyping

Circumnavigating the state does not mean that there will be no opposition to social learning. The state will continue to intervene to promote centralization and standardization in the name of egalitarianism.

Two interesting bottom-up initiatives in Canada—a new way to structure discussions among the federal, provincial, and local levels of government around the notion of fiscal imbalance, and a new agora in a Council of the Federation—have recently been dismissed out of hand by the Canadian federal government and its epigoni, largely on ideological grounds, as the liberal constitutional project presumes that the federal government knows best (Carter 1998).

The first initiative was a way to cast the raw power debates among federal, provincial, and local agencies in a new light, by examining the match or mismatch between fiscal resources and responsibilities. Many federal cabinet ministers immediately reacted by propounding that a fiscal imbalance could not logically exist in Canada as taxes can always be raised as needed by the various levels of government. This is not only intellectually dishonest, but analytically wrong. Any first-year economics student would recognize that the citizen cannot be squeezed separately and independently by any one level of government without eroding the potential tax base of the others (Paquet 2002b).

The possible use of this framework for discussion—likely to underpin a reasoned way to recast the contours of Canadian fiscal federalism—was simply squashed because any such discussion could only lead to a shift toward subsidiarity-based governance, depriving the federal organs of many of their powers (Paquet 1999c).

The second initiative is the proposal for a Council of the Federation. It has been caricatured by the centralized-mindset tribe as nothing but an additional layer of bureaucracy, and a ploy by the provinces to put pressure on the federal government (Cohen 2003). In Ottawa, there is little understanding of the importance of drawing up forums and mechanisms. Raw politics and the commitment to egalitarianism-cum-centralization are the ruling dogmas. The fact that educational issues, city issues, and inter-regional trade issues cannot be resolved without these tripartite conversations would appear to not be understood.

This lack of comprehension about the usefulness of dialogue is hardly surprising. The "liberal constitutional project" (as Stephen Carter labels it) is predicated on the belief that only the central government has the capacity to appreciate the nature of today's problems, and to suggest meaningful solutions to them. "Solutionism" or "ultrasolutionism" is indeed the name of the game: issues are interpreted as puzzles to which there is a solution, rather than problems to which there may be a response (Paquet 2004b).

Social learning calls for exactly the converse: prototyping, i.e., the development of rough and ready arrangements, around which collaboration and negotiations might be built. Schrage (2000) has shown that rough prototypes serve as social media and mechanisms to create dialogue and cooperation, and are the source of much of the innovation in all sectors. Prototypes create shared space, turn transactors into partners, are the platform for much co-development and evolutionary development, and provide tools for accelerated social learning. Indeed, it may even be said that prototyping is the basis for all learning—from language to values (Paquet 2003b).

When Microsoft made 400,000 beta-version copies (the prototype of the final product) of Windows 95 freely available to organizations and individuals ready to detect bugs and flaws or to suggest improvements in exchange for receiving the product in advance and for free, it was suggested that it had created a shared space with this prototype, and that it probably received over $1 billion worth of added value from the counsels of its customers and potential users.

The modern comptrollership initiative currently underway in Canada may well provide an extraordinary experimental ground for the study of e-government, and a most useful introduction to the reconstruction of Canadian governance in a digital world, if it were to make full use of prototyping. To the extent that it avoids the perils of the centralized mindset, while keeping fully in sight the possibilities of the new ICTs, and the need to experiment with new HR regimes, the modern comptrollership initiative might be seen as 100 meaningful experiments to rethink the ways in which the federal government might help reframe its participation in 100 shared spaces. This might be sufficient to identify what works and what does not, the best way to partition the public service anew to face the new network age, and the ways in which the new technologies may help not only in revamping Canadian government, but in reframing Canadian governance (Paquet 2004b).

(d) The tipping effect of new accountability mechanisms

If prototypes can serve as a useful device to kickstart cumulative learning, what will trigger a coalescence of these mechanisms into a pattern that will strengthen the required "*faire émerger*" capabilities?

While there is a *prima-facie* case for putting in place shared space for multilogue—promising due to the possibility of it triggering a massive propagation effect in the subversive intervention tableau—the lack of predictability regarding the impact of agora-building has led impatient interventionists to search for better tipping points.

There can be no governance without accountability. And accountability has to do with who can request information when, from whom, about what, and under what conditions. One of the features of mobius-web-type governance—effective coordination when resources, power, and information are in a multiplicity of hands—is the absence of a single focal point as well as a simple overarching accountability framework. The absence of specific and specified links between the various elements of the system, coupled with the absence of a single focal point, suggest the development *ab ovo* of an optimal governance/accountability scheme to be unlikely. The best hope is for the development of a performance report that would force into existence this governance/accountability scheme.

Much can be accomplished through performance reporting, because it often has a trigger or tipping effect on the performance and governance of the system. As agents and groups are inserted into a cycle of reporting, monitoring, and rendering of accounts, gaps become more visible, and one may expect that these gaps being exposed will lead to the development of mechanisms to fill them.

As multiple accountabilities come to be regarded as a fact of life, and soft accountabilities as legitimate, there will be recognition that effective coordination requires an array of informal mechanisms of collaboration, that trust has to be built, and that collective intelligence and social learning are the underpinnings of evolution.

There has been much learning internationally following the GATT era. Those were the days of mutual accountabilities; no executive power existed. As a result, the very notion of accountability (like the notion of property rights) was considerably transformed: it became less "absolute"; imperial powers were dwarfed, and the possibility of a contagion of changes throughout the system were heralded, while specific interventions in engineering appropriate mechanisms resulted in some accountability linkages being increased dramatically.

Conclusion

There is no truly general theory providing the necessary and sufficient conditions for good geo-governance.

Many observers have sketched plausible schemes, from the most decentralized to the most centralized, but, as we have suggested earlier, these efforts at "grand scheming" are not very promising. What is most likely to materialize over time is the sort of step-by-step integration that has been effected in Europe, and is under way in the Americas. This is also in progress for "ocean territories" as well as for "territories of the mind".

Such a work in progress is bound to be somewhat messy and forever fundamentally incomplete. It is also bound to be only partially controllable, and subject at best to *bricolage*. The fact that it will retain a baroque flavour is inevitable.

As for the chaordic nature of the geo-governance likely to ensue: it is in the making, and remains a hypothesis for now. However, it appears to meet with less and less skepticism as the work progresses (Hock 1999; Rosenau 2003).

Acknowledgments

Although they have been modified a number of times, important segments of several chapters have been drawn from previously published papers.

Introduction and Chapter 3

2001. The New Governance, Subsidiarity and the Strategic State. In W. Michalski et al. (ed). *Governance in the 21st Century*. Paris: OECD. 183–214.

Chapter 1

1995. Institutional Evolution in an Information Age. In T. J. Courchene (ed.). *Technology, Information and Public Policy. The Bell Canada Papers in Economics and Public Policy, 3*. Kingston: John Deutsch Institute for the Study of Economic Policy. 197–229.

Chapter 2

1997. States, Communities and Markets: The Distributed Governance Scenario. In T. J. Courchene (ed). *The Nation-State in a Global Information Era: Policy Challenges. The Bell Canada Papers in Economics and Public Policy, 5*. Kingston: John Deutsch Institute for the Study of Economic Policy. 25–46.

Chapter 4

2003. Ecologies of Governance and Institutional Metissage (with R. Hubbard). *Optimumonline* 32(4): 25–34.

Chapter 5

2000. *On Hemispheric Governance. Transactions of the Royal Society of Canada.* 6(10): 9–21.

Chapter 6

1998. Technonationalism and Meso Innovation Systems. In R. Anderson et al (eds). *Innovation Systems in a Global Context.* Montreal: McGill-Queen's University Press. 58–75.

Chapter 7

2001. Smart Communities and the Geo-governance of Social Learning. *Optimumonline.* 31(2): 33–50.

Chapter 8

The governance of sustainability. A social learning approach. Inaugural address to the First National Colloquium on the Governance of Sustainable Development. (January 26, 2004).

Chapter 9–10

2002. *Ocean Governance: An Inquiry into Stakeholding* (with K. Wilkins). Ottawa: Centre on Governance.

Chapter 11

2003. Toward a Baroque Governance in 21ˢᵗ Century Canada. In C. Gaffield and K. L. Gould (eds). *The Canadian Distinctiveness into the 21st Century.* Ottawa: The University of Ottawa Press. 59–88.

Chapter 12

2004. Governance and Emergent Transversal Citizenship, Pluralism and Governance: Toward a New Nexus of Moral Contracts. In P. Boyer, L. Cardinal and D. Headon (eds). *From Subjects to Citizens: One Hundred Years of Citizenship in Australia and Canada.* Ottawa: The University of Ottawa Press. 231–61.

Bibliography

Abrahamson, E. and C. J. Fombrun. 1994. Macrocultures: Determinants and consequences. *Academy of Management Review.* 19(4): 728–55.

Acs, Z., J. de la Mothe, and G. Paquet. 1996. Local systems of innovation: Toward an enabling strategy. In P. Howitt, ed. *The implications of knowledge-based growth for microeconomic policies.* Calgary: University of Calgary Press. 339–58.

Adelman, I. 1973. Social and economic development at the micro level. In E. B. Ayal, ed. *Micro aspects of development.* New York: Praeger. 3–13.

Adger, W. N. et al. 2002. *Governance for sustainability: Towards a 'thick' understanding of environmental decision making.* University of East Anglia: CSERGE Working Paper EDM 02–04.

Agamben, G. 1993. *The coming community.* Minneapolis: The University of Minnesota Press.

———. 2000. *Means without end: Notes on politics.* Minneapolis: The University of Minnesota Press.

Amin, A. and N.Thrift. 1995. Institutional issues for the European regions: From markets and plans to socioeconomics and powers of association. *Economy and Society.* 24(1): 43–66.

Anderson, W. T. 2001. *All connected now.* Cambridge, MA: Westview Press.

Angus, D. E. and M. Bégin. 2000. Governance in health care: Dysfunctions and challenges. In *Transactions of the Royal Society of Canada.* 6(10): 171–93.

Angus, I., 2001. *Emergent publics.* Winnipeg: Arbeiter Ring Publishing.

Archibugi, D., ed. 2003. *Debating cosmopolitics.* London: Verso.

Argyris, C. 1996. Prologue: towards a comprehensive theory of management. In B. Moingeon and A. Edmonsdon, eds. *Organizational learning and competitive advantage.* London: Sage.

———— and D. A. Schön. 1974. *Theory in practice*. San Francisco: Jossey-Bass.

————. 1978. *Organizational learning: A theory of action perspective*. Reading, MA: Addison-Wesley.

———— et al. 1985. *Action Science*. San Francisco: Jossey-Bass.

Arthur, W.B. 1988. Self-reinforcing mechanisms in economics. In P. W. Anderson et al., eds. *The economy as an evolving complex system*. Reading, MA: Addison-Wesley. 9–31.

————. 1990. 'Silicon Valley' locational clusters: When do increasing returns imply monopoly? *Mathematical Social Sciences*. 19: 235–51.

————. 1994. *Increasing returns and path dependence in the economy*. Ann Arbor: The University of Michigan Press.

Ashby, W. R. 1960. *Design for a brain*. London: Chapman.

————. 1970. *An introduction to cybernetics*. London: Chapman & Hall.

Atkins, G. P. 1993. Institutional arrangements for hemispheric free trade. *The Annals of the American Academy of Political and Social Science*. 526 (March): 183–94.

Atkinson, D. B., and B. Bennett. 1994. Proceedings of a northern cod workshop held in St. John's Newfoundland, 27–29 January 1993. Canadian Technical Report of Fisheries and Aquatic Sciences. Department of Fisheries and Oceans Canada.

Auditor General of Canada. 1991. Report to the House of Commons for fiscal year ended 31 March 1991, Ottawa.

Australian Citizenship Council. 2000. *Australian citizenship for a new century*. Canberra.

Axelrod, R. and M. D. Cohen. 1999. *Harnessing complexity*. New York: The Free Press.

Axline, W. A. 1997. NAFTA, ALADI and the proliferation of bilateralism in the Americas. *Canadian Journal of Latin American and Caribbean Studies*. 22(44): 101–26.

Badaracco, J. L. 2002. *Leading quietly*. Boston: Harvard Business School Press.

Bakan, J. 2004. *The Corporation*. Toronto: Viking Canada.

Baland, J. M. and J. P. Platteau. 1996. *Halting degradation of natural resources: is there a role for rural communities?* Oxford: Clarendon Press.

Balladur, E. 2005. *La fine de l'illusion jacobine*. Paris: Fayard.

Banting, K. G. 1999. Social citizenship and the multicultural welfare state. In A. C. Cairns et al., eds. *Citizenship, diversity and pluralism: Canadian and comparative perspectives*. Montreal: McGill-Queen's University Press. 108–36.

Barlow, J. P. 1993. The economy of ideas. *Wired*. 2(3): 84.

————. 1995. Is there a there in cyberspace? *Utne Reader*. 68: 53–6.

Barnard, C. 1968 (1938). *The functions of the executive*. Cambridge: Harvard University Press.

Baron, J. and J. Jurney. 1993. Norms against voting for coerced reform. *Journal of Personality and Social Psychology*. 64: 347–55.

Baudrillard, J. and M. Guillaume. 1994. *Figures de l'altérité*. Paris: Descartes & Cie.

Bauman, Z. 2000. *Liquid modernity*. Cambridge: Polity Press.

Baumard, P. 1996. *Organisations déconcertées*. Paris: Masson.

Bazerman, M. 1986. *Judgement in managerial decision-making*. New York: Wiley.

Bean. 1990. *An economic analysis of compliance and enforcement in the Quahang Fishery of Narragansett Bay*. Unpublished master's thesis. University of Rhode Island.

Becker, T. L. 1991. *Quantum politics*. New York: Praeger.

Beer, S. 1974. *Designing freedom*. The 13ᵗʰ Massey Lectures. Toronto: CBC.

Beiner, R. and W. Norman, eds. 2001. *Canadian political philosophy*. Toronto: Oxford.

Bélanger, G. 2002. Peut-on décentraliser la centralisation? *Optimumonline*. 32(4): 21–4.

Bell, D. 1976. *The coming of post-industrial society: A venture in social forecasting*. New York: Basic Books.

Bellah, R., N. R. Madsen, W. M. Sullivan, A. Swidler, and S. M. Tipton. 1991. *The good society*. New York: Alfred A. Knopf.

Benko, G. and A. Lipietz, eds. 1992. *Les régions qui gagnent*. Paris: Presses Universitaires de France.

Bennis, W. 1976. Have we gone overboard on the 'right to know'? *Saturday Review*, June 3: 18–21.

——— and O'Toole, J. 1992. Our federalist future. *California Management Review*. 34(4): 73–90.

Bergson, H. 1932. *Les deux sources de la morale et de la religion*. 3rd ed. Paris: Alcan.

Berkes, F., ed. 1989. *Common property resources: Ecology and community-based sustainable development*. London: Belhaven Press.

Berry, A., L. Waverman, and A. Weston. 1992. Canada and the Enterprise for the Americas Initiative: A case of reluctant regionalism. *Business Economics*. 27(2): 31–9.

Bes, M. P. 1993. Partage des informations au sein des systèmes locaux d'innovation. *Revue d'économie régionale et urbaine*. 3: 565–77.

Bessières, F. 1969. The concept of separability and the optimization of economic organization. *European Economic Review*. Fall: 74–91.

Best, M. 1990. *The new competition*. Cambridge: Harvard University Press.

Bettis, R. A. and C. K. Prahalad. 1995. The dominant logic: Retrospective and extension. *Strategic Management Journal*. 16(5): 5–14.

Bhagwati, J. 1997. Fast track to nowhere. *The Economist*. October 18ᵗʰ.

Bhalla, A. S. and P. Bhalla. 1997. *Regional blocks*. New York: St Martin's Press.

Bleischwitz, R. and T. Langrock. 2003. *Governance of sustainable development: Co-evolution of corporate and political strategies*.

Boisot, M. 1987. *Information and organizations*. London: Fontana/Collins.

———. 1995. *Information space: A framework for learning in organizations, institutions and culture*. London: Routledge.

Boland, R. J., R. Ramkrishna, and V. Tenkasi. 1996. *Communication and collaboration in distributed cognition*. Los Angeles: Center for Effective Organizations, University of Southern California.

Boswell, J. 1990. *Community and the economy*. London: Routledge.

Boudon, R. 2003. *Raison, bonnes raisons*. Paris: Presses Universitaires de France.

Boulding, K. E. 1970. *A primer on social dynamics*. New York: The Free Press.

Bourdieu, P. 1972. *Esquisse d'une théorie de la pratique*. Genève: Droz.

Bourdieu, P. 1994. *Raisons pratiques*. Paris: Le Seuil.

Braithwaite, V. and M. Levi, eds. 1998. *Trust and governance*. New York: Russell Sage Foundation.

Brandenburger, A. M. and B. J. Nalebuff. 1996. *Co-opetition*. New York: Currency Doubleday.

Braybrooke, D. and G. Paquet. 1987. Human dimensions of global change: The challenges to the humanities and social sciences. *Transactions of the Royal Society of Canada*. 4(25): 269–91.

Bregha, F. 2002. *Governance and sustainable development*. Ottawa: Stratos.

Bressand, A., C. Distler, and K. Nicolaidis. 1989. Vers une économie de réseaux. *Politique industrielle*. 155–68.

Breton, R. 1984. The production and allocation of symbolic resources: An analysis of the linguistic and ethnocultural fields in Canada. *Canadian Review of Sociology and Anthropology*. 21(2): 123–44.

Bromley, D. W. 1991. *Environment and economy: Property rights and public policy*. Oxford: Blackwell.

———, ed. 1992. *Making the commons work: Theory, practice, and policy*. San Francisco: Institute for Contemporary Studies Press.

Brown, J. S. and P. Duguid. 1991. Organizational learning and communities in practice: Toward a unified view of working, learning and innovating. *Organization Science*. 2(1): 40–57.

Brundtland Commission. 1987. *Our common future: Report of the World Commission on Environment and Development*. New York: Oxford University Press.

Buchanan, J. M. and Y. J. Yoon. 2000. Symmetric tragedies: Commons and anticommons. *Journal of Law and Economics*. 43(1): 1–13.

Buckley, W. F. 1990. *Gratitude*. New York: Random House.

Burelle, A. 1995. *Le mal canadien*. Montréal: Fides.

Business Week. 1993. *The virtual corporation*. February 8, 1993: 98–103.

Cairncross, F. and N. McRae. 1975. *The second great crash*. London: Methuen.

Cairns, A. C. et al., eds. *Citizenship, diversity and pluralism: Canadian and comparative perspectives*. Montreal: McGill-Queen's University Press.

Caldwell, G. 2001. *La culture publique commune*. Quebec: Editions Note bene.

Campbell, V. P. and R. D. Masser. 1991. *The impact of GIS on local government in Great Britain*. Proceedings of the Association for Geographic Information. London: Conference of the Association for Geographic Information. 251–256.

Canada—Senate Committee on Social Affairs, Science and Technology. 1999. *On social cohesion.*

Canada—Advisory Council on Science and Technology. 2000. *Stepping up: Skills and opportunities in the knowledge economy:* B Report of the Expert Panel on Skills.

Canadian Centre for Management Development. 1996. *The Toronto Waterfront Regeneration Trust,* Report on the Deputy Ministers' Task Force on Service Delivery Models, Case Studies Vol 2. Ottawa. 231–40.

Cardinal, L. and C. Andrew, eds. 2001. *La démocratie à l'épreuve de la gouvernance.* Ottawa: Ottawa University Press.

Carlsson, I. and S. Ramphal, eds. 1995. *Our global neighbourhood: The report of the Commission on Global Governance.* Oxford: Oxford University Press.

Carter, S. L. 1998. *The dissent of the governed.* Cambridge: Harvard University Press.

Cassiers, W. 1999. Juger: dire les droits, dire le droit. In F. A. Druet and E. Ganty, eds. *Rendre justice au droit.* Namur: Presses Universitaires de Namur. 235–50.

Castells, M. 1989. *The informational city.* Oxford: Blackwell.

———. 1996. *The rise of the network society.* Oxford: Blackwell.

———. 1997. *The power of identity.* Oxford: Blackwell.

———. 1998. *End of millennium.* Oxford: Blackwell.

Choate, P. and J. Linger. 1988. Tailored trade: Dealing with the world as it is. *Harvard Business Review* 66(1): 86–93.

Chrétien, J. 2000. *The Canadian way in the 21st century.* Speech at the conference on Progressive Governance in the 21st Century in Berlin (June 2–3).

Christie, K. H. 1993. *Different strokes: Regionalism and Canada's economic diplomacy.* Ottawa: DFAIT Policy Staff Paper B No. 93(8).

Ciborra, C.U. 1992. Innovation, networks and organizational learning. In C. Antonelli, ed. *The economics of information networks.* New York: North Holland. 91–102.

Cicourel, A. V. 1990. The integration of distributed knowledge in collaborative medical diagnosis. In J. Galagher, R. E. Kraut, and C. Egido, eds. *Intellectual teamwork: Social and technological foundations of cooperative work.* New Jersey: Lawrence Erlbaum Associates. 221–42.

Clark, C. 1981. Bioeconomics of the ocean. *BioScience.* 233–4.

Clark, T. W. and R. P. Reading. 1994. A professional perspective: Improving problem solving, communication and effectiveness. In T. W. Clark, R. P. Reading, and A. L. Clarke, eds. *Endangered species recovery: Finding the lessons, improving the process.* Washington D.C.: Island Press. 351–70.

Clark, W. C. and R. E. Munn, eds. 1986. *Sustainable development of the biosphere.* Cambridge: Cambridge University Press.

Cleveland, H. 1982. Information as a resource. *The Futurist.* (December): 34–9.

———. 2002. Innovative technology: The institutional challenge. *Chaordic Commons.* 2(1).

Cohen, A. 2003. Ten little men short of ideas. *The Ottawa Citizen*. July 15 (A–14).
———. 2003. *While Canada Slept*. Toronto: McClelland & Stewart.
Cohen, W. M. and D. A. Levinthal. 1989. Innovation and learning: The two faces of r & d. *The Economic Journal*. 99: 569–96.
———. 1990. Absorptive capacity: A new perspective on learning and innovation. *Administrative Science Quarterly*. 35: 128–52.
Coleman, J. S. 1988. Social capital and the creation of human capital. *American Journal of Sociology*. 94 (Supplement): 95–120.
Commons, J. R. 1934. *Institutional economics*. New York: MacMillan.
Conseil des Sciences du Canada. 1984. *Le développement industriel au Canada: Quelques propositions d'action*. Ottawa: Conseil des sciences du Canada. 37.
Constanza, R. 1998. Principles for sustainable governance of the oceans. *Science*. 281(5374): 198.
———, F. Andrade, P. Antunes, M. van den Belt, D. Boesch, D. Boersma, F. Catarino, S. Hanna, K. Limburg, B. Low, M. Molitor, J. Pereira, S. Rayner, R. Santos, J. Wilson, M. Young. 1999. Ecological economics and sustainable governance of the oceans. *Ecological Economics*. 31: 171–87.
Cooke, P. and K. Morgan. 1993. The network paradigm: New departures in corporate and regional development. *Environment and Planning D: Society and Space*. 11: 543–64.
Cooper, R. N. 1997. States, citizens and markets in the 21st century. In T. J. Courchene, ed. *The Nation State in a Global/Information Era: Policy Challenges*. The Bell Canada Papers on Economic and Public Policy 5. Kingston: John Deutsch Institute for the Study of Economic Policy. 15–24.
Côté, M. 1991. *By way of advice*. Oakville: Mosaic Press.
Courchene, T. J. 1995. Glocalization: The regional/international interface. *Canadian Journal of Regional Science*. 18(1): 1–20.
——— and C. R. Telmer. 1998. *From heartland to North American region state*. Toronto: University of Toronto, Faculty of Management.
Coward, L. A. 1990. *Pattern thinking*. New York: Praeger.
Crozier, M. 1987. État modeste. *État moderne*. Paris: Fayard.
Dagan, H. and M. Heller. 2001. The liberal commons. *The Yale Law Journal*. 110: 549–623.
Dahl, R. A. 1989. *Democracy and its critics*. New Haven: Yale University Press.
Dahmen, E. 1988. Development blocks in industrial economics. *Scandinavian Economic History Review*. 36(1): 3–14.
Dahrendorf, R. 1995. A precarious balance: Economic opportunity, civil society and political liberty. *The Responsive Society*. 5(3): 13–39.
Dale, A. 1998. *Framework for governance*. http://www.royalroads.ca/ste/research/addialogue/conclusi.html
———. 2001. *At the edge: Sustainable development in the 21st century*. Vancouver: UBC Press.

Dalum, B. et al. 1992. Public policy in the learning society. In B. Lundvall, ed. *National systems of innovation*. London: Pinter. 296–317.

Daly, H. E. and J.B. Cobb JR. 1989. *For the common good*. New York: Beacon Press.

Daniels, S. E., G. B. Walker, J. R. Boeder, and J. E. Means. 1994. Managing ecosystems and social conflict. In P. S. Jensen and P. S. Bourgeron, eds. *Ecosystem Management: principles and applications*. US Forest Service General Technical Report PNW-318.

Daudelin, J. and E. J. Dosman. 1998. Canada and hemispheric governance: The new challenges. In F. O. Hampson and M. A. Molot, eds. *Leadership and dialogue B Canada among nations 1998*. Toronto: Oxford University Press. 211–38.

Davidow, W. H. and M. S. Malone. 1992. *The virtual corporation*. New York: HarperBusiness.

Debray, R. 1991. *Cours de médiologie générale*. Paris: Gallimard.

————.1994. *Manifestes médiologiques*. Paris: Gallimard.

———— ,ed.1997. Anciennes nations, nouveaux réseaux. *Les Cahiers de médiologie*. No. 3.

Debresson, C. and F. Amesse. 1991. Networks of innovators: A review and introduction to the issue. *Research Policy*. 20(5): 363–79.

de Geus, A. 1997. The living company. *Harvard Business Review*. 75(2): 51–9.

De la Mothe, J. and G. Paquet. 1994a. The dispersive revolution. *Optimum*. 25(1): 42–8.

————. 1994b. The technology-trade nexus: Liberalization, warring blocs, or negotiated access? *Technology in Society*. 16(1): 97–118.

————. 1994c. The shock of the new: A techno-economic paradigm for small economies. In M. Stevenson, ed. *The entry into new economic communities: Swedish and Canadian perspectives on the European Economic Community and North American Free Trade Accord*. Toronto: Swedish-Canadian Academic Foundation. 13–27.

————. 1994d. Circumstantial evidence: A note on science policy in Canada. *Science and Public Policy*. 21(4): 261–68.

————, eds. 1996. Evolutionary economics and the new international political economy. London: Pinter.

Devall, B. and E. Session. 1985. *Deep ecology: Living as if nature mattered*. Salt Lake City: Gibbs M. Smith.

De Young, B., and G. A. Rose. 1993. On recruitment and distribution of Atlantic Cod (Gadus Morhua) off Newfoundland. *Canadian Journal of Fisheries and Aquatic Science*. 50: 2729–41.

Diduck, A. P. and A. J. Sinclair. 1999. The concept of critical environmental assessment education. *The Canadian Geographer*. 41(3): 294–307.

Diebold, J. 1985. *Business in the age of information*. New York: Amacom.

Dionne, E. J. 1991. *Why Americans hate politics*. New York: Simon and Schuster.

Doerr, A. 2003. *Perspectives on policy and science: Building bridges for sustainable development.* (mimeo)

Donaldson, T. and T. W. Dunfee. 1994. Towards a unified conception of business ethics: Integrative social contracts theory. *The Academy of Management Review.* 19(2): 252–84.

Dosi, G. and L. Marengo. 1994. Some elements of an evolutionary theory of organizational competences. In R. W. England, ed. *Evolutionary concepts in contemporary economics.* Ann Arbor: The University of Michigan Press. 157–78.

Dosi, G. and R. R. Nelson. 1994. An introduction to evolutionary theories in economics. *Journal of Evolutionary Economics.* 4(3): 153–72.

Douglas, M. 1986. *How institutions think.* Syracuse, NY: Syracuse University Press.

Drezner, D. 1998. *The resurgent state.* The Washington Quarterly. 21(1): 209–25.

Dror, Y. 1997. Delta-type senior civil service for the 21st century. *International Review of Administrative Sciences.* 63(1): 7–23.

———. 2001. *The capacity to govern.* London: Frank Cass.

Drucker, P. F. 1989. *The new realities in government and politics, in economics and business, in society and world view.* New York: Harper.

———. 1994. The age of social transformation. *The Atlantic Monthly.* 274(5): 53–80.

Drummond, L. 1981–2. Analyse sémiotique de l'ethnicité au Québec. *Question de culture.* 2: 139–53.

Dubnick, M. J. 1996. *Clarifying accountability: An ethical theory framework.* Paper presented at the Fifth International Conference of Ethics in the Public Service, in Brisbane, Australia on August 5–9, 1996.

Duncan, G. 1985. A crisis of social democracy? *Parliamentary Affairs.* 38(3): 267–81.

Durlauf, S. N. 1998. *What should policymakers know about economic complexity?* The Washington Quarterly. 21(1): 157–65.

Dwivedi, O. P. and J. I. Gow. 1999. *From bureaucracy to public management.* Toronto: Broadview Press/IPAC.

Edwards, J. and L. Doucette. 1987. Ethnic salience, identity and symbolic ethnicity. *Canadian Ethnic Studies.* 14(1): 52–62.

Elkins, D. J. 1995. *Beyond sovereignty: Territory and political economy in the 21st century.* Toronto: The University of Toronto Press.

Elliott, S. R., T.A. Coe, J. A. Helfield, and R. J. Naiman. 1998. Spatial variation in environmental characteristics of Atlantic salmon (Salmo salar) rivers. *Canadian Journal of Fisheries and Aquatic Science.* 55(suppl.1): 267–80

El-Sabh, M., S. Demers, and D. Lafontaine. 1998. Coastal management and sustainable development: from Stockholm to Rimouski. *Ocean & Coastal Management.* 39(1–2): 1–24.

Elster, J. 1998. A plea for mechanisms. In P. Hedström and R. Swedberg, eds. *Social mechanisms: An analytical approach to social theory.* Cambridge: Cambridge University Press. 45–73.

Emery, F. E. and E. L. Trist. 1965. The causal texture of organizational environments. *Human Relations.* 18: 21–32.

Emmott, B. 1999. Freedom's journey: A survey of the 20th century. *The Economist.* Sept. 11th.

Endter-Wada, J., D. Blahna, R. Krannich, and M. Brunson. 1998. A framework for understanding social science contributions to ecosystem management. *Ecological Applications.* 8(3): 891–904.

Endter-Wada, J. and R. Lilieholm, eds. 1995. Proceedings of the Symposium: Conflicts in natural resource management: Integrating social and ecological concerns. *Natural Resources and Environmental Issues.* Vol. 3. College of Natural Resources, Utah State University.

Estabrooks, M. 1988. *Programmed capitalism.* London: M.E. Sharpe Inc.

Ettlinger, N. 1994. The localization of development in comparative perspective. *Economic Geography.* 70(2): 144–66.

Etzioni, A. 1983. *An immodest agenda.* New York: McGraw Hill.

Euston, S. R. and W. E. Gibson. 1995. The ethic of sustainability. *Earth Ethics.* 6: 5–7.

Falk, R. 1999. The future of sovereign states and international order. *Harvard International Review.* 21(3): 30–5.

Fauconnier, G. and M. Turner. 1998. Conceptual integration networks. *Cognitive Science.* 22(2): 133–87 (expanded web version 10 February 2001: htttp:// markturner.org/cin.web/cin.html).

Feeny, D., S. Hanna, and A. F. McEvoy. 1996. Questioning the assumptions of the "tragedy of the commons" model of fisheries. *Land Economics.* 72(2): 187–206.

Felt, L. and L. Locke. 1995. 'It were well to live mainly off fish': The collapse of Newfoundland's fishery and beyond. In R. Arnason and L. Felt, eds. *The North Atlantic Fisheries: Successes, Failures and Challenges.* Charlottetown, PEI: Institute of Island Studies. 197–236.

Fish, S. 1999. *The trouble with principles.* Cambridge: Harvard University Press.

Fleiner, T. 2001. *Models of citizen rights.* Ottawa: Forum of the Federations.

Florida, R. 1995. Toward the learning region. *Futures.* 27(5): 527–36.

———— and M. Kenny. 1993. Innovation-mediated production. *Futures.* 25(5): 637–51.

Foa, U. G. 1971. Interpersonal and economic resources. *Science.* 3969:345–51.

Folke, C. 2003. Social-ecological resilience and behavioural responses. In A. Biel et al., eds. *Individual and structural determinants of environmental practice.* London: Ashgate.

Foray, D. and B. A. Lundvall. 1996. The knowledge-based economy: From the economics of knowledge to the learning economy. In *Employment and growth in the knowledge-based economy.* Paris: OECD. 11–32.

Franklin, U. 1990. *The real world of technology*. Toronto: CBC Enterprises.

Friedmann, J. 1978. The Epistemology of Social Practice. *Theory and Society.* 6(1): 75–92.

———. 1987. Planning in the public domain: From knowledge to action. New Jersey: Princeton University Press.

——— and G. Abonyi. 1976. Social learning: A model for policy research. *Environment and Planning.* A(8): 927–40.

Fritzsche, D. J. 1997. *Business ethics: A global and managerial perspective*. New York: The McGraw-Hill Companies.

Fukuyama, F. 1995. Trust: *The social virtues and the creation of prosperity*. London: Hamish Hamilton.

Furlong, W. J. 1991. The deterrent effect of regulatory enforcement in the fishery. *Land Economics.* 67: 116–29.

Gairdner, W. D. 1996. *On higher ground*. Toronto: Stoddart.

Gallie, W. P. 1964. *Philosophy and the historical understanding*. London: Chatto & Windus.

Galston, W. A. 1998. A public philosophy for the 21st century. *The Responsive Community.* 8(3): 18–36.

Gans, H. 1979. Symbolic ethnicity. *Ethnic and Racial Studies.* 2: 1–20.

Garcia, J. 1997. America's agreements: An interim stage in building the free trade of the Americas. *Columbia Journal of Transnational Law.* 35(1): 63–130.

Gauchet, M. 1998. *La religion dans la démocratie*. Paris: Gallimard.

Geertz, C. 1986. The uses of diversity. *Michigan Quarterly Review.* 25(1): 105–23.

Gell-Mann, M. 1994. *The quark and the jaguar*. New York: W.H. Freeman.

Genschel, P. 1993. *Matching institutions and coordination problems*. Paper presented at the international research seminar on Institutional Change and Network Evolution. Stockholm.

Gibbons, M., et al. 1994. *The new production of knowledge*. London: Sage Publications.

Gill, J. H. 2000. *The tacit mode*. Albany: State University of New York.

Gilles, W. and G. Paquet. 1989. On delta knowledge. In G. Paquet and M. Von Zur Muehlen, eds. *Edging toward the year 2000*. Ottawa: Canadian Federation of Deans of Management and Administrative Sudies. 15–30.

Gladwell, M. 2000. *The tipping point*. New York: Little, Brown & Company.

Glouberman, S. and B. Zimmerman. 2002. *Complicated and complex systems: What would successful reform of medicare look like*. Discussion paper no. 8. Commission on the Future of Health Care in Canada (Romanow Commission).

Gluckman, M. 1967. *The judicial process among the Barotse of Northern Rhodesia*. 2nd ed. Manchester: Manchester University Press.

Goldberg, V. P. 1980. Relational exchange: Economics and complex contracts. *American Behavioral Scientist.* 23: 337–52.

———. 1989. *Readings in the economics of contract law*. Cambridge: Cambridge University Press.

Gordon, H. S. 1954. The economic theory of a common property resource: The fishery. *Journal of Political Economy*. 62: 124–42.

———. 1975. The political economy of big questions and small ones. *Canadian Public Policy*. 1(1): 97–106.

Gordon, B. K. 1998. The natural market fallacy: Slim pickings in Latin America. *Foreign Affairs*. 77(3): 13–16.

Gow, J. I. 1994. *Learning from others*. Toronto: IPAC/CCMD.

Graham, S. 1994. Networking cities: Telmatics and urban policy: A critical review. *International Journal of Urban and Regional Research*. 18(3): 416–32.

Granovetter, M. 1973. The strength of weak ties. *American Journal of Sociology*. 78(6): 1360–80.

Gray, B. 1985. Conditions facilitating interorganizational collaboration. *Human Relations*. 38: 930–1.

———. 1989. *Collaborating: Finding common ground for multiparty problems*. San Francisco: Jossey-Bass.

——— and D. J. Wood. 1991. Collaborative alliances, moving from practice to theory. *Journal of Applied Behavioural Science*. 27: 3–22.

Guéhenno, J. M. 1993. *La fin de la démocratie*. Paris: Flammarion.

Guerrieri, P. 1992. Technological and trade competition: The changing positions of the United States, Japan and Germany. In M. Caldwell Harris and G. E. Moore, eds. *Linking trade and technology policies*. Washington: National Academy Press. 29–59.

Guillaume, M. 1999. *L'empire des réseaux*. Paris: Descartes & Cie.

Habermas, J. 1973. *Legitimation crisis*. Boston: Beacon.

Hackett, S., E. Schlager, and J. Walker. 1994. The role of communication in resolving commons dilemmas: Experimental evidence with heterogeneous appropriators. *Journal of Environmental Economics and Management*. 27: 99–126.

Hampden-Turner, C. and A. Trompenaars. 1993. *The seven cultures of capitalism*. New York: Currency Doubleday.

Handy, C. 1992. Balancing corporate power: A new federalist paper. *Harvard Business Review*. 70(6): 59–72.

———. 1994. *The age of paradox*. Boston: Harvard Business School Press.

———.1995a. *Beyond certainty*. London: Hutchinson.

———.1995b. Trust and the virtual organization. *Harvard Business Review*. 73(3): 40–50.

Hardin, G. 1968. The tragedy of the commons. *Science*. 162: 1243–8.

Hardin, H. 1974. *A nation unaware: The Canadian economic culture*. Vancouver: J. J. Douglas.

Harris, L. K., R. H. Gimblett, and W. W. Shaw. 1995. Multiple-use management: Using a GIS model to understand conflicts between recreationists and sensitive wildlife. *Society and Natural Resources*. 8(6): 559–72.

Harris, M. 1998. *Lament for an ocean: The collapse of the Atlantic cod fishery: A true crime story*. Toronto: McClelland & Stewart.

Harvey, D. 1988. Urban places in the global village: Reflections on the urban condition in late 20th century. In L. Mazza, ed. *World cities and the future of the metropolis*. Milan: Electra.

Hasenclever, A., P. Mayer, and V. Rittberger. 1997. *Theories of international regimes*. New York: Cambridge Press.

Heath, J. 2001. *The efficient society*. Toronto: Penguin/Viking.

————. 2003. The disappearance of big ideas. *Policy Options*. 24(4): 35.

Hedström, P. and R. Swedberg, eds. 1998. *Social mechanisms: An analytical approach to social theory*. Cambridge: Cambridge University Press.

Held, D. 1995. *Democracy and the global order*. Stanford: Stanford University Press.

Helliwell, J. F. 1996. *Trust and social capital in the United States and Canadian provinces: An exploratory empirical survey*. (mimeo)

Hendriks, P. H. J. 2000. An organizational learning perspective on GIS. *International Journal of Geographical Information Science*. 14(4): 373–96.

Henton, D., J. Melville, and K. Walesh. 1997. *Grassroots Leaders for a New Economy*. San Francisco: Jossey-Bass.

Heritage Canada. 1995. *Partnership resource kit*. Ottawa.

Héritier, A., ed. 2002. *Common goods: Reinventing European and international governance*. London: Rowman & Littlefield.

Hilgartner, S. and C. Bosk. 1988. The rise and fall of social problems: A public arenas model. *American Journal of Sociology*. 94: 53–78.

Hine, V. H. 1977. The basic paradigm of a future socio-cultural system. *World Issues*. (April/May): 19–22.

Hirsch, F. 1976. *Social limits to growth*. Cambridge: Harvard University Press.

Hock, D. 1995. The chaordic organization: Out of control and into order. *World Business Academy Perspectives*. 9(1): 5–18.

————. 1999. *Birth of the chaordic age*. San Francisco: Berrett-Koehler Publishers Inc.

Hofstadter, D. R. 1979. *Godel, Escher, Bach: An eternal golden braid*. New York: Basic Books.

Holland, J. H. 1988. The global economy as an adaptive process. In P. W. Anderson et al., eds. *The economy as an evolving complex system*. Reading, MA: Addison-Wesley. 117–24.

————. 1995. *Hidden order*. Reading, MA: Addison-Wesley.

————. 1998. *Emergence*. Reading, MA: Addison-Wesley.

Holland, M. 1996. Ensuring sustainability of natural resources: Focus on institutional arrangements. *Canadian Journal of Fisheries and Aquatic Science*. 53(S1): 432–9.

Holling, C. S. 1973. Resilience and stability of ecological systems. *Annual Review of Ecology and Systematics*. 4: 1–23.

———— and G. K. Meffe. 1996. Command-and-control and the pathology of natural resource management. *Conservation Biology.* 10(2): 328–37.

Hollingsworth, R. 1994. Variation among nations in the logic of manufacturing sectors and international competitiveness. In D. Foray and C. Freeman, eds. *Technology and the wealth of nations.* London: Pinter. 301–31.

Horsman, M. and A. Marshall. 1994. *After the nation-state: Citizens, tribalism and the new world disorder.* London: HarperCollins.

Howard-Hassmann, R. E. 1999. 'Canadian' as an ethnic category: Implications for multiculturalism and national unity. *Canadian Public Policy.* 24(4): 523–37.

Howlett, M. 2001. Complex network management and the governance of the environment: Prospects for policy change and policy stability over the long term. In E. Parson, ed. *Governing the environment: Persistent challenges, uncertain innovations.* Toronto: University of Toronto Press. 303–44.

Hubbard, R. and G. Paquet. 2002. Ecologies of governance and institutional métissage. *Optimumonline.* 31(4): 25–34.

Huffbauer, G. C. and J. J. Schott. 1994. *Western hemisphere economic integration.* Washington, DC: Institute for International Economics.

Huntington, S. P. 1993. The clash of civilizations? *Foreign Affairs.* 72(3): 22–8.

————. 1996. *The clash of civilizations and the remaking of the world order.* New York: Simon and Schuster.

Hutchins, E. 1991. Organizing work by adaptation. *Organization Science.* 2(1): 14–39.

Hutchins, J. A. 1996. Spatial and temporal variation in the density of northern cod and a review of hypotheses for the stock's collapse. *Canadian Journal of Fisheries and Aquatic Sciences.* 53(5): 943–62.

Hymer, S. 1972. The multinational corporation and the law of uneven development. In J. Bhagwati, ed. *Economics and world order from the 1970s to the 1990s.* New York: Collier-Macmillan.

Iglesias, E. V. and G. Rosenthal, eds. 1995. *Trade liberalization in the western hemisphere.* Washington, DC: Inter-American Development Bank/Economic Commission for Latin America and the Caribbean.

Ignatieff, M. 1985. *The needs of strangers.* New York: Viking.

————. 1993. *Blood and belonging.* New York: Viking.

————. 2000. *The rights revolution.* Toronto: Anansi.

Integral Governance Initiative. 2002.

Iyer, P. 2000. *The global soul.* New York: Alfred A. Knopf.

Jackson, R. 2000. *The global covenant.* Oxford: Oxford University Press.

Jacobs, J. 1985. Cities and the wealth of nations. New York: Vintage Books.

————. 1992. *Systems of survival.* New York: Random House.

Jaques, E. 2002. *The life and behavior of living organisms.* London: Praeger.

Jacquet, P., J. Pisani-Ferry, and L.Tubiana. 2002. De quelques principes pour une gouvernance hybride. *Problèmes économiques.* 2755: 1–6; 2767: 1–4.

Janoski, T. 1998. *Citizenship and civil society*. Cambridge: Cambridge University Press.

Jenson, J. and M. Papillon. 1999. *The changing boundaries of citizenship: A review and a research agenda*. Ottawa: CPRN.

———. 2000. *Citizenship and the recognition of cultural diversity: the Canadian experience*. Ottawa: CPRN.

Jentoft, S. 1989. Fisheries co-management: delegating government responsibility to fisheries organizations. *Marine Policy*. 13: 137–54.

———. 2000. Co-managing the coastal zone: is the task too complex? *Ocean & Coastal Management*. 43(6): 527–35.

——— and T. Kristoffersen. 1989. Fishermen's co-management: The case of the Lofoten fishery. *Human Organization*. 48(4): 355–65.

Johnson, B. 1992. Institutional learning. In B. A. Lundvall, ed. *National systems of innovation: Towards a theory of innovation and interactive learning*. London: Pinter. 23–44.

Johnson, M. 1993. *Moral imagination*. Chicago: The University of Chicago Press.

Johnson, S. 2001. *Emergence*. New York: Scribner.

Juillet, L. and G. Paquet. 2002. The neurotic state. In G. B. Doern, ed. *How Ottawa spends 2002–2003: The security aftermath and national priorities*. Don Mills: Oxford University Press. 69–87.

——— and F. Scala. 2001. Gouvernance collaborative, imputabilités douces et contrats moraux: un cadre d'analyse. *Gouvernance*. 2(1–2): 85–95.

Kahn, A. E. 1966. Tyranny of small decisions. *Kyklos*. 19: 23–46.

Kanter, R. M. 1994. Collaborative advantage: The art of alliances. *Harvard Business Review*. 72(4): 96–108.

Kaplan, R. D. 1994. The coming anarchy. *The Atlantic Monthly* (February): 44–76.

Kauffmann, S. A. 1993. *The origins of order*. Oxford: Oxford University Press.

Kay, J. and E. D. Schneider. 1994. Embracing complexity: The challenge of the ecosystem approach. *Alternatives*. 20(3): 32–8.

——— et al. 1999. An ecosystem approach to sustainability: Addressing the challenge of complexity. *Futures*. 31(7): 721–42.

Keating, D. P. 1995. The Learning Society in the Information Age. In S. A. Rosell et al. *Changing maps: Governing in a world of rapid change*. Ottawa: Carleton University Press. 205–29.

Keen, P. G. W. 1999. Transforming intellectual property into intellectual capital: Competing in the trust economy. In N. Imparato, ed. *Capital for our Time*. Stanford: Hoover Institution Press. 3–35.

Kekes, J. 1993. *The morality of pluralism*. Princeton: Princeton University Press.

Kelly, K. 1993. Cypherpunks, e-money and the technologies of disconnection. *Whole Earth Review*. 79 (Summer): 40–59.

———. 1994. *Out of control*. Reading, MA: Addison-Wesley.

————. 1999. *New rules for the new economy*. New York: Viking.

Kemp, R. and D. Loorbach. 2003. *Governance for sustainability through transition management*. (November version).

Kennedy, J. J. and T. M. Quigley. 1993. Evolution of Forest Service organizational culture and adaptation issues in embracing ecosystem management. In P. S. Jensen and P. S. Bourgeron, eds. *Ecosystem Management: principles and applications*. US Forest Service General Technical Report PNW-318.

Killick, T. 1995. *The flexible economy*. London: Routledge.

Kim, D. H. 1993. The link between individual and organizational learning. *Sloan Management Review*. 35(1): 37–50.

King, A. 1975. Overload: Problems of governing in the seventies. *Political Studies*. June–September: 284–96.

———— and B. Schneider. 1991. *Questions de survie*. Paris: Calmann-Lévy.

Klandermans, B. 1992. Persuasive communication: Measures to overcome real-life social dilemmas. In B. G. L. Wim, D. M. Messick, and H. A. M. Wilke, eds. *Social dilemmas: Theoretical issues and research findings*. Oxford: Pergamon. 307–18.

Kling, R. et al. 1996. *Transforming coordination: The promise and problems of information technology in coordination*. http://www.slis.indiana.edu/kling/pubs

Kohlberg, L. 1981. *The philosophy of moral development*. New York: Harper & Row.

Kollock, P. 1998. Social dilemmas: The anatomy of cooperation. *Annals of the Review of Sociology*. 24: 183–214.

Kooiman, J., ed. 1993. *Modern governance*. London: Sage Publications.

Kosko, B. 1991. *Neural networks and fuzzy systems*. Englewood Cliffs, NJ: Prentice-Hall.

Krasner, S. P. 1993. *International regimes*. Ithaca: Cornell University Press.

Krugman, P. 1996. *The self-organizing economy*. Oxford: Blackwell.

Kumar, K. and H. G. Van Dissel. 1996. Sustainable collaboration: Managing conflict and cooperation in interorganizational systems. *MIS Quarterly*. Sept.: 279–300.

Kumon, S. 1992. Japan as a network society. In S. Kumon and H. Rosovsky, eds. *The political economy of Japan: Volume 3*. Stanford: Stanford University Press. 109–41.

Kuperan, K. and J. G. Sutinen. 1998. Blue waters crime: Deterrence, legitimacy, and compliance in fisheries. *Law & Society Review*. 32(2): 309–37.

Kymlicka, W. 1998. *Finding our way*. Toronto: Oxford University Press.

————. 2001. *Politics in the vernacular*. Toronto: Oxford.

Lachmann, L. M. 1971. *The legacy of Max Weber*. Berkeley: The Glendessary Press.

Lane, D. E. and R. L. Stephenson. 1997. Fisheries management science: Integrating the roles of science, economics, sociology and politics in effective fisheries management. In D. A. Hancock et al., eds. *Developing and Sustaining World*

Fisheries Resources: The State of Science and Management. Proceedings of the 2nd World Fisheries Congress. Brisbane: CSIRO Publishing. 177–82.

———. 2000. Institutional arrangements for fisheries: Alternate structures and impediments to change. *Marine Policy.* 24: 385–93.

Larkin, P. A. 1997. The costs of fisheries management information and fisheries research. In D. A. Hancock et al., eds. *Developing and Sustaining World Fisheries Resources: The State of Science and Management.* Proceedings of the 2nd World Fisheries Congress. Brisbane: CSIRO Publishing.

Laurendeau, A. 1962. *La crise de la conscription 1942.* Montréal: Les Éditions du Jour.

Laurent, P. and G. Paquet. 1991. Intercultural relations: A Myrdal-Tocqueville-Girard interpretative scheme. *International Political Science Review.* 12(3): 173–85.

———. 1994. Préliminaires à une étude des relations de pouvoir dans les réseaux stratégiques. *Les Cahiers Lyonnais de Recherche en Gestion.* 15 (avril): 288–316.

———. 1998. *Epistémologie et économie de la relation: coordination et gouvernance distribuée.* Lyon/Paris: Vrin.

Leadbeater, C. 1999. *Living on thin air.* London: Viking.

Leblond, A. and G. Paquet. 1988. Stratégie et structure de l'entreprise de l'an 2000. In J. Jabes, ed. *Gestion stratégique internationale.* Paris/Reims: Economica/Groupe E.S.C. 19–37.

Lecoq, B. 1989. Réseau et système productif régional. *Dossiers de l'IRER.* 23.

Lefebvre, H. 1961. Utopie expérimentale: pour un nouvel urbanisme. *Revue française de sociologie.* 2(3): 191–8.

Leibenstein, H. 1976. *Beyond economic man.* Cambridge: Harvard University Press.

Lenihan, D. G. 2002. *Post-industrial governance: Designing a Canadian cultural institution for the global village.* Changing Government Series: Vol. 5. Center for Collaborative Government.

———, G. Robertson and R. Tassé. 1994. *Reclaiming the middle ground.* Montreal: Institute for Research on Public Policy.

Leroy, R. 1990. L'économiste du travail en quête du social. In F. Michon and D. Segrestin, eds. *L'emploi, l'entreprise et la société.* Paris: Economica. 27–40.

Lévy, P. 1994. *L'intelligence collective.* Paris: La Découverte.

———. 2000. *World philosophie.* Paris: Editions Odile Jacob.

Lind, M. 1992. The catalytic state. *The National Interest.* 27 (Spring): 3–12.

———. 2000. A national good. *Prospect.* 56 (October): 44–9.

Lindblom, C. E. 1990. *Inquiry and Change.* New Haven: Yale University Press.

Lipnack, J. and J. Stamps. 1994. *The age of the network.* Essex Junction, VT: Omneo.

Lipsey, R. G. and P. Meller, eds. 1997. *Western hemisphere trade integration.* New York: St Martin's Press.

Loasby, B. J. 1991. *Equilibrium and evolution*. Manchester: Manchester University Press.

Loorbach, D. 2002. *Transition management: Governance for sustainability*.

Lovelock, J. E. 1979. *GAIA: A new look at life on earth*. Oxford University Press.

Lowi, T. J. 1975. Toward a politics of economics: The state of permanent receivership. In L. N. Lindberg, et al. *Stress and Contradiction in Modern Capitalism*. Lexington, MA: D.C. Heath and Co. 115–24.

Luke, T. W. 1991. The discipline of security studies and the codes of containment. *Alternatives*. 16(3): 315–44.

Lundvall, B. A. 1992. *National systems of innovation: Towards a theory of innovation and interactive learning*. London: Pinter.

——— and B. Johnson. 1994. The learning economy. *Journal of Industry Studies*. 1(2): 23–42.

Lussato, B. 1989. *Le défi culturel*. Paris: Nathan.

Luttwak, E. N. 1990. From geo-politics to geo-economics: Logic of conflict, grammar of commerce. *The National Interest*. 20: 17–24.

Maddox, J. and H. Gee. 1994. Mexico's bid to join the world. *Nature*. 6474: 789–804.

Magee, B. 1973. *Popper*. London: Fontana.

Maillat, D. 1992. Milieux et dynamique territoriale de l'innovation. *Canadian Journal of Regional Science*. 15(2): 199–218.

Mandel, M. 1996. *The high-risk society*. New York: Random House.

March, J. G. 1991. Exploration and exploitation in organizational learning. *Organization Science* 2(1): 71–7.

———. and J. P. Olsen. 1995. *Democratic governance*. New York: The Free Press.

Marengo, L. 1993. Knowledge distribution and coordination in organizations: On some social aspects of the exploitation vs exploration trade-off. *Revue internationale de systémique*. 7(5): 553–71.

Margalit, A. 1996. *The decent society*. Cambridge, MA: Harvard University Press.

Markell, P. 2000. The recognition of politics. *Constellation*. 7(4): 496–506.

Marquand, D. 1988. *The unprincipled society*. London: Fontana Press.

Marshall, A. 1920. *Principles of economics*. London: Macmillan.

Marshall, T. H. 1964. *Class, citizenship and social development*. Chicago: The University of Chicago Press.

Masuda, Y. 1982. Information epochs and human society. *World Future Society Bulletin*. (November–December): 17–23.

———. 1990. *Managing in the information society*. Oxford: Blackwell.

May, R. 1972. *Power and innocence*. New York: Norton.

McCallum, J. 1995. National borders matter: Canada–US regional trade patterns. *American Economic Review*. 85(3): 615–23.

McCay, B. 1995. The ocean commons and community. *Dalhousie Review*. 74(3): 310–38.

———— and J. M. Acheson. 1987. *The question of the commons: the culture and ecology of communal resources*. Tucson: The University of Arizona Press.

———— and S. Jentoft. 1998. Market or community failure? Critical perspectives on common property research. *Human Organization*. 57(1): 21–30.

McColl, J. C. and R. A. Stephens. 1997. Australian Fisheries Management Authority: Organizational structure and management philosophy. In D. A. Hancock et al. (eds). *Developing and Sustaining World Fisheries Resources: The State of Science and Management. Proceedings of the 2nd World Fisheries Congress*. Brisbane: CSIRO Publishing. 655–60.

McDonald, H. P. 2004. *John Dewey and environmental philosophy*. Albany: State University of New York Press.

McGinnis, M. D., ed. 1999a. *Polycentric governance and development*. Ann Arbor: The University of Michigan Press.

————, ed. 1999b. *Polycentricity and local public economies*. Ann Arbor: The University of Michigan Press.

————, ed. 2000. *Polycentric games and institutions*. Ann Arbor: The University of Michigan Press.

McKean, M. 1992. Success on the commons: A comparative examination of institutions for common property resource management. *Journal of Theoretical Politics*. 4(3): 247–81.

McLaughlin, J. 1966. *Information technology and survival of the firm*. Homewood, IL: Irwin.

McPhail, T. L. 1981. *Electronic colonialism*. Beverly Hills, CA: Sage Publications.

Mead, L. 1986. *Beyond entitlement: The social obligations of citizenship*. New York: The Free Press.

Mesthene, E. G. 1970. *Technological change*. New York: Mentor Books.

Metcalfe, L. 1993. Public management: From imitation to innovation. In J. Kooiman, ed. *Modern governance: New government–society interactions*. London: Sage Publications. 173–89.

————. 1998. Flexible integration in and after the Amsterdam Treaty. In M. den Boer, A. Guggenbühl, and S. Vanhoonacker, eds. *Coping with flexibility and legitimacy after Amsterdam*.Maastricht: European Institute of Public Administration. 11–30.

Michael, D. N. 1980. *The new competence: The organization as a learning system*. San Francisco: Values and Lifestyles Program.

————. 1988a. The search for values in the information age. *Western City*. 64(9): 10–18.

————. 1988b. *Can leaders tell the truth and still remain leaders?* Paris: 20th Anniversary Conference of the Club of Rome. 20 pp. (mimeo).

————. 1993. Governing by learning: Boundaries, myths and metaphors. *Futures*. January–February: 81–9.

Miller, R. and R. Côté. 1987. *Growing the next Silicon Valley*. Lexington, Mass.: D.C. Heath.

Millon-Delsol, C. 1992. *L'état subsidiaire*. Paris: Presses Universitaires de France.

Mintzberg, H. 1976. Planning on the left side and managing on the right. *Harvard Business Review*. 54 (4): 49–58.

————. 1987. Crafting strategy. *Harvard Business Review*. 6(4): 66–75.

Mitchell, B., ed. 1995. *Resource and environmental management in Canada: Addressing conflict and uncertainty*. Toronto: Oxford University Press.

Moati, P. and E. M. Mouhoud. 1994. Information et organisation de la production: vers une division cognitive du travail. *Economie appliquée*. 46(1): 47–73.

Monbiot, G. 2003. *The age of consent*. London: Flamingo.

Moore, J. F. 1996. *The death of competition*. New York: Harper Collins.

————. 1998. The rise of a new corporate form. *The Washington Quarterly*. 21(1): 167–81.

Moreau Defarges, P. 2003. *La gouvernance*. Paris: Presses Universitaires de France.

Morgan, G. 1988. *Riding the waves of change*. San-Francisco: Jossey-Bass.

Mouffe, C. 1993. *The return of the political*. London: Verso.

Mowery, D. C. and N. Rosenberg. 1993. The U.S, National Innovation System. In R. R. Nelson (ed.). *National innovation systems*. 29–75.

Mulgan, G. 1997. *Connexity*. Boston: Harvard Business School.

Naisbitt, J. 1994. *Global paradox: The bigger the world economy, the more powerful its smallest players* New York: William Morrow.

Nardi, B. A. and V. A. O'Day. 1999. *Information ecologies: using technology with heart*. Cambridge, Mass.: MIT Press.

Nash, M. 1989. *The cauldron of ethnicity in the modern world*. Chicago: University of Chicago Press.

National Round Table on Environment and the Economy. 1998. Sustainable strategies for oceans: A co-management guide.

Neill, R. F. 1972. *A new theory of value—The Canadian economics of H. A. Innis*. Toronto: University of Toronto Press.

Nelson, R. R., ed. 1993. *National innovation systems*. New York: Oxford University Press.

————and S. G. Winter. 1977. In search of a useful theory of innovation. *Research Policy*. 6(1): 36–46.

Nichols, S., M. Sutherland and K.Wilkins. 2002. Web-geographic information systems and coastal and marine governance. *Optimumonline*. 32(1): 21–5.

Niosi, J. et al. 1992. Les systèmes nationaux d'innovation: A la recherche d'un concept utilisable. *Revue française d'économie*. 7(1): 125–44.

Nitsch, V. 2000. National borders and international trade: Evidence from the European Union. *Canadian Journal of Economics*. 33(4): 1091–105.

Nohria, N. and R. G. Eccles, eds. 1992. *Networks and organizations*. Boston: Harvard Business School Press.

Norgaard, R. B. 1988. Sustainable development: A co-evolutionary view. *Futures*. 606–20.

———. 1994. *Development betrayed: The end of progress and a co-evolutionary revisioning of the future*. London: Routledge.

———. 1999. *Vision and methods of ecological economics*. Buenos Aires: Universidad de Buenos Aires. 16p.

——— and J. A. Dixon. 1984. Pluralistic project design : An argument for combining economic and co-evolutionary methodologies. *Policy Sciences*. 19(3): 297–317.

Norrie, K. and D. Owram. 1991. *A history of the Canadian economy*. Toronto: Harcourt, Brace, Jovanovich Canada.

North, D. C. 1990. *Institutions, institutional change and economic performance*. Cambridge: Cambridge University Press.

———. 1991. Institutions. *Journal of Economic Perspectives*. 5(1): 91–112.

———. 1993. *Economic performance through time*. Nobel Prize lecture in Economics.

Nozick, R. 1981. *Philosophical explanations*. Cambridge: Harvard University Press.

O'Connor, J. 1973. *The fiscal crisis of the state*. New York: St Martin's Press.

OECD. 1979. *Interfuturs*. Paris: OECD.

———. 1998. *21st century technologies: Promises and perils of a dynamic future*. Paris: OECD.

———. 1999. *The future of the global economy: Toward a long-boom?* Paris: OECD.

———. 2000. *The creative society of the 21st century*. Paris: OECD.

———. 2001. *Governance in the 21st century*. Paris: OECD.

Ogilvy, J. A. 1986–7. Scenarios for the future of governance. *The Bureaucrat*. 15(4): 13–16.

Ohmae, K. 1993. The rise of the region state. *Foreign Affairs*. 72 (Spring): 78–87.

———.1995. The end of the nation state: The rise of regional economies. New York: The Free Press.

Oldfield, A. 1990. *Citizenship and community*. London: Routledge.

Olson, M. 1982. *The rise and decline of nations: Economic growth, stagflation, & social rigidities*. New Haven, CT: Yale University Press.

O'Neill, O. 2002. *A question of trust*. Cambridge: Cambridge University Press.

Orgogozo, I. and H. Sérieyx. 1989. *Changer le changement*. Paris: Seuil.

Orléan, A., ed. 1994. *Analyse économique des conventions*. Paris: Presses universitaires de France.

Orr, J. 1990. *Talking about machines: A ethnography of a modern job*. Ph.D. thesis, Cornell University.

Osborne, D. and T. Gaebler. 1992. *Reinventing government*. New York: Addison-Wesley.

Ostrom, E. 1990. *Governing the commons: The evolution of institutions for collective action*. Cambridge: Cambridge University Press.

———. 1998. Self-governance of common-pool resources. In P. Newman, ed. *The New Palgrave Dictionary of Economics and the Law*. London: MacMillan. 424–33.

———, R. Gardner and J. Walker. 1994. *Rules, games, and common-pool resources*. Ann Arbor: University of Michigan Press.

———, J. Burger , C. B. Field , R. B. Norgaard and D. Policansky. 1999. Revisiting the commons: local lessons, global challenges. *Science*. 284(5412): 278–82.

Ostry, S. 1997. *The post Cold War trading system*. Chicago: The University of Chicago Press.

O'Toole, J. 1995. *Leading change*. San Francisco: Jossey-Bass.

——— and W. Bennis. 1992. Our federalist future: The leadership imperative. *California Management Review*. 34(4): 73–90.

Ò Tuathail, G., S. Dalby, P. Routledge (eds). 1998. *The geopolitics reader*. London: Routledge.

Paquet, G. 1977. Federalism as social technology. In J. Evans, ed. *Options*. Toronto: The University of Toronto Press. 281–302.

———. 1978. The regulatory process and economic performance. In G. Bruce Doern, ed. *The regulatory process in Canada*. Toronto: MacMillan. 34–67.

———. 1987. Le goût de l'improbable: à propos d'une stratégie de sortie crise pour les sciences humaines. In G. Paquet and M. von Zur Muehlen, eds. *Education Canada?* Ottawa: Canadian Higher Education Research Network. 61–92.

———. 1988. La solution Catoblépas: le pari sur l'innovation à Montréal. *Revue des petites et moyennes organisations*. 3(2): 48–56.

———. 1989a. Pour une notion renouvelée de citoyenneté. *Transactions of the Royal Society of Canada*. Fourth Series Volume XXVII: 83–100.

———. 1989b. Science and technology policy under free trade. *Technology in Society*. 11: 221–34.

———. 1989c. Vers une nouvelle dynamique de la localisation des entreprises. In *Les conditions du développement technologique de l'entreprise*. Québec: Conseil de la science et de la technologie du Québec: 73–94.

———. 1990. Internationalization of domestic firms and governments: Anamorphosis of a palaver. *Science and Public Policy*. 17(5): 327–32.

———. 1991–2a. Betting on moral contracts. *Optimum*. 22(3): 45–53.

———. 1991–2b. The best is enemy of the good. *Optimum*. 22 (1): 7–15.

———. 1992a. Le kaléidoscope de l'ethnicité: un approche constructiviste. In C. Andrew et al. *L'ethnicité à l'heure de la mondialisation*. Ottawa: ACFAS-Outaouais. 21–33.

———. 1992b. The strategic state. In J. Chrétien, ed. *Finding Common Ground*. Hull: Voyageur Publishing. 85–101.

———. 1993. Sciences transversales et savoirs d'expérience: the art of trespassing. *Revue générale de droit*. 24(2): 269–81.

The New Geo-Governance

———. 1994a. From the information economy to evolutionary cognitive economics. In R. E. Babe, ed. *Information and communication in economics*. Boston: Kluwer Academic Publishers, 34–40.

———. 1994b. Reinventing governance. *Opinion Canada*. 2(2): 1–5.

———. 1994c. La citoyenneté dans la société de l'information: une réalité transversale et paradoxale. *Transactions of the Royal Society of Canada*. 6(5): 59–78.

———. 1994d. New patterns of governance. *PRIME Working Paper* 94.59.

———. 1994e. Paradigms of governance. In M. Cottrell-Boyd (ed.) *Rethinking Government*. Ottawa: Canadian Center for Management Development. 29–42.

———. 1994f. Political philosophy of multiculturalism. In J. Berry and J. Laponce, eds. *Ethnicity and culture in Canada*. Toronto: University of Toronto Press. 60–80.

———. 1995a. Gouvernance distribuée et habitus centralisateur. *Mémoires de la Société royale du Canada*. Série VI, Tome VI: 93–107.

———. 1995b. Institutional evolution in an information age. In T. J. Courchene, ed. *Technology, information and public policy: The Bell Canada Papers on Economic and Public Policy 3*. Kingston: John Deutsch Institute for the Study of Economic Policy. 197–229.

———. 1996a. Distributed gouvernance and transversal leadership. In John E. Trent, Robert Young and Guy Lachapelle, eds. *Québec-Canada: What is the Path Ahead?/ Nouveaux sentiers vers l'avenir*. Ottawa: The University of Ottawa Press. 317–332.

———. 1996b. La grisaille institutionnelle. In S. Coulombe and G. Paquet, eds. *La ré-invention des institutions et le rôle de l'état*. Montréal: Association des économistes québécois. 393–421

———. 1996c. Le fruit dont l'ignorance est la saveur. In J. Bourgault et al., eds. *Hard choices, no choices: Assessing program review*. Toronto: Institute of Public Administration of Canada. 47–58.

———. 1996–7. The strategic state. *Ciencia Ergo Sum*. 3(3): 257–61 (Part 1); 4(1): 28–34 (Part 2); 4(2): 148–54 (Part 3).

———. 1997a. Et si la Révolution Tranquille n'avait pas eu lieu... *L'Agora*. 4(2) : 35–6.

———. 1997b. Nothing is more rational than a rationalization: Words of caution about public policy marksmanship. In D. Zéghal, ed. *Public Sector Accounting: Shifting the Focus to Results*. Ottawa: CGA Accounting Research Center. 37–48.

———. 1997c. Slouching toward a new governance. *Optimum* 27(3): 44–50.

———. 1997d. States, communities and markets: The distributed governance scenario. In T. J. Courchene, ed. *The nation state in a global information era: Policy challenges: The Bell Canada Papers on Economic and Public Policy, 5*. Kingston: John Deutsch Institute for the Study of Economic Policy. 25–46.

———. 1997e. Canada as a disconcerted learning economy: A governance challenge. *Transactions of the Royal Society of Canada*. 6(8): 69–98.

Bibliography

————. 1997f. The Burden of Office, Ethics and Connoisseurship. *Canadian Public Administration*. 40(1): 55–71.

————. 1998. Canada as a disconcerted learning economy: A governance challenge. In D. M. Hayne, ed. *Transactions of the Royal Society of Canada* 6(8): 69–98.

————. 1999a. Governance and social cohesion: Survivability in the 21st century. In *Transactions of the Royal Society of Canada*. 6(9): 85–116.

————. 1999b. *Governance through social learning*. Ottawa: University of Ottawa Press.

————. 1999c. Innovations in governance in Canada. *Optimum*. 29 (2/3): 71–81.

————. 1999d. La résilience dans l'économie. *L'Agora*. 7(1): 14–17.

————. 1999e. *Oublier la révolution tranquille*. Montréal: Liber.

————. 1999f. Tectonic changes in Canadian governance. In L. A Pal (ed.) *How Ottawa Spends 1999–2000*. Toronto: Oxford University Press. 75–111.

————. 2000a. André Laurendeau et la démocratie des communautés. *Les cahiers d'histoire du Québec au Xxe siècle*. 10: 45–54.

————. 2000b. Canada 2015: The Governance Challenge. *Ivey Business Journal*. 64(3): 57–61.

————. 2000c. Gouvernance distribuée, socialité et engagement civique. *Gouvernance*. 1(1) : 52–66 (68?).

————. 2000d. E-gouvernance, gouvernementalité et État commutateur. *Relations Industrielles/ Industrial Relations*. 55(4): 746–69.

————. 2000e. On hemispheric governance. In *Transactions of the Royal Society of Canada*, 6(10): 37–79.

————. 2001a. Betting on diversity: The problématique of cultural diversity. In R. Higham, ed. *Building plurality*. Ottawa: Centre on Governance. 31–45.

————. 2001b. Governance in the face of bricolage and sabotage. *Canadian Parliamentary Review*. 24(3): 11–17.

————. 2001c. La gouvernance en tant que conditions auxiliaires. In L. Cardinal and C. Andrew, eds. *Gouvernance et démocratie*. Ottawa: Les Presses de l'Université d'Ottawa. 213–37.

————. 2001d. Le droit à l'épreuve de la gouvernance. *Gouvernance*. 2(1-2): 74–84.

————. 2002a. Pepin-Robarts Redux: socialité, régionalité et gouvernance. In J. P. Wallot, ed. *La Commission Pépin-Roberts: quelques vingt ans après*. Ottawa: Les Presses de l'Université d'Ottawa.

————. 2002b. Déséquilibre fiscal et gouvernance. *Optimumonline*. 32(2): 21–33.

————. 2002c. L'éthique est une sagesse toujours en chantier. Réflexions sur l'éthique et la gouvernance. Ethique publique. 4(1): 62–76.

————. 2003a. Quelle éthique pour la science? *Optimumonline*. 33(2): 24–35.

————. 2003b. Toward a baroque governance in the 21st century. In C. Gaffield (ed.) *The Canadian distinctiveness into the 21st century*. Ottawa: The University of Ottawa Press. 59–88.

————. 2004a. *Pathologies de gouvernance*. Montréal: Liber.

————. 2004b. There is more to governance than public candelabras: e-governance and Canada's public service. In L. Oliver and L. Sanders (eds.) *E-governance in the 21ˢᵗ Century*. Regina: Canadian Plains Research Center. 181–203.

————. 2005a. Productivity and innovation in Canada: a case of governance failure. *Policy Options*. 26(3): 38–42.

————. 2005b. *Gouvernance: une invitation à la subversion*. Montréal: Liber.

———— and Roy, J. 1992. *The prosperity challenge: Canada in the 1990s*. Discussion paper for the Canadian Center for Management Development, September.

————.1994. Towards a political economy of Canada's postindustrial transformation. *PRIME Working Paper*. 94(12).

————. 1995a. *Canada 2005: A Phoenician strategy*. Mimeo.

————. 1995b. Prosperity through networks: The bottom-up strategy (/the small business strategy?) that might have been. In S. Phillips (ed.) *How Ottawa Spends 1995–96*. Ottawa: Carleton University Press. 137–158.

————. 1998. *Governance in Canada*. Ottawa: Centre on Governance.

Paquet, G. and R. Shepherd. 1996. The program review process: A deconstruction. In G. Swimmer (ed.). *How Ottawa Spends – Life Under the Knife*, Ottawa: Carleton University Press. 39–72.

Paquet, G. and J. P. Wallot. 1987. Nouvelle France/Quebec/Canada: A world of limited identities. In N. Canny and A. Pagden (eds.) *Colonial identity in the Atlantic world, 1500–1800*. Princeton: Princeton University Press. 95–114.

Paquet, G. and K. Wilkins. 2002. *Ocean governance: An inquiry into stakeholding*. Ottawa: Centre on Governance.

Parker, E. B. 1975. *Social implications of computer telecommunications systems: Stanford Programs in Information Technology and Telecommunications, Report No. 16* (with the assistance of Marc Porat).

Pascale, R. et al. 1997. Changing the way we change. *Harvard Business Review*. 75(6): 127–39.

Pateman, C. 1972. *Participation and democratic theory*. Cambridge University Press.

Perrin, J. 1976. Pour un nouveau tableau de bord de l'entreprise. *Revue française de gestion*. No. 2: 35–40.

Perrings, C. 1987. *Economy and environment*. Cambridge: Cambridge University Press.

Perroux, F. 1960. *Economie et société*. Paris: Presses Universitaires de France.

Peternoster, R., R. Bachman, R. Brame, L. Sherman. 1997. Do fair procedures matter? The effect of procedural justice on spouse assault. *Law and Society Review*. 31: 163–204.

Peters, T. 1992. *Liberation management*. New York: Alfred A. Knopf.

————. 1994. *Crazy times call for crazy organizations*. New York: Vintage.

Petrella, R. 1995. A global agora vs. gated city-regions. *New Perspectives Quarterly*. 12 (1): 21–22.

Pettit, P. 1995. The cunning of trust. *Philosophy & Public Affairs.* 24: 202–25.

Pinkerton, E., ed. 1989. *Co-operative management of local fisheries: New directions for improved management and community development.* Vancouver: University of British Columbia Press.

Piore, M. J. 1995. *Beyond individualism.* Cambridge: Harvard University Press.

Polanyi, K. 1957. The economy as instituted process. In K. Polanyi et al., eds. *Trade and markets in the early empires.* New York: The Free Press. 243–70.

———.1968. The economy as instituted process. In K. Polanyi. *Primitive, archaic and modern economies.* New York: Anchor Books.

M. Polanyi, M. 1964. *Personal knowledge.* New York: Harper & Row.

———. 1966. *The tacit dimension.* Garden City, N.Y.: Doubleday.

Popper, K. 1942.*The open society and its enemies.* London: Routledge and Kegan Paul.

Porat, M. U. 1977. *The information economy.* Washington, DC: Department of Commerce.

Porter, J. E. 1965. *The vertical mosaic.* Toronto: The University of Toronto Press.

Porter, J. N. 1979. On multiculturalism as a limit of Canadian life. In H. Bouraoui, ed. *The Canadian alternative: Cultural; pluralism and Canadian unity.* Downsview: ECW Press. 64–79.

Prahalad, C. K. and R. A. Bettis. 1986. The dominant logic: A new linkage between diversity and performance. *Strategic Management Journal.* 7: 485–501.

Preston, L. E. and D. Windsor. 1992. *The rules of the game in the global economy.* Boston: Kluwer Academic Publishers.

Public Policy Forum. 1993. *Private–public sector cooperation as a means of improving a country's economic performance: A survey of practices in Canada, the US, Europe and Japan.* Ottawa: Public Policy Forum.

Purvis, A. 1999. New force in the hemisphere. *Time Magazine.* 153(25).

Putnam, R. D. 1993. *Making democracy work.* Princeton: Princeton University Press.

———. 1995. Bowling alone: America's declining social capital. *Journal of Democracy.* 6(1): 65–78.

———. 2000. Bowling alone: The collapse and revival of American community. New York: Simon and Schuster.

Ramos, A. G. 1981. *The new science of organizations.* Toronto: University of Toronto Press.

Raymond, E. S. 1999. *The cathedral and the bazaar.* Cambridge: O'Reilly.

Redclift, M. 1987. *Sustainable development: Exploring the contradictions.* London: Methuen.

Resnick, M. 1994a. Changing the centralized mind. *Technology Review.* 97(5): 32–40.

———. 1994b. *Turtles, termites and traffic jams.* Cambridge: The MIT Press.

Reszler, A. 1990. *Le pluralisme.* Genève: Georg.

Reynolds, C. W. 1987. Flocks, herds, and schools: A distributed behavioral model. *Computer Graphics*. 21(4): 25–34.

Rheingold, R. 1993. *The virtual community*. Reading, MA: Addison-Wesley.

———. 2002. *Smart mobs*. Cambridge: Perseus.

Richardson, G. B. 1960. *Information and investment*. Oxford: Oxford University Press.

Rittel, H. W. J. and M. M. Webber. 1973. Dilemmas in a general theory of planning. *Policy Sciences*. 4: 155–69.

Rivlin, A. M. 1992. *Reviving the American Dream*. Washington: The Brookings Institution.

Roberts, A. 2000. The informational commons at risk. In D. Drache, ed. *The market or the public domain*. London: Routledge. 175–201.

Roberts, L. W. and R. A. Clifton. 1982. Exploring the ideology of Canadian multiculturalism. *Journal of Canadian Studies*. 17(1): 88–94.

Rocard, M. 1996. *Ethique et démocratie*. Genève: Labor et Fides.

Rocha, E. M. 1997. A ladder of empowerment. *The Journal of Planning Education and Research*. 17: 31–44.

Rocher, G. 1997. Du pluralisme à l'égalitarisme. *Le Devoir*. 18 décembre.

Rorty, R. 1989. *Contingency, irony and solidarity*. Cambridge: Cambridge University Press.

Rosell, S. A. 2000. *Renewing governance*. Don Mills: Oxford University Press.

Rosenau, J. N. 2003. *Distant proximities*. Princeton: Princeton University Press.

Ross, M. 1954. *Our sense of identity*. Toronto: The Ryerson Press.

Sabel, C. F. 1993. Studied trust: Building new forms of cooperation in a volatile economy. In D. Foray and C. Freeman (eds.) *Technology and the Wealth of Nations*. London: Pinter. 332–52.

Sacconi, L. 2000. *The social contract of the firm*. London: Springer.

Saez, R. E. 1997. Trade and investment between Canada and the LAIA countries. In R. G. Lipsey and P. Meller (eds.) *Western hemisphere trade integration*. 232–48.

Saint-Onge, H. 1996. Tacit knowledge: The key to the strategic alignment of intellectual capital. *Strategy and Leadership*, March–April: 10–14.

Saxenian, A. 1994. *Regional advantage*.Cambridge: Harvard University Press.

Schaffer, D. L. 1988. Theodore J. Lowi and the administrative state. *Administration and Society*. 19(4): 371–98.

Scheffler, S. 1997. Relationships and responsibilities. *Philosophy & Public Affairs*. 26 (3): 189–209.

Schelling, T. C. 1960. *The Strategy of Conflict*. Cambridge: Harvard University Press.

Schick, F. 1984. *Having reasons*. Princeton: Princeton University Press.

Schön, D. A. 1970. *The future of American industry*. The Listener (July).

———. 1971. *Beyond the stable state*. New York: Norton.

———. 1983. *The reflective practitioner*. New York: Basic Books.

————. 1995. Causality and causal inference in the study of organizations. In R. F. Goodman and W. R. Fisher, eds. *Rethinking knowledge*. Albany: State University of New York Press. 69–101.

———— and M. Rein. 1994. *Frame reflection*. New York: Basic Books.

Schrage, M. 2000. *Serious play*. Boston: Harvard Business School Press.

Schroeder, P. C., P. R. Boudreau, C. E. W. Brehme, A. M. Boyce , A. J. Evans, A. Rahmani. 2001. The Gulf of Maine environmental information exchange: Participation, observations, conversation. *Environment and Planning B: Planning and Design*. 28(6): 865–87.

Schultz, R. 1982. Partners in a game without masters: Reconstructing the telecommunications regulatory system. In R. J. Buchan et al., eds. *Telecommunications Regulation and the Constitution*. Montreal: The Institute for Research on Public Policy. 41–114.

Schumacher, E. F. 1977. *A guide for the perplexed*. New York: Harper & Row.

Schumpeter, J. 1949. Science and ideology. *The American Economic Review*. 39: 345–59.

Semprini, A. 2003. *La société de flux*. Paris: L'Harmattan.

Sen, A. 1987. *On ethics and economics*. Oxford: Basil Blackwell.

————. 1999a. *Development as freedom*. New York: Knopf.

————. 1999b. Galbraith and the art of description. In H. Sassoon, ed. *Between friends*. New York: Houghton-Mifflin. 139–45.

————. 2003. The end and means of sustainability. In *Transition to sustainability in the 21ˢᵗ century*. Wahington: The National Academices Press. 2–16.

Sérieyx, H. 1994. *L'effet Gulliver*. Paris: Calmann-Levy.

Sheck, C., et al. 1994. Canada in the Americas: New opportunities and challenges. *DFAIT Policy Staff Paper B*. 94(06).

Shepherd, J. G. and J. M. McGlade. 1992. *Techniques for biological assessment in fisheries management*. (Forschungszentrum Julich GmbH, Julich, Germany).

Sheppard, E., H. Coucilis, S. Graham, J. W. Harrington and H. Onsrud. 1999. Geographies of he information society. *International Journal of Geographical Information Science*. 13: 797–823.

Shklar, J. 1989. Giving injustice its due. *Yale Law Journal*. 98: 1135–51.

Simpson, J. 2001. *The friendly dictatorship*. Toronto: McLelland & Stewart.

Sinclair, A. J. and A. P. Diduck. 1995. Public education: an undervalued component of the environmental assessment public involvement process. *Environmental Impact Assessment Review*. 15: 219–40.

Solomon, R. C. and F. Flores. 2001. *Building trust*. New York: Oxford University Press.

Solow, R. M. 1992. *An almost practical step toward sustainability*. Washington: Resources for the Future.

Spinosa, C., F. Flores, and H. L. Dreyfus. 1997. *Disclosing new worlds*. Cambridge: The MIT Press.

Stephenson, R., K.Rodman, D. Aldous, and D. Lane. 1999. An in-season approach to management under uncertainty: The case of the SW Nova Scotia herring fishery. *ICES Journal of Marine Science.* 56: 1005–13.

Stoffaes, C. 1987. *Fins de mondes.* Paris: Editions Odile Jacob.

Storper, M. 1992. The limits of globalization: Tecnology districts and international trade. *Economic Geography.* 68(1): 60–93.

———. 1993. Regional worlds of production: Leaning and innovation in the technology districts of France, Italy and the USA. *Regional Studies.* 27(5): 433–55.

———. 1996. Institutions of the knowledge-based economy. In *Employment and Growth in the Knowledge-Based Economy.* Paris: OECD. 255–83.

——— and B. Harrison. 1991. Flexibility, hierarchy and regional development: The changing structure of industrial production systems and their forms of governance in the 1990s. *Research Policy.* 20(5): 407–22.

Strange, S. 1996. The retreat of the state: The diffusion of power in the world economy. Cambridge: Cambridge University Press.

Stratos Inc. 2003. *Building confidence: Corporate sustainability reporting in Canada.* Ottawa.

Sutinen, J. G. and J. R.Gauvin. 1989. An econometric study of regulatory enforcement and compliance in the commercial inshore lobster fishery of Massachusetts. In P. A. Neher, R. Arnason and N. Mollet, eds. *Rights based fishing.* Boston: Kluwer Academic Publishers. 415–31.

Talen, E. 2000. Bottom-up GIS: A new tool for individual and group expression in participatory planning. *Journal of the American Planning Association.* 66(3): 279–94.

Tapié, V. L. 1961. *Le baroque.* Paris: Presses Universitaires de France.

Tapscott, D. and D. Agnew. 1999. Governance in the Digital Economy. *Finance and Development,* December: 34–7.

Tarondeau, J. C. and R. W. Wright. 1995. La transversalité dans les organisations ou le contrôle par les processus. *Revue française de gestion.* 104: 112–21.

Taylor, C. 1985. Alternative futures. In A. Cairns and C. Williams, eds. *Constitutionalism, citizenship and society in Canada.* Toronto: University of Toronto Press. 183–229.

———. 1993. *Reconciling the solitudes.* Montreal: McGill-Queen's University Press.

———. 2004. *Modern social imaginaries.* Durham, N.C.: Duke University Press.

Taylor, W. C. 1994. Control in an age of chaos. *Harvard Business Review.* 72(6): 64–76.

Tenkasi, R. V. and R. J. Boland. 1996. Exploring knowledge diversity in knowledge intensive firms: a new role for information systems. *Journal of Organizational Change Management.* 9(1): 79–91.

The Economist. 1990. *The state of the nation-state.* 22 December: 43–6.

————. 1994. *Welcome to Cascadia*. May 21: 52.

————. 1995. *No place like home: Domestic management of fishing policy would serve fish-stock conservation better than international disputes*. April 22, 335(7911): 17.

Thompson, B. H. 2000. Tragically difficult: the obstacles to governing the commons. *Environmental Law*. 30(2): 241.

Thuderoz, C., V. Mangematin, D. Harrisson, eds. 1999. *La confiance*. Paris: Gaëtan Morin Europe.

Time Magazine. 1999. *Canada 2005*. 153(25).

Toffler, A. 1975. *The eco-spasm report*. New York: Morrow.

Törnqvist, G. 1968. Flows of information and the location of economic activities. *Lund University Studies in Geography*. 30.

Toulmin, S. 1990. *Cosmopolis*. Chicago: The University of Chicago Press.

Touraine, A. 1999. Le désenchantement de la politique. *Le Monde des Débats*. Décembre: 39.

Trist, E. L. 1977. Collaboration in work settings: A personal perspective. *Journal of Applied Behavioural Science*. 13(3): 268–78.

Tully, J., ed. 1994. *Philosophy in a age of pluralism*. Cambridge: Cambridge University Press.

————. 2000. Struggles over recognition and distribution. *Constellation*. 7(4): 469–82.

————. 2001. Democracy and globalization: A defeasible sketch. In R. Beiner and W. Norman, eds. op.cit., 36–62.

Tully, S. 1993. The modular corporation. *Fortune*. February 8. 106–14.

Turner, M. 2001. *Cognitive dimensions of social science*. New York: Oxford University Press.

Tussman, J. 1977. *Government and the mind*. New York: Oxford University Press.

————. 1989. *The burden of office*. Vancouver: Talonbooks.

Tyler, T. R., J. D. Casper and B. Fisher. 1989. Maintaining allegiance toward political authorities: The role of prior attitudes and the use of fair procedures. *American Journal of Political Science*. 33: 629–42.

Vaillancourt Rosenau, P. 2000. *Public private policy partnerships*. Cambridge: The MIT Press.

Valaskakis, K. 1990. *Canada in the nineties: Meltdown or renaissance?* Montréal: The Gamma Institute Press.

Van Gunsteren, H. 1998. *A theory of citizenship*. Wetsview: Boulder.

Van Vugt, M. and D. de Cremer. 1999. Leadership in social dilemmas: The effects of group identification on collective actions to provide public goods. *Journal of Personality & Social Psychology*. 76: 587–99.

Varela, F. J. 1989. *Connaître les sciences cognitives: tendances et perspectives*. Paris: Seuil.

Vertinsky, I. 1987. An ecological model of resilient decision-making: An application to the study of public and private sector decision-making in Japan. *Ecological Modelling.* 38: 141–58.

Vickers, G. 1965. *The art of judgment.* London: Methuen.

———. 1968. *Value systems and social process.* Penguin Books.

———. 1983. *Human systems are different.* London: Harper & Row.

———. 1987. *Policy-making, communications and social learning.* New Brunswick, N.J.: Transaction.

Vipond, R. C. 1996. Citizenship and the Charter of Rights: The two sides of Pierre Trudeau. *International Journal of Canadian Studies.* 14: 179–92.

Von Martin, A. 1944. *Sociology of the Renaissance.* London: Kegan, Paul, Trench and Trubner.

Wade, R. 1987. The management of common property resources: Collective action as an alternative to privatisation or state regulation. *Cambridge Journal of Economics.* 11: 95–106.

Wade-Benzoni, K. A., A. E. Tenbrunsel and M. H. Bazerman. 1996. Egocentric interpretations of fairness in asymmetric environmental social dilemmas: Explaining harvesting behaviour and the role of communications. *Organizational Behaviour and Human Communication Processes.* 67: 111–26.

Waldo, D. 1985. An agenda for future reflections: A conversation with Dwight Waldo. *Public Administration Review.* July–August: 459–67.

Walker, R. B. J. 1991. State sovereignty and the articulation of political space/time. *Millenium.* 20(3): 445–61.

Walzer, M. 1983. *Spheres of justice.* Oxford: Martin Robertson.

Waterfront Regeneration Trust. 1995. *Lake Ontario Greenway strategy.*

———. 1995. *Lake Ontario Greenway strategy: Next steps.*

Webber, A. M. 1993. What's so new about the new economy? *Harvard Business Review.* 71(1) 24–42.

Weinberg, A. M. 1972. Science and trans-science. *Minerva.* 10: 209–222.

Weintraub, S. 1993. Western hemisphere free trade: Probability or pipe dream? *The Annals of the American Academy of Political and Social Science.* 526 (March): 9–24.

Weiss, L. 1998. *The myth of the powerless state.* Ithaca, NY: Cornell University Press.

Wenger, E., R. McDermott and W.M. Snyder. 2002. *Cultivating communities of practice.* Boston: Harvard Business School Press.

Wheeler, W. M. 1928. *Emergent evolution and the development of societies.* New York: W.W. Norton and Co.

Whitman, M. V. N. 1999. *New world, new rules.* Boston: Harvard Business School Press.

Wiener, N. 1948. *Cybernetics.* Cambridge: MIT Press.

Wikström, S. and R. Normann. 1994. *Knowledge and value: A new perspective on corporate transformation*. London: Routledge.

Wilensky, H. L. 1967. *Organizational intelligence*. New York: Basic Books.

Wiley, N. 1977. Review of Habermas' legitimation crisis in contemporary sociology. 6(4): 416–24.

Williamson, O. E. 1975. *Markets and hierarchies*. New York: Free Press.

———. 1985. *The economic institutions of capitalism*. New York: Free Press.

Wilson, J. A., J. M. Acheson, M. Metcalfe, and P. Kleban. 1994. Chaos, complexity and community management of fisheries. *Marine Policy*. 18(4): 291–305.

Wilson, R. 1975. Informational economies of scale. *The Bell Journal of Economics*. (Spring): 184–95.

Wolfe, A. 1989. *Whose keeper?* Berkeley: The University of California Press.

Wolfe, R. 2001. Rendering onto Ceasar. In G. Smith and D. Wolfish (eds.) *Who's afraid of the state?* Toronto: The University of Toronto Press. 259–309.

Wondelleck, J. M. and S. L. Yaffee. 2000. *Making collaboration work*. Washington: Island Press.

Wonnacott, R. J. 1996. Trade and investment in a hub-and-spoke system versus a free trade area. *The World Economy*. 19: 237–52.

World Bank. 1999. *World development indicators*. Washington.

Wright, R. 2000. *Nonzero: The logic of human destiny*. New York: Vintage.

Wriston, W. B. 1992. *The twilight of sovereignty*. New York: Scribner's.

Wrobel, P.S. 1998. A free trade area of the Americas in 2005? *International Affairs*. 74(3): 547–61.

Yankelovich, D. 1999. *The magic of dialogue*. New York: Simon & Schuster.

Young, O. 1999. *Governance in world affairs*. Ithaca: Cornell University Press.

Young, O. R. 2002.

Ziman, J. 1991. A neural net model of innovation. *Science and Public Policy*. 18(1): 65–75

Index

intervention experiment, 146
investment, 88–92
Iyer, Pico, 242

Jacobs, Jane, 35, 71–72, 78, 291
Japan, 34, 35, 73, 98
jurisdictional gridlock, 201–02

Kanizsa square, 25
Kauffman, Stuart, 30
Kay, James, 167
Kelly, Kevin, 30–31
Keynesian state, 59–60, 124
knowledge, 7–8, 27. *See also*
    information; learning; smart
    communities
    deficit, 105
    delta, 148
    organization of, 117–21
    systems, 20
    tacit, 135
knowledge economy, 15, 23
Krasner, Stephen, 77, 292

Labour, 94, 104–05
labour market restructuring, 94
Laing, R.D., 244
Latin America, 88–102, 106–07
Latin American Free Trade Association
    (LAFTA), 88
Latin American Integration Association
    (ALADI), 101
Latin American Integration Association
    (LAIA), 88, 101
Latin America/the Caribbean (LAC), 91,
    98, 100, 105
Laurendeau, André, 296
law of requisite variety, 155, 162, 240
leadership, 219–20, 305–06, 308–09
learning, 2, 4, 6–10, 294. *See also* smart
    communities; social learning
    collective, 53, 63, 64, 119, 142, 162, 243
    diversity and, 120–21, 173–75
    drivers of, 117
    experimentation and, 175
    institutional, 24–32
    multilogue and, 173–75

organizational, 4, 6–7, 197–200
    single- and double-loop, 182–83
    territorialization of, 123
learning economy, 7–10, 96–97, 243–44
learning networks, 138
learning organizations, 96
learning systems, 116
Lefebvre, Henri, 147
legitimate peripheral participation, 120
legitimation deficit, 59
Lévy, Pierre, 54
liberal constitutional project, 315
Lind, Michael, 98
Lindblom, Charles, 57–58
Loasby, Brian, 118
logic of flows, 8–9
loyalty, 34, 47–48

Macro social contract, 214
management, 117, 164. *See also*
    leadership
management advisory committees
    (MACs), 208–09
management science, 40–41
March, James, 118
market approach to sustainability, 159
market economy, 42
market failure, 171
markets, 29, 34, 39–46. *See also* economy
    bureaucratic systems and, 44
    forums vs., 27
    new, for Canada, 100–09
Marshall, Alfred, 118, 132
Marshall, T.H., 269
mechanism-based approach, 303–12
mechanisms, 143–44
    of collaboration, 140–41
    cooperation-amplifying, 312–17
    for distributed governance, 303, 304–12
    monitoring, 140–41, 143–44
membership, 120
Mercosur, 86–91, 93, 95
meso innovation systems, 121–24, 124
Metcalfe, Les, 170
Mexico, 95, 101, 102, 128, 129
micro social contract, 214
milieu, 122, 135–36

tribalism, 116, 123
Trudeau, Pierre Elliott, 241
trust, 34, 37, 64, 120, 183, 218, 245, 305–09
turbulence, 20–21, 24, 45–46, 63, 104, 181, 187. *See also* change
Tussman, Joseph, 70
type I and II errors, 158, 168, 179–80, 182

Ultrasolutionism, 315
unfreedoms, 285
ungovernance, 47
United Nations, 5, 309
United States, 88, 91–92, 94, 96, 99, 100, 102, 128, 129, 288, 289
 and American nations, 88, 91–92, 94, 96
 centralized mindset in, 129
 competitiveness effect in, 128
 federalism in, 288, 289
 sub-national units in, 128
 trade relations of, 99, 100
unwritten plan, 62, 63

Vickers, Geoffrey, 162, 164, 173, 175
vigilant trust, 34
virtual communities, 32
virtual organizations, 19
VISA credit card company, 74–75, 76, 192–93, 215, 234, 297
vivisystems, 30
voluntary agreements, 80

Waldo, Dwight, 69–70
Waterfront Regeneration Trust, 200–03
wealth, 7–8, 114–15, 128
welfare state era, 24
Westminster government, 58
Westphalian nation, 1–2, 3
work, 119, 250–51
workable meta-vision, 36
worlds, new, 66–68
World Trade Organization (WTO), 29–30

Yankelovich, Daniel, 173

zero power, 22